# DATA SCIENCE PROJECTS WITH PYTHON

## SECOND EDITION

A case study approach to gaining valuable insights from real data with machine learning

Stephen Klosterman

# DATA SCIENCE PROJECTS WITH PYTHON
## SECOND EDITION

**Author:** Stephen Klosterman

**Reviewers:** Ashish Jain and Deepti Miyan Gupta

**Managing Editor:** Mahesh Dhyani

**Acquisitions Editors:** Sneha Shinde and Anindya Sil

**Production Editor:** Shantanu Zagade

**Editorial Board:** Megan Carlisle, Mahesh Dhyani, Heather Gopsill, Manasa Kumar, Alex Mazonowicz, Monesh Mirpuri, Bridget Neale, Abhishek Rane, Brendan Rodrigues, Ankita Thakur, Nitesh Thakur, and Jonathan Wray

First published: April 2019

Second edition: July 2021

Production reference: 1280721

ISBN: 978-1-80056-448-0

Published by Packt Publishing Ltd.

Livery Place, 35 Livery Street

Birmingham B3 2PB, UK

# Table of Contents

## Chapter 3: Details of Logistic Regression and Feature Exploration 113

# Chapter 6: Gradient Boosting, XGBoost, and SHAP Values

# PREFACE

## ABOUT THE BOOK

If data is the new oil, then machine learning is the drill. As companies gain access to ever-increasing quantities of raw data, the ability to deliver state-of-the-art predictive models that support business decision-making becomes more and more valuable.

In this book, you'll work on an end-to-end project based around a realistic data set and split up into bite-sized practical exercises. This creates a case-study approach that simulates the working conditions you'll experience in real-world data science projects.

You'll learn how to use key Python packages, including pandas, Matplotlib, and scikit-learn, and master the process of data exploration and data processing, before moving on to fitting, evaluating, and tuning algorithms such as regularized logistic regression and random forest.

Now in its second edition, this book will take you through the end-to-end process of exploring data and delivering machine learning models. Updated for 2021, this edition includes brand new content on XGBoost, SHAP values, algorithmic fairness, and the ethical concerns of deploying a model in the real world.

By the end of this data science book, you'll have the skills, understanding, and confidence to build your own machine learning models and gain insights from real data.

## ABOUT THE AUTHOR

*Stephen Klosterman* is a Machine Learning Data Scientist with a background in math, environmental science, and ecology. His education includes a Ph.D. in Biology from Harvard University, where he was an assistant teacher of the Data Science course. His professional experience includes work in the environmental, health care, and financial sectors. At work, he likes to research and develop machine learning solutions that create value, and that stakeholders understand. In his spare time, he enjoys running, biking, paddleboarding, and music.

## OBJECTIVES

- Load, explore, and process data using the pandas Python package
- Use Matplotlib to create effective data visualizations
- Implement predictive machine learning models with scikit-learn and XGBoost
- Use lasso and ridge regression to reduce model overfitting

- Build ensemble models of decision trees, using random forest and gradient boosting

- Evaluate model performance and interpret model predictions

- Deliver valuable insights by making clear business recommendations

## AUDIENCE

*Data Science Projects with Python – Second Edition* is for anyone who wants to get started with data science and machine learning. If you're keen to advance your career by using data analysis and predictive modeling to generate business insights, then this book is the perfect place to begin. To quickly grasp the concepts covered, it is recommended that you have basic experience with programming in Python or another similar language (R, Matlab, C, etc). Additionally, knowledge of statistics that would be covered in a basic course, including topics such as probability and linear regression, or a willingness to learn about these on your own while reading this book would be useful.

## APPROACH

*Data Science Projects with Python* takes a practical case study approach to learning, teaching concepts in the context of a real-world dataset. Clear explanations will deepen your knowledge, while engaging exercises and challenging activities will reinforce it with hands-on practice.

## ABOUT THE CHAPTERS

*Chapter 1, Data Exploration and Cleaning*, gets you started with Python and Jupyter notebooks. The chapter then explores the case study dataset and delves into exploratory data analysis, quality assurance, and data cleaning using pandas.

*Chapter 2, Introduction to Scikit-Learn and Model Evaluation*, introduces you to the evaluation metrics for binary classification models. You'll learn how to build and evaluate binary classification models using scikit-learn.

*Chapter 3, Details of Logistic Regression and Feature Exploration*, dives deep into logistic regression and feature exploration. You'll learn how to generate correlation plots of many features and a response variable and interpret logistic regression as a linear model.

*Chapter 4, The Bias-Variance Trade-Off*, explores the foundational machine learning concepts of overfitting, underfitting, and the bias-variance trade-off by examining how the logistic regression model can be extended to address the overfitting problem.

*Chapter 5, Decision Trees and Random Forests*, introduces you to tree-based machine learning models. You'll learn how to train decision trees for machine learning purposes, visualize trained decision trees, and train random forests and visualize the results.

*Chapter 6, Gradient Boosting, XGBoost, and SHAP Values*, introduces you to two key concepts: gradient boosting and **shapley additive explanations** (**SHAP**). You'll learn to train XGBoost models and understand how SHAP values can be used to provide individualized explanations for model predictions from any dataset.

*Chapter 7, Test Set Analysis, Financial Insights, and Delivery to the Client*, presents several techniques for analyzing a model test set for deriving insights into likely model performance in the future. The chapter also describes key elements to consider when delivering and deploying a model, such as the format of delivery and ways to monitor the model as it is being used.

## HARDWARE REQUIREMENTS

For the optimal student experience, we recommend the following hardware configuration:

- Processor: Intel Core i5 or equivalent
- Memory: 4 GB RAM
- Storage: 35 GB available space

## SOFTWARE REQUIREMENTS

You'll also need the following software installed in advance:

- OS: Windows 7 SP1 64-bit, Windows 8.1 64-bit or Windows 10 64-bit, Ubuntu Linux, or the latest version of OS X
- Browser: Google Chrome/Mozilla Firefox Latest Version
- Notepad++/Sublime Text as IDE (this is optional, as you can practice everything using the Jupyter Notebook on your browser)
- Python 3.8+ (This book uses Python 3.8.2) installed (from https://python.org, or via Anaconda as recommended below) . At the time of writing, the SHAP library used in *Chapter 6, Gradient Boosting, XGBoost, and SHAP Values*, is not compatible with Python 3.9. Hence, if you are using Python 3.9 as your base environment, we suggest that you set up a Python 3.8 environment as described in the next section.

- Python libraries as needed (Jupyter, NumPy, Pandas, Matplotlib, and so on, installed via Anaconda as recommended below)

## INSTALLATION AND SETUP

Before you start this book, it is recommended to install the Anaconda package manager and use it to coordinate installation of Python and its packages.

## CODE BUNDLE

Please find the code bundle for this book, hosted on GitHub at https://github.com/ PacktPublishing/Data-Science-Projects-with-Python-Second-Ed.

## ANACONDA AND SETTING UP YOUR ENVIRONMENT

You can install Anaconda by visiting the following link: https://www.anaconda.com/ products/individual. Scroll down to the bottom of the page and download the installer relevant to your system.

It is recommended to create an environment in Anaconda to do the exercises and activities in this book, which have been tested against the software versions indicated here. Once you have Anaconda installed, open a Terminal, if you're using macOS or Linux, or a Command Prompt window in Windows, and do the following:

1. Create an environment with most required packages. You can call it whatever you want; here it's called **dspwp2**. Copy and paste, or type the entire statement here on one line in the terminal:

```
conda create -n dspwp2 python=3.8.2 jupyter=1.0.0 pandas=1.2.1 scikit-learn=0.23.2 numpy=1.19.2 matplotlib=3.3.2 seaborn=0.11.1 python-graphviz=0.15 xlrd=2.0.1
```

2. Type **'y'** and press [Enter] when prompted.

3. Activate the environment:

```
conda activate dspwp2
```

4. Install the remaining packages:

```
conda install -c conda-forge xgboost=1.3.0 shap=0.37.0
```

5. Type **'y'** and [Enter] when prompted.

6. You are ready to use the environment. To deactivate it when finished:

```
conda deactivate
```

We also have other code bundles from our rich catalog of books and videos available at https://github.com/PacktPublishing/. Check them out!

## CONVENTIONS

Code words in the text, database table names, folder names, filenames, file extensions, pathnames, dummy URLs, user input, and Twitter handles are shown as follows: "By typing **conda list** at the command line, you can see all the packages installed in your environment."

A block of code is set as follows:

```
import numpy as np #numerical computation
import pandas as pd #data wrangling
import matplotlib.pyplot as plt #plotting package
#Next line helps with rendering plots
%matplotlib inline
import matplotlib as mpl #add'l plotting functionality
mpl.rcParams['figure.dpi'] = 400 #high res figures
import graphviz #to visualize decision trees
```

New terms and important words are shown in bold. Words that you see on the screen, for example, in menus or dialog boxes, appear in the text like this: "Create a new Python 3 notebook from the **New** menu as shown."

## CODE PRESENTATION

Lines of code that span multiple lines are split using a backslash ( \ ). When the code is executed, Python will ignore the backslash, and treat the code on the next line as a direct continuation of the current line.

For example:

```
my_new_lr = LogisticRegression(penalty='l2', dual=False,\
                        tol=0.0001, C=1.0,\
                        fit_intercept=True,\
                        intercept_scaling=1,\
                        class_weight=None,\
                        random_state=None,\
                        solver='lbfgs',\
                        max_iter=100,\
```

```
multi_class='auto',\
verbose=0, warm_start=False,\
n_jobs=None, l1_ratio=None)
```

Comments are added into code to help explain specific bits of logic. Single-line comments are denoted using the # symbol, as follows:

```
import pandas as pd
import matplotlib.pyplot as plt #import plotting package
#render plotting automatically
%matplotlib inline
```

## GET IN TOUCH

Feedback from our readers is always welcome.

**General feedback**: If you have any questions about this book, please mention the book title in the subject of your message and email us at `customercare@packtpub.com`.

**Errata**: Although we have taken every care to ensure the accuracy of our content, mistakes do happen. If you have found a mistake in this book, we would be grateful if you could report this to us. Please visit www.packtpub.com/support/errata and complete the form.

**Piracy**: If you come across any illegal copies of our works in any form on the internet, we would be grateful if you could provide us with the location address or website name. Please contact us at `copyright@packt.com` with a link to the material.

**If you are interested in becoming an author**: If there is a topic that you have expertise in, and you are interested in either writing or contributing to a book, please visit authors.packtpub.com.

## PLEASE LEAVE A REVIEW

Let us know what you think by leaving a detailed, impartial review on Amazon. We appreciate all feedback – it helps us continue to make great products and help aspiring developers build their skills. Please spare a few minutes to give your thoughts – it makes a big difference to us. You can leave a review by clicking the following link: https://packt.link/r/1800564481.

# 1

# DATA EXPLORATION AND CLEANING

**OVERVIEW**

In this chapter, you will take your first steps with Python and Jupyter notebooks, some of the most common tools data scientists use. You'll then take the first look at the dataset for the case study project that will form the core of this book. You will begin to develop an intuition for quality assurance checks that data needs to be put through before model building. By the end of the chapter, you will be able to use pandas, the top package for wrangling tabular data in Python, to do exploratory data analysis, quality assurance, and data cleaning.

# INTRODUCTION

Most businesses possess a wealth of data on their operations and customers. Reporting on this data in the form of descriptive charts, graphs, and tables is a good way to understand the current state of the business. However, in order to provide quantitative guidance on future business strategies and operations, it is necessary to go a step further. This is where the practices of machine learning and predictive modeling are needed. In this book, we will show how to go from descriptive analyses to concrete guidance for future operations, using predictive models.

To accomplish this goal, we'll introduce some of the most widely used machine learning tools via Python and many of its packages. You will also get a sense of the practical skills necessary to execute successful projects: inquisitiveness when examining data and communication with the client. Time spent looking in detail at a dataset and critically examining whether it accurately meets its intended purpose is time well spent. You will learn several techniques for assessing data quality here.

In this chapter, after getting familiar with the basic tools for data exploration, we will discuss a few typical working scenarios for how you may receive data. Then, we will begin a thorough exploration of the case study dataset and help you learn how you can uncover possible issues, so that when you are ready for modeling, you may proceed with confidence.

## PYTHON AND THE ANACONDA PACKAGE MANAGEMENT SYSTEM

In this book, we will use the Python programming language. Python is a top language for data science and is one of the fastest-growing programming languages. A commonly cited reason for Python's popularity is that it is easy to learn. If you have Python experience, that's great; however, if you have experience with other languages, such as C, Matlab, or R, you shouldn't have much trouble using Python. You should be familiar with the general constructs of computer programming to get the most out of this book. Examples of such constructs are **for** loops and **if** statements that guide the **control flow** of a program. No matter what language you have used, you are likely familiar with these constructs, which you will also find in Python.

A key feature of Python that is different from some other languages is that it is zero-indexed; in other words, the first element of an ordered collection has an index of **0**. Python also supports negative indexing, where the index **−1** refers to the last element of an ordered collection and negative indices count backward from the end. The slice operator, **:**, can be used to select multiple elements of an ordered collection from within a range, starting from the beginning, or going to the end of the collection.

## INDEXING AND THE SLICE OPERATOR

Here, we demonstrate how indexing and the slice operator work. To have something to index, we will create a **list**, which is a **mutable** ordered collection that can contain any type of data, including numerical and string types. "Mutable" just means the elements of the list can be changed after they are first assigned. To create the numbers for our list, which will be consecutive integers, we'll use the built-in **range()** Python function. The **range()** function technically creates an **iterator** that we'll convert to a list using the **list()** function, although you need not be concerned with that detail here. The following screenshot shows a list of the first five positive integers being printed on the console, as well as a few indexing operations, and changing the first item of the list to a new value of a different data type:

```
>>> example_list = list(range(1,6))
>>> example_list
[1, 2, 3, 4, 5]
>>> example_list[0]
1
>>> example_list[-1]
5
>>> example_list[-2]
4
>>> example_list[:3]
[1, 2, 3]
>>> example_list[0] = 'a string'
>>> example_list
['a string', 2, 3, 4, 5]
>>>
```

Figure 1.1: List creation and indexing

A few things to notice about *Figure 1.1*: the endpoint of an interval is open for both slice indexing and the **range()** function, while the starting point is closed. In other words, notice how when we specify the start and end of **range()**, endpoint 6 is not included in the result but starting point 1 is. Similarly, when indexing the list with the slice **[:3]**, this includes all elements of the list with indices up to, but not including, 3.

We've referred to ordered collections, but Python also includes unordered collections. An important one of these is called a **dictionary**. A dictionary is an unordered collection of **key:value** pairs. Instead of looking up the values of a dictionary by integer indices, you look them up by keys, which could be numbers or strings. A dictionary can be created using curly braces **{ }** and with the **key:value** pairs separated by commas. The following screenshot is an example of how we can create a dictionary with counts of fruit – examine the number of apples, then add a new type of fruit and its count:

```
>>> example_dict = {'apples':5, 'oranges':8}
>>> example_dict['apples']
5
>>> example_dict['bananas'] = 13
>>> example_dict
{'apples': 5, 'oranges': 8, 'bananas': 13}
>>>
```

Figure 1.2: An example dictionary

There are many other distinctive features of Python and we just want to give you a flavor here, without getting into too much detail. In fact, you will probably use packages such as **pandas (pandas)** and **NumPy (numpy)** for most of your data handling in Python. NumPy provides fast numerical computation on arrays and matrices, while pandas provides a wealth of data wrangling and exploration capabilities on tables of data called **DataFrames**. However, it's good to be familiar with some of the basics of Python—the language that sits at the foundation of all of this. For example, indexing works the same in NumPy and pandas as it does in Python.

One of the strengths of Python is that it is open source and has an active community of developers creating amazing tools. We will use several of these tools in this book. A potential pitfall of having open source packages from different contributors is the dependencies between various packages. For example, if you want to install pandas, it may rely on a certain version of NumPy, which you may or may not have installed. Package management systems make life easier in this respect. When you install a new package through the package management system, it will ensure that all the dependencies are met. If they aren't, you will be prompted to upgrade or install new packages as necessary.

For this book, we will use the **Anaconda** package management system, which you should already have installed. While we will only use Python here, it is also possible to run R with Anaconda.

> **NOTE: ENVIRONMENTS**
>
> It is recommended to create a new Python 3.x environment for this book. Environments are like separate installations of Python, where the set of packages you have installed can be different, as well as the version of Python. Environments are useful for developing projects that need to be deployed in different versions of Python, possibly with different dependencies. For general information on this, see https://docs.conda.io/projects/conda/en/latest/user-guide/tasks/manage-environments.html. See the *Preface* for specific instructions on setting up an Anaconda environment for this book before you begin the upcoming exercises.

## EXERCISE 1.01: EXAMINING ANACONDA AND GETTING FAMILIAR WITH PYTHON

In this exercise, you will examine the packages in your Anaconda installation and practice with some basic Python control flow and data structures, including a `for` loop, `dict`, and `list`. This will confirm that you have completed the installation steps in the preface and show you how Python syntax and data structures may be a little different from other programming languages you may be familiar with. Perform the following steps to complete the exercise:

> **NOTE**
>
> Before executing the exercises and the activity in this chapter, please make sure you have followed the instructions regarding setting up your Python environment as mentioned in the *Preface*. The code file for this exercise can be found here: https://packt.link/N0RPT.

1. Open up Terminal, if you're using macOS or Linux, or a Command Prompt window in Windows. If you're using an environment, activate it using **conda activate <name_of_your_environment>**. Then type **conda list** at the command line. You should observe an output similar to the following:

```
requests                 2.21.0                          py37_0
rope                     0.11.0                          py37_0
ruamel_yaml              0.15.46                   py37h1de35cc_0
scikit-image             0.14.1                   py37h0a44026_0
scikit-learn             0.20.1                   py37h27c97d8_0
scipy                    1.1.0                    py37h1410ff5_2
seaborn                  0.9.0                           py37_0
send2trash               1.5.0                           py37_0
setuptools               40.6.3                          py37_0
simplegeneric            0.8.1                           py37_2
singledispatch           3.4.0.3                         py37_0
sip                      4.19.8                   py37h0a44026_0
six                      1.12.0                          py37_0
snappy                   1.1.7                     he62c110_3
snowballstemmer          1.2.1                           py37_0
```

Figure 1.3: Selection of packages from conda list

You can see all the packages installed in your environment, including the packages we will directly interact with, as well as their dependencies which are needed for them to function. Managing dependencies among packages is one of the main advantages of a package management system.

> **NOTE**
>
> For more information about Anaconda and command-line interaction, check out this "cheat sheet": https://docs.conda.io/projects/conda/en/latest/_downloads/843d9e0198f2a193a3484886fa28163c/conda-cheatsheet.pdf.

2. Type **python** in Terminal to open a command-line Python interpreter. You should obtain an output similar to the following:

```
Python 3.7.1 (default, Dec 14 2018, 13:28:58)
[Clang 4.0.1 (tags/RELEASE_401/final)] :: Anaconda, Inc. on darwin
Type "help", "copyright", "credits" or "license" for more information.
>>>
```

Figure 1.4: Command-line Python

You should see some information about your version of Python, as well as the Python Command Prompt (**>>>**). When you type after this prompt, you are writing Python code.

> **NOTE**
>
> Although we will be using the Jupyter notebook in this book, one of the aims of this exercise is to go through the basic steps of writing and running Python programs on the Command Prompt.

3.  Write a **for** loop at the Command Prompt to print values from 0 to 4 using the following code (note that the three dots at the beginning of the second and third lines appear automatically if you are writing code in the command-line Python interpreter; if you're instead writing in a Jupyter notebook, these won't appear):

```
for counter in range(5):
...     print(counter)
...
```

Once you hit *Enter* when you see **. . .** on the prompt, you should obtain this output:

**Figure 1.5: Output of a for loop at the command line**

Notice that in Python, the opening of the **for** loop is followed by a colon, and **the body of the loop requires indentation**. It's typical to use four spaces to indent a code block. Here, the **for** loop prints the values returned by the **range()** iterator, having repeatedly accessed them using the **counter** variable with the **in** keyword.

> **NOTE**
>
> For many more details on Python code conventions, refer to the following:
> https://www.python.org/dev/peps/pep-0008/.

Now, we will return to our dictionary example. The first step here is to create the dictionary.

4. Create a dictionary of fruits (**apples**, **oranges**, and **bananas**) using the following code:

```
example_dict = {'apples':5, 'oranges':8, 'bananas':13}
```

5. Convert the dictionary to a list using the **list()** function, as shown in the following snippet:

```
dict_to_list = list(example_dict)
dict_to_list
```

Once you run the preceding code, you should obtain the following output:

```
['apples', 'oranges', 'bananas']
```

Notice that when this is done and we examine the contents, only the keys of the dictionary have been captured in the list. If we wanted the values, we would have had to specify that with the **.values()** method of the list. Also, notice that the list of dictionary keys happens to be in the same order that we wrote them when creating the dictionary. This is not guaranteed, however, as dictionaries are unordered collection types.

One convenient thing you can do with lists is to append other lists to them with the **+** operator. As an example, in the next step, we will combine the existing list of fruit with a list that contains just one more type of fruit, overwriting the variable containing the original list, like this: **list(example_dict.values());** the interested readers can confirm this for themselves.

6. Use the **+** operator to combine the existing list of fruits with a new list containing only one fruit (**pears**):

```
dict_to_list = dict_to_list + ['pears']
dict_to_list
```

Your output will be as follows:

```
['apples', 'oranges', 'bananas', 'pears']
```

**What if we wanted to sort our list of fruit types?**

Python provides a built-in **sorted()** function that can be used for this; it will return a sorted version of the input. In our case, this means the list of fruit types will be sorted alphabetically.

7. Sort the list of fruits in alphabetical order using the **sorted()** function, as shown in the following snippet:

```
sorted(dict_to_list)
```

Once you run the preceding code, you should see the following output:

```
['apples', 'bananas', 'oranges', 'pears']
```

That's enough Python for now. We will show you how to execute the code for this book, so your Python knowledge should improve along the way. While you have the Python interpreter open, you may wish to run the code examples shown in *Figures 1.1* and *1.2*. When you're done with the interpreter, you can type **quit()** to exit.

> **NOTE**
>
> As you learn more and inevitably want to try new things, consult the official Python documentation: https://docs.python.org/3/.

# DIFFERENT TYPES OF DATA SCIENCE PROBLEMS

Much of your time as a data scientist is likely to be spent wrangling data: figuring out how to get it, getting it, examining it, making sure it's correct and complete, and joining it with other types of data. pandas is a widely used tool for data analysis in Python, and it can facilitate the data exploration process for you, as we will see in this chapter. However, one of the key goals of this book is to start you on your journey to becoming a machine learning data scientist, for which you will need to master the art and science of **predictive modeling**. This means using a mathematical model, or idealized mathematical formulation, to learn relationships within the data, in the hope of making accurate and useful predictions when new data comes in.

For predictive modeling use cases, data is typically organized in a tabular structure, with **features** and a **response variable**. For example, if you want to predict the price of a house based on some characteristics about it, such as **area** and **number of bedrooms**, these attributes would be considered the features and the **price of the house** would be the response variable. The response variable is sometimes called the **target variable** or **dependent variable**, while the features may also be called the **independent variables**.

If you have a dataset of 1,000 houses including the values of these features and the prices of the houses, you can say you have 1,000 **samples** of **labeled** data, where the labels are the known values of the response variable: the prices of different houses. Most commonly, the tabular data structure is organized so that different rows are different samples, while features and the response occupy different columns, along with other metadata such as sample IDs, as shown in *Figure 1.6*:

| House ID | Area (m²) | Number of Bedrooms | Price ($) |
|----------|-----------|--------------------|-----------|
| 1 | 1,500 | 3 | 200,000 |
| 2 | 2,500 | 5 | 600,000 |
| 3 | 3,500 | 3 | 500,000 |

Figure 1.6: Labeled data (the house prices are the known target variable)

**Regression Problem**

Once you have trained a model to learn the relationship between the features and response using your labeled data, you can then use it to make predictions for houses where you don't know the price, based on the information contained in the features. The goal of predictive modeling in this case is to be able to make a prediction that is close to the true value of the house. Since we are predicting a numerical value on a continuous scale, this is called a **regression problem**.

## Classification Problem

On the other hand, if we were trying to make a qualitative prediction about the house, to answer a **yes** or **no** question such as "will this house go on sale within the next 5 years?" or "will the owner default on the mortgage?", we would be solving what is known as a **classification problem**. Here, we would hope to answer the yes or no question correctly. The following figure is a schematic illustrating how model training works, and what the outcomes of regression or classification models might be:

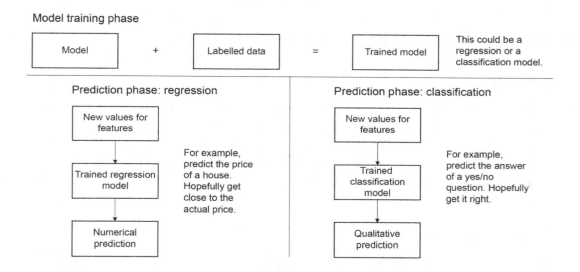

**Figure 1.7: Schematic of model training and prediction for regression and classification**

Classification and regression tasks are called **supervised learning**, which is a class of problems that relies on labeled data. These problems can be thought of as needing "supervision" by the known values of the target variable. By contrast, there is also **unsupervised learning**, which relates to more open-ended questions of trying to find some sort of structure in a dataset that does not necessarily have labels. Taking a broader view, any kind of applied math problem, including fields as varied as **optimization**, **statistical inference**, and **time series modeling**, may potentially be considered an appropriate responsibility for a data scientist.

# LOADING THE CASE STUDY DATA WITH JUPYTER AND PANDAS

Now it's time to take a first look at the data we will use in our case study. We won't do anything in this section other than ensure that we can load the data into a **Jupyter notebook** correctly. Examining the data, and understanding the problem you will solve with it, will come later.

The data file is an Excel spreadsheet called `default_of_credit_card_ clients__courseware_version_1_21_19.xls`. We recommend you first open the spreadsheet in Excel or the spreadsheet program of your choice. Note the number of rows and columns. Look at some example values. This will help you know whether or not you have loaded it correctly in the Jupyter notebook.

> **NOTE**
>
> The dataset can be obtained from the following link: https://packt.link/ wensZ. This is a modified version of the original dataset, which has been sourced from the UCI Machine Learning Repository [http://archive.ics.uci. edu/ml]. Irvine, CA: University of California, School of Information and Computer Science.

**What is a Jupyter notebook?**

Jupyter notebooks are interactive coding environments that allow for inline text and graphics. They are great tools for data scientists to communicate and preserve their results, since both the methods (code) and the message (text and graphics) are integrated. You can think of the environment as a kind of web page where you can write and execute code. Jupyter notebooks can, in fact, be rendered as web pages, as is done on GitHub. Here is an example notebook: https://packt.link/pREet. Look it over and get a sense of what you can do. An excerpt from this notebook is displayed here, showing code, graphics, and prose, which is known as **Markdown** in this context:

```
+ cardio_years[map_index]

map_quantity(country_names, quantity_to_map, map_title)
```

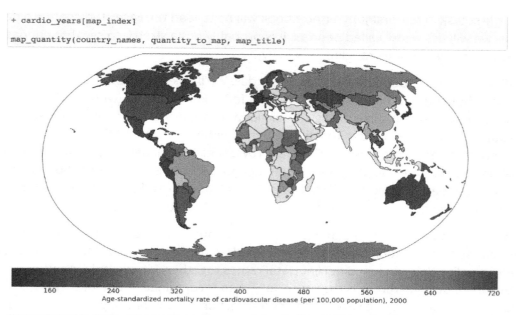

Age-standardized mortality rate of cardiovascular disease (per 100,000 population), 2000

Northern Central Asia, Russia, and parts of Eastern Europe seem to have the highest incidences. The Middle East and much of Africa have moderately high but variable rates, while Western Europe, the Americas, Australia, and Eastern Asian countries have relatively low rates of cardiovascular disease.

**Figure 1.8: Example of a Jupyter notebook showing code, graphics, and Markdown text**

One of the first things to learn about Jupyter notebooks is how to navigate around and make edits. There are two modes available to you. If you select a cell and press *Enter*, you are in **edit mode** and you can edit the text in that cell. If you press *Esc*, you are in **command mode** and you can navigate around the notebook.

> **NOTE**
>
> If you're reading the print version of this book, you can download and browse the color versions of some of the images in this chapter by visiting the following link: https://packt.link/T5EIH.

When you are in command mode, there are many useful hotkeys you can use. The *Up* and *Down* arrows will help you select different cells and scroll through the notebook. If you press *y* on a selected cell in command mode, it changes it to a **code cell**, in which the text is interpreted as code. Pressing *m* changes it to a **Markdown cell**, where you can write formatted text. *Shift + Enter* evaluates the cell, rendering the Markdown or executing the code, as the case may be. You'll get some practice with a Jupyter notebook in the next exercise.

Our first task in our first Jupyter notebook will be to load the case study data. To do this, we will use a tool called **pandas**. It is probably not a stretch to say that pandas is the pre-eminent data-wrangling tool in Python.

A DataFrame is a foundational class in pandas. We'll talk more about what a class is later, but you can think of it as a template for a data structure, where a data structure is something like the lists or dictionaries we discussed earlier. However, a DataFrame is much richer in functionality than either of these. A DataFrame is similar to spreadsheets in many ways. There are rows, which are labeled by a row index, and columns, which are usually given column header-like labels that can be thought of as a column index. **Index** is, in fact, a data type in pandas used to store indices for a DataFrame, and columns have their own data type called **Series**.

You can do a lot of the same things with a DataFrame that you can do with Excel sheets, such as creating pivot tables and filtering rows. pandas also includes SQL-like functionality. You can join different DataFrames together, for example. Another advantage of DataFrames is that once your data is contained in one of them, you have the capabilities of a wealth of pandas functionality at your fingertips, for data analysis. The following figure is an example of a pandas DataFrame:

| | ID | LIMIT_BAL | SEX | EDUCATION | MARRIAGE | AGE | PAY_1 |
|---|---|---|---|---|---|---|---|
| 0 | b730d678-5446 | 20000 | 2 | 2 | 1 | 24 | 2 |
| 1 | 99a3ae70-57a8 | 120000 | 2 | 2 | 2 | 26 | -1 |
| 2 | 90194006-f94a | 90000 | 2 | 2 | 2 | 34 | 0 |
| 3 | 19acf9a3-2b01 | 50000 | 2 | 2 | 1 | 37 | 0 |
| 4 | 70d7bc16-a6a4 | 50000 | 1 | 2 | 1 | 57 | -1 |

Figure 1.9: Example of a pandas DataFrame with an integer row index at the left and a column index of strings

The example in *Figure 1.9* is in fact the data for the case study. As the first step with Jupyter and pandas, we will now see how to create a Jupyter notebook and load data with pandas. There are several convenient functions you can use in pandas to explore your data, including `.head()` to see the first few rows of the DataFrame, `.info()` to see all columns with datatypes, `.columns` to return a list of column names as strings, and others we will learn about in the following exercises.

## EXERCISE 1.02: LOADING THE CASE STUDY DATA IN A JUPYTER NOTEBOOK

Now that you've learned about Jupyter notebooks, the environment in which we'll write code, and pandas, the data wrangling package, let's create our first Jupyter notebook. We'll use pandas within this notebook to load the case study data and briefly examine it. Perform the following steps to complete the exercise:

> **NOTE**
>
> The Jupyter notebook for this exercise can be found at https://packt.link/GHPSn.

1. Open a Terminal (macOS or Linux) or a Command Prompt window (Windows) and type `jupyter notebook` (first activating your Anaconda environment if you're using one).

   You will be presented with the Jupyter interface in your web browser. If the browser does not open automatically, copy and paste the URL from the Terminal into your browser. In this interface, you can navigate around your directories starting from the directory you were in when you launched the notebook server.

2. Navigate to a convenient location where you will store the materials for this book, and create a new Python 3 notebook from the **New** menu, as shown here:

**Figure 1.10: Jupyter home screen**

3. Make your very first cell a Markdown cell by typing *m* while in command mode (press *Esc* to enter command mode), then type a number sign, **#**, at the beginning of the first line, followed by a space, for a heading. Add a title for your notebook here. On the next few lines, place a description.

Here is a screenshot of an example, including other kinds of Markdown such as bold, italics, and the way to write code-style text in a Markdown cell:

# First Jupyter notebook
Welcome to your first jupyter notebook! The first thing to know about Jupyter notebooks is that there are two kinds of cells. This is a markdown cell.

There are a lot of different ways to mark up the text in markdown cells, including __bold__ and *italics*.

The next one will be a `code` cell.

Figure 1.11: Unrendered Markdown cell

Note that it is good practice to add a title and brief description for your notebook, to identify its purpose to readers.

4.  Press *Shift + Enter* to render the Markdown cell.

    This should also create a new cell, which will be a code cell. You can change it to a Markdown cell by pressing *m*, and back to a code cell by pressing *y*. You will know it's a code cell because of the **In [ ]:** next to it.

5.  Type **import pandas as pd** in the new cell, as shown in the following screenshot:

**First Jupyter notebook**

Welcome to your first jupyter notebook! The first thing to know about Jupyter notebooks is that there are two kinds of cells. This is a markdown cell.

There are a lot of different ways to mark up the text in markdown cells, including **bold** and *italics*.

The next one will be a `code` cell.

```
In [ ]:  import pandas as pd
```

Figure 1.12: Rendered Markdown cell and code cell

After you execute this cell, the **pandas** module will be loaded into your computing environment. It's common to import modules with **as** to create a short alias such as **pd**. Now, we are going to use pandas to load the data file. It's in Microsoft Excel format, so we can use **pd.read_excel**.

> **NOTE**
>
> For more information on all the possible options for **pd.read_excel**, refer to the following documentation: https://pandas.pydata.org/pandas-docs/stable/reference/api/pandas.read_excel.html.

6. Import the dataset, which is in the Excel format, as a DataFrame using the **pd.read_excel()** method, as shown in the following snippet:

```
df = pd.read_excel('../../Data/default_of_credit_card_clients'\
                    '__courseware_version_1_21_19.xls')
```

Note that you need to point the Excel reader to wherever the file is located. If it's in the same directory as your notebook, you could just enter the filename. The **pd.read_excel** method will load the Excel file into a **DataFrame**, which we've called **df**. By default, the first sheet of the spreadsheet is loaded, which in this case is the only sheet. The power of pandas is now available to us.

Let's do some quick checks in the next few steps. First, does the number of rows and columns match what we know from looking at the file in Excel?

7. Use the **.shape** method to review the number of rows and columns, as shown in the following snippet:

```
df.shape
```

Once you run the cell, you will obtain the following output:

```
Out[3]:  (30000, 25)
```

This should match your observations from the spreadsheet. If it doesn't, you would then need to look into the various options of **pd.read_excel** to see if you needed to adjust something.

With this exercise, we have successfully loaded our dataset into the Jupyter notebook. You may also wish to try the **.info()** and **.head()** methods on the DataFrame, which will tell you information about all the columns, and show you the first few rows of the **DataFrame**, respectively. Now you're up and running with your data in pandas.

As a final note, while this may already be clear, observe that if you define a variable in one code cell, it is available to you in other code cells within the notebook. This is because the code cells within a notebook are said to share **scope** as long as the notebook is running, as shown in the following screenshot:

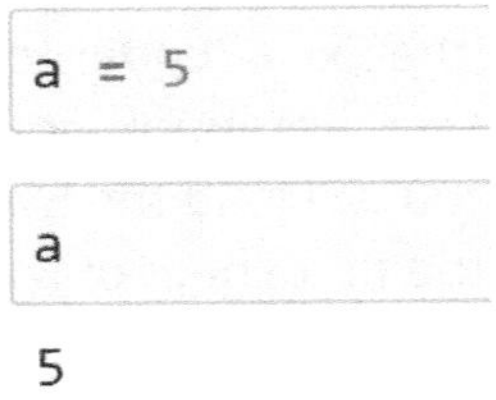

```
a = 5
```

```
a
```

5

**Figure 1.13: Variable in scope between cells**

Every time you launch a Jupyter notebook, while the code and markdown cells are saved from your previous work, the environment starts fresh and you will need to reload all modules and data to start working with them again. You can also shut down or restart the notebook manually using the **Kernel** menu of the notebook. More details on Jupyter notebooks can be found in the documentation here: https://jupyter-notebook.readthedocs.io/en/stable/.

> **NOTE**
>
> In this book, each new exercise and activity will be done in a new Jupyter notebook. However, some exercise notebooks also contain additional Python code and outputs presented in the sections preceding the exercises. There are also reference notebooks that contain the entirety of each chapter. For example, the notebook for *Chapter 1*, *Data Exploration and Cleaning*, can be found here: https://packt.link/zwofX.

## GETTING FAMILIAR WITH DATA AND PERFORMING DATA CLEANING

Now let's take a first look at this data. In your work as a data scientist, there are several possible scenarios in which you may receive such a dataset. These include the following:

1. You created the SQL query that generated the data.

2. A colleague wrote a SQL query for you, with your input.

3. A colleague who knows about the data gave it to you, but without your input.

4. You are given a dataset about which little is known.

In cases 1 and 2, your input was involved in generating/extracting the data. In these scenarios, you probably understood the business problem and then either found the data you needed with the help of a data engineer or did your own research and designed the SQL query that generated the data. Often, especially as you gain more experience in your data science role, the first step will be to meet with the business partner to understand and refine the mathematical definition of the business problem. Then, you would play a key role in defining what is in the dataset.

Even if you have a relatively high level of familiarity with the data, doing data exploration and looking at **summary statistics** of different variables is still an important first step. This step will help you select good features, or give you ideas about how you can engineer new features. However, in the third and fourth cases, where your input was not involved or you have little knowledge about the data, data exploration is even more important.

Another important initial step in the data science process is examining the **data dictionary**. A data dictionary is a document that explains what the data owner thinks should be in the data, such as definitions of the column labels. It is the data scientist's job to go through the data carefully to make sure that these definitions match the reality of what is in the data. In cases 1 and 2, you will probably need to create the data dictionary yourself, which should be considered essential project documentation. In cases 3 and 4, you should seek out the dictionary if at all possible.

The case study data we'll use in this book is similar to case 3 here.

## THE BUSINESS PROBLEM

Our client is a credit card company. They have brought us a dataset that includes some demographics and recent financial data, over the past 6 months, for a sample of 30,000 of their account holders. This data is at the credit account level; in other words, there is one row for each account (you should always clarify what the definition of a row is, in a dataset). Rows are labeled by whether, in the next month after the 6-month historical data period, an account owner has defaulted, or in other words, failed to make the minimum payment.

**Goal**

Your goal is to develop a predictive model for whether an account will default next month, given demographics and historical data. Later in the book, we'll discuss the practical application of the model.

The data is already prepared, and a data dictionary is available. The dataset supplied with the book, **default_of_credit_card_clients__courseware_version_1_21_19.xls**, is a modified version of this dataset in the UCI Machine Learning Repository: https://archive.ics.uci.edu/ml/datasets/default+of+credit+card+clients. Have a look at that web page, which includes the data dictionary.

## DATA EXPLORATION STEPS

Now that we've understood the business problem and have an idea of what is supposed to be in the data, we can compare these impressions to what we actually see in the data. Your job in data exploration is to not only look through the data both directly and using numerical and graphical summaries but also to think critically about whether the data make sense and match what you have been told about it. These are helpful steps in data exploration:

1. How many columns are there in the data?

   These may be features, responses, or metadata.

2. How many rows (samples) are there?

3. What kind of features are there? Which are **categorical** and which are **numerical**?

   Categorical features have values in discrete classes such as "Yes," "No," or "Maybe."

   Numerical features are typically on a continuous numerical scale, such as dollar amounts.

4. What does the data look like in these features?

   To see this, you can examine the range of values in numeric features, or the frequency of different classes in categorical features, for example.

5. Is there any missing data?

We have already answered questions 1 and 2 in the previous section; there are 30,000 rows and 25 columns. As we start to explore the rest of these questions in the following exercise, pandas will be our go-to tool. We begin by verifying basic data integrity in the next exercise.

> **NOTE**
>
> Note that compared to the website's description of the data dictionary, **X6-X11** are called **PAY_1-PAY_6** in our data. Similarly, **X12-X17** are **BILL_AMT1-BILL_AMT6**, and **X18-X23** are **PAY_AMT1-PAY_AMT6**.

## EXERCISE 1.03: VERIFYING BASIC DATA INTEGRITY

In this exercise, we will perform a basic check on whether our dataset contains what we expect and verify whether there is the correct number of samples.

The data is supposed to have observations for 30,000 credit accounts. While there are 30,000 rows, we should also check whether there are 30,000 unique account IDs. It's possible that, if the SQL query used to generate the data was run on an unfamiliar schema, values that are supposed to be unique are in fact not unique.

To examine this, we can check if the number of unique account IDs is the same as the number of rows. Perform the following steps to complete the exercise:

> **NOTE**
>
> The Jupyter notebook for this exercise can be found here: https://packt.link/EapDM.

1. Import pandas, load the data, and examine the column names by running the following command in a cell, using *Shift + Enter*:

```
import pandas as pd
df = pd.read_excel('../Data/default_of_credit_card'\
                   '_clients__courseware_version_1_21_19.xls')
df.columns
```

The `.columns` method of the DataFrame is employed to examine all the column names. You will obtain the following output once you run the cell:

```
Index(['ID', 'LIMIT_BAL', 'SEX', 'EDUCATION', 'MARRIAGE', 'AGE', 'PAY_1',
       'PAY_2', 'PAY_3', 'PAY_4', 'PAY_5', 'PAY_6', 'BILL_AMT1', 'BILL_AMT2',
       'BILL_AMT3', 'BILL_AMT4', 'BILL_AMT5', 'BILL_AMT6', 'PAY_AMT1',
       'PAY_AMT2', 'PAY_AMT3', 'PAY_AMT4', 'PAY_AMT5', 'PAY_AMT6',
       'default payment next month'],
      dtype='object')
```

Figure 1.14: Columns of the dataset

As can be observed, all column names are listed in the output. The account ID column is referenced as **ID**. The remaining columns appear to be our features, with the last column being the response variable. Let's quickly review the dataset information that was given to us by the client:

**LIMIT_BAL**: Amount of credit provided (in New Taiwanese (NT) dollar) including individual consumer credit and the family (supplementary) credit.

**SEX**: Gender (1 = male; 2 = female).

> **NOTE**
>
> We will not be using the gender data to decide credit-worthiness owing to ethical considerations.

**EDUCATION**: Education (1 = graduate school; 2 = university; 3 = high school; 4 = others).

**MARRIAGE**: Marital status (1 = married; 2 = single; 3 = others).

**AGE**: Age (year).

**PAY_1**–**PAY_6**: A record of past payments. Past monthly payments, recorded from April to September, are stored in these columns.

**PAY_1** represents the repayment status in September; **PAY_2** is the repayment status in August; and so on up to **PAY_6**, which represents the repayment status in April.

The measurement scale for the repayment status is as follows: -1 = pay duly; 1 = payment delay for 1 month; 2 = payment delay for 2 months; and so on up to 8 = payment delay for 8 months; 9 = payment delay for 9 months and above.

**BILL_AMT1–BILL_AMT6**: Bill statement amount (in NT dollar).

**BILL_AMT1** represents the bill statement amount in September; **BILL_AMT2** represents the bill statement amount in August; and so on up to **BILL_AMT6**, which represents the bill statement amount in April.

**PAY_AMT1–PAY_AMT6**: Amount of previous payment (NT dollar). **PAY_AMT1** represents the amount paid in September; **PAY_AMT2** represents the amount paid in August; and so on up to **PAY_AMT6**, which represents the amount paid in April.

Let's now use the `.head()` method in the next step to observe the first few rows of data. By default, this will return the first 5 rows.

2. Run the following command in the subsequent cell:

```
df.head()
```

Here is a portion of the output you should see:

| | ID | LIMIT_BAL | SEX | EDUCATION | MARRIAGE | AGE | PAY_1 |
|---|---|---|---|---|---|---|---|
| 0 | 798fc410-45c1 | 20000 | 2 | 2 | 1 | 24 | 2 |
| 1 | 8a8c8f3b-8eb4 | 120000 | 2 | 2 | 2 | 26 | -1 |
| 2 | 85698822-43f5 | 90000 | 2 | 2 | 2 | 34 | 0 |
| 3 | 0737c11b-be42 | 50000 | 2 | 2 | 1 | 37 | 0 |
| 4 | 3b7f77cc-dbc0 | 50000 | 1 | 2 | 1 | 57 | -1 |

5 rows × 25 columns

Figure 1.15: .head() of a DataFrame

The ID column seems like it contains unique identifiers. Now, to verify whether they are in fact unique throughout the whole dataset, we can count the number of unique values using the **.nunique()** method on the Series (aka column) **ID**. We first select the column using square brackets.

3.  Select the column (**ID**) and count unique values using the following command:

```
df['ID'].nunique()
```

Here's the output:

```
29687
```

As can be seen from the preceding output, the number of unique entries is **29,687**.

4.  Run the following command to obtain the number of rows in the dataset:

```
df.shape
```

As can be observed in the following output, the total number of rows in the dataset is **30,000**:

```
(30000, 25)
```

We see here that the number of unique IDs is less than the number of rows. This implies that the ID is not a unique identifier for the rows of the data. So we know that there is some duplication of IDs. But how much? Is one ID duplicated many times? How many IDs are duplicated?

We can use the **.value_counts()** method on the ID Series to start to answer these questions. This is similar to a **group by/count** procedure in SQL. It will list the unique IDs and how often they occur. We will perform this operation in the next step and store the value counts in the **id_counts** variable.

5.  Store the value counts in the variable defined as **id_counts** and then display the stored values using the **.head()** method, as shown:

```
id_counts = df['ID'].value_counts()
id_counts.head()
```

You will obtain the following output:

```
e50d8395-da32    2
4534975d-bf92    2
a3a5c0fc-fdd6    2
0d66d575-c461    2
fd6033f4-cc72    2
Name: ID, dtype: int64
```

**Figure 1.16: Getting value counts of the account IDs**

Note that `.head()` returns the first five rows by default. You can specify the number of items to be displayed by passing the required number in the parentheses, `()`.

6.  Display the number of duplicated entries by running another value count:

```
id_counts.value_counts()
```

You will obtain the following output:

```
1    29374
2      313
Name: ID, dtype: int64
```

**Figure 1.17: Getting value counts of the account IDs**

Here, we can see that most IDs occur exactly once, as expected. However, 313 IDs occur twice. So, no ID occurs more than twice. With this information, we are ready to begin taking a closer look at this data quality issue and go about fixing it. We will create Boolean masks to do this.

## BOOLEAN MASKS

To help clean the case study data, we introduce the concept of a **logical mask**, also known as a **Boolean mask**. A logical mask is a way to filter an array, or Series, by some condition. For example, we can use the "is equal to" operator in Python, **==**, to find all locations of an array that contain a certain value. Other comparisons, such as "greater than" (**>**), "less than" (**<**), "greater than or equal to" (**>=**), and "less than or equal to" (**<=**), can be used similarly. The output of such a comparison is an array or Series of **True/False** values, also known as **Boolean** values. Each element of the output corresponds to an element of the input, is **True** if the condition is met, and is **False** otherwise. To illustrate how this works, we will use **synthetic data**. Synthetic data is data that is created to explore or illustrate a concept. First, we are going to import the NumPy package, which has many capabilities for generating random numbers, and give it the alias **np**. We'll also import the default random number generator from the random module within NumPy:

```
import numpy as np
from numpy.random import default_rng
```

Now we use what's called a **seed** for the random number generator. If you set the seed, you will get the same results from the random number generator across runs. Otherwise, this is not guaranteed. This can be a helpful option if you use random numbers in some way in your work and want to have consistent results every time you run a notebook. We arbitrarily set the seed to **12345**:

```
rg = default_rng(12345)
```

Next, we generate 100 random integers, using the **integers** method of **rg**, with the appropriate arguments. We generate integers from between 1 and 4. Note the **high** argument specifies an open endpoint by default, that is, the upper limit of the range is not included:

```
random_integers = rg.integers(low=1,high=5,size=100)
```

Let's look at the first five elements of this array, with **random_integers[:5]**. The output should appear as follows:

```
array ([3, 1, 4, 2, 1])
```

Suppose we wanted to know the locations of all elements of **random_integers** equal to 3. We could create a Boolean mask to do this:

```
is_equal_to_3 = random_integers == 3
```

From examining the first 5 elements, we know the first element is equal to 3, but none of the rest are. So in our Boolean mask, we expect **True** in the first position and **False** in the next 4 positions. Is this the case?

```
is_equal_to_3[:5]
```

The preceding code should give this output:

```
array([ True, False, False, False, False])
```

This is what we expected. This shows the creation of a Boolean mask. But what else can we do with them? Suppose we wanted to know how many elements were equal to 3. To know this, you can take the sum of a Boolean mask, which interprets **True** as 1 and **False** as 0:

```
sum(is_equal_to_3)
```

This should give us the following output:

```
31
```

This makes sense, as with a random, equally likely choice of 4 possible values, we would expect each value to appear about 25% of the time. In addition to seeing how many values in the array meet the Boolean condition, we can also use the Boolean mask to select the elements of the array that meet that condition. Boolean masks can be used directly to index arrays, as shown here:

```
random_integers[is_equal_to_3]
```

This outputs the elements of **random_integers** meeting the Boolean condition we specified. In this case, the 31 elements equal to 3:

```
array([3, 3, 3, 3, 3, 3, 3, 3, 3, 3, 3, 3, 3, 3, 3, 3, 3, 3, 3, 3, 3, 3])
```

Figure 1.18: Using the Boolean mask to index an array

Now you know the basics of Boolean arrays, which are useful in many situations. In particular, you can use the `.loc` method of DataFrames to index the rows by a Boolean mask, and the columns by label, to get values of various columns meeting a condition in a potentially different column. Let's continue exploring the case study data with these skills.

> **NOTE**
>
> The Jupyter notebook containing the code and the corresponding outputs presented in the preceding section can be found at https://packt.link/pT9gT.

## EXERCISE 1.04: CONTINUING VERIFICATION OF DATA INTEGRITY

In this exercise, with our knowledge of Boolean arrays, we will examine some of the duplicate IDs we discovered. In *Exercise 03*, *Verifying Basic Data Integrity*, we learned that no ID appears more than twice. We can use this learning to locate the duplicate IDs and examine them. Then we take action to remove rows of dubious quality from the dataset. Perform the following steps to complete the exercise:

> **NOTE**
>
> The Jupyter notebook for this exercise can be found here:
> https://packt.link/snAP0.

1. Continuing where we left off in *Exercise 1.03*, *Verifying Basic Data Integrity*, we need to get the locations of the **id_counts** Series, where the count is **2**, to locate the duplicates. First, we load the data and get the value counts of IDs to bring us to where we left off in *Exercise 03*, *Verifying Basic Data Integrity*, then we create a Boolean mask locating the duplicated IDs with a variable called **dupe_mask** and display the first five elements. Use the following commands:

```
import pandas as pd
df = pd.read_excel('../../Data/default_of_credit_card_clients'\
                   '__courseware_version_1_21_19.xls')
id_counts = df['ID'].value_counts()
id_counts.head()

dupe_mask = id_counts == 2
dupe_mask[0:5]
```

You will obtain the following output (note the ordering of IDs may be different in your output, as **value_counts** sorts on frequency, not the index of IDs):

```
47d9ee33-0df0      True
db903e22-a55a      True
9878723a-0b58      True
8d3a2576-a958      True
956cbf4a-d24e      True
Name: ID, dtype: bool
```

Figure 1.19: A Boolean mask to locate duplicate IDs

Note that in the preceding output, we are displaying only the first five entries using **dupe_mask** to illustrate the contents of this array. You can edit the integer indices in the square brackets (**[]**) to change the number of entries displayed.

Our next step is to use this logical mask to select the IDs that are duplicated. The IDs themselves are contained as the index of the **id_count** Series. We can access the index in order to use our logical mask for selection purposes.

2. Access the index of **id_count** and display the first five rows as context using the following command:

```
id_counts.index[0:5]
```

With this, you will obtain the following output:

```
Index(['47d9ee33-0df0', 'db903e22-a55a', '9878723a-0b58', '8d3a2576-a958',
       '956cbf4a-d24e'],
    dtype='object')
```

Figure 1.20: Duplicated IDs

3. Select and store the duplicated IDs in a new variable called **dupe_ids** using the following command:

```
dupe_ids = id_counts.index[dupe_mask]
```

4. Convert **dupe_ids** to a list and then obtain the length of the list using the following commands:

```
dupe_ids = list(dupe_ids)
len(dupe_ids)
```

You should obtain the following output:

```
313
```

We changed the **dupe_ids** variable to a **list**, as we will need it in this form for future steps. The list has a length of **313**, as can be seen in the preceding output, which matches our knowledge of the number of duplicate IDs from the value count.

5.  We verify the data in **dupe_ids** by displaying the first five entries using the following command:

```
dupe_ids[0:5]
```

We obtain the following output:

```
['47d9ee33-0df0',
 'db903e22-a55a',
 '9878723a-0b58',
 '8d3a2576-a958',
 '956cbf4a-d24e']
```

**Figure 1.21: Making a list of duplicate IDs**

We can observe from the preceding output that the list contains the required entries of duplicate IDs. We're now in a position to examine the data for the IDs in our list of duplicates. In particular, we'd like to look at the values of the features, to see what, if anything, might be different between these duplicate entries. We will use the .**isin** and .**loc** methods of the DataFrame **df** for this purpose.

Using the first three IDs on our list of dupes, **dupe_ids[0:3]**, we will plan to first find the rows containing these IDs. If we pass this list of IDs to the .**isin** method of the ID Series, this will create another logical mask we can use on the larger DataFrame to display the rows that have these IDs. The .**isin** method is nested in a .**loc** statement indexing the DataFrame in order to select the location of all rows containing **True** in the Boolean mask. The second argument of the .**loc** indexing statement is **:**, which implies that all columns will be selected. By performing the following steps, we are essentially filtering the DataFrame in order to view all the columns for the first three duplicate IDs.

6. Run the following command in your notebook to execute the plan we formulated in the previous step:

```
df.loc[df['ID'].isin(dupe_ids[0:3]),:]
```

| | ID | LIMIT_BAL | SEX | EDUCATION | MARRIAGE | AGE | PAY_1 | PAY_2 | PAY_3 | PAY_4 | ... | BILL_AMT4 | BILL_AMT5 |
|---|---|---|---|---|---|---|---|---|---|---|---|---|---|
| 11769 | 9878723a-0b58 | 130000 | 1 | 5 | 1 | 44 | 0 | 0 | 0 | 0 | ... | 54668 | 22780 |
| 11869 | 9878723a-0b58 | 0 | 0 | 0 | 0 | 0 | 0 | 0 | 0 | 0 | ... | 0 | 0 |
| 14979 | db903e22-a55a | 50000 | 1 | 2 | 2 | 55 | 2 | 0 | 0 | 0 | ... | 15848 | 16026 |
| 15079 | db903e22-a55a | 0 | 0 | 0 | 0 | 0 | 0 | 0 | 0 | 0 | ... | 0 | 0 |
| 23377 | 47d9ee33-0df0 | 550000 | 2 | 2 | 1 | 32 | 2 | 0 | 0 | 0 | ... | 548020 | 530672 |
| 23477 | 47d9ee33-0df0 | 0 | 0 | 0 | 0 | 0 | 0 | 0 | 0 | 0 | ... | 0 | 0 |

6 rows × 25 columns

**Figure 1.22: Examining the data for duplicate IDs**

What we observe here is that each duplicate ID appears to have one row with what seems like valid data, and one row that's entirely zeros. Take a moment and think to yourself what you would do with this knowledge.

After some reflection, it should be clear that you ought to delete the rows with all zeros. Perhaps these arose through a faulty join condition in the SQL query that generated the data? Regardless, a row of all zeros is definitely invalid data as it makes no sense for someone to have an age of 0, a credit limit of 0, and so on.

One approach to deal with this issue would be to find rows that have all zeros, except for the first column, which has the IDs. These would be invalid data in any case, and it may be that if we get rid of all of these, we would also solve our problem of duplicate IDs. We can find the entries of the DataFrame that are equal to zero by creating a Boolean matrix that is the same size as the whole DataFrame, based on the "is equal to zero" condition.

7. Create a Boolean matrix of the same size as the entire DataFrame using ==, as shown:

```
df_zero_mask = df == 0
```

In the next steps, we'll use **df_zero_mask**, which is another DataFrame containing Boolean values. The goal will be to create a Boolean Series, **feature_zero_mask**, that identifies every row where all the elements starting from the second column (the features and response, but not the IDs) are 0. To do so, we first need to index **df_zero_mask** using the integer indexing (**.iloc**) method. In this method, we pass (**:**) to examine all rows and (**1:**) to examine all columns starting with the second one (index **1**). Finally, we will apply the **all()** method along the column axis (**axis=1**), which will return **True** if and only if every column in that row is **True**. This is a lot to think about, but it's pretty simple to code, as will be observed in the following step. The goal is to get one Series, that is the same length as the DataFrame, telling us which rows have all zeros besides the ID.

8. Create the Boolean Series **feature_zero_mask**, as shown in the following code:

```
feature_zero_mask = df_zero_mask.iloc[:,1:].all(axis=1)
```

9. Calculate the sum of the Boolean Series using the following command:

```
sum(feature_zero_mask)
```

You should obtain the following output:

```
315
```

The preceding output tells us that 315 rows have zeros for every column but the first one. This is greater than the number of duplicate IDs (313), so if we delete all the "zero rows," we may get rid of the duplicate ID problem.

10. Clean the DataFrame by eliminating the rows with all zeros, except for the ID, using the following code:

```
df_clean_1 = df.loc[~feature_zero_mask,:].copy()
```

While performing the cleaning operation in the preceding step, we return a new DataFrame called **df_clean_1**. Notice that here we've used the **.copy()** method after the **.loc** indexing operation to create a copy of this output, as opposed to a view on the original DataFrame. You can think of this as creating a new DataFrame, as opposed to referencing the original one. Within the **.loc** method, we used the logical not operator, **~**, to select all the rows that don't have zeros for all the features and the response variable, and **:** to select all columns. This is the valid data we wish to keep. After doing this, we now want to know if the number of remaining rows is equal to the number of unique IDs.

11. Verify the number of rows and columns in **df_clean_1** by running the following code:

```
df_clean_1.shape
```

You will obtain the following output:

```
(29685, 25)
```

12. Obtain the number of unique IDs by running the following code:

```
df_clean_1['ID'].nunique()
```

Here's the output:

```
29685
```

From the preceding output, we can see that we have successfully eliminated duplicates, as the number of unique IDs is equal to the number of rows. Now take a breath and pat yourself on the back. That was a whirlwind introduction to quite a few pandas techniques for indexing and characterizing data. Now that we've filtered out the duplicate IDs, we're in a position to start looking at the actual data itself: the features, and eventually, the response variable.

After completing this exercise, save your progress as follows, to a CSV (comma-separated value) file. Notice we don't include the index of the DataFrame when saving, as this is not necessary and can create extra columns when we load it later:

```
df_clean_1.to_csv('../../Data/df_clean_1.csv', index=False)
```

## EXERCISE 1.05: EXPLORING AND CLEANING THE DATA

Thus far, we have identified a data quality issue related to the metadata: we had been told that every sample from our dataset corresponded to a unique account ID, but found that this was not the case. We were able to use logical indexing and pandas to correct this issue. This was a fundamental data quality issue, having to do simply with what samples were present, based on the metadata. Aside from this, we are not really interested in the metadata column of account IDs: these will not help us develop a predictive model for credit default.

Now, we are ready to start examining the values of the features and response variable, the data we will use to develop our predictive model. Perform the following steps to complete this exercise:

> **NOTE**
>
> The Jupyter notebook for this exercise can be found here: https://packt.link/q0huQ.

1. Load the results of the previous exercise and obtain the data type of the columns in the data by using the `.info()` method as shown:

```
import pandas as pd
df_clean_1 = pd.read_csv('../../Data/df_clean_1.csv')
df_clean_1.info()
```

You should see the following output:

```
df_clean_1.info()

<class 'pandas.core.frame.DataFrame'>
Int64Index: 29685 entries, 0 to 29999
Data columns (total 25 columns):
ID                          29685 non-null object
LIMIT_BAL                   29685 non-null int64
SEX                         29685 non-null int64
EDUCATION                   29685 non-null int64
MARRIAGE                    29685 non-null int64
AGE                         29685 non-null int64
PAY_1                       29685 non-null object
PAY_2                       29685 non-null int64
PAY_3                       29685 non-null int64
PAY_4                       29685 non-null int64
PAY_5                       29685 non-null int64
PAY_6                       29685 non-null int64
BILL_AMT1                   29685 non-null int64
BILL_AMT2                   29685 non-null int64
BILL_AMT3                   29685 non-null int64
BILL_AMT4                   29685 non-null int64
BILL_AMT5                   29685 non-null int64
BILL_AMT6                   29685 non-null int64
PAY_AMT1                    29685 non-null int64
PAY_AMT2                    29685 non-null int64
PAY_AMT3                    29685 non-null int64
PAY_AMT4                    29685 non-null int64
PAY_AMT5                    29685 non-null int64
PAY_AMT6                    29685 non-null int64
default payment next month  29685 non-null int64
dtypes: int64(23), object(2)
memory usage: 5.9+ MB
```

Figure 1.23: Getting column metadata

We can see in *Figure 1.23* that there are 25 columns. Each row has 29,685 **non-null** values, according to this summary, which is the number of rows in the DataFrame. This would indicate that there is no missing data, in the sense that each cell contains some value. However, if there is a fill value to represent missing data, that would not be evident here.

We also see that most columns say `int64` next to them, indicating they are an **integer** data type, that is, numbers such as ..., -2, -1, 0, 1, 2,... . The exceptions are `ID` and `PAY_1`. We are already familiar with `ID`; this contains strings, which are account IDs. What about `PAY_1`? According to the data dictionary, we'd expect this to contain integers, like all the other features. Let's take a closer look at this column.

2. Use the `.head(n)` pandas method to view the top **n** rows of the `PAY_1` Series:

```
df_clean_1['PAY_1'].head(5)
```

You should obtain the following output:

```
0        2
1       -1
2        0
3        0
4       -1
Name: PAY_1, dtype: object
```

**Figure 1.24: Examine a few columns' contents**

The integers on the left of the output are the DataFrame index, which is simply consecutive integers starting with 0. The data from the `PAY_1` column is shown on the right. This is supposed to be the payment status of the most recent month's bill, using the values –1, 1, 2, 3, and so on. However, we can see that there are values of 0 here, which are not documented in the data dictionary. According to the data dictionary, *"The measurement scale for the repayment status is: -1 = pay duly; 1 = payment delay for one month; 2 = payment delay for two months; . . .; 8 = payment delay for eight months; 9 = payment delay for nine months and above"* (https://archive.ics.uci.edu/ml/datasets/default+of+credit+card+clients). Let's take a closer look, using the value counts of this column.

3. Obtain the value counts for the **PAY_1** column by using the `.value_counts()` method:

```
df_clean_1['PAY_1'].value_counts()
```

You should see the following output:

```
0                13087
-1                5047
1                 3261
Not available     3021
-2                2476
2                 2378
3                  292
4                   63
5                   23
8                   17
6                   11
7                    9
Name: PAY_1, dtype: int64
```

**Figure 1.25: Value counts of the PAY_1 column**

The preceding output reveals the presence of two undocumented values: 0 and –2, as well as the reason this column was imported by pandas as an **object** data type, instead of **int64** as we would expect for integer data: there is a **'Not available'** string present in this column, symbolizing missing data. Later on in the book, we'll come back to this when we consider how to deal with missing data. For now, we'll remove rows of the dataset in which this feature has a missing value.

4. Use a logical mask with the **!=** operator (which means "does not equal" in Python) to find all the rows that don't have missing data for the **PAY_1** feature:

```
valid_pay_1_mask = df_clean_1['PAY_1'] != 'Not available'
valid_pay_1_mask[0:5]
```

By running the preceding code, you will obtain the following output:

```
0       True
1       True
2       True
3       True
4       True
Name: PAY_1, dtype: bool
```

**Figure 1.26: Creating a Boolean mask**

5.  Check how many rows have no missing data by calculating the sum of the mask:

```
sum(valid_pay_1_mask)
```

You will obtain the following output:

```
26664
```

We see that 26,664 rows do not have the value **'Not available'** in the **PAY_1** column. We saw from the value count that 3,021 rows do have this value. Does this make sense? From *Figure 1.23* we know there are 29,685 entries (rows) in the dataset, and 29,685 – 3,021 = 26,664, so this checks out.

6.  Clean the data by eliminating the rows with the missing values of **PAY_1** as shown:

```
df_clean_2 = df_clean_1.loc[valid_pay_1_mask,:].copy()
```

7.  Obtain the shape of the cleaned data using the following command:

```
df_clean_2.shape
```

You will obtain the following output:

```
(26664, 25)
```

After removing these rows, we check that the resulting DataFrame has the expected shape. You can also check for yourself whether the value counts indicate the desired values have been removed like this: **df_clean_2['PAY_1'].value_counts()**.

Lastly, so this column's data type can be consistent with the others, we will cast it from the generic **object** type to **int64** like all the other features, using the **.astype** method. Then we select a couple of columns, including **PAY_1**, to examine the data types and make sure it worked.

8.  Run the following command to convert the data type for **PAY_1** from **object** to **int64** and show the column metadata for **PAY_1** and **PAY_2** by using a list to select multiple columns:

```
df_clean_2['PAY_1'] = df_clean_2['PAY_1'].astype('int64')
df_clean_2[['PAY_1', 'PAY_2']].info()
```

This is the output you will obtain:

```
<class 'pandas.core.frame.DataFrame'>
Int64Index: 26664 entries, 0 to 29684
Data columns (total 2 columns):
 #   Column  Non-Null Count  Dtype
---  ------  --------------  -----
 0   PAY_1   26664 non-null  int64
 1   PAY_2   26664 non-null  int64
dtypes: int64(2)
memory usage: 624.9 KB
```

**Figure 1.27: Check the data type of the cleaned column**

Congratulations, you have completed your second data cleaning operation! However, if you recall, during this process we also noticed the undocumented values of –2 and 0 in **PAY_1**. Now, let's imagine we got back in touch with our business partner and learned the following information:

- -2 means the account started that month with a zero balance and never used any credit.

- -1 means the account had a balance that was paid in full.

- 0 means that at least the minimum payment was made, but the entire balance wasn't paid (that is, a positive balance was carried to the next month).

We thank our business partner since this answers our questions, for now. Maintaining a good line of communication and working relationship with the business partner is important, as you can see here, and may determine the success or failure of a project.

In your notebook, save your progress from this exercise like this:

```
df_clean_2.to_csv('../../Data/df_clean_2.csv', index=False)
```

# DATA QUALITY ASSURANCE AND EXPLORATION

So far, we remedied two data quality issues just by asking basic questions or by looking at the `.info()` summary. Let's now take a look at the first few columns of data. Before we get to the historical bill payments, we have the credit limits of the **LIMIT_BAL** accounts, and the **SEX**, **EDUCATION**, **MARRIAGE**, and **AGE** demographic features. Our business partner has reached out to us, to let us know that gender should not be used to predict credit-worthiness, as this is **unethical** by their standards. So we keep this in mind for future reference. Now we'll explore the rest of these columns, making any corrections that are necessary.

In order to further explore the data, we will use **histograms**. Histograms are a good way to visualize data that is on a continuous scale, such as currency amounts and ages. A histogram groups similar values into bins and shows the number of data points in these bins as a bar graph.

To plot histograms, we will start to get familiar with the graphical capabilities of pandas. pandas relies on another library called **Matplotlib** to create graphics, so we'll also set some options using **matplotlib**. Using these tools, we'll also learn how to get quick statistical summaries of data in pandas.

## EXERCISE 1.06: EXPLORING THE CREDIT LIMIT AND DEMOGRAPHIC FEATURES

In this exercise, we'll start our exploration of data with the credit limit and age features. We will visualize them and get summary statistics to check that the data contained in these features is sensible. Then we will look at the education and marriage categorical features to see if the values there make sense, correcting them as necessary. **LIMIT_BAL** and **AGE** are numerical features, meaning they are measured on a continuous scale. Consequently, we'll use histograms to visualize them. Perform the following steps to complete the exercise:

> **NOTE**
>
> The Jupyter notebook for this exercise found here: https://packt.link/PRdtP.

1. In addition to pandas, import **matplotlib** and set up some plotting options with this code snippet. Note the use of comments in Python with **#**. Anything appearing after a **#** on a line will be ignored by the Python interpreter:

```
import pandas as pd

import matplotlib.pyplot as plt #import plotting package

#render plotting automatically
%matplotlib inline

import matplotlib as mpl #additional plotting functionality

mpl.rcParams['figure.dpi'] = 400 #high resolution figures
```

This imports **matplotlib** and uses **.rcParams** to set the resolution (**dpi** = dots per inch) for a nice crisp image; you may not want to worry about this last part unless you are preparing things for presentation, as it could make the images quite large in your notebook.

2. Load our progress from the previous exercise using the following code:

```
df_clean_2 = pd.read_csv('../Data/df_clean_2.csv'),
```

3. Run **df_clean_2[['LIMIT_BAL', 'AGE']].hist()** and you should see the following histograms:

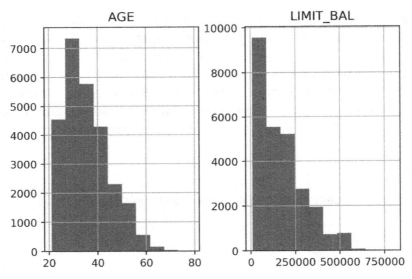

Figure 1.28: Histograms of the credit limit and age data

This is a nice visual snapshot of these features. We can get a quick, approximate look at all of the data in this way. In order to see statistics such as the mean and median (that is, the 50th percentile), there is another helpful pandas function.

4. Generate a tabular report of summary statistics using the following command:

```
df_clean_2[['LIMIT_BAL', 'AGE']].describe()
```

You should see the following output:

| | LIMIT_BAL | AGE |
|---|---|---|
| count | 26664.000000 | 26664.000000 |
| mean | 167919.054905 | 35.505213 |
| std | 129839.453081 | 9.227442 |
| min | 10000.000000 | 21.000000 |
| 25% | 50000.000000 | 28.000000 |
| 50% | 140000.000000 | 34.000000 |
| 75% | 240000.000000 | 41.000000 |
| max | 800000.000000 | 79.000000 |

Figure 1.29: Statistical summaries of credit limit and age data

Based on the histograms and the convenient statistics computed by `.describe()`, which include a count of non-nulls, the mean and standard deviation, minimum, maximum, and quartiles, we can make a few judgments.

**LIMIT_BAL**, the credit limit, seems to make sense. The credit limits have a minimum of 10,000. This dataset is from Taiwan; the exact unit of currency (NT dollar) may not be familiar, but intuitively, a credit limit should be above zero. You are encouraged to look up the conversion to your local currency and consider these credit limits. For example, 1 US dollar is about 30 NT dollars.

The **AGE** feature also looks reasonably distributed, with no one under the age of 21 having a credit account.

For the categorical features, a look at the value counts is useful, since there are relatively few unique values.

5.  Obtain the value counts for the **EDUCATION** feature using the following code:

```
df_clean_2['EDUCATION'].value_counts()
```

You should see this output:

```
2       12458
1        9412
3        4380
5         245
4         115
6          43
0          11
Name: EDUCATION, dtype: int64
```

Figure 1.30: Value counts of the EDUCATION feature

Here, we see undocumented education levels 0, 5, and 6, as the data dictionary describes only **Education (1 = graduate school; 2 = university; 3 = high school; 4 = others)**. Our business partner tells us they don't know about the others. Since they are not very prevalent, we will lump them in with the **others** category, which seems appropriate.

6.  Run this code to combine the undocumented levels of the **EDUCATION** feature into the level for **others** and then examine the results:

```
df_clean_2['EDUCATION'].replace(to_replace=[0, 5, 6],\
                                value=4, inplace=True)
df_clean_2['EDUCATION'].value_counts()
```

The pandas **.replace** method makes doing the replacements described in the preceding step pretty quick. Once you run the code, you should see this output:

```
2       12458
1        9412
3        4380
4         414
Name: EDUCATION, dtype: int64
```

Figure 1.31: Cleaning the EDUCATION feature

Note that here we make this change **in place** (`inplace=True`). This means that, instead of returning a new DataFrame, this operation will make the change on the existing DataFrame.

7. Obtain the value counts for the **MARRIAGE** feature using the following code:

```
df_clean_2['MARRIAGE'].value_counts()
```

You should obtain the following output:

```
2      14158
1      12172
3        286
0         48
Name: MARRIAGE, dtype: int64
```

Figure 1.32: Value counts of the raw MARRIAGE feature

The issue here is similar to that encountered for the **EDUCATION** feature; there is a value, 0, which is not documented in the data dictionary: `1 = married; 2 = single; 3 = others`. So we'll lump it in with `others`.

8. Change the values of 0 in the **MARRIAGE** feature to 3 and examine the result with this code:

```
df_clean_2['MARRIAGE'].replace(to_replace=0, value=3, \
                               inplace=True)
df_clean_2['MARRIAGE'].value_counts()
```

The output should be as follows:

```
2      14158
1      12172
3        334
Name: MARRIAGE, dtype: int64
```

Figure 1.33: Value counts of the cleaned MARRIAGE feature

We've now accomplished a lot of exploration and cleaning of the data. We will do some more advanced visualization and exploration of the financial history features that come after this in the DataFrame, later. First, we'll consider the meaning of the **EDUCATION** feature, a categorical feature in our dataset.

Save your progress from this exercise as follows:

```
df_clean_2.to_csv('../../Data/df_clean_2_01.csv', index=False)
```

# DEEP DIVE: CATEGORICAL FEATURES

Machine learning algorithms only work with numbers. If your data contains text features, for example, these would require transformation to numbers in some way. We learned above that the data for our case study is, in fact, entirely numerical. However, it's worth thinking about how it got to be that way. In particular, consider the **EDUCATION** feature.

This is an example of what is called a **categorical feature**: you can imagine that as raw data, this column consisted of the text labels `graduate school`, `university`, `high school`, and `others`. These are called the **levels** of the categorical feature; here, there are four levels. It is only through a mapping, which has already been chosen for us, that this data exists as the numbers 1, 2, 3, and 4 in our dataset. This particular assignment of categories to numbers creates what is known as an **ordinal feature**, since the levels are mapped to numbers in order. As a data scientist, at a minimum, you need to be aware of such mappings, if you are not choosing them yourself.

### What are the implications of this mapping?

It makes some sense that the education levels are ranked, with 1 corresponding to the highest level of education in our dataset, 2 to the next highest, 3 to the next, and 4 presumably including the lowest levels. However, when you use this encoding as a numerical feature in a machine learning model, it will be treated just like any other numerical feature. For some models, this effect may not be desired.

### What if a model seeks to find a straight-line relationship between the features and response?

This may seem like an arbitrary question, although later in the book you will learn the importance of distinguishing between linear and non-linear models. In this section, we will briefly introduce the concept that some models do look for linear relationships between features and the response variable. Whether or not this would work well in the case of the education feature depends on the actual relationship between different levels of education and the outcome we are trying to predict.

Here, we examine two hypothetical cases of synthetic data with ordinal categorical variables, each with 10 levels. The levels measure the self-reported satisfaction of customers visiting a website. The average number of minutes spent on the website for customers reporting each level is plotted on the y-axis. We've also plotted the line of best fit in each case to illustrate how a linear model would deal with this data, as shown in the following figure:

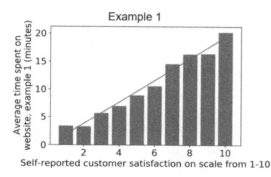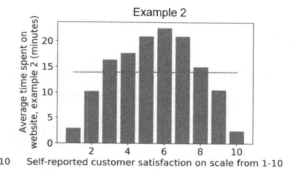

Figure 1.34: Ordinal features may or may not work well in a linear model

We can see that if an algorithm assumes a linear (straight-line) relationship between the features and response variable, this may or may not work well depending on the true relationship. Notice that in this synthetic example, we are modeling a regression problem: the response variable takes on a continuous range of numbers. While our case study involves a classification problem, some classification algorithms such as **logistic regression** also assume a linear effect of the features. We will discuss this in greater detail later when we get into modeling the data for our case study.

Roughly speaking, for a binary classification problem, meaning the response variable only has two outcomes, which we'll assume are coded as 0 and 1, you can look at the different levels of a categorical feature in terms of the average values of the response variable within each level. These average values represent the "rates" of the positive class (that is, the samples where the response variable = 1) for each level. This can give you an idea of whether an ordinal encoding will work well with a linear model. Assuming you've imported the same packages in your Jupyter notebook as in the previous sections, you can quickly look at this using a **groupby/agg**regate procedure and a bar plot in pandas.

This will group the data by the values in the **EDUCATION** feature and then within each group aggregate the data together using the average of the **default payment next month** response variable:

```
df_clean_2 = pd.read_csv('../../Data/df_clean_2_01.csv')
df_clean_2.groupby('EDUCATION').agg({'default payment next '\
                                    'month':'mean'})\
                          .plot.bar(legend=False)
plt.ylabel('Default rate')
plt.xlabel('Education level: ordinal encoding')
```

Once you run the code, you should obtain the following output:

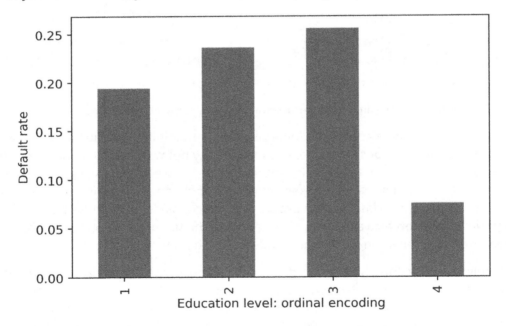

**Figure 1.35: Default rate within education levels**

Similar to *Example 2* in *Figure 1.34*, it looks like a straight-line fit would probably not be the best description of the data here. In case a feature has a non-linear effect like this, it may be better to use a more complex algorithm such as a **decision tree** or **random forest**. Or, if a simpler and more interpretable linear model such as logistic regression is desired, we could avoid an ordinal encoding and use a different way of encoding categorical variables. A popular way of doing this is called **one-hot encoding (OHE)**.

OHE is a way to transform a categorical feature, which may consist of text labels in the raw data, into a numerical feature that can be used in mathematical models.

Let's learn about this in an exercise. And if you are wondering why a logistic regression is more interpretable and a random forest is more complex, we will be learning about these concepts in detail in later chapters.

## EXERCISE 1.07: IMPLEMENTING OHE FOR A CATEGORICAL FEATURE

In this exercise, we will "reverse engineer" the **EDUCATION** feature in the dataset to obtain the text labels that represent the different education levels, then show how to use pandas to create an OHE. As a preliminary step, please set up the environment and load in the progress from previous exercises:

```
import pandas as pd
import matplotlib as mpl #additional plotting functionality
mpl.rcParams['figure.dpi'] = 400 #high resolution figures
df_clean_2 = pd.read_csv('../../Data/df_clean_2_01.csv')
```

First, let's consider our **EDUCATION** feature before it was encoded as an ordinal. From the data dictionary, we know that 1 = graduate school, 2 = university, 3 = high school, 4 = others. We would like to recreate a column that has these strings, instead of numbers. Perform the following steps to complete the exercise:

> **NOTE**
>
> The Jupyter notebook for this exercise found here: https://packt.link/akAYJ.

1. Create an empty column for the categorical labels called **EDUCATION_CAT**. Using the following command, every row will contain the string **'none'**:

```
df_clean_2['EDUCATION_CAT'] = 'none'
```

2. Examine the first few rows of the DataFrame for the **EDUCATION** and **EDUCATION_CAT** columns:

```
df_clean_2[['EDUCATION', 'EDUCATION_CAT']].head(10)
```

The output should appear as follows:

| | EDUCATION | EDUCATION_CAT |
|---|---|---|
| 0 | 2 | none |
| 1 | 2 | none |
| 2 | 2 | none |
| 3 | 2 | none |
| 4 | 2 | none |
| 5 | 1 | none |
| 6 | 1 | none |
| 7 | 2 | none |
| 8 | 3 | none |
| 9 | 3 | none |

Figure 1.36: Selecting columns and viewing the first 10 rows

We need to populate this new column with the appropriate strings. pandas provides a convenient functionality for mapping all values of a Series onto new values. This function is in fact called `.map` and relies on a dictionary to establish the correspondence between the old values and the new values. Our goal here is to map the numbers in **EDUCATION** onto the strings they represent. For example, where the **EDUCATION** column equals the number 1, we'll assign the `'graduate school'` string to the **EDUCATION_CAT** column, and so on for the other education levels.

3. Create a dictionary that describes the mapping for education categories using the following code:

```
cat_mapping = {1: "graduate school",\
               2: "university",\
               3: "high school",\
               4: "others"}
```

4. Apply the mapping to the original **EDUCATION** column using `.map` and assign the result to the new **EDUCATION_CAT** column:

```
df_clean_2['EDUCATION_CAT'] = df_clean_2['EDUCATION']\
                              .map(cat_mapping)
df_clean_2[['EDUCATION', 'EDUCATION_CAT']].head(10)
```

After running those lines, you should see the following output:

| | EDUCATION | EDUCATION_CAT |
|---|---|---|
| 0 | 2 | university |
| 1 | 2 | university |
| 2 | 2 | university |
| 3 | 2 | university |
| 4 | 2 | university |
| 5 | 1 | graduate school |
| 6 | 1 | graduate school |
| 7 | 2 | university |
| 8 | 3 | high school |
| 9 | 3 | high school |

Figure 1.37: Examining the string values corresponding to the ordinal encoding of EDUCATION

Excellent! Note that we could have skipped *Step 1*, where we assigned the new column with `'none'`, and gone straight to *Steps 3* and *4* to create the new column. However, sometimes it's useful to create a new column initialized with a single value, so it's worth knowing how to do that.

Now we are ready to one-hot encode. We can do this by passing a Series of a **DataFrame** to the pandas **get_dummies()** function. The function got this name because one-hot encoded columns are also referred to as **dummy variables**. The result will be a new DataFrame, with as many columns as there are levels of the categorical variable.

5. Run this code to create a one-hot encoded DataFrame of the **EDUCATION_CAT** column. Examine the first 10 rows:

```
edu_ohe = pd.get_dummies(df_clean_2['EDUCATION_CAT'])
edu_ohe.head(10)
```

This should produce the following output:

| | graduate school | high school | none | others | university |
|---|---|---|---|---|---|
| 0 | 0 | 0 | 0 | 0 | 1 |
| 1 | 0 | 0 | 0 | 0 | 1 |
| 2 | 0 | 0 | 0 | 0 | 1 |
| 3 | 0 | 0 | 0 | 0 | 1 |
| 4 | 0 | 0 | 0 | 0 | 1 |
| 5 | 1 | 0 | 0 | 0 | 0 |
| 6 | 1 | 0 | 0 | 0 | 0 |
| 7 | 0 | 0 | 0 | 0 | 1 |
| 8 | 0 | 1 | 0 | 0 | 0 |
| 9 | 0 | 1 | 0 | 0 | 0 |

Figure 1.38: DataFrame of one-hot encoding

You can now see why this is called "one-hot encoding": across all these columns, any particular row will have a 1 in exactly 1 column, and 0s in the rest. For a given row, the column with the 1 should match up to the level of the original categorical variable. To check this, we need to concatenate this new DataFrame with the original one and examine the results side by side. We will use the pandas **concat** function, to which we pass the list of DataFrames we wish to concatenate, and the **axis=1** keyword saying to concatenate them horizontally; that is, along the column axis. This basically means we are combining these two DataFrames "side by side," which we know we can do because we just created this new DataFrame from the original one: we know it will have the same number of rows, which will be in the same order as the original DataFrame.

6. Concatenate the one-hot encoded DataFrame to the original DataFrame as follows:

```
df_with_ohe = pd.concat([df_clean_2, edu_ohe], axis=1)
df_with_ohe[['EDUCATION_CAT', 'graduate school',\
             'high school', 'university', 'others']].head(10)
```

You should see this output:

| | EDUCATION_CAT | graduate school | high school | university | others |
|---|---|---|---|---|---|
| 0 | university | 0 | 0 | 1 | 0 |
| 1 | university | 0 | 0 | 1 | 0 |
| 2 | university | 0 | 0 | 1 | 0 |
| 3 | university | 0 | 0 | 1 | 0 |
| 4 | university | 0 | 0 | 1 | 0 |
| 5 | graduate school | 1 | 0 | 0 | 0 |
| 6 | graduate school | 1 | 0 | 0 | 0 |
| 7 | university | 0 | 0 | 1 | 0 |
| 8 | high school | 0 | 1 | 0 | 0 |
| 9 | high school | 0 | 1 | 0 | 0 |

Figure 1.39: Checking the one-hot encoded columns

Alright, looks like this has worked as intended. OHE is another way to encode categorical features that avoids the implied numerical structure of an ordinal encoding. However, notice what has happened here: we have taken a single column, **EDUCATION**, and exploded it out into as many columns as there were levels in the feature. In this case, since there are only four levels, this is not such a big deal. However, if your categorical variable had a very large number of levels, you may want to consider an alternate strategy, such as grouping some levels together into single categories.

This is a good time to save the DataFrame we've created here, which encapsulates our efforts at cleaning the data and adding an OHE column.

Write the latest DataFrame to a file like this: **df_with_ohe.to_csv('../../Data/Chapter_1_cleaned_data.csv', index=False)**.

# EXPLORING THE FINANCIAL HISTORY FEATURES IN THE DATASET

We are ready to explore the rest of the features in the case study dataset. First set up the environment and load data from the previous exercise. This can be done using the following snippet:

```
import pandas as pd
import matplotlib.pyplot as plt #import plotting package
#render plotting automatically
%matplotlib inline
import matplotlib as mpl #additional plotting functionality
mpl.rcParams['figure.dpi'] = 400 #high resolution figures
import numpy as np
df = pd.read_csv('../../Data/Chapter_1_cleaned_data.csv')
```

> **NOTE**
>
> The path to your CSV file may be different depending on where you saved it.

The remaining features to be examined are the financial history features. They fall naturally into three groups: the status of the monthly payments for the last 6 months, and the billed and paid amounts for the same period. First, let's look at the payment statuses. It is convenient to break these out as a list so we can study them together. You can do this using the following code:

```
pay_feats = ['PAY_1', 'PAY_2', 'PAY_3', 'PAY_4', 'PAY_5', \
             'PAY_6']
```

We can use the **.describe** method on these six Series to examine summary statistics:

```
df[pay_feats].describe()
```

This should produce the following output:

```
df[pay_feats].describe()
```

| | PAY_1 | PAY_2 | PAY_3 | PAY_4 | PAY_5 | PAY_6 |
|---|---|---|---|---|---|---|
| count | 26664.000000 | 26664.000000 | 26664.000000 | 26664.000000 | 26664.000000 | 26664.000000 |
| mean | -0.017777 | -0.133363 | -0.167679 | -0.225023 | -0.269764 | -0.293579 |
| std | 1.126769 | 1.198640 | 1.199165 | 1.167897 | 1.131735 | 1.150229 |
| min | -2.000000 | -2.000000 | -2.000000 | -2.000000 | -2.000000 | -2.000000 |
| 25% | -1.000000 | -1.000000 | -1.000000 | -1.000000 | -1.000000 | -1.000000 |
| 50% | 0.000000 | 0.000000 | 0.000000 | 0.000000 | 0.000000 | 0.000000 |
| 75% | 0.000000 | 0.000000 | 0.000000 | 0.000000 | 0.000000 | 0.000000 |
| max | 8.000000 | 8.000000 | 8.000000 | 8.000000 | 8.000000 | 8.000000 |

Figure 1.40: Summary statistics of payment status features

Here, we observe that the range of values is the same for all of these features: -2, -1, 0, ... 8. It appears that the value of 9, described in the data dictionary as *payment delay for nine months and above*, is never observed.

We have already clarified the meaning of all of these levels, some of which were not in the original data dictionary. Now let's look again at the **value_counts()** of **PAY_1**, now sorted by the values we are counting, which are the **index** of this Series:

```
df[pay_feats[0]].value_counts().sort_index()
```

This should produce the following output:

```
-2       2476
-1       5047
 0      13087
 1       3261
 2       2378
 3        292
 4         63
 5         23
 6         11
 7          9
 8         17
Name: PAY_1, dtype: int64
```

**Figure 1.41: Value counts of the payment status for the previous month**

Compared to the positive integer values, most of the values are either -2, -1, or 0, which correspond to an account that was in good standing last month: not used, paid in full, or made at least the minimum payment.

Notice that, because of the definition of the other values of this variable (1 = payment delay for 1 month; 2 = payment delay for 2 months, and so on), this feature is sort of a hybrid of categorical and numerical features. Why should no credit usage correspond to a value of -2, while a value of 2 means a 2-month late payment, and so forth? We should acknowledge that the numerical coding of payment statuses -2, -1, and 0 constitute a decision made by the creator of the dataset on how to encode certain categorical features, which were then lumped in with a feature that is truly numerical: the number of months of payment delay (values of 1 and larger). Later on, we will consider the potential effects of this way of doing things on the predictive capability of this feature.

For now, we will continue to explore the data. This dataset is small enough, with 18 of these financial features and a handful of others, that we can afford to individually examine every feature. If the dataset had thousands of features, we would likely forgo this and instead explore **dimensionality reduction** techniques, which are ways to condense the information in a large number of features down to a smaller number of derived features, or, alternatively, methods of **feature selection**, which can be used to isolate the important features from a candidate field of many. We will demonstrate and explain some feature selection techniques later. But on this dataset, it's feasible to visualize every feature. As we know from the last chapter, a histogram is a good way to get a quick visual interpretation of the same kind of information we would get from tables of value counts. You can try this on the most recent month's payment status features with `df[pay_feats[0]].hist()`, to produce this:

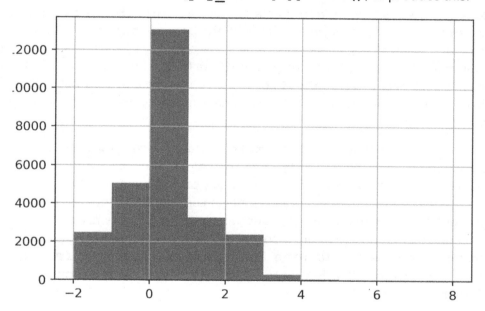

Figure 1.42: Histogram of PAY_1 using default arguments

Now we're going to take an in-depth look at how this graphic is produced and consider whether it is as informative as it should be. A key point about the graphical functionality of pandas is that **pandas plotting actually calls matplotlib under the hood**. Notice that the last available argument to the pandas `.hist()` method is **\*\*kwds**, which the documentation indicates are `matplotlib` keyword arguments.

> **NOTE**
>
> For more information, refer to the following: https://pandas.pydata.org/pandas-docs/stable/reference/api/pandas.DataFrame.hist.html.

Looking at the `matplotlib` documentation for `matplotlib.pyplot.hist` shows additional arguments you can use with the pandas `.hist()` method, such as the type of histogram to plot (see https://matplotlib.org/api/_as_gen/matplotlib.pyplot.hist.html for more details). In general, to get more details about plotting functionality, it's important to be aware of `matplotlib`, and in some scenarios, you will want to use `matplotlib` directly, instead of pandas, to have more control over the appearance of plots.

You should be aware that pandas uses `matplotlib`, which in turn uses NumPy. When plotting histograms with `matplotlib`, the numerical calculation for the values that make up the histogram is actually carried out by the NumPy `.histogram` function. This is a key example of code reuse, or "not reinventing the wheel." If a standard functionality, such as plotting a histogram, already has a good implementation in Python, there is no reason to create it anew. And if the mathematical operation to create the histogram data for the plot is already implemented, this should be leveraged as well. This shows the interconnectedness of the Python ecosystem.

We'll now address a couple of key issues that arise when calculating and plotting histograms.

**Number of bins**

Histograms work by grouping together values into what are called **bins**. The number of bins is the number of vertical bars that make up the discrete histogram plot we see. If there are a large number of unique values on a continuous scale, such as the histogram of ages we viewed earlier, histogram plotting works relatively well "out of the box," with default arguments. However, when the number of unique values is close to the number of bins, the results may be a little misleading. The default number of bins is 10, while in the **PAY_1** feature, there are 11 unique values. In cases like this, it's better to manually set the number of histogram bins to the number of unique values.

In our current example, since there are very few values in the higher bins of **PAY_1**, the plot may not look much different. But in general, this is important to keep in mind when plotting histograms.

**Bin edges**

The locations of the edges of the bins determine how the values get grouped in the histogram. Instead of indicating the number of bins to the plotting function, you could alternatively supply a list or array of numbers for the **bins** keyword argument. This input would be interpreted as the bin edge locations on the x-axis. The way values are grouped into bins in **matplotlib**, using the edge locations, is important to understand. All bins, except the last one, group together values as low as the left edge, and up to **but not including** values as high as the right edge. In other words, the left edge is closed but the right edge is open for these bins. However, the last bin includes both edges; it has a closed left and right edge. This is of more practical importance when you are binning a relatively small number of unique values that may land on the bin edges.

For control over plot appearance, it's usually better to specify the bin edge locations. We'll create an array of 12 numbers, which will result in 11 bins, each one centered around 1 of the unique values of **PAY_1**:

```
pay_1_bins = np.array(range(-2,10)) - 0.5
pay_1_bins
```

The output shows the bin edge locations:

```
array([-2.5, -1.5, -0.5, 0.5, 1.5, 2.5,\
       3.5,4.5, 5.5, 6.5, 7.5,8.5])
```

As a final point of style, it is important to always *label your plots* so that they are interpretable. We haven't yet done this manually, because in some cases, pandas does it automatically, and in other cases, we simply left the plots unlabeled. From now on, we will follow best practice and label all plots. We use the **xlabel** and **ylabel** functions in **matplotlib** to add axis labels to this plot. The code is as follows:

```
df[pay_feats[0]].hist(bins=pay_1_bins)
plt.xlabel('PAY_1')
plt.ylabel('Number of accounts')
```

The output should look like this:

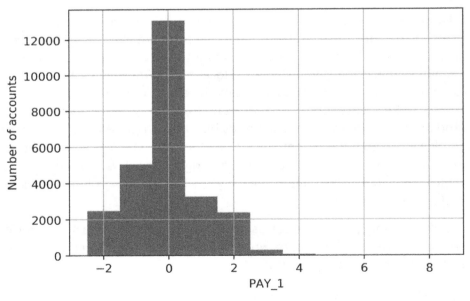

Figure 1.43: A better histogram of PAY_1

*Figure 1.43* represents an improved histogram, since the bars are centered over the actual values in the data, and there is 1 bar per unique value. While it's tempting, and often sufficient, to just call plotting functions with the default arguments, one of your jobs as a data scientist is to create *accurate and representative data visualizations*. To do that, sometimes you need to dig into the details of plotting code, as we've done here.

**What have we learned from this data visualization?**

Since we already looked at the value counts, this confirms for us that most accounts are in good standing (values -2, -1, and 0). For those that aren't, it's more common for the "months late" to be a smaller number. This makes sense; likely, most people are paying off their balances before too long. Otherwise, their account may be closed or sold to a collection agency. Examining the distribution of your features and making sure it seems reasonable is a good thing to confirm with your client, as the quality of this data underlies the predictive modeling you seek to do.

Now that we've established some good plotting style for histograms, let's use pandas to plot multiple histograms together, and visualize the payment status features for each of the last 6 months. We can pass our list of column names **pay_feats** to access multiple columns to plot with the **.hist()** method, specifying the bin edges we've already determined, and indicating we'd like a 2 by 3 grid of plots. First, we set the font size small enough to fit between these **subplots**. Here is the code for this:

```
mpl.rcParams['font.size'] = 4
df[pay_feats].hist(bins=pay_1_bins, layout=(2,3))
```

The plot titles have been created automatically for us based on the column names. The y-axes are understood to be counts. The resulting visualizations are as follows:

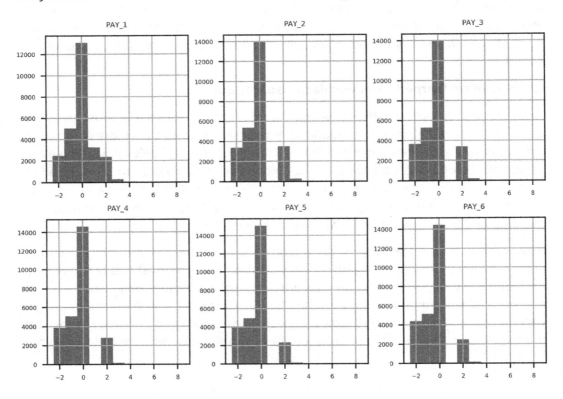

**Figure 1.44: Grid of histogram subplots**

We've already seen the first of these, and it makes sense. What about the rest of them? Remember the definitions of the positive integer values of these features, and what each feature means. For example, **PAY_2** is the repayment status in August, **PAY_3** is the repayment status in July, and the others go further back in time. A value of 1 means a payment delay for 1 month, while a value of 2 means a payment delay for 2 months, and so forth.

Did you notice that something doesn't seem right? Consider the values between July (**PAY_3**) and August (**PAY_2**). In July, there are very few accounts that had a 1-month payment delay; this bar is not really visible in the histogram. However, in August, there are suddenly thousands of accounts with a 2-month payment delay. This does not make sense: the number of accounts with a 2-month delay in a given month should be less than or equal to the number of accounts with a 1-month delay in the previous month.

Let's take a closer look at accounts with a 2-month delay in August and see what the payment status was in July. We can do this with the following code, using a Boolean mask and .loc, as shown in the following snippet:

```
df.loc[df['PAY_2']==2, ['PAY_2', 'PAY_3']].head()
```

The output of this should appear as follows:

|  | PAY_2 | PAY_3 |
| --- | --- | --- |
| 0 | 2 | -1 |
| 1 | 2 | 0 |
| 13 | 2 | 2 |
| 15 | 2 | 0 |
| 47 | 2 | 2 |

Figure 1.45: Payment status in July (PAY_3) of accounts with a 2-month payment delay in August (PAY_2)

From *Figure 1.45*, it's clear that accounts with a 2-month delay in August have nonsensical values for the July payment status. The only way to progress to a 2-month delay should be from a 1-month delay the previous month, yet none of these accounts indicate that.

When you see something like this in the data, you need to either check the logic in the query used to create the dataset or contact the person who gave you the dataset. After double-checking these results, for example using .value_counts() to view the numbers directly, we contact our client to inquire about this issue.

The client lets us know that they had been having problems with pulling the most recent month of data, leading to faulty reporting for accounts that had a 1-month delay in payment. In September, they had mostly fixed these problems (although not entirely; that is why there were missing values in the PAY_1 feature, as we found). So, in our dataset, the value of 1 is underreported in all months except for September (the PAY_1 feature). In theory, the client could create a query to look back into their database and determine the correct values for PAY_2, PAY_3, and so on up to PAY_6. However, for practical reasons, they won't be able to complete this retrospective analysis in time for us to receive it and include it in our project.

Because of this, only the most recent month of our payment status data is correct. This means that, of all the payment status features, only **PAY_1** is representative of future data, those that will be used to make predictions with the model we develop. This is a key point: *a predictive model relies on getting the same kind of data to make predictions as it was built with*. This means we can use **PAY_1** as a feature in our model, but not **PAY_2** or the other payment status features from previous months.

This episode shows the importance of a thorough examination of data quality. Only by carefully combing through the data did we discover this issue. It would have been nice if the client had told us up front that they had been having reporting issues over the last few months, when our dataset was collected, and that the reporting procedure was not **consistent** during that time period. However, ultimately it is our responsibility to build a credible model, so we need to be sure we believe the data is correct, by making this kind of detailed exploration. We explain to the client that we can't use the older features since they are not representative of the future data the model will be **scored** on (that is, to make predictions on future months), and ask them to let us know of any further data issues they are aware of. There are none at this time.

## ACTIVITY 1.01: EXPLORING THE REMAINING FINANCIAL FEATURES IN THE DATASET

In this activity, you will examine the remaining financial features in a similar way to how we examined **PAY_1**, **PAY_2**, **PAY_3**, and so on. In order to better visualize some of this data, we'll use a mathematical function that should be familiar: the logarithm. You'll use pandas' **apply** method, which serves to apply any function to an entire column or DataFrame in the process. Once you complete the activity, you should have the following set of histograms of logarithmic transformations of non-zero payments:

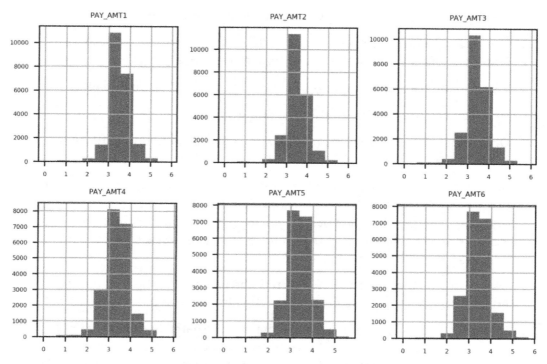

**Figure 1.46: Expected set of histograms**

Perform the following steps to complete the activity:

Before beginning, set up your environment and load in the cleaned dataset as follows:

```
import pandas as pd
import matplotlib.pyplot as plt #import plotting package
#render plotting automatically
%matplotlib inline
import matplotlib as mpl #additional plotting functionality
mpl.rcParams['figure.dpi'] = 400 #high resolution figures
mpl.rcParams['font.size'] = 4 #font size for figures
from scipy import stats
import numpy as np
df = pd.read_csv('../../Data/Chapter_1_cleaned_data.csv')
```

1.  Create lists of feature names for the remaining financial features.

2.  Use `.describe()` to examine statistical summaries of the bill amount features. Reflect on what you see. Does it make sense?

3.  Visualize the bill amount features using a 2 by 3 grid of histogram plots.

    Hint: You can use 20 bins for this visualization.

4.  Obtain the `.describe()` summary of the payment amount features. Does it make sense?

5.  Plot a histogram of the bill payment features similar to the bill amount features, but also apply some rotation to the x-axis labels with the **xrot** keyword argument so that they don't overlap. In any plotting function, you can include the **xrot=<angle>** keyword argument to rotate x-axis labels by a given angle in degrees. Consider the results.

6.  Use a Boolean mask to see how much of the payment amount data is exactly equal to 0. Does this make sense given the histogram in the previous step?

7.  Ignoring the payments of 0 using the mask you created in the previous step, use pandas' `.apply()` and NumPy's `np.log10()` to plot histograms of logarithmic transformations of the non-zero payments. Consider the results.

    Hint: You can use `.apply()` to apply any function, including **log10**, to all the elements of a DataFrame or a column using the following syntax: `.apply(<function_name>)`.

    > **NOTE**
    >
    > The Jupyter notebook containing the Python code and corresponding outputs for this activity can be found here: https://packt.link/FQQOB. Detailed step-wise solution to this activity can be found on page 364.

# SUMMARY

In this introductory chapter, we made extensive use of pandas to load and explore the case study data. We learned how to check for basic consistency and correctness by using a combination of statistical summaries and visualizations. We answered such questions as "Are the unique account IDs truly unique?", "Is there any missing data that has been given a fill value?", and "Do the values of the features make sense given their definition?"

You may notice that we spent nearly all of this chapter identifying and correcting issues with our dataset. This is often the most time-consuming stage of a data science project. While it is not necessarily the most exciting part of the job, it gives you the raw materials necessary to build exciting models and insights. These will be the subjects of most of the rest of this book.

Mastery of software tools and mathematical concepts is what allows you to execute data science projects, at a technical level. However, managing your relationships with clients, who are relying on your services to generate insights from their data, is just as important to successful projects. You must make as much use as you can of your business partner's understanding of the data. They are likely going to be more familiar with it than you, unless you are already a subject matter expert in the area. However, even in that case, your first step should be a thorough and critical review of the data you are using.

In our data exploration, we discovered an issue that could have undermined our project: the data we had received was not internally consistent. Most of the months of the payment status features were plagued by a data reporting issue, included nonsensical values, and were not representative of the most recent month of data, or the data that would be available to the model going forward. We only uncovered this issue by taking a careful look at all of the features. While this is not always possible, especially when there are very many features, you should always take the time to spot-check as many features as you can. If you can't examine every feature, it's useful to check a few of every category of feature, when the features fall into categories, such as financial or demographic features.

When discussing data issues like this with your client, make sure you are respectful and professional. The client may simply have forgotten about the issue when presenting you with the data. Or, they may have known about it but assumed it wouldn't affect your analysis for some reason. In any case, you are doing them an essential service by bringing it to their attention and explaining why it would be a problem to use flawed data to build a model. Be as specific as you can, presenting the kinds of graphs and tables you used to discover the issue.

In the next chapter, we will examine the response variable for our case study problem, which completes the initial data exploration. Then we will start to get some hands-on experience with machine learning models and learn how we can decide whether a model is useful or not. These skills will be important when we start building models using the case study data.

# 2

# INTRODUCTION TO SCIKIT-LEARN AND MODEL EVALUATION

## OVERVIEW

After exploring the response variable of the case study data, this chapter introduces the core functionality of scikit-learn for training models and making predictions, through simple use cases of logistic and linear regression. Evaluation metrics for binary classification models, including **true and false positive rates**, the **confusion matrix**, the **receiver operating characteristic (ROC) curve**, and the **precision-recall curve**, are demonstrated both from scratch and using convenient scikit-learn functionality. By the end of this chapter, you'll be able to build and evaluate binary classification models using scikit-learn.

# INTRODUCTION

In the previous chapter, you became familiar with basic Python and then learned about the pandas tool for data exploration. Using Python and pandas, you performed operations such as loading a dataset, verifying data integrity, and performing exploratory analysis of the features, or independent variables, in the data.

In this chapter, we will finish our exploration of the data by examining the response variable. After we've concluded that the data is of high quality and makes sense, we will be ready to move forward with developing machine learning models. We will take our first steps with scikit-learn, one of the most popular machine learning packages available in the Python language. Before learning the details of how mathematical models work in the next chapter, here we'll start to get comfortable with the syntax for using them in scikit-learn.

We will also learn some common techniques for answering the question, "Is this model good or not?" There are many possible ways to approach model evaluation. For business applications, a financial analysis to determine the value that could be created by a model is an important way to understand the potential impact of your work. Usually, it's best to scope the business opportunity of a project at the very beginning. However, as the emphasis of this book is on machine learning and predictive modeling, we will demonstrate a financial analysis in the final chapter.

There are several important model evaluation criteria that are considered standard knowledge in data science and machine learning. We will cover a few of the most widely used classification model performance metrics here.

# EXPLORING THE RESPONSE VARIABLE AND CONCLUDING THE INITIAL EXPLORATION

We have now looked through all the **features** to see whether any data is missing, as well as to generally examine them. The features are important because they constitute the **inputs** to our machine learning algorithm. On the other side of the model lies the **output**, which is a prediction of the **response variable**. For our problem, this is a binary flag indicating whether or not a credit account will default next month.

The key task for the case study project is to come up with a predictive model for this target. Since the response variable is a yes/no flag, this problem is called a **binary classification** task. In our labeled data, the samples (accounts) that defaulted (that is, `'default payment next month'` = 1) are said to belong to the **positive class**, while those that didn't belong to the **negative class**.

The main piece of information to examine regarding the response of a binary classification problem is this: what is the proportion of the positive class? This is an easy check.

Before we perform this check, we load the packages we need with the following code:

```
import numpy as np #numerical computation
import pandas as pd #data wrangling
import matplotlib.pyplot as plt #plotting package
#Next line helps with rendering plots
%matplotlib inline
import matplotlib as mpl #add'l plotting functionality
mpl.rcParams['figure.dpi'] = 400 #high res figures
```

Now we load the cleaned version of the case study data like this:

```
df = pd.read_csv('../../Data/Chapter_1_cleaned_data.csv')
```

> **NOTE**
>
> The cleaned dataset should have been saved as a result of your work in *Chapter 1, Data Exploration and Cleaning*. The path to the cleaned data in the preceding code snippet may be different if you saved it in a different location.

Now, to find the proportion of the positive class, all we need to do is get the average of the response variable over the whole dataset. This has the interpretation of the default rate. It's also worthwhile to check the number of samples in each class, using **groupby** and **count** in pandas. This is presented in the following screenshot:

```
df['default payment next month'].mean()
```

```
0.2217971797179718
```

```
df.groupby('default payment next month')['ID'].count()
```

```
default payment next month
0    20750
1     5914
Name: ID, dtype: int64
```

Figure 2.1: Class balance of the response variable

Since the target variable is **1** or **0**, taking the mean of this column indicates the fraction of accounts that defaulted: 22%. The proportion of samples in the positive class (default = 1), also called the **class fraction** for this class, is an important statistic. In binary classification, datasets are described in terms of being **balanced** or **imbalanced**: are the proportions of the positive and negative classes equal or not? Most machine learning classification models are designed to work with balanced data: a 50/50 split between the classes.

However, in practice, real data is rarely balanced. Consequently, there are several methods geared toward dealing with imbalanced data. These include the following:

- **Undersampling** the majority class: Randomly throwing out samples from the majority class until the class fractions are equal, or at least less imbalanced.

- **Oversampling** the minority class: Randomly adding duplicate samples of the minority class to achieve the same goal.

- **Weighting samples**: This method is performed as part of the training step, so the minority class collectively has as much "emphasis" as the majority class in the trained model. The effect of this is similar to oversampling.

- More sophisticated methods, such as **Synthetic Minority Over-sampling Technique (SMOTE)**.

While our data is not, strictly speaking, balanced, we also note that a positive class fraction of 22% is not particularly imbalanced, either. Some domains, such as fraud detection, typically deal with much smaller positive class fractions: on the order of 1% or less. This is because the proportion of "bad actors" is quite small compared to the total population of transactions; at the same time, it is important to be able to identify them if possible. For problems like this, it is more likely that using a method to address class imbalance will lead to substantially better results.

Now that we've explored the response variable, we have concluded our initial data exploration. However, data exploration should be considered an ongoing task that you should continually have in mind during any project. As you create models and generate new results, it's always good to think about what those results imply about the data, which usually requires a quick iteration back to the exploration phase. A particularly helpful kind of exploration, which is also typically done before model building, is examining the relationship between features and the response. We gave a preview of that in *Chapter 1, Data Exploration and Cleaning*, when we were grouping by the **EDUCATION** feature and examining the mean of the response variable. We will also do more of this later. However, this has more to do with building a model than checking the inherent quality of the data.

The initial perusal through all the data that we have just completed is an important foundation to lay at the beginning of a project. As you do this, you should ask yourself the following questions:

- Is the data **complete**?

  Are there missing values or other anomalies?

- Is the data **consistent**?

  Does the distribution change over time, and if so, is this expected?

- Does the data **make sense**?

  Do the values of the features fit with their definition in the data dictionary?

The latter two questions help you determine whether you think the data is **correct**. If the answer to any of these questions is "no," this should be addressed before continuing the project.

Also, if you think of any alternative or additional data that might be helpful to have and is possible to get, now would be a good point in the project life cycle to augment your dataset with it. Examples of this may include postal code-level demographic data, which you could **join** to your dataset if you had the addresses associated with accounts. We don't have these for the case study data and have decided to proceed on this project with the data we have now.

## INTRODUCTION TO SCIKIT-LEARN

While pandas will save you a lot of time loading, examining, and cleaning data, the machine learning algorithms that will enable you to do predictive modeling are located in other packages. Scikit-learn is a foundational machine learning package for Python that contains many useful algorithms and has also influenced the design and syntax of other machine learning libraries in Python. For this reason, we focus on scikit-learn to develop skills in the practice of predictive modeling. While it's impossible for any one package to offer everything, scikit-learn comes pretty close in terms of accommodating a wide range of classic approaches for classification, regression, and unsupervised learning. However, it does not offer much functionality for some more recent advancements, such as deep learning.

Here are a few other related packages you should be aware of:

**SciPy**:

- Most of the packages we've used so far, such as NumPy and pandas, are actually part of the SciPy ecosystem.

- SciPy offers lightweight functions for classic methods such as linear regression and linear programming.

**StatsModels**:

- More oriented toward statistics and maybe more comfortable for users familiar with R

- Can get p-values and confidence intervals on regression coefficients

- Capability for time series models such as ARIMA

**XGBoost and LightGBM**:

- Offer a suite of state-of-the-art ensemble models that often outperform random forests. We will learn about XGBoost in *Chapter 6, Gradient Boosting, SHAP Values, and Dealing with Missing Data*.

**TensorFlow, Keras, and PyTorch**:

- Deep learning capabilities

There are many other Python packages that may come in handy, but this gives you an idea of what's out there.

Scikit-learn offers a wealth of different models for various tasks, but, conveniently, the syntax for using them is consistent. In this section, we will illustrate model syntax using a **logistic regression** model. Logistic regression, despite its name, is actually a classification model. This is one of the simplest, and therefore most important, classification models. In the next chapter, we will go through the mathematical details of how logistic regression works. Until then, you can simply think of it as a black box that can learn from labeled data, then make predictions.

From the first chapter, you should be familiar with the concept of training an algorithm on labeled data so that you can use this trained model to then make predictions on new data. Scikit-learn encapsulates these core functionalities in the `.fit` method for training models, and the `.predict` method for making predictions. Because of the consistent syntax, you can call `.fit` and `.predict` on any scikit-learn model from linear regression to classification trees.

The first step is to choose some model, in this example a logistic regression model, and instantiate it from the **class** provided by scikit-learn. In Python, classes are templates for creating objects, which are collections of functions, like `.fit`, and data, such as information learned from the model fitting process. When you instantiate a model class from scikit-learn, you are taking the blueprint of the model that scikit-learn makes available to you and creating a useful **object** out of it. You can train this object on your data and then save it to disk for later use. The following snippets can be used to perform this task. The first step is to import the class:

```
from sklearn.linear_model import LogisticRegression
```

The code to instantiate the class into an object is as follows:

```
my_lr = LogisticRegression()
```

The object is now a variable in our workspace. We can examine it using the following code:

```
my_lr
```

This should give the following output:

```
LogisticRegression()
```

Notice that the act of creating the model object involves essentially no knowledge of what logistic regression is or how it works. Although we didn't select any particular options when creating the logistic regression model object, we are now in fact using many **default options** for how the model is formulated and would be trained. In effect, these are choices we have made regarding the details of model implementation without having been aware of it. The danger of an easy-to-use package such as scikit-learn is that it has the potential to obscure these choices from you. However, any time you use a machine learning model that has been prepared for you as scikit-learn models have been, your first job is to understand all the options that are available. A best practice in such cases is to explicitly provide every keyword parameter to the model when you create the object. Even if you are just selecting all the default options, this will help increase your awareness of the choices that are being made.

We will review the interpretation of these choices later on, but for now here is the code for instantiating a logistic regression model with all the default options:

```
my_new_lr = LogisticRegression(penalty='l2', dual=False,\
                               tol=0.0001, C=1.0,\
                               fit_intercept=True,\
                               intercept_scaling=1,\
```

```
                                        class_weight=None, \
                                        random_state=None, \
                                        solver='lbfgs', \
                                        max_iter=100, \
                                        multi_class='auto', \
                                        verbose=0, warm_start=False, \
                                        n_jobs=None, l1_ratio=None)
```

Even though the object we've created here in **my_new_lr** is identical to **my_lr**, being explicit like this is especially helpful when you are starting out and learning about different kinds of models. Once you're more comfortable, you may wish to just instantiate with the default options and make changes later as necessary. Here, we show how this may be done. The following code sets two options and displays the current state of the model object:

```
my_new_lr.C = 0.1
my_new_lr.solver = 'liblinear'
my_new_lr
```

This should produce the following:

```
Out[11]:LogisticRegression(C=0.1, solver='liblinear')
```

Notice that only the options we have updated from the default values are displayed. Here, we've taken what is called a **hyperparameter** of the model, **C**, and updated it from its default value of **1** to **0.1**. We've also specified a solver. For now, it is enough to understand that hyperparameters are options that you supply to the model, before fitting it to the data. These options specify the way in which the model will be trained. Later, we will explain in detail what all the options are and how you can effectively choose values for them.

To illustrate the core functionality, we will fit this nearly default logistic regression to some data. Supervised learning algorithms rely on labeled data. That means we need both the features, customarily contained in a variable called **X**, and the corresponding responses, in a variable called **y**. We will borrow the first 10 samples of one feature, and the response, from our dataset to illustrate:

```
X = df['EDUCATION'][0:10].values.reshape(-1,1)
X
```

That should show the values of the **EDUCATION** feature for the first 10 samples:

```
array([[2],
       [2],
       [2],
       [2],
       [2],
       [1],
       [1],
       [2],
       [3],
       [3]])
```

**Figure 2.2: First 10 values of a feature**

The corresponding first 10 values of the response variable can be obtained as follows:

```
y = df['default payment next month'][0:10].values
y
```

Here is the output:

```
Out[13]: array([1, 1, 0, 0, 0, 0, 0, 0, 0, 0])
```

Here, we have selected a couple of Series (that is, columns) from our DataFrame: the **EDUCATION** feature we've been discussing, and the response variable. Then we selected the first 10 elements of each and finally used the **.values** method to return NumPy arrays. Also notice that we used the **.reshape** method to reshape the features. Scikit-learn expects that the first dimension (that is, the number of rows) of the array of features will be equal to the number of samples, so we need to make that reshaping for **X**, but not for **y**. The **−1** in the first positional argument of **.reshape** means to make the output array shape flexible in that dimension, according to how much data goes in. Since we just have a single feature in this example, we specified the number of columns as the second argument, **1**, and let the **−1** argument indicate that the array should "fill up" along the first dimension with as many elements as necessary to accommodate the data, in this case, 10 elements. Note that while we've extracted the data into NumPy arrays to show how this can be done, it's also possible to use pandas Series as direct input to scikit-learn.

Let's now use this data to fit our logistic regression. This is accomplished with just one line:

```
my_new_lr.fit(X, y)
```

Here is the output:

```
Out[14]:LogisticRegression(C=0.1, solver='liblinear')
```

That's all there is to it. Once the data is prepared and the model is specified, fitting the model almost seems like an afterthought. Of course, we are ignoring all the important options and what they mean right now. But, technically speaking, fitting a model is very easy in terms of the code. You can see that the output of this cell just prints the same options we've already seen. While the fitting procedure did not return anything aside from this output, a very important change has taken place. The **my_new_lr** model object is now a trained model. We say that this change happened **in place** since no new object was created; the existing object, **my_new_lr**, has been modified. This is similar to modifying a DataFrame in place. We can now use our trained model to make predictions using the features of new samples, that the model has never "seen" before. Let's try the next 10 rows from the **EDUCATION** feature.

We can select and view these features using a new variable, **new_X**:

```
new_X = df['EDUCATION'][10:20].values.reshape(-1,1)
new_X
```

```
array([[3],
       [1],
       [2],
       [2],
       [1],
       [3],
       [1],
       [1],
       [1],
       [3]])
```

**Figure 2.3: New features to make predictions for**

Making predictions is done like this:

```
my_new_lr.predict(new_X)
```

Here is the output:

```
array([0, 0, 0, 0, 0, 0, 0, 0, 0, 0])
```

We can also view the true values corresponding to these predictions, since this data is labeled:

```
df['default payment next month'][10:20].values
```

Here is the output:

```
Out[17]:array([0, 0, 0, 1, 0, 0, 1, 0, 0, 0])
```

Here, we've illustrated several things. After getting our new feature values, we've called the `.predict` method on the trained model. Notice that the only argument to this method is a set of features, that is, an "X" that we've called **new_X**.

How well did our little model do? We may naively observe that since the model predicted all 0s, and 80% of the true labels are 0s, we were right 80% of the time, which seems pretty good. On the other hand, we entirely failed to successfully predict any 1s. So, if those were important, we did not actually do very well. While this is just an example to get you familiar with how scikit-learn works, it's worth considering what a "good" prediction might look like for this problem. We will get into the details of assessing model predictive capabilities shortly. For now, congratulate yourself on having gotten your hands dirty with some real data and fitting your first machine learning model.

## GENERATING SYNTHETIC DATA

In the following exercise, you will walk through the model fitting process on your own. We'll motivate this process using a linear regression, one of the best-known mathematical models, which should be familiar from basic statistics. It's also called a line of best fit. If you don't know what it is, you could consult a basic statistics resource, although the intent here is to illustrate the mechanics of model fitting in sci-kit learn, as opposed to understanding the model in detail. We'll work on that later in the book for other mathematical models that we'll apply to the case study, such as logistic regression. In order to have data to work with, you will generate your own **synthetic data**. Synthetic data is a valuable learning tool for exploring models, illustrating mathematical concepts, and for conducting thought experiments to test various ideas. In order to make synthetic data, we will again illustrate here how to use NumPy's **random** library to generate random numbers, as well as matplotlib's **scatter** and **plot** functions to create scatter and line plots. In the exercise, we'll use scikit-learn for the linear regression part.

To get started, we use NumPy to make a one-dimensional array of feature values, **X**, consisting of 1,000 random real numbers (in other words, not just integers but decimals as well) between 0 and 10. We again use a **seed** for the random number generator. Next, we use the `.uniform` method of **default_rng** (random number generator), which draws from the uniform distribution: it's equally likely to choose any number between **low** (inclusive) and **high** (exclusive), and will return an array of whatever **size** you specify. We create a one-dimensional array (that is, a vector) with 1,000 elements, then examine the first 10. All of this can be done using the following code:

```
from numpy.random import default_rng
rg = default_rng(12345)
X = rg.uniform(low=0.0, high=10.0, size=(1000,))
X[0:10]
```

The output should appear as follows:

```
array ([2.27336022),   3.1675834 ,   7.97365457,   6.76254671,   3.91109551,
          3.32813928 ,   5.98308754,   1.86734186,   6.72756044,   9.41802865])
```

**Figure 2.4: Creating random, uniformly distributed numbers with NumPy**

## DATA FOR LINEAR REGRESSION

Now we need a response variable. For this example, we'll generate data that follows the assumptions of linear regression: the data will exhibit a linear trend against the feature, but have normally distributed errors:

$$y = ax + b + N(\mu, \sigma)$$

**Figure 2.5: Linear equation with Gaussian noise**

Here, $a$ is the slope, $b$ is the intercept, and the Gaussian noise has a mean of $\mu$ with a standard deviation of $\sigma$. In order to write code to implement this, we need to make a corresponding vector of responses, **y**, which are calculated as the slope times the feature array, **X**, plus some Gaussian noise (again using NumPy), and an intercept. The noise will be an array of 1,000 data points with the same shape (**size**) as the feature array, **X**, where the mean of the noise (**loc**) is 0 and the standard deviation (**scale**) is 1. This will add a little "spread" to our linear data:

```
slope = 0.25
intercept = -1.25
y = slope * X + rg.normal(loc=0.0, scale=1.0, size=(1000,))\
        + intercept
```

Now we'd like to visualize this data. We will use matplotlib to plot **y** against the feature **X** as a scatter plot. First, we use **.rcParams** to set the resolution (**dpi** = dots per inch) for a nice crisp image. Then we create the scatter plot with **plt.scatter**, where **X** and **y** are the first two arguments, respectively, and the **s** argument specifies a size for the dots.

This code can be used for plotting:

```
mpl.rcParams['figure.dpi'] = 400
plt.scatter(X,y,s=1)
plt.xlabel('X')
plt.ylabel('y')
```

After executing these cells, you should see something like this in your notebook:

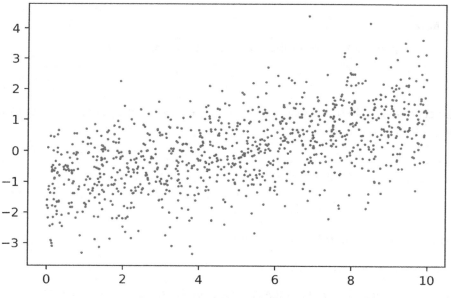

Figure 2.6: Plot the noisy linear relationship

Looks like some noisy linear data, just like we hoped. Now let's model it.

> **NOTE**
>
> If you're reading the print version of this book, you can download and browse the color versions of some of the images in this chapter by visiting the following link: https://packt.link/0dbUp.

## EXERCISE 2.01: LINEAR REGRESSION IN SCIKIT-LEARN

In this exercise, we will take the synthetic data we just generated and determine a line of best fit, or linear regression, using scikit-learn. The first step is to import a linear regression model class from scikit-learn and create an object from it. The import is similar to the **LogisticRegression** class we worked with previously. As with any model class, you should observe what all the default options are. Notice that for linear regression, there are not that many options to specify: you will use the defaults for this exercise. The default settings include **fit_intercept=True**, meaning the regression model will include an intercept term. This is certainly appropriate since we added an intercept to the synthetic data. Perform the following steps to complete the exercise, noting that the code creating the data for linear regression from the preceding section must be run first in the same notebook (as seen on GitHub):

> **NOTE**
>
> The Jupyter notebook for this exercise can be found here:
> https://packt.link/laoyM.

1.  Execute this code to import the linear regression model class and instantiate it with all the default options:

```
from sklearn.linear_model import LinearRegression
lin_reg = LinearRegression(fit_intercept=True, normalize=False, \
                           copy_X=True, n_jobs=None)
lin_reg
```

You should see the following output:

```
Out[11]:LinearRegression()
```

No options are displayed since we used all the defaults. Now we can fit the model using our synthetic data, remembering to reshape the feature array (as we did earlier) so that that samples are along the first dimension. After fitting the linear regression model, we examine **lin_reg.intercept_**, which contains the intercept of the fitted model, as well as **lin_reg.coef_**, which contains the slope.

2. Run this code to fit the model and examine the coefficients:

```
lin_reg.fit(X.reshape(-1,1), y)
print(lin_reg.intercept_)
print(lin_reg.coef_)
```

You should see this output for the intercept and slope:

```
-1.2522197212675905
[0.25711689]
```

We again see that actually fitting a model in scikit-learn, once the data is prepared and the options for the model are decided, is a trivial process. This is because all the algorithmic work of determining the model parameters is abstracted away from the user. We will discuss this process later, for the logistic regression model we'll use on the case study data.

**What about the slope and intercept of our fitted model?**

These numbers are fairly close to the slope and intercept we indicated when creating the model. However, because of the random noise, they are only approximations.

Finally, we can use the model to make predictions on feature values. Here, we do this using the same data used to fit the model: the array of features, **X**. We capture the output of this as a variable, **y_pred**. This is very similar to the example shown in *Figure 2.7*, only here we are making predictions on the same data used to fit the model (previously, we made predictions on different data) and we put the output of the **.predict** method into a variable.

3. Run this code to make predictions:

```
y_pred = lin_reg.predict(X.reshape(-1,1))
```

We can plot the predictions, **y_pred**, against feature **X** as a line plot over the scatter plot of the feature and response data, like we made in *Figure 2.6*. Here, we make the addition of **plt.plot**, which produces a line plot by default, to plot the feature and the model-predicted response values for the model training data. Notice that we follow the **X** and **y** data with **'r'** in our call to **plt.plot**. This keyword argument causes the line to be red and is part of a shorthand syntax for plot formatting.

4.  This code can be used to plot the raw data, as well as the fitted model predictions on this data:

```
plt.scatter(X,y,s=1)
plt.plot(X,y_pred,'r')
plt.xlabel('X')
plt.ylabel('y')
```

After executing this cell, you should see something like this:

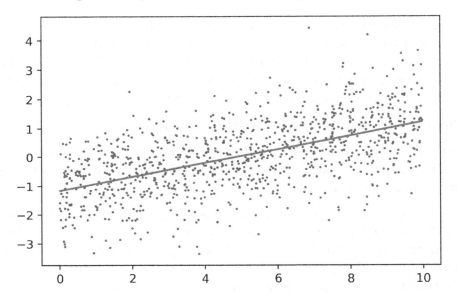

Figure 2.7: Plotting the data and the regression line

The plot looks like a line of best fit, as expected.

In this exercise, as opposed to when we called `.predict` with logistic regression, we made predictions on the same data **X** that we used to train the model. This is an important distinction. While here, we are seeing how the model "fits" the same data that it was trained on, we previously examined model predictions on new, unseen data. In machine learning, we are usually concerned with predictive capabilities: we want models that can help us know the likely outcomes of future scenarios. However, it turns out that model predictions on both the **training data** used to fit the model and the **test data**, which was not used to fit the model, are important for understanding the workings of the model. We will formalize these notions later in *Chapter 4, The Bias-Variance Trade-Off*, when we discuss the **bias-variance trade-off**.

# MODEL PERFORMANCE METRICS FOR BINARY CLASSIFICATION

Before we start building predictive models in earnest, we would like to know how we can determine, once we've created a model, whether it is "good" in some sense of the word. As you may imagine, this question has received a lot of attention from researchers and practitioners. Consequently, there is a wide variety of model performance metrics to choose from.

> **NOTE**
>
> For an idea of the range of options, have a look at the scikit-learn model evaluation page: https://scikit-learn.org/stable/modules/model_evaluation.html#model-evaluation.

When selecting a model performance metric to assess the predictive quality of a model, it's important to keep two things in mind.

**Appropriateness of the metric for the problem**

Metrics are typically only defined for a specific class of problems, such as classification or regression. For a binary classification problem, several metrics characterize the correctness of the yes or no question that the model answers. An additional level of detail here is how often the model is correct for each class, the positive and negative classes. We will go into detail on these metrics here. On the other hand, regression metrics are aimed at measuring how close a prediction is to the target quantity. If we are trying to predict the price of a house, how close did we come? Are we systematically over- or under-estimating? Are we getting the more expensive houses wrong but the cheaper ones right? There are many possible ways to look at regression metrics.

**Does the metric answer the business question?**

Whatever class of problem you are working on, there will be many choices for the metric. Which one is the right one? And even then, how do you know if a model is "good enough" in terms of the metric? At some level, this is a subjective question. However, we can be objective when we consider what the goal of the model is. In a business context, typical goals are to increase profit or reduce loss. Ultimately, you need to unify your business question, which is often related to money in some way, and the metric you will use to judge your model.

For example, in our credit default problem, is there a particularly high cost associated with not correctly identifying accounts that will default? Is this more important than potentially misclassifying some of the accounts that won't default?

Later in the book, we'll incorporate the concept of relative costs and benefits of correct and incorrect classifications in our problem and conduct a financial analysis. First, we'll introduce you to the most common metrics used to assess the predictive quality of binary classification models, the kinds of model we need to build for our case study.

## SPLITTING THE DATA: TRAINING AND TEST SETS

In the scikit-learn introduction of this chapter, we introduced the concept of using a trained model to make predictions on new data that the model had never "seen" before. It turns out this is a foundational concept in predictive modeling. In our quest to create a model that has predictive capabilities, we need some kind of measure of how well the model can make predictions on data that were not used to fit the model. This is because in fitting a model, the model becomes "specialized" at learning the relationship between features and response on the specific set of labeled data that were used for fitting. While this is nice, in the end we want to be able to use the model to make accurate predictions on new, unseen data, for which we don't know the true value of the labels.

For example, in our case study, once we deliver the trained model to our client, they will then generate a new dataset of features like those we have now, except instead of spanning the period from April to September, they will span from May to October. And our client will be using the model with these features, to predict whether accounts will default in November.

In order to know how well we can expect our model to predict which accounts will actually default in November (which won't be known until December), we can take our current dataset and reserve some of the data we have, with known labels, from the model training process. This data is referred to as **test data** and may also be called **out-of-sample data** since it consists of samples that were not used in training the model. Those samples used to train the model are called **training data**. The practice of holding out a set of test data gives us an idea of how the model will perform when it is used for its intended purpose, to make predictions on samples that were not included during model training. In this chapter, we'll create an example train/test split to illustrate different binary classification metrics.

We will use the convenient **train_test_split** functionality of scikit-learn to split the data so that 80% will be used for training, holding 20% back for testing. These percentages are a common way to make such a split; in general, you want enough training data to allow the algorithm to adequately "learn" from a representative sample of data. However, these percentages are not set in stone. If you have a very large number of samples, you may not need as large a percentage of training data, since you will be able to achieve a pretty large, representative training set with a lower percentage. We encourage you to experiment with different sizes and see the effect. Also, be aware that every problem is different with respect to how much data is needed to effectively train a model. There is no hard and fast rule for sizing your training and test sets.

For our 80/20 split, we can use the code shown in the following snippet:

```
from sklearn.model_selection import train_test_split
X_train, X_test, y_train, y_test = train_test_split\
                        (df['EDUCATION']\
                        .values.reshape(-1,1),\
                        df['default payment\
                        ' next month']\
                        .values, test_size=0.2,\
                        random_state=24)
```

Notice that we've set **test_size** to **0.2**, or 20%. The size of the training data will be automatically set to the remainder, 80%. Let's examine the shapes of our training and test data, to see whether they are as expected, as shown in the following output:

```
print(X_train.shape)
print(X_test.shape)
print(y_train.shape)
print(y_test.shape)

(21331, 1)
(5333, 1)
(21331,)
(5333,)
```

**Figure 2.8: Shape of training and test sets**

You should confirm for yourself that the number of samples (rows) in the training and test sets is consistent with an 80/20 split.

In making the train/test split, we've also set the **random_state** parameter, which is a random number seed. Using this parameter allows a consistent train/test split across runs of this notebook. Otherwise, the random splitting procedure would select a different 20% of the data for testing each time the code was run.

The first argument to **train_test_split** is the features, in this case just **EDUCATION**, and the second argument is the response. There are four outputs: the features of the samples in the training and test sets, respectively, and the corresponding response variables that go with these sets of features. All this function has done is randomly select 20% of the row indices from the dataset and subset out these features and responses as test data, leaving the rest for training. Now that we have our training and test data, it's good to make sure the nature of the data is the same between these sets. In particular, is the fraction of the positive class similar? You can observe this in the following output:

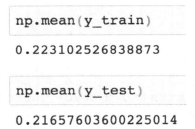

```
np.mean(y_train)
```

0.223102526838873

```
np.mean(y_test)
```

0.21657603600225014

**Figure 2.9: Class fractions in training and test data**

The positive class fractions in the training and test data are both about 22%. This is good, as we can say that the training set is representative of the test set. In this case, since we have a pretty large dataset with tens of thousands of samples, and the classes are not too imbalanced, we didn't have to take precautions to ensure this happens.

However, you can imagine that if the dataset were smaller, and the positive class very rare, it may be that the class fractions would be noticeably different between the training and test sets, or worse yet, there might be no positive samples at all in the test set. In order to guard against such scenarios, you could use **stratified sampling**, with the **stratify** keyword argument of **train_test_split**. This procedure also makes a random split of the data into training and test sets but guarantees that the class fractions will be equal or very similar.

> **NOTE**
>
> **Out-of-time testing**
>
> If your data contains both features and responses that span a substantial period of time, it's a good practice to try making your train/test split over time. For example, if you have two years of data with features and responses from every month, you may wish to try sequentially training the model on 12 months of data and testing on the next month, or the month after that, depending on what is operationally feasible when the model will be used. You could repeat this until you've exhausted your data, to get a few different test scores. This will give you useful insights into model performance because it simulates the actual conditions the model will face when it is deployed: a model trained on old features and responses will be used to make predictions on new data. In the case study, the responses only come from one point in time (credit defaults within one month), so this is not an option here.

## CLASSIFICATION ACCURACY

Now we proceed to fit an example model to illustrate binary classification metrics. We will continue to use logistic regression with near-default options, choosing the same options we demonstrated in *Chapter 1, Data Exploration and Cleaning*:

```
from sklearn.linear_model import LogisticRegression
```

```
example_lr = LogisticRegression(C=0.1, class_weight=None,
                                dual=False, fit_intercept=True,
                                intercept_scaling=1, max_iter=100,
                                multi_class='auto', n_jobs=None,
                                penalty='l2', random_state=None,
                                solver='liblinear', tol=0.0001,
                                verbose=0, warm_start=False)
```

Figure 2.10: Loading the model class and creating a model object

Now we proceed to train the model, as you might imagine, using the labeled data from our training set. We proceed immediately to use the trained model to make predictions on the features of the samples from the held-out test set:

```
example_lr.fit(X_train, y_train)

LogisticRegression(C=0.1, solver='liblinear')

y_pred = example_lr.predict(X_test)
```

Accuracy

**Figure 2.11: Training a model and making predictions on the test set**

We've stored the model-predicted labels of the test set in a variable called **y_pred**. How should we now assess the quality of these predictions? We have the true labels, in the **y_test** variable. First, we will compute what is probably the simplest of all binary classification metrics: **accuracy**. Accuracy is defined as the proportion of samples that were correctly classified.

One way to calculate accuracy is to create a logical mask that is **True** whenever the predicted label is equal to the actual label, and **False** otherwise. We can then take the average of this mask, which will interpret **True** as 1 and **False** as 0, giving us the proportion of correct classifications:

```
is_correct = y_pred == y_test

np.mean(is_correct)
0.7834239639977498
```

**Figure 2.12: Calculating classification accuracy with a logical mask**

This indicates that the model is correct 78% of the time. While this is a pretty straightforward calculation, there are actually easier ways to calculate accuracy using the convenience of scikit-learn. One way is to use the trained model's **.score** method, passing the features of the test data to make predictions on, as well as the test labels. This method makes the predictions and then does the same calculation we performed previously, all in one step. Or, we could import scikit-learn's **metrics** library, which includes many model performance metrics, such as **accuracy_ score**. For this, we pass the true labels and the predicted labels:

```
example_lr.score(X_test, y_test)
```

0.7834239639977498

```
from sklearn import metrics
```

```
metrics.accuracy_score(y_test, y_pred)
```

0.7834239639977498

**Figure 2.13: Calculating classification accuracy with scikit-learn**

These all give the same result, as they should. Now that we know how accurate the model is, how do we interpret this metric? On the surface, an accuracy of 78% may sound good. We are getting most of the predictions right. However, an important test for the accuracy of binary classification is to compare things to a very simple hypothetical model that only makes one prediction: this hypothetical model predicts the majority class for every sample, no matter what the features are. While in practice this model is useless, it provides an important extreme case with which to compare the accuracy of our trained model. Such extreme cases are sometimes referred to as null models.

Think about what the accuracy of such a null model would be. In our dataset, we know that about 22% of the samples are positive. So, the negative class is the majority class, with the remaining 78% of the samples. Therefore, a null model for this dataset, which always predicts the majority negative class, will be right 78% of the time. Now when we compare our trained model here to such a null model, it becomes clear that an accuracy of 78% is actually not very useful. We can get the same accuracy with a model that doesn't pay any attention to the features.

While we can interpret accuracy in terms of a majority-class null model, there are other binary classification metrics that delve a little deeper into how the model is performing for negative, as well as positive samples separately.

## TRUE POSITIVE RATE, FALSE POSITIVE RATE, AND CONFUSION MATRIX

In binary classification, there are just two labels to consider: positive and negative. As a more descriptive way to look at model performance than the accuracy of prediction across all samples, we can also look at the accuracy of only those samples that have a positive label. The proportion of these that we successfully predict as positive is called the **true positive rate** (**TPR**). If we say that **P** is the number of samples in the **positive class** in the test data, and **TP** is the number of **true positives**, defined as the number of positive samples that were predicted to be positive by the model, then the TPR is as follows:

$$TPR = \frac{TP}{P}$$

Figure 2.14: TPR equation

The flip side of the true positive rate is the **false negative rate** (**FNR**). This is the proportion of positive test samples that we incorrectly predicted as negative. Such errors are called **false negatives** (**FN**) and the **false negative rate** (**FNR**) is calculated as follows:

$$FNR = \frac{FN}{P}$$

Figure 2.15: FNR equation

Since all the positive samples are either correctly or incorrectly predicted, the sum of the number of true positives and the number of false negatives equals the total number of positive samples. Mathematically, $P = TP + FN$, and therefore, using the definitions of TPR and FNR, we have the following:

$$TPR + FNR = 1$$

Figure 2.16: The relation between the TPR and FNR

Since the TPR and FNR sum to 1, it's sufficient to just calculate one of them.

Similar to the TPR and FNR, there is the **true negative rate (TNR)** and the **false positive rate (FPR)**. If **N** is the number of **negative** samples, the sum of **true negative** samples (**TN**) is the number of these that are correctly predicted, and the sum of **false positive** (**FP**) samples is the number incorrectly predicted as positive:

$$TNR = \frac{TN}{N}$$

**Figure 2.17: TNR equation**

$$FPR = \frac{FP}{N}$$

**Figure 2.18: FPR equation**

$$TNR + FPR = 1$$

**Figure 2.19: Relation between the TNR and FPR**

True and false positives and negatives can be conveniently summarized in a table called a **confusion matrix**. A confusion matrix for a binary classification problem is a 2 x 2 matrix where the true class is along one axis and the predicted class is along the other. The confusion matrix gives a quick summary of how many true and false positives and negatives there are:

|  |  | Predicted class | |
|---|---|---|---|
|  |  | N | P |
| True class | N | TN | FP |
|  | P | FN | TP |

**Figure 2.20: The confusion matrix for binary classification**

Since we hope to make correct classifications, we hope that the **diagonal** entries (that is, the entries along a diagonal line from the top left to the bottom right: TN and TP) of the confusion matrix are relatively large, while the off-diagonals are relatively small, as these represent incorrect classifications. The accuracy metric can be calculated from the confusion matrix by adding up the entries on the diagonal, which are predictions that are correct, and dividing by the total number of all predictions.

## EXERCISE 2.02: CALCULATING THE TRUE AND FALSE POSITIVE AND NEGATIVE RATES AND CONFUSION MATRIX IN PYTHON

In this exercise, we'll use the test data and model predictions from the logistic regression model we created previously, using only the **EDUCATION** feature. We will illustrate how to manually calculate the true and false positive and negative rates, as well as the numbers of true and false positives and negatives needed for the confusion matrix. Then we will show a quick way to calculate a confusion matrix with scikit-learn. Perform the following steps to complete the exercise, noting that some code from the previous section must be run before doing this exercise (as seen on GitHub):

> **NOTE**
>
> The Jupyter notebook for this exercise can be found here: https://packt.link/S02kz.

1. Run this code to calculate the number of positive samples:

```
P = sum(y_test)
P
```

The output should appear like this:

```
1155
```

Now we need the number of true positives. These are samples where the true label is 1 and the prediction is also 1. We can identify these with a logical mask for the samples that are positive (**y_test==1**) **AND** (**&** is the logical **AND** operator in Python) have a positive prediction (**y_pred==1**).

2. Use this code to calculate the number of true positives:

```
TP = sum( (y_test==1) & (y_pred==1) )
TP
```

Here is the output:

```
0
```

The true positive rate is the proportion of true positives to positives, which of course would be 0 here.

3. Run the following code to obtain the TPR:

```
TPR = TP/P
TPR
```

You will obtain the following output:

```
0.0
```

Similarly, we can identify the false negatives.

4. Calculate the number of false negatives with this code:

```
FN = sum( (y_test==1) & (y_pred==0) )
FN
```

This should output the following: 1155

We'd also like the FNR.

5. Calculate the FNR with this code:

```
FNR = FN/P
FNR
```

This should output the following:

```
1.0
```

### What have we learned from the true positive and false negative rates?

First, we can confirm that they sum to 1. This fact is easy to see because the TPR = 0 and the FPR = 1. What does this tell us about our model? On the test set, at least for the positive samples, the model has in fact acted as a majority-class null model. Every positive sample was predicted to be negative, so none of them was correctly predicted.

6. Let's find the TNR and FPR of our test data. Since these calculations are very similar to those we looked at previously, we show them all at once and illustrate a new Python function:

```
N = sum(y_test==0)
N
```

```
4178
```

```
TN = sum( (y_test==0) & (y_pred==0))
TN
```

```
4178
```

```
FP = sum( (y_test==0) & (y_pred==1))
FP
```

```
0
```

```
TNR = TN/N
FPR = FP/N
print('The true negative rate is {} and the false positive rate is {}'.format(TNR, FPR))
```

```
The true negative rate is 1.0 and the false positive rate is 0.0
```

**Figure 2.21: Calculating true negative and false positive rates and printing them**

In addition to calculating the TNR and FPR in a similar way that we had previously with the TPR and FNR, we demonstrate the **print** function in Python along with the **.format** method for strings, which allows substitution of variables in locations marked by curly braces **{}**. There is a range of options for formatting numbers, such as including a certain number of decimal places.

> **NOTE**
>
> For additional details, refer to
> https://docs.python.org/3/tutorial/inputoutput.html.

Now, what have we learned here? In fact, our model behaves exactly like the majority-class null model for all samples, both positive and negative. It's clear we're going to need a better model.

While we have manually calculated all the entries of the confusion matrix in this exercise, in scikit-learn there is a quick way to do this. Note that in scikit-learn, the true class is along the vertical axis and the predicted class is along the horizontal axis of the confusion matrix, as we presented earlier.

7.  Create a confusion matrix in scikit-learn with this code:

```
metrics.confusion_matrix(y_test, y_pred)
```

You will obtain the following output:

```
array([[4178,    0],
       [1155,    0]])
```

**Figure 2.22: The confusion matrix for our example model**

All the information we need to calculate the TPR, FNR, TNR, and FPR is contained in the confusion matrix. We also note that there are many more classification metrics that can be derived from the confusion matrix. In fact, some of these are actually synonyms for ones we've already examined here. For example, the TPR is also called **recall** and **sensitivity**. Along with recall, another metric that is often used for binary classification is **precision**: this is the proportion of positive predictions that are correct (as opposed to the proportion of positive samples that are correctly predicted). We'll get more experience with precision in the activity for this chapter.

> **NOTE**
>
> **Multiclass classification**
>
> Our case study involves a binary classification problem, with only two possible outcomes: the account does or does not default. Another important type of machine learning classification problem is multiclass classification. In multiclass classification, there are several possible mutually exclusive outcomes. A classic example is image recognition of handwritten digits; a handwritten digit should be only one of 0, 1, 2, … 9. Although multiclass classification is outside the scope of this book, the metrics we are learning now for binary classification can be extended to the multiclass setting.

## DISCOVERING PREDICTED PROBABILITIES: HOW DOES LOGISTIC REGRESSION MAKE PREDICTIONS?

Now that we're familiar with accuracy, true and false positives and negatives, and the confusion matrix, we can explore new ways of using logistic regression to learn about more advanced binary classification metrics. So far, we've only considered logistic regression as a "black box" that can learn from labeled training data and then make binary predictions on new features. While we will learn about the workings of logistic regression in detail later in the book, we can begin to peek inside the black box now.

One thing to understand about how logistic regression works is that the raw predictions – in other words, the direct outputs from the mathematical equation that defines logistic regression – are not binary labels. They are actually **probabilities** on a scale from 0 to 1 (although, technically, the equation never allows the probabilities to be exactly equal to 0 or 1, as we'll see later). These probabilities are only transformed into binary predictions through the use of a **threshold**. The threshold is the probability above which a prediction is declared to be positive, and below which it is negative. The threshold in scikit-learn is 0.5. This means any sample with a predicted probability of at least 0.5 is identified as positive, and any with a predicted probability < 0.5 is decided to be negative. However, we are free to use any threshold we want. In fact, choosing the threshold is one of the key flexibilities of logistic regression, as well as other machine learning classification algorithms that estimate probabilities of class membership.

## EXERCISE 2.03: OBTAINING PREDICTED PROBABILITIES FROM A TRAINED LOGISTIC REGRESSION MODEL

In the following exercise, we will get familiar with the predicted probabilities of logistic regression and how to obtain them from a scikit-learn model.

We can begin to discover predicted probabilities by further examining the methods available to us on the logistic regression model object that we trained earlier in this chapter. Recall that before, once we trained the model, we could then make binary predictions using the values of features from new samples by passing these values to the `.predict` method of the trained model. These are predictions made on the assumption of a threshold of 0.5.

However, we can directly access the predicted probabilities of these samples, using the `.predict_proba` method. Perform the following steps to complete the exercise, keeping in mind that you will need to recreate the same model trained previously in the chapter if you are starting a new notebook:

> **NOTE**
>
> The Jupyter notebook for this exercise can be found here:
> https://packt.link/yDyQn. The notebook contains the prerequisite steps of training the model and should be executed prior to the first step shown here.

1. Obtain the predicted probabilities for the test samples using this code:

```
y_pred_proba = example_lr.predict_proba(X_test)
y_pred_proba
```

The output should be as follows:

```
array([[0.77423402, 0.22576598],
       [0.77423402, 0.22576598],
       [0.78792915, 0.21207085],
       ...,
       [0.78792915, 0.21207085],
       [0.78792915, 0.21207085],
       [0.78792915, 0.21207085]])
```

Figure 2.23: Predicted probabilities of the test data

We see in the output of this, which we've stored in **y_pred_proba**, that there are two columns. This is because there are two classes in our classification problem: negative and positive. Assuming the negative labels are coded as 0 and the positives as 1, as they are in our data, scikit-learn will report the probability of negative class membership as the first column, and positive class membership as the second.

Since the two classes are mutually exclusive and are the only options, the sum of predicted probabilities for the two classes should equal 1 for every sample. Let's confirm this.

First, we can use **np.sum** over the first dimension (columns) to calculate the sum of probabilities for each sample.

2. Calculate the sum of predicted probabilities for each sample with this code:

```
prob_sum = np.sum(y_pred_proba,1)
prob_sum
```

The output is as follows:

```
array([1., 1., 1., ..., 1., 1., 1.])
```

It certainly looks like all 1s. We should check to see that the result is the same shape as the array of test data labels.

3. Check the array shape with this code:

```
prob_sum.shape
```

This should output the following:

```
(5333,)
```

Good; this is the expected shape. Now, to check that each value is 1. We use **np.unique** to show all the unique elements of this array. This is similar to **DISTINCT** in SQL. If all the probability sums are indeed 1, there should only be one unique element of the probability array: 1.

4. Show all unique array elements with this code:

```
np.unique(prob_sum)
```

This should output the following:

```
array([1.])
```

After confirming our belief in the predicted probabilities, we note that since class probabilities sum to 1, it's sufficient to just consider the second column, the predicted probability of positive class membership. Let's capture these in an array.

5.  Run this code to put the second column of the predicted probabilities array (predicted probability of membership in the positive class) in an array:

```
pos_proba = y_pred_proba[:,1]
pos_proba
```

The output should be as follows:

```
array([0.22576598, 0.22576598, 0.21207085, ..., 0.21207085, 0.21207085,
       0.21207085])
```

Figure 2.24: Predicted probabilities of positive class membership

What do these probabilities look like? One way to find out, and a good diagnostic for model output, is to plot the predicted probabilities. A histogram is a natural way to do this, for which we can use the matplotlib function, **hist()**. Note that if you execute a cell with only the histogram function, you will get the output of the NumPy histogram function returned before the plot. This includes the number of samples in each bin and the locations of the bin edges.

6.  Execute this code to see histogram output and an unformatted plot (not shown here):

```
plt.hist(pos_proba)
```

The output is as follows:

```
(array([1883.,    0.,    0., 2519.,    0.,    0., 849.,    0.,    0.,
          82.]),
 array([0.21207085, 0.21636321, 0.22065556, 0.22494792, 0.22924027,
        0.23353263, 0.23782498, 0.24211734, 0.24640969, 0.25070205,
        0.2549944 ]),
 <BarContainer object of 10 artists>)
```

Figure 2.25: Details of histogram calculation

This may be useful information for you and could also be obtained directly from the **np.histogram()** function. However, here we're mainly interested in the plot, so we adjust the font size and add some axis labels.

7.  Run this code for a formatted histogram plot of predicted probabilities:

```
mpl.rcParams['font.size'] = 12
plt.hist(pos_proba)
plt.xlabel('Predicted probability of positive class '\
           'for test data')
plt.ylabel('Number of samples')
```

The plot should look like this:

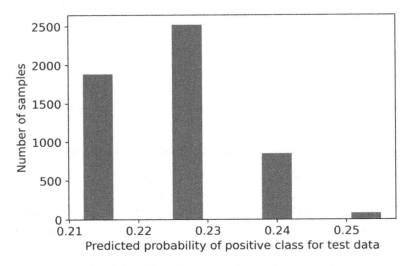

Figure 2.26: Histogram plot of predicted probabilities

Notice that in the histogram of probabilities, there are only four bins that actually have samples in them, and they are spaced fairly far apart. This is because there are only four unique values for the **EDUCATION** feature, which is the only feature in our example model.

Also, notice that all the predicted probabilities are below 0.5. This is the reason every sample was predicted to be negative, using the 0.5 threshold. We can imagine that if we set our threshold below 0.5, we would get different results. For example, if we set the threshold at 0.25, all of the samples in the smallest bin to the far right of *Figure 2.26* would be classified as positive, since the predicted probability for all of these is above 0.25. It would be informative for us if we could see how many of these samples actually had positive labels. Then we could see whether moving our threshold down to 0.25 would improve the performance of our classifier by classifying the samples in the rightmost bin as positive.

In fact, we can visualize this easily, using a **stacked histogram**. This will look a lot like the histogram in *Figure 2.27*, except that the negative and positive samples will be colored differently. First, we need to distinguish between positive and negative samples in the predicted probabilities. We can do this by indexing our array of predicted probabilities with logical masks; first to get positive samples, where **y_test == 1**, and then to get negative samples, where **y_test == 0**.

8. Isolate the predicted probabilities for positive and negative samples with this code:

```
pos_sample_pos_proba = pos_proba[y_test==1]
neg_sample_pos_proba = pos_proba[y_test==0]
```

Now we want to plot these as a stacked histogram. The code is similar to the histogram we already created, except that we will pass a list of arrays to be plotted, which are the arrays of probabilities for positive and negative samples we just created, and a keyword indicating we'd like the bars to be stacked, as opposed to plotted side by side. We'll also create a legend so that the colors are clearly identifiable on the plot.

9. Plot a stacked histogram using this code:

```
plt.hist([pos_sample_pos_proba, neg_sample_pos_proba],\
         histtype='barstacked')
plt.legend(['Positive samples', 'Negative samples'])
plt.xlabel('Predicted probability of positive class')
plt.ylabel('Number of samples')
```

The plot should look like this:

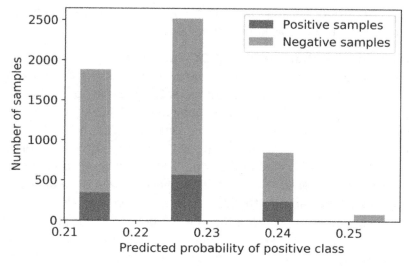

Figure 2.27: Stacked histogram of predicted probabilities by class

The plot shows us the true labels of the samples for each predicted probability. Now we can consider what the effect would be of lowering the threshold to 0.25. Take a moment and think about what this would mean, keeping in mind that any sample with a predicted probability at or above the threshold would be classified as positive.

Since nearly all the samples in the small bin to the right of *Figure 2.28* are negative samples, if we were to decrease the threshold to 0.25, we would erroneously classify these as positive samples and increase our FPR. At the same time, we still wouldn't have managed to classify many, if any, positive samples correctly, so our TPR wouldn't increase very much at all. Making this change would appear to decrease the accuracy of the model.

## THE RECEIVER OPERATING CHARACTERISTIC (ROC) CURVE

Deciding on a threshold for a classifier is a question of finding the "sweet spot" where we are successfully recovering enough true positives, without incurring too many false positives. As the threshold is lowered more and more, there will be more of both. A good classifier will be able to capture more true positives without the expense of a large number of false positives. What would be the effect of lowering the threshold even more, with the predicted probabilities from the previous exercise? It turns out there is a classic method of visualization in machine learning, with a corresponding metric that can help answer this kind of question.

The **receiver operating characteristic** (**ROC**) curve is a plot of the pairs of TPRs (*y-axis*) and FPRs (*x-axis*) that result from lowering the threshold down from 1 all the way to 0. You can imagine that if the threshold is 1, there are no positive predictions since a logistic regression only predicts probabilities strictly between 0 and 1 (endpoints not included). Since there are no positive predictions, the TPR and the FPR are both 0, so the ROC curve starts out at (0, 0). As the threshold is lowered, the TPR will start to increase, hopefully faster than the FPR if it's a good classifier. Eventually, when the threshold is lowered all the way to 0, every sample is predicted to be positive, including all the samples that are, in fact, positive, but also all the samples that are actually negative. This means the TPR is 1 but the FPR is also 1. In between these two extremes are the reasonable options for where you may want to set the threshold, depending on the relative costs and benefits of true and false positives and negatives for the specific problem being considered. In this way, it is possible to get a complete picture of the performance of the classifier at all different thresholds to decide which one to use.

We could write the code to determine the TPRs and FPRs of the ROC curve by using the predicted probabilities and varying the threshold from 1 to 0. Instead, we will use scikit-learn's convenient functionality, which will take the true labels and predicted probabilities as inputs and return arrays of TPRs, FPRs, and the thresholds that lead to them. We will then plot the TPRs against the FPRs to show the ROC curve. Run this code to use scikit-learn to generate the arrays of TPRs and FPRs for the ROC curve, importing the **metrics** module if needed:

```
from sklearn import metrics
fpr, tpr, thresholds = metrics.roc_curve(y_test, pos_proba)
```

Now we need to produce a plot. We'll use **plt.plot**, which will make a line plot using the first argument as the *x* values (FPRs), the second argument as the *y* values (TPRs), and the shorthand `'*-'` to indicate a line plot with star symbols where the data points are located. We add a straight-line plot from (0, 0) to (1, 1), which will appear in red (`'r'`) and as a dashed line (`'--'`). We've also given the plot a legend (which we'll explain shortly), as well as axis labels and a title. This code produces the ROC plot:

```
plt.plot(fpr, tpr, '*-')
plt.plot([0, 1], [0, 1], 'r--')
plt.legend(['Logistic regression', 'Random chance'])
plt.xlabel('FPR')
plt.ylabel('TPR')
plt.title('ROC curve')
```

And the plot should look like this:

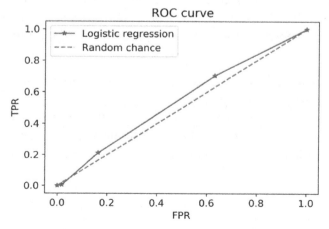

Figure 2.28: ROC curve for our logistic regression, with a line of random chance shown for comparison

What have we learned from our ROC curve? We can see that it starts at (0,0) with a threshold high enough so that there are no positive classifications. Then the first thing that happens, as we imagined previously when lowering the threshold to about 0.25, is that we get an increase in the FPR, but very little increase in the TPR. The effects of continuing to lower the threshold so that the other bars from our stacked histogram plot in *Figure 2.28* would be included as positive classifications are shown by the subsequent points on the line. We can see the thresholds that lead to these rates by examining the threshold array, which is not part of the plot. View the thresholds used to calculate the ROC curve using this code:

```
thresholds
```

The output should be as follows:

```
array([1.2549944 , 0.2549944 , 0.24007604, 0.22576598, 0.21207085])
```

Notice that the first threshold is actually above 1; practically speaking, it just needs to be a threshold that's high enough that there are no positive classifications.

Now consider what a "good" ROC curve would look like. As we lower the threshold, we want to see the TPR increase, which means our classifier is doing a good job of correctly identifying positive samples. At the same time, ideally the FPR should not increase that much. The ROC curve of an effective classifier would hug the upper left corner of the plot: high TPR, low FPR. You can imagine that a perfect classifier would get a TPR of 1 (recovers all the positive samples) and an FPR of 0 and appear as a sort of square starting at (0,0), going up to (0,1), and finishing at (1,1). While in practice this kind of performance is highly unlikely, it gives us a limiting case.

Further consider what the **area under the curve (AUC)** of such a classifier would be, remembering integrals from calculus if you have studied it. The AUC of a perfect classifier would be 1, because the shape of the curve would be a square on the unit interval [0, 1].

On the other hand, the line labeled as "Random chance" in our plot is the ROC curve that theoretically results from flipping an unbiased coin as a classifier: it's just as likely to get a true positive as a false positive, so lowering the threshold introduces more of each in equal proportion and the TPR and FPR increase at the same rate. The AUC under this ROC would be half of the perfect classifier's, as you can see graphically, and would be 0.5.

So, in general, the ROC AUC is going to be between 0.5 and 1 (although values below 0.5 are technically possible). Values close to 0.5 indicate the model can do little better than random chance (coin flip) as a classifier, while values closer to 1 indicate better performance. The **ROC AUC** is a key metric for the quality of a classifier and is widely used in machine learning. The ROC AUC may also be referred to as the **C-statistic** (concordance statistic).

Being such an important metric, scikit-learn has a convenient way to calculate the ROC AUC. Let's see what the ROC AUC of the logistic regression classifier is, where we can pass the same information that we did to the `roc_curve` function. Calculate the area under the ROC curve with this code:

```
metrics.roc_auc_score(y_test, pos_proba)
```

And observe the output:

```
0.5434650477972642
```

The ROC AUC for the logistic regression is pretty close to 0.5, meaning it's not a very effective classifier. This may not be surprising, considering we have expended no effort to determine which features out of the candidate pool are actually useful at this point. We're just getting used to model fitting syntax and learning the way to calculate model quality metrics using a simple model containing only the **EDUCATION** feature. Later on, by considering other features, hopefully we'll get a higher ROC AUC.

> **NOTE**
>
> **ROC curve: How did it get that name?**
>
> During World War II, radar receiver operators were evaluated on their ability to judge whether something that appeared on their radar screen was in fact an enemy aircraft or not. These decisions involved the same concepts of true and false positives and negatives that we are interested in for binary classification. The ROC curve was devised as a way to measure the effectiveness of operators of radar receiver equipment.

## PRECISION

Before embarking on the activity, we will consider the classification metric briefly introduced previously: **precision**. Like the ROC curve, this diagnostic is useful over a range of thresholds. Precision is defined as follows:

$$precision = \frac{TP}{TP + FP}$$

**Figure 2.29: Precision equation**

Consider the interpretation of this, in the sense of varying the threshold across the range of predicted probabilities, as we did for the ROC curve. At a high threshold, there will be relatively few samples predicted as positive. As we lower the threshold, more and more will be predicted as positive. Our hope is that as we do this, the number of true positives increases more quickly than the number of false positives, as we saw on the ROC curve. Precision looks at the ratio of the number of true positives to the sum of true and false positives. Think about the denominator here: what is the sum of true and false positives?

This sum is in fact the total number of positive predictions, since all positive predictions will be either correct or incorrect. So, precision measures the ratio of positive predictions that are correct to all positive predictions. For this reason, it is also called the **positive predictive value**. If there are very few positive samples, precision gives a more critical assessment of the quality of a classifier than the ROC AUC. As with the ROC curve, there is a convenient function in scikit-learn to calculate precision, together with recall (also known as the TPR), over a range of thresholds: `metrics.precision_recall_curve`. Precision and recall are often plotted together to assess the quality of positive predictions as far as what fraction are correct, while at the same time considering what fraction of the positive class a model is able to identify. We'll plot a precision-recall curve in the following activity.

Why might precision be a useful measure of classifier performance? Imagine that for every positive model prediction, you are going to take some expensive course of action, such as a time-consuming review of content that was flagged as inappropriate by an automated procedure. False positives would waste the valuable time of human reviewers. You would want to be sure that you were making the right decisions on what content received a detailed review. Precision could be a good metric to use in this situation.

## ACTIVITY 2.01: PERFORMING LOGISTIC REGRESSION WITH A NEW FEATURE AND CREATING A PRECISION-RECALL CURVE

In this activity, you'll train a logistic regression model using a feature besides **EDUCATION**. Then you will graphically assess the trade-off between precision and recall, as well as calculate the area underneath a precision-recall curve. You will also calculate the ROC AUC on both the training and test sets and compare them.

Perform the following steps to complete the activity:

> **NOTE**
>
> The code and the resulting output for this activity have been loaded in a Jupyter notebook that can be found here: https://packt.link/SvAOD.

1. Use scikit-learn's `train_test_split` to make a new set of training and test data. This time, instead of **EDUCATION**, use **LIMIT_BAL**, the account's credit limit, as the feature.

2. Train a logistic regression model using the training data from your split.

3. Create the array of predicted probabilities for the test data.

4. Calculate the ROC AUC using the predicted probabilities and the true labels of the test data. Compare this to the ROC AUC from using the **EDUCATION** feature.

5. Plot the ROC curve.

6. Calculate the data for the **precision-recall curve** on the test data using scikit-learn's functionality.

7. Plot the precision-recall curve using matplotlib.

8. Use scikit-learn to calculate the area under the precision-recall curve. You should get a value of approximately 0.315.

9. Now recalculate the ROC AUC, except this time do it for the training data. How is this different, conceptually and quantitatively, from your earlier calculation?

> **NOTE**
>
> The Jupyter notebook containing the Python code solution for this activity can be found here: https://packt.link/SvAOD. Detailed step-wise solution to this activity can be found on page 372.

# SUMMARY

In this chapter, we finished the initial exploration of the case study data by examining the response variable. Once we became confident in the completeness and correctness of the dataset, we were prepared to explore the relation between features and response and build models.

We spent much of this chapter getting used to model fitting in scikit-learn at the technical, coding level, and learning about metrics we could use with the binary classification problem of the case study. When trying different feature sets and different kinds of models, you will need some way to tell if one approach is working better than another. Consequently, you'll need to use model performance metrics like those we learned in this chapter.

While accuracy is a familiar and intuitive metric as the percentage of correct classifications, we learned why it may not give a useful assessment of the performance of a classifier. We learned how to use a majority-class null model to tell whether an accuracy rate is truly good, or no better than what would result from simply predicting the most common class for all samples. When the data is imbalanced, accuracy is usually not the best way to judge a classifier.

In order to have a more nuanced view of how a model is performing, it's necessary to separate the positive and negative classes and assess the accuracy of them independently. From the resulting counts of true and false positive and negative classifications, which can be summarized in a confusion matrix, we can derive several other metrics: true and false positive and negative rates. Combining true and false positives and negatives with the concept of predicted probabilities and a variable threshold of prediction, we can further characterize the usefulness of a classifier using the ROC curve, the precision-recall curve, and the areas under these curves.

With these tools, you are well equipped to answer general questions about the performance of a binary classifier in any domain you may be working in. Later in the book, we will learn about application-specific ways to assess model performance by attaching costs and benefits to true and false positives and negatives. Before that, starting in the next chapter, we will begin learning the details behind what is possibly the most popular and simplest classification model: **logistic regression**.

# 3

# DETAILS OF LOGISTIC REGRESSION AND FEATURE EXPLORATION

## OVERVIEW

This chapter teaches you how to evaluate features quickly and efficiently, in order to know which ones will probably be most important for a machine learning model. Once we get a taste for this, we'll explore the inner workings of logistic regression so you can continue your journey to mastery of this fundamental technique. After reading this chapter, you will be able to make a correlation plot of many features and a response variable and interpret logistic regression as a linear model.

# INTRODUCTION

In the previous chapter, we developed a few example machine learning models using scikit-learn, to get familiar with how it works. However, the features we used, **EDUCATION** and **LIMIT_BAL**, were not chosen in a systematic way.

In this chapter, we will start to develop techniques that can be used to assess features for their usefulness in modeling. This will enable you to make a quick pass over all candidate features, to have an idea of which will be the most important. For the most promising features, we will see how to create visual summaries that serve as useful communication tools.

Next, we will begin our detailed examination of logistic regression. We'll learn why logistic regression is considered to be a linear model, even if the formulation involves some non-linear functions. We'll learn what a decision boundary is and see that as a key consequence of its linearity, the decision boundary of logistic regression could make it difficult to accurately classify the response variable. Along the way, we'll get more familiar with Python, by using list comprehensions and writing functions.

## EXAMINING THE RELATIONSHIPS BETWEEN FEATURES AND THE RESPONSE VARIABLE

In order to make accurate predictions of the response variable, good features are necessary. We need features that are clearly linked to the response variable in some way. Thus far, we've examined the relationship between a couple of features and the response variable, either by calculating the **groupby/mean** of a feature and the response variable, or using individual features in a model and examining performance. However, we have not yet done a systematic exploration of how all the features relate to the response variable. We will do that now and begin to capitalize on all the hard work we put in when we were exploring the features and making sure the data quality was good.

A popular way of getting a quick look at how all the features relate to the response variable, as well as how the features are related to each other, is by using a **correlation plot**. We will first create a correlation plot for the case study data, then discuss how to interpret it, along with some mathematical details.

In order to create a correlation plot, the necessary inputs include all features that we plan to explore, as well as the response variable. Since we are going to use most of the column names from the DataFrame for this, a quick way to get the appropriate list in Python is to start with all the column names and remove those that we don't want. As a preliminary step, we start a new notebook for this chapter and load packages and the cleaned data from *Chapter 1, Data Exploration and Cleaning*, with this code:

```
import numpy as np #numerical computation
import pandas as pd #data wrangling
import matplotlib.pyplot as plt #plotting package
#Next line helps with rendering plots
%matplotlib inline
import matplotlib as mpl #add'l plotting functionality
import seaborn as sns #a fancy plotting package
mpl.rcParams['figure.dpi'] = 400 #high res figures
df = pd.read_csv('../../Data/Chapter_1_cleaned_data.csv')
```

> **NOTE**
>
> The path to your cleaned data file may be different, depending on where
> you saved it in *Chapter 1*, *Data Exploration and Cleaning*. The code and the
> outputs presented in this section are also present in the reference notebook:
> https://packt.link/pMvWa.

Notice that this notebook starts out in a very similar way to the previous chapter's
notebook, except we also import the **Seaborn** package, which has many convenient
plotting features that build on **Matplotlib**. Now let's make a list of all the columns of
the DataFrame and look at the first and last five:

```
features_response = df.columns.tolist()
```

```
features_response[:5]
```

```
['ID', 'LIMIT_BAL', 'SEX', 'EDUCATION', 'MARRIAGE']
```

```
features_response[-5:]
```

```
['EDUCATION_CAT', 'graduate school', 'high school', 'others', 'university']
```

Figure 3.1: Get a list of column names

Recall that we are not to use the **gender** variable due to ethical concerns, and we learned that **PAY_2**, **PAY_3**,..., **PAY_6** are incorrect and should be ignored. Also, we are not going to examine the one-hot encoding we created from the **EDUCATION** variable, since the information from those columns is already included in the original feature, at least in some form. We will just use the **EDUCATION** feature directly. Finally, it makes no sense to use **ID** as a feature, since this is simply a unique account identifier and has nothing to do with the response variable. Let's make another list of column names that are neither features nor the response. We want to exclude these from our analysis:

```
items_to_remove = ['ID', 'SEX',\
                   'PAY_2', 'PAY_3', 'PAY_4', 'PAY_5', 'PAY_6',\
                   'EDUCATION_CAT',\
                   'graduate school', 'high school', 'none',\
                   'others', 'university']
```

To have a list of column names that consists only of the features and response we will use, we want to remove the names in **items_to_remove** from the current list contained in **features_response**. There are several ways to do this in Python. We will use this opportunity to learn about a particular way of building a list in Python, called a **list comprehension**. When people talk about certain constructions as being **Pythonic**, or idiomatic to the Python language, list comprehensions are often one of the things that are mentioned.

What is a list comprehension? Conceptually, it is basically the same as a **for** loop. However, list comprehensions enable the creation of lists, which may be spread across several lines in an actual **for** loop, to be written in one line. They are also slightly faster than **for** loops, due to optimizations within Python. While this likely won't save us much time here, this is a good chance to become familiar with them. Here is an example list comprehension:

```
example_list_comp = [item for item in range(5)]
example_list_comp
```

```
[0, 1, 2, 3, 4]
```

**Figure 3.2: Example of a list comprehension**

That's all there is to it.

We can also use additional clauses to make the list comprehensions flexible. For example, we can use them to reassign the **features_response** variable with a list containing everything that's not in the list of strings we wish to remove:

```
features_response = [item for item in features_response if item not in items_to_remove]
features_response
```

```
['LIMIT_BAL',
 'EDUCATION',
 'MARRIAGE',
 'AGE',
 'PAY_1',
 'BILL_AMT1',
 'BILL_AMT2',
 'BILL_AMT3',
 'BILL_AMT4',
 'BILL_AMT5',
 'BILL_AMT6',
 'PAY_AMT1',
 'PAY_AMT2',
 'PAY_AMT3',
 'PAY_AMT4',
 'PAY_AMT5',
 'PAY_AMT6',
 'default payment next month']
```

Figure 3.3: Using a list comprehension to prune down the column names

The use of **if** and **not in** within the list comprehension is fairly self-explanatory. Easy readability in structures such as list comprehensions is one of the reasons for the popularity of Python.

> **NOTE**
>
> The Python documentation (https://docs.python.org/3/tutorial/datastructures.html) defines list comprehensions as the following:
>
> *"A list comprehension consists of brackets containing an expression followed by a for clause, then zero or more for or if clauses."*
>
> Thus, list comprehensions can enable you to do things with less code, in a way that is usually pretty readable and understandable.

## PEARSON CORRELATION

Now we are ready to create our correlation plot. Underlying a correlation plot is a **correlation matrix**, which we must calculate first. pandas makes this easy. We just need to select our columns of features and response values using the list we just created and call the `.corr()` method on these columns. As we calculate this, note that the type of correlation available to us in pandas is **linear correlation**, also known as **Pearson correlation**. Pearson correlation is used to measure the strength and direction (that is, positive or negative) of the linear relationship between two variables:

|  | LIMIT_BAL | EDUCATION | MARRIAGE | AGE | PAY_1 |
|---|---|---|---|---|---|
| LIMIT_BAL | 1.000000 | -0.232688 | -0.111873 | 0.149157 | -0.273396 |
| EDUCATION | -0.232688 | 1.000000 | -0.137097 | 0.179035 | 0.112653 |
| MARRIAGE | -0.111873 | -0.137097 | 1.000000 | -0.412828 | 0.019759 |
| AGE | 0.149157 | 0.179035 | -0.412828 | 1.000000 | -0.044277 |
| PAY_1 | -0.273396 | 0.112653 | 0.019759 | -0.044277 | 1.000000 |

**Figure 3.4: First five rows and columns of the correlation matrix**

After creating the correlation matrix, notice that the row and column names are the same. Then, for each possible comparison between all pairs of features, as well as all features and the response, which we can't yet see here in the first five rows and columns, there is a number. This number is called the **correlation** between these two columns. All the correlations are between -1 and 1; a column has a correlation of 1 with itself (the diagonal of the correlation matrix), and there is repetition: each comparison appears twice since each column name from the original DataFrame appears as both a row and column in the correlation matrix. Before saying more about correlation, we'll use Seaborn to make a nice plot of it. Here is the plotting code, followed by the output (please see the notebook on GitHub for a color figure if you're reading in black and white; it's necessary here - https://packt.link/pMvWa):

```
sns.heatmap(corr,
            xticklabels=corr.columns.values,
            yticklabels=corr.columns.values,
            center=0)
```

You should see the following output:

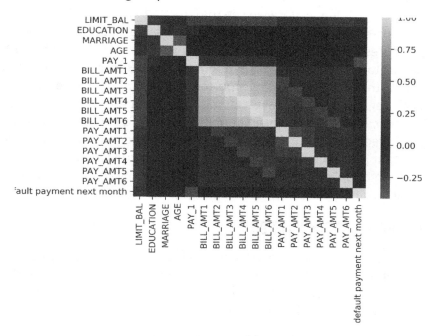

Figure 3.5: Heatmap of the correlation plot in Seaborn

The Seaborn **heatmap** feature makes an obvious visualization of the correlation matrix, according to the color scale on the right of *Figure 3.5*, which is called a **colorbar**. Notice that when calling **sns.heatmap**, in addition to the matrix, we supplied the **tick labels** for the *x* and *y* axes, which are the features and response names, and indicated that the center of the colorbar should be 0, so that positive and negative correlation are distinguishable as red and blue, respectively.

> **NOTE**
>
> If you're reading the print version of this book, you can download and browse the color versions of some of the images in this chapter by visiting the following link: https://packt.link/veMmT.

What does this plot tell us? At a high level, if two features, or a feature and the response, are **highly correlated** with each other, you can say there is a strong association between them. Features that are highly correlated to the response will be good features to use for prediction. This high correlation could be positive or negative; we'll explain the difference shortly.

To see the correlation with the response variable, we look along the bottom row, or equivalently, the last column. Here we see that the **PAY_1** feature is probably the most strongly correlated feature to the response variable. We can also see that a number of features are highly correlated to each other, in particular the **BILL_AMT** features. We will talk in the next chapter about the importance of features that are correlated with each other; this is important to know about for certain models, such as logistic regression, that make assumptions about the correlations between features. For now, we make the observation that **PAY_1** is likely going to be one of the best, most predictive features for our model. The other feature that looks like it may be important is **LIMIT_BAL**, which is negatively correlated. Depending on how astute your vision is, only these two really appear to be any color other than black (meaning 0 correlation) in the bottom row of *Figure 3.5*.

## MATHEMATICS OF LINEAR CORRELATION

What is linear correlation, mathematically speaking? If you've taken basic statistics, you are likely familiar with linear correlation already. Linear correlation works very similarly to linear regression. For two columns, $X$ and $Y$, linear correlation $\rho$ (the lowercase Greek letter "rho") is defined as the following:

$$\rho = \frac{E[(X - \mu_X)(Y - \mu_Y)]}{\sigma_X \sigma_Y}$$

**Figure 3.6: Linear correlation equation**

This equation describes the **expected value** (*E*, which you can think of as the average) of the difference between the elements of $X$ and their average, $\mu_x$, multiplied by the difference between the corresponding elements of $Y$ and their average, $\mu_y$. The average for $E$ is taken over pairs of $X$, $Y$ values. You can imagine that if, when $X$ is relatively large compared to its mean, $\mu_x$, $Y$ also tends to be similarly large, then the terms of the multiplication in the numerator will both tend to be positive, leading to a positive product and **positive correlation** after the expected value, $E$, is taken. Similarly, if $Y$ tends to be small when $X$ is small, both terms in the numerator will be negative and again lead to positive correlation. Conversely, if $Y$ tends to decrease as $X$ increases, they will have **negative correlation**. The denominator (the product of the **standard deviations** of $X$ and $Y$) serves to normalize linear correlation to the scale of [-1, 1]. Because Pearson correlation is adjusted for the mean and standard deviation of the data, the actual values of the data are not as important as the relationship between $X$ and $Y$. *Stronger linear correlations are closer to 1 or -1. If there is no linear relation between X and Y, the correlation will be close to 0.*

It's worth noting that, while it is regularly used in this context by data science practitioners, Pearson correlation is not strictly appropriate for a binary response variable, as we have in the case study problem. Technically speaking, among other restrictions, Pearson correlation is only valid for **continuous data**, such as the data we used for our linear regression exercise in *Chapter 2, Introduction to Scikit-Learn and Model Evaluation*. However, Pearson correlation can still accomplish the purpose of giving a quick idea of the potential usefulness of features. It is also conveniently available in software libraries such as pandas.

In data science in general, you will find that certain widely used techniques may be applied to data that violate their formal statistical assumptions. It is important to be aware of the formal assumptions underlying analytical methods. In fact, knowledge of these assumptions may be tested during interviews for data science jobs. However, in practice, as long as a technique can help us on our way to understanding the problem and finding an effective solution, it can still be a valuable tool.

That being said, linear correlation will not be an effective measure of the predictive power of all features. In particular, it only picks up on linear relationships. Shifting our focus momentarily to a hypothetical regression problem, have a look at the following examples and discuss what you expect the linear correlations to be. Notice that the values of the data on the *x* and *y* axes are not labeled; this is because the location (mean) and standard deviation (scale) of data does not affect the Pearson correlation, only the relationship between the variables, which can be discerned by plotting them together:

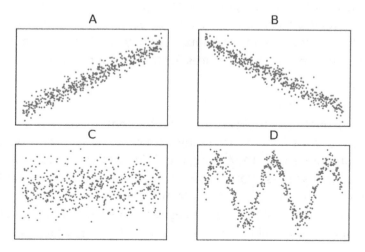

Figure 3.7: Scatter plots of the relationship between example variables

For *examples A* and *B*, the actual Pearson correlations of these datasets are 0.96 and -0.97, respectively, according to the formula given previously. From looking at the plots, it's pretty clear that a correlation close to 1 or -1 has provided useful insight into the relationship between these variables. For *example C*, the correlation is 0.06. A correlation closer to 0 looks like an effective indication of the lack of an association here: the value of Y doesn't really seem to have much to do with the value of X. However, in *example D*, there is clearly some relationship between the variables. But the linear correlation is actually lower than the previous example, at 0.02. Here, X and Y tend to "move together" over smaller scales, but this is averaged out over all samples when the linear correlation is calculated.

> **NOTE**
>
> The code to generate the plots presented in this and the preceding section can be found here: https://packt.link/XrUJU.

Ultimately, any summary statistic such as correlation that you may choose is only that: a summary. It could hide important details. For this reason, it is usually a good idea to visually examine the relationship between the features and response. This potentially takes up a lot of space on the page, so we won't demonstrate it here for all features in the case study. However, both pandas and Seaborn offer functions to create what's called a **scatter plot matrix**. A scatter plot matrix is similar to a correlation plot, but it actually shows all the data as a grid of scatter plots of all features and the response variable. This allows you to examine the data directly in a concise format. Since this could potentially be a lot of data and plots, you may need to downsample your data and look at a reduced number of features for the function to run efficiently.

## F-TEST

While Pearson correlation is theoretically valid for continuous response variables, the binary response variable for the case study data could be considered categorical data, with only two categories: 0 and 1. Among the different kinds of tests we can run, to see whether features are associated with a categorical response, is the **ANOVA F-test**, available in scikit-learn as `f_classif`. **ANOVA** stands for **analysis of variance**. The ANOVA F-test can be contrasted with the **regression F-test**, which is very similar to Pearson correlation, also available in scikit-learn as `f_regression`.

We will do an ANOVA F-test using the candidate features for the case study data in the following exercise. You will see that the output consists of F-statistics, as well as **p-values**. How can we interpret this output? We will focus on the p-value, for reasons that will become clear in the exercise. The p-value is a useful concept across a wide variety of statistical measures. For instance, although we didn't examine them, each of the Pearson correlations calculated for the preceding correlation matrix has a corresponding p-value. There is a similar concept of a p-value corresponding to linear regression coefficients, logistic regression coefficients, and other measures.

In the context of the F-test, the p-value answers the question: "For the samples in the positive class, how likely is it that the average value of this feature is the same as that of samples in the negative class?" If the data indicated that a feature has very different average values between the positive and negative classes, the following will be the case:

- It will be very unlikely that those average values are the same (low p-value).

- It will probably be a good feature in our model because it will help us discriminate between positive and negative classes.

Keep these points in mind during the following exercise.

## EXERCISE 3.01: F-TEST AND UNIVARIATE FEATURE SELECTION

In this exercise, we'll use the F-test to examine the relationship between the features and response variable. We will use this method to do what is called **univariate feature selection**: the practice of testing features one by one against the response variable, to see which ones have predictive power. Perform the following steps to complete the exercise:

> **NOTE**
>
> The Jupyter notebook for this exercise can be found here: https://packt.link/ZDPYf. This notebook also contains the prerequisite steps of loading the cleaned data and importing the necessary libraries. These steps should be executed before step 1 of this exercise.

1. Our first step in doing the ANOVA F-test is to separate out the features and response as NumPy arrays, taking advantage of the list we created, as well as integer indexing in pandas:

```
X = df[features_response].iloc[:,:-1].values
y = df[features_response].iloc[:,-1].values
print(X.shape, y.shape)
```

The output should show the shapes of the features and response:

```
(26664, 17) (26664, )
```

There are 17 features, and both the features and response arrays have the same number of samples as expected.

2. Import the **f_classif** function and feed in the features and response:

```
from sklearn.feature_selection import f_classif
[f_stat, f_p_value] = f_classif(X, y)
```

There are two outputs from **f_classif**: the **F-statistic** and the **p-value**, for the comparison of each feature to the response variable. Let's create a new DataFrame containing the feature names and these outputs, to facilitate our inspection. One way to specify a new DataFrame is by using a **dictionary**, with **key:value** pairs of column names and the data to be contained in each column. We show the DataFrame sorted (ascending) on p-value.

3. Use this code to create a DataFrame of feature names, F-statistics, and p-values, and show it sorted on p-value:

```
f_test_df = pd.DataFrame({'Feature':features_response[:-1],
                          'F statistic':f_stat,
                          'p value':f_p_value})
f_test_df.sort_values('p value')
```

The output should look like this:

| | Feature | F statistic | p value |
|---|---|---|---|
| 4 | PAY_1 | 3156.672300 | 0.000000e+00 |
| 0 | LIMIT_BAL | 651.324071 | 5.838366e-142 |
| 11 | PAY_AMT1 | 140.612679 | 2.358354e-32 |
| 12 | PAY_AMT2 | 101.408321 | 8.256124e-24 |
| 13 | PAY_AMT3 | 90.023873 | 2.542641e-21 |
| 15 | PAY_AMT5 | 85.843295 | 2.090120e-20 |
| 16 | PAY_AMT6 | 80.420784 | 3.219565e-19 |
| 14 | PAY_AMT4 | 79.640021 | 4.774112e-19 |
| 1 | EDUCATION | 32.637768 | 1.122175e-08 |
| 2 | MARRIAGE | 18.078027 | 2.127555e-05 |
| 5 | BILL_AMT1 | 11.218406 | 8.110226e-04 |
| 7 | BILL_AMT3 | 5.722938 | 1.675157e-02 |
| 6 | BILL_AMT2 | 5.668454 | 1.727965e-02 |
| 3 | AGE | 5.479140 | 1.925206e-02 |
| 8 | BILL_AMT4 | 3.434740 | 6.384965e-02 |
| 9 | BILL_AMT5 | 1.216082 | 2.701409e-01 |
| 10 | BILL_AMT6 | 1.049561 | 3.056176e-01 |

Figure 3.8: Results of the ANOVA F-test

Note that for every decrease in p-value, there is an increase in the F-statistic, so the information in these columns is identical in terms of ranking features.

The conclusions we can draw from the DataFrame of F-statistics and p-values are similar to what we observed in the correlation plot: **PAY_1** and **LIMIT_BAL** appear to be the most useful features. They have the smallest p-values, indicating the average values of these features are **significantly different** between the positive and negative classes, and these features will help predict which class a sample belongs to.

In scikit-learn, measures such as the F-test help us perform **univariate feature selection**. This may be helpful if you have a very large number of features, many of which may be totally useless, and would like a quick way to get a short list of which ones might be most useful. For example, if we wanted to retrieve only the 20% of features with the highest F-statistics, we could do this easily with the **SelectPercentile** class. Also note there is a similar class for the selection of the top "*k*" features (where *k* is any number you specify), called **SelectKBest**. Here we demonstrate how to select the top 20%.

4. To select the top 20% of features according to the F-test, first import the **SelectPercentile** class:

```
from sklearn.feature_selection import SelectPercentile
```

5. Instantiate an object of this class, indicating we'd like to use the same feature selection criteria, ANOVA F-test, that we've already been considering in this exercise, and that we'd like to select the top 20% of features:

```
selector = SelectPercentile(f_classif, percentile=20)
```

6. Use the **.fit** method to fit the object on our features and response data, similar to how a model would be fit:

```
selector.fit(X, y)
```

The output should appear like this:

```
SelectPercentile(percentile=20)
```

There are several ways to access the selected features directly, which you may learn about in the scikit-learn documentation (that is, the **.transform** method, or in the same step as fitting with **.fit_transform**). However, these methods will return NumPy arrays, which don't tell you the names of the features that were selected, just the values. For that, you can use the **.get_support** method of the feature selector object, which will give you the column indices of the feature array that were selected.

7. Capture the indices of the selected features in an array named **best_feature_ix**:

```
best_feature_ix = selector.get_support()
best_feature_ix
```

The output should appear as follows, indicating a logical index that can be used with an array of feature names, as well as values, assuming they're in the same order as the features array supplied to **SelectPercentile**:

```
array([ True, False, False, False,  True, False, False, False, False,
       False, False,  True,  True, False, False, False, False])
```

8. The feature names can be obtained using all but the last element (the **name** response variable) of our **features_response** list by indexing with **:-1**:

```
features = features_response[:-1]
```

9. Use the index array we created in *Step 7* with a list comprehension and the **features** list, to find the selected feature names, as follows:

```
best_features = [features[counter]
                 for counter in range(len(features))
                 if best_feature_ix[counter]]
best_features
```

The output should be as follows:

```
['LIMIT_BAL', 'PAY_1', 'PAY_AMT1', 'PAY_AMT2']
```

In this code, the list comprehension has looped through the number of elements in the **features** array (**len(features)**) with the **counter** loop increment, using the **best_feature_ix** Boolean array, representing selected features, in the **if** statement to test whether each feature was selected and capturing the name if so.

The selected features agree with the top four rows of our DataFrame of F-test results, so the feature selection has worked as expected. While it's not strictly necessary to do things both ways, since they both lead to the same result, it's good to check your work, especially as you are learning new concepts. You should be aware that with convenient methods such as **SelectPercentile**, you don't get visibility of the F-statistics or p-values. However, in some situations, it may be more convenient to use these methods, as the p-values may not necessarily be important, outside of their utility in ranking features.

## FINER POINTS OF THE F-TEST: EQUIVALENCE TO THE T-TEST FOR TWO CLASSES AND CAUTIONS

When we use an F-test to look at the difference in means between just two groups, as we've done here for the binary classification problem of the case study, the test we are performing actually reduces to what's called a **t-test**. An F-test is extensible to three or more groups and so is useful for multiclass classification. A t-test just compares the means between two groups of samples, to see whether the difference in those means is **statistically significant**.

While the F-test served our purposes here of univariate feature selection, there are a few cautions to keep in mind. Going back to the concept of formal statistical assumptions, for the F-test these include that the data is **normally distributed**. We have not checked this. Also, in comparing the same response variable, $y$, to many potential features from the matrix, $X$, we have performed what is known in statistics as **multiple comparisons**. In short, this means that by examining multiple features in comparison to the same response over and over, the odds increase that we'll find what we think is a "good feature" just by random chance. However, such features may not generalize to new data. There are statistical **corrections for multiple comparisons** that amount to adjusting the p-values to account for this.

Even if we have not followed all the statistical rules that go along with these methods, we can still get useful results from them. The multiple comparisons correction is more of a concern when p-values are the ultimate quantity of interest, for example, when making statistical inferences. Here, p-values are just a means to an end of ranking the feature list. The order of this ranking would not change if the p-values were corrected for multiple comparisons.

In addition to knowing which features are likely to be useful for modeling, it is good to have a deeper understanding of the important features. Consequently, we will do a detailed graphical exploration of these in the next exercise. We will also look at other methods for feature selection later that don't make the same assumptions as those we've introduced here and are more directly integrated with the predictive models that we will build.

## HYPOTHESES AND NEXT STEPS

According to our univariate feature exploration, the feature with the strongest association with the response variable is **PAY_1**. Does this make sense? What is the interpretation of **PAY_1**? **PAY_1** is the payment status of the account, in the most recent month. As we learned in the initial data exploration, there are some values that indicate that the account was in good standing: -2 means no account usage, -1 means balance paid in full, and 0 means at least the minimum payment was made. On the other hand, positive integer values indicate a delay of payment by that many months. Accounts with delayed payments last month were accounts that could be considered in default. This means that, essentially, this feature captures historical values of the response variable. Features such as this are extremely important as *one of the best predictors for just about any machine learning problem is historical data on the same thing you are trying to predict (that is, the response variable).* This should make sense: people who have defaulted before are probably at the highest risk of defaulting again.

How about **LIMIT_BAL**, the credit limit of accounts? Thinking about how credit limits are assigned, it is likely that our client has assessed how risky a borrower is when deciding their credit limit. Riskier clients should be given lower limits, so the creditor is less exposed. Therefore, we may expect to see a higher probability of default for accounts with lower values for **LIMIT_BAL**.

What have we learned from our univariate feature selection exercise? We have an idea of what the most important features in our model are likely to be. And, from the correlation matrix, we have some idea of how they are related to the response variable. However, knowing the limitations of the tests we used, it is a good idea to visualize these features for a closer look at the relationship between the features and response variable. We have also started to develop **hypotheses** about these features: why do we think they are important? Now, by visualizing the relationships between the features and the response variable, we can determine whether our ideas are compatible with what we can see in the data.

Such hypotheses and visualizations are often a key part of presenting your results to a client, who may be interested in how a model works, not just the fact that it does work.

## EXERCISE 3.02: VISUALIZING THE RELATIONSHIP BETWEEN THE FEATURES AND RESPONSE VARIABLE

In this exercise, you will further your knowledge of plotting functions from Matplotlib that you used earlier in this book. You'll learn how to customize graphics to better answer specific questions with the data. As you pursue these analyses, you will create insightful visualizations of how the **PAY_1** and **LIMIT_BAL** features relate to the response variable, which may possibly provide support for the hypotheses you formed about these features. This will be done by becoming more familiar with the Matplotlib **Application Programming Interface** (**API**), in other words, the syntax you use to interact with Matplotlib. Perform the following steps to complete the exercise:

> **NOTE**
>
> Before beginning step 1 of this exercise, make sure that you have imported the necessary libraries and have loaded the correct dataframe. You can refer to the following notebook for the prerequisite steps along with the code for this exercise: https://packt.link/DOrZ9.

1. Calculate a baseline for the response variable of the default rate across the whole dataset using pandas' **.mean()**:

```
overall_default_rate = df['default payment next month'].mean()
overall_default_rate
```

The output of this should be the following:

```
0.2217971797179718
```

What would be a good way to visualize default rates for different values of the **PAY_1** feature?

Recall our observation that this feature is sort of like a hybrid categorical and numerical feature. We'll choose to plot it in a way that is typical for categorical features, due to the relatively small number of unique values. In *Chapter 1, Data Exploration and Cleaning*, we did **value_counts** of this feature as part of data exploration, then later we learned about **groupby/mean** when looking at the **EDUCATION** feature. **groupby/mean** would be a good way to visualize the default rate again here, for different payment statuses.

2. Use this code to create a **groupby/mean** aggregation:

```
group_by_pay_mean_y = df.groupby('PAY_1').agg(
```

{'default payment next month':np.mean})

```
group_by_pay_mean_y
```

The output should look as follows:

```
group_by_pay_mean_y = df.groupby('PAY_1').agg({'default payment next month':np.mean})
group_by_pay_mean_y
```

| PAY_1 | default payment next month |
|---|---|
| -2 | 0.131664 |
| -1 | 0.170002 |
| 0 | 0.128295 |
| 1 | 0.336400 |
| 2 | 0.694701 |
| 3 | 0.773973 |
| 4 | 0.682540 |
| 5 | 0.434783 |
| 6 | 0.545455 |
| 7 | 0.777778 |
| 8 | 0.588235 |

Figure 3.9: Mean of the response variable by groups of the PAY_1 feature

Looking at these values, you may already be able to discern the trend. Let's go straight to plotting them. We'll take it step by step and introduce some new concepts. You should put all the code from *Steps 3* through *6* in a single code cell.

In Matplotlib, every plot exists on an axes, and within a **figure** window. By creating objects for **axes** and **figure**, you can directly access and change their properties, including axis labels and other kinds of annotation on the axes.

3.  Create an **axes** object in a variable also called **axes**, using the following code:

```
axes = plt.axes()
```

4.  Plot the overall default rate as a red horizontal line.

    Matplotlib makes this easy; you just have to indicate the *y* intercept of this line with the **axhline** function. Notice that instead of calling this function from **plt**, now we are calling it as a method on our **axes** object:

```
axes.axhline(overall_default_rate, color='red')
```

    Now, over this line, we want to plot the default rate within each group of **PAY_1** values.

5.  Use the **plot** method of the DataFrame of grouped data we created. Specify to include an **'x'** marker along the line plot, to not have a **legend** instance, which we'll create later, and that the **parent axes** of this plot should be the axes we are already working with (otherwise, pandas would erase what was already there and create new axes):

```
group_by_pay_mean_y.plot(marker='x', legend=False, ax=axes)
```

    This is all the data we want to plot.

6.  Set the *y*-axis label and create a **legend** instance (there are many possible options for controlling the legend appearance, but a simple way is to provide a list of strings, indicating the labels for the graphical elements in the order they were added to the axes):

```
axes.set_ylabel('Proportion of credit defaults')
axes.legend(['Entire dataset', 'Groups of PAY_1'])
```

7. Executing all the code from *Steps 3* through *6* in a single code cell should result in the following plot:

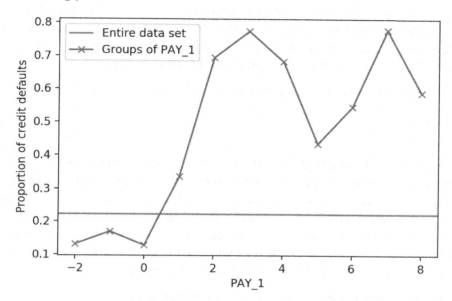

**Figure 3.10: Credit default rates across the dataset**

Our visualization of payment statuses has revealed a clear, and probably expected, story: those who defaulted before are in fact more likely to default again. The default rate of accounts in good standing is well below the overall default rate, which we know from before is about 22%. However, over 30% of the accounts that were in default last month will be in default again next month, according to this. This is a good visual to share with our business partner as it shows the effect of what may be one of the most important features in our model.

Now we turn our attention to the feature ranked as having the second strongest association with the target variable: **LIMIT_BAL**. This is a numerical feature with many unique values. A good way to visualize features such as this, for a classification problem, is to plot multiple histograms on the same axis, with different colors for the different classes. As a way to separate the classes, we can index them from the DataFrame using logical arrays.

8.  Use this code to create logical masks for positive and negative samples:

```
pos_mask = y == 1
neg_mask = y == 0
```

To create our dual histogram plot, we'll make another **axes** object, then call the **.hist** method on it twice for the positive and negative class histograms. We supply a few additional keyword arguments: the first histogram will have black edges and white bars, while the second will use **alpha** to create transparency, so we can see both histograms in the places they overlap. Once we have the histograms, we rotate the *x*-axis tick labels to make them more legible and create several other annotations that should be self-explanatory.

9.  Use the following code to create the dual histogram plot with the aforementioned properties:

```
axes = plt.axes()
axes.hist(df.loc[neg_mask, 'LIMIT_BAL'],\
          edgecolor='black', color='white')
axes.hist(df.loc[pos_mask, 'LIMIT_BAL'],\
          alpha=0.5, edgecolor=None, color='black')
axes.tick_params(axis='x', labelrotation=45)
axes.set_xlabel('Credit limit (NT$)')
axes.set_ylabel('Number of accounts')
axes.legend(['Not defaulted', 'Defaulted'])
axes.set_title('Credit limits by response variable')
```

The plot should appear like this:

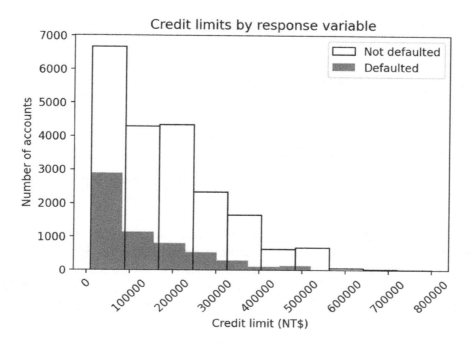

Figure 3.11: Dual histograms of credit limits

While this plot has accomplished all the formatting we wished to present, it's not quite as interpretable as it could be. What we hope to gain from looking at it is some knowledge of how the credit limit may be a good way to distinguish between accounts that default and those that do not. However, the primary visual takeaway here is that the transparent histogram is bigger than the gray one. This is due to the fact that fewer accounts default than don't default. We already know this from examining the class fractions.

It would be more informative to show something about how the shapes of these histograms are different, not just their sizes. To emphasize this, we can make the total plotted area of the two histograms the same, by **normalizing** them. Matplotlib provides a keyword argument that makes this easy, creating what might be considered an empirical version of a **probability mass function**. This means that the integral or area contained within each histogram will be equal to 1 after normalization, since probabilities sum to 1.

After some experimentation, we decide to make a histogram with 16 bins. Since the maximum credit limit is NT$800,000, we use **range** with an increment of NT$50,000. Here is the code that you can use:

```
df['LIMIT_BAL'].max()
```

10. Create and display the histogram bin edges with this code:

```
bin_edges = list(range(0,850000,50000))
print(bin_edges)
```

The output should be as follows:

```
[0, 50000, 100000, 150000, 200000, 250000, 300000, 350000, 40000,
450000,
500000, 550000, 600000, 650000, 700000, 750000, 800000]
```

The plotting code for the normalized histograms is similar to before, with a few key changes: the use of the **bins** keyword to define bin edge locations, **density=True** to normalize the histograms, and changes to the plot annotations. The most complex part is that we need to adjust the **y-axis tick labels**, so that the heights of the histogram bins have the interpretation of proportions, which is more intuitive than the default output.

*Y*-axis tick labels are the text labels displayed next to the ticks on the *y* axis and are usually simply the values of the ticks at those locations. However, you are able to manually change this if you want.

> **NOTE**
>
> According to the Matplotlib documentation, for a normalized histogram, the bin heights are calculated by *"dividing the count by the number of observations times the bin width"* (https://matplotlib.org/api/_as_gen/ matplotlib.pyplot.hist.html). So, we need to multiply the *y*-axis tick labels by the bin width of NT$50,000, for the bin heights to represent the proportion of the total number of samples in each bin. Notice the two lines where we get the tick locations of the *y*-axis, then set the labels to a modified version. The rounding to two decimal places with **np.round** is needed due to slight errors of floating-point arithmetic.

11. Run this code to produce normalized histograms:

```
mpl.rcParams['figure.dpi'] = 400
axes = plt.axes()
axes.hist(
    df.loc[neg_mask, 'LIMIT_BAL'],
    bins=bin_edges, density=True,
    edgecolor='black', color='white')
axes.hist(
    df.loc[pos_mask, 'LIMIT_BAL'],
    bins=bin_edges, density=True, alpha=0.5,
    edgecolor=None, color='black')
axes.tick_params(axis='x', labelrotation=45)
axes.set_xlabel('Credit limit (NT$)')
axes.set_ylabel('Proportion of accounts')
y_ticks = axes.get_yticks()
axes.set_yticklabels(np.round(y_ticks*50000,2))
axes.legend(['Not defaulted', 'Defaulted'])
axes.set_title('Normalized distributions of '\
               'credit limits by response variable')
```

The plot should look like this:

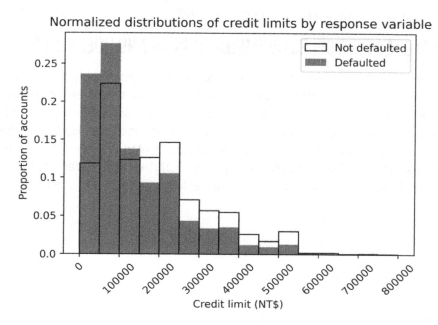

Figure 3.12: Normalized dual histograms

You can see that plots in Matplotlib are highly customizable. In order to view all the different things you can get from and set on Matplotlib axes, have a look here: https://matplotlib.org/stable/api/axes_api.html.

What can we learn from this plot? It looks like the accounts that default tend to have a higher proportion of lower credit limits. Accounts with credit limits less than NT$150,000 are relatively more likely to default, while the opposite is true for accounts with limits higher than this. We should ask ourselves, does this make sense? Our hypothesis was that the client would give riskier accounts lower limits. This intuition is compatible with the higher proportions of defaulters with lower credit limits that we observed here.

Depending on how the model building goes, if the features we examined in this exercise turn out to be important for predictive modeling as we expect, it would be good to show these graphs to our client, as part of a presentation of our work. This would give the client insight into how the model works, as well as insights into their data.

A key learning from this section is that effective visual presentations take substantial time to produce. It is good to budget some time in your project workflow for this. Convincing visuals are worth the effort since they should be able to quickly and effectively communicate important findings to the client. They are usually a better choice than adding lots of text to the materials that you create. Visual communication of quantitative concepts is a core data science skill.

## UNIVARIATE FEATURE SELECTION: WHAT IT DOES AND DOESN'T DO

In this chapter, we have learned techniques for going through features one by one to see whether they have predictive power. This is a good first step, and if you already have features that are very predictive of the outcome variable, you may not need to spend much more time considering features before modeling. However, there are drawbacks to univariate feature selection. In particular, it does not consider the **interactions** between features. For example, what if the credit default rate is very high specifically for people with both a certain education level and a certain range of credit limit?

Also, with the methods we used here, only the linear effects of features are captured. If a feature is more predictive when it's undergone some type of **transformation**, such as a **polynomial** or **logarithmic** transformation, or **binning (discretization)**, linear techniques of univariate feature selection may not be effective. Interactions and transformations are examples of **feature engineering**, or creating new features, in these cases from existing features. The shortcomings of linear feature selection methods can be remedied by non-linear modeling techniques including decision trees and methods based on them, which we will examine later. But there is still value in looking for simple relationships that can be found by linear methods for univariate feature selection, and it is quick to do.

## UNDERSTANDING LOGISTIC REGRESSION AND THE SIGMOID FUNCTION USING FUNCTION SYNTAX IN PYTHON

In this section, we will open the "black box" of logistic regression all the way: we will gain a comprehensive understanding of how it works. We'll start off by introducing a new programming concept: **functions**. At the same time, we'll learn about a mathematical function, the sigmoid function, which plays a key role in logistic regression.

In the most basic sense, a function in computer programming is a piece of code that takes inputs and produces outputs. You have been using functions throughout the book: functions that were written by someone else. Any time that you use syntax such as this: `output = do_something_to(input)`, you have used a function. For example, NumPy has a function you can use to calculate the mean of the input:

```
np.mean([1, 2, 3, 4, 5])
3.0
```

Functions **abstract** away the operations being performed so that, in our example, you don't need to see all the lines of code that it takes to calculate a mean, every time you need to do this. For many common mathematical functions, there are already pre-defined versions available in packages such as NumPy. You do not need to "reinvent the wheel." The implementations in popular packages are likely popular for a reason: people have spent time thinking about how to create them in the most efficient way. So, it would be wise to use them. However, since all the packages we are using are **open source**, if you are interested in seeing how the functions in the libraries we use are implemented, you are able to look at the code within any of them.

Now, for the sake of illustration, let's learn Python function syntax by writing our own function for the arithmetic mean. Function syntax in Python is similar to **for** or **if** blocks, in that the body of a function is indented and the declaration of the function is followed by a colon. Here is the code for a function to compute the mean:

```
def my_mean(input_argument):
    output = sum(input_argument)/len(input_argument)
    return(output)
```

After you execute the code cell with this definition, the function is available to you in other code cells in the notebook. Take the following example:

```
my_mean([1, 2, 3, 4, 5])
3.0
```

The first part of defining a function, as shown here, is to start a line of code with **def**, followed by a space, followed by the name you'd like to call the function. After this come parentheses, inside which the names of the **parameters** of the function are specified. Parameters are names of the input variables, where these names are internal to the body of the function: the variable names defined as parameters are available within the function when it is **called** (used), but not outside the function. There can be more than one parameter; they would be comma-separated. After the parentheses comes a colon.

The body of the function is indented and can contain any code that operates on the inputs. Once these operations are done, the last line should start with **return** and contain the output variable(s), comma-separated if there is more than one. We are leaving out many fine points in this very simple introduction to functions, but those are the essential parts you need to get started.

The power of a function comes when you use it. Notice how after we define the function, in a separate code block we can **call** it by the name we've given it, and it operates on whatever inputs we **pass** it. It's as if we've copied and pasted all the code to this new location. But it looks much nicer than actually doing that. And if you are going to use the same code many times, a function can greatly reduce the overall length of your code.

As a brief additional note, you can optionally specify the inputs using the parameter names explicitly, which can be clearer when there are many inputs:

```
my_mean(input_argument=[1, 2, 3])
2.0
```

Now that we're familiar with the basics of Python functions, we are going to consider a mathematical function that's important to logistic regression, called **sigmoid**. This function may also be called the **logistic function**. The definition of sigmoid is as follows:

$$f(X) = sigmoid(X) = \frac{1}{1 + e^{-X}}$$

**Figure 3.13: The sigmoid function**

We will break down the different parts of this function. As you can see, the sigmoid function involves the **irrational number e**, which is also known as the base of the **natural logarithm**, in contrast to the base-10 logarithms we used earlier for data exploration. In order to compute $e^{-X}$ using Python, we don't actually need to perform the exponentiation manually. NumPy has a convenient function, **exp**, that takes **e** to the input exponent automatically. If you look at the documentation, you will see this process is called taking the "exponential," which sounds vague. But it is assumed to be understood that the base of the exponent is $e$ in this case. In general, if you want to take an exponent in Python, such as $2^3$ ("two to the third power"), the syntax is two asterisks: **2\*\*3**, which equals 8, for example.

Consider how inputs may be passed to the **np.exp** function. Since NumPy's implementation is **vectorized**, this function can take individual numbers as well as arrays or matrices as input. To illustrate individual arguments, we compute the exponential of 1, which shows the approximate value of $e$, as well as $e0$, which of course equals 1, as does the zeroth power of any base:

```
np.exp(1)
2.718281828459045
np.exp(0)
1.0
```

To illustrate the vectorized implementation of **np.exp**, we create an array of numbers using NumPy's **linspace** function. This function takes as input the starting and stopping points of a range, both inclusive, and the number of values you'd like within that range, to create an array of that many linearly spaced values. This function performs a somewhat similar role to Python's **range**, but can also produce decimal values:

```
X_exp = np.linspace(-4,4,81)
print(X_exp[:5])
print(X_exp[-5:])

[-4.  -3.9 -3.8 -3.7 -3.6]
[3.6 3.7 3.8 3.9 4. ]

Y_exp = np.exp(X_exp)
Y_exp[:5]
```

Figure 3.14: Using np.linspace to make an array

Since **np.exp** is vectorized, it will compute the exponential of the whole array at once, in an efficient manner. Here is the code with output, to calculate the exponential of our **X_exp** array and examine the first five values:

```
Y_exp = np.exp(X_exp)
Y_exp[:5]
```

array([0.01831564, 0.02024191, 0.02237077, 0.02472353, 0.02732372])

Figure 3.15: NumPy's exp function

## EXERCISE 3.03: PLOTTING THE SIGMOID FUNCTION

In this exercise, we will use **X_exp** and **Y_exp**, created previously, to make a plot of what the exponential function looks like over the interval **[-4, 4]**. You need to have run all the code in *Figures 3.14* and *3.15* to have these variables available for this exercise. Then we will define a function for the sigmoid, create a plot of that, and consider how it is related to the exponential function. Perform the following steps to complete the exercise:

> **NOTE**
>
> Before beginning step 1 of this exercise, make sure that you have imported the necessary libraries. The code for importing the libraries along with that for rest of the steps in the exercise can be found here: https://packt.link/Uq012.

1.  Use this code to plot the exponential function:

```
plt.plot(X_exp, Y_exp)
plt.title('Plot of $e^X$')
```

The plot should look like this:

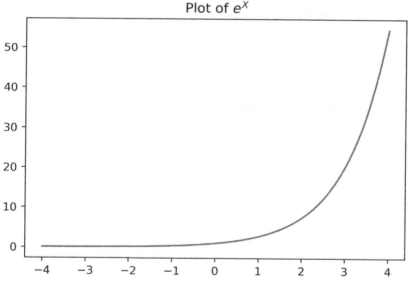

Figure 3.16: Plotting the exponential function

Notice that in titling the plot, we've taken advantage of a kind of syntax called **LaTeX**, which enables the formatting of mathematical notation. We won't go into the details of LaTeX here, but suffice to say that it is very flexible. Note that enclosing part of the title string in dollar signs causes it to be rendered using LaTeX, and that superscript can be created using ^.

Also note in *Figure 3.16* that many points spaced close together create the appearance of a smooth curve, but in fact, it is a graph of discrete points connected by line segments.

**What can we observe about the exponential function?**

It is never negative: as $X$ approaches negative infinity, $Y$ approaches 0.

As $X$ increases, $Y$ increases slowly at first, but very quickly "blows up." This is what is meant when people say "exponential growth" to signify a rapid increase.

**How can you think about the sigmoid in terms of the exponential?**

First, the sigmoid involves $e^{-x}$, as opposed to $e^x$. The graph of $e^{-x}$ is just the reflection of $e^x$ about the $y$ axis. This can be plotted easily and annotated using curly braces for multiple-character superscript in the plot title.

2. Run this code to see the plot of $e^{-x}$:

```
Y_exp = np.exp(-X_exp)
plt.plot(X_exp, Y_exp)
plt.title('Plot of $e^{-X}$')
```

The output should appear like this:

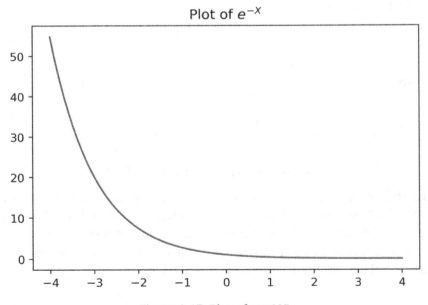

Figure 3.17: Plot of exp(-X)

Now, in the sigmoid function, $e^{-x}$ is in the denominator, with 1 added to it. The numerator is 1. So, what happens to the sigmoid as $X$ approaches negative infinity? We know that $e^{-x}$ "blows up," becoming very large. Overall, the denominator becomes very large and the fraction approaches 0. What about when $X$ increases toward positive infinity? We can see that $e^{-x}$ becomes very close to 0. So, in this case, the sigmoid function would be approximately *1/1 = 1*. This should give you an intuition that the sigmoid function stays between 0 and 1. Let's now implement a sigmoid function in Python and use it to create a plot to see how reality matches this intuition.

3. Define a sigmoid function like this:

```
def sigmoid(X):
    Y = 1 / (1 + np.exp(-X))
    return Y
```

4. Make a larger range of *x* values to plot over and plot the sigmoid. Use this code:

```
X_sig = np.linspace(-7,7,141)
Y_sig = sigmoid(X_sig)
plt.plot(X_sig,Y_sig)
plt.yticks(np.linspace(0,1,11))
plt.grid()
plt.title('The sigmoid function')
```

The plot should look like this:

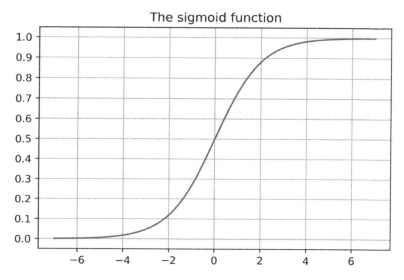

**Figure 3.18: A sigmoid function plot**

This plot matches what we expected. Further, we can see that **sigmoid(0) = 0.5**. What is special about the sigmoid function? The output of this function is strictly bounded between 0 and 1. This is a good property for a function that should predict probabilities, which are also required to be between 0 and 1. Technically, probabilities can be exactly equal to 0 and 1, while the sigmoid never is. But the sigmoid can be close enough that this is not a practical limitation.

Recall that we described logistic regression as producing **predicted probabilities** of class membership, as opposed to directly predicting class membership. This enables a more flexible implementation of logistic regression, allowing the selection of the threshold probability. The sigmoid function is the source of these predicted probabilities. Shortly, we will see how the different features are used in the calculation of the predicted probabilities.

## SCOPE OF FUNCTIONS

As you begin to use functions, you should develop an awareness of the concept of **scope**. Notice that when we wrote the **sigmoid** function, we created a variable, **Y**, inside the function. Variables created inside functions are different from those created outside functions. They are effectively created and destroyed within the function itself when it is called. These variables are said to be **local** in scope: local to the function. If you have been running all the code as written in this chapter in a single notebook in sequence, notice that you are not able to access the **Y** variable after using the **sigmoid** function:

```
-------------------------------------------------------------------
NameError                                 Traceback (most recent call last)
<ipython-input-6-c881daf1af41> in <module>
----> 1 Y

NameError: name 'Y' is not defined
```

**Figure 3.19: The Y variable not in the scope of the notebook**

The **Y** variable is not in the **global** scope of the notebook. However, global variables created outside of functions are available within the local scope of functions, even if they are not inputted as parameters to the function. Here we demonstrate creating a variable outside of a function, which is global in scope, and then accessing it within a function. The function actually doesn't take any parameters at all, but as you can see, it can work with the value of the global variable to create an output:

```
example_global_variable = 1
```

```
def example_function():
    output = example_global_variable + 1
    return(output)
```

```
example_function()
```

2

Figure 3.20: Global variable available within the local scope of the function

> **NOTE**
>
> **More details on scope**
>
> The scope of variables can potentially be confusing but is good to know when you start making more advanced use of functions. While this knowledge isn't required for the book, you may wish to get a more in-depth perspective on variable scope in Python here: https://nbviewer.jupyter.org/github/rasbt/python_reference/blob/master/tutorials/scope_resolution_legb_rule.ipynb.
>
> **Sigmoid curves in scientific applications**
>
> Besides being fundamental to logistic regression, sigmoid curves are used in a variety of applications. In biology, they can be used to describe the growth of an organism, which starts slowly, then has a rapid phase, followed by a smooth tapering off as the final size is reached. Sigmoids can also be used to describe population growth, which has a similar trajectory, increasing rapidly but then slowing as the carrying capacity of the environment is reached.

# WHY IS LOGISTIC REGRESSION CONSIDERED A LINEAR MODEL?

We mentioned previously that logistic regression is considered a **linear model**, while we were exploring whether the relationship between features and response resembled a linear relationship. Recall that we plotted **groupby/mean** of the **EDUCATION** feature in *Chapter 1, Data Exploration and Cleaning*, as well as for the **PAY_1** feature in this chapter, to see whether the default rates across values of these features exhibited a linear trend. While this is a good way to get a quick approximation of how "linear or not" these features may be, here we formalize the notion of why logistic regression is a linear model.

A model is considered linear if the transformation of features that is used to calculate the prediction is a **linear combination** of the features. The possibilities for a linear combination are that each feature can be multiplied by a numerical constant, these terms can be added together, and an additional constant can be added. For example, in a simple model with two features, $X_1$ and $X_2$, a linear combination would take the following form:

$$Linear\ combination\ of\ X_1\ and\ X_2 = \theta_0 + \theta_1 X_1 + \theta_2 X_2$$

Figure 3.21: Linear combination of $X_1$ and $X_2$

The constants $\theta_i$ can be any number, positive, negative, or zero, for *i = 0, 1, and 2* (although if a coefficient is 0, this removes a feature from the linear combination). A familiar example of a linear transformation of one variable is a straight line with the equation *y = mx + b*, as discussed *Chapter 2, Introduction to Scikit-Learn and Model Evaluation*. In this case, $\theta_0$ = *b* and $\theta_1$ = *m*. $\theta_0$ is called the **intercept** of a linear combination, which should be familiar from algebra.

What kinds of things are "not allowed" in linear transformations? Any other mathematical expressions besides what was just described, such as the following:

- Multiplying a feature by itself; for example, $X_1^2$ or $X_1^3$. These are called polynomial terms.

- Multiplying features together; for example, $X_1 X_2$. These are called interactions.

- Applying non-linear transformations to features; for example, log and square root.

- Other complex mathematical functions.

- "If then" types of statements. For example, "if $X_1 > a$, then *y = b*."

However, while these transformations are not part of the basic formulation of a linear combination, they could be added to a linear model by **engineering features**, for example, defining a new feature, $X^3 = X_1^2$.

Earlier, we learned that the predictions of logistic regression, which take the form of probabilities, are made using the sigmoid function. Taking another look here, we see that this function is clearly non-linear:

$$sigmoid(x) = \frac{1}{1 + e^{-x}}$$

**Figure 3.22: Non-linear sigmoid function**

Why, then, is logistic regression considered a linear model? It turns out that the answer to this question lies in a different formulation of the sigmoid equation, called the `logit` function. We can derive the `logit` function by solving the sigmoid function for $X$; in other words, finding the inverse of the sigmoid function. First, we set the sigmoid equal to $p$, which we interpret as the probability of observing the positive class, then solve for $X$ as shown in the following:

$$p = \frac{1}{1 + e^{-X}}$$

$$1 + e^{-X} = \frac{1}{p}$$

$$e^{-X} = \frac{1}{p} - 1$$

$$e^{-X} = \frac{1 - p}{p}$$

$$e^{X} = \frac{p}{1 - p}$$

$$X = \log\left(\frac{p}{1 - p}\right)$$

**Figure 3.23: Solving for X**

Here, we've used some laws of exponents and logs to solve for $X$. You may also see `logit` expressed as follows:

$$X = \log\left(\frac{p}{q}\right)$$

**Figure 3.24: The logit function**

In this expression, the **probability of failure**, $q$, is expressed in terms of the **probability of success**, $p$; $q = 1 - p$, because probabilities sum to 1. Even though in our case, credit default would probably be considered a failure in the sense of real-world outcomes, the positive outcome (response variable = 1 in a binary problem) is conventionally considered "success" in mathematical terminology. The `logit` function is also called the **log odds**, because it is the natural logarithm of the **odds ratio**, $p/q$. Odds ratios may be familiar from the world of gambling, via phrases such as "the odds are 2 to 1 that team $a$ will defeat team $b$."

In general, what we've called capital $X$ in these manipulations can stand for a linear combination of all the features. For example, this would be $X = \theta_0 + \theta_1 X_1 + \theta_2 X_2$ in our simple case of two features. Logistic regression is considered a linear model because the features included in $X$ are, in fact, only subject to a linear combination when the response variable is considered to be the log odds. This is an alternative way of formulating the problem, as compared to the sigmoid equation.

Putting the pieces together, the features $X_1, X_2, ..., X_j$ look like this in the sigmoid equation version of logistic regression:

$$p = \frac{1}{1 + e^{-(\theta_0 + \theta_1 X_1 + \theta_2 X_2 + \cdots \theta_j X_j)}}$$

**Figure 3.25: Sigmoid version of logistic regression**

But they look like this in the log odds version, which is why logistic regression is called a linear model:

$$\theta_0 + \theta_1 X_1 + \theta_2 X_2 + \cdots \theta_j X_j = \log\left(\frac{p}{q}\right)$$

**Figure 3.26: Log odds version of logistic regression**

Because of this way of looking at logistic regression, ideally, the features of a logistic regression model would be **linear in the log odds** of the response variable. We will see what is meant by this in the following exercise.

Logistic regression is part of a broader class of statistical models called **Generalized Linear Models** (**GLMs**). GLMs are connected to the fundamental concept of ordinary linear regression, which may have one feature (that is, the **line of best fit**, $y = mx + b$, for a single feature, $x$) or more than one in **multiple linear regression**. The mathematical connection between GLMs and linear regression is the **link function**. The link function of logistic regression is the logit function we just learned about.

## EXERCISE 3.04: EXAMINING THE APPROPRIATENESS OF FEATURES FOR LOGISTIC REGRESSION

In *Exercise 3.02, Visualizing the Relationship between the Features and Response Variable*, we plotted a `groupby/mean` of what might be the most important feature of the model, according to our exploration so far: the **PAY_1** feature. By grouping samples by the values of **PAY_1**, and then looking at the mean of the response variable, we are effectively looking at the probability, $p$, of default within each of these groups.

In this exercise, we will evaluate the appropriateness of **PAY_1** for logistic regression. We will do this by examining the log odds of default within these groups to see whether the response variable is linear in the log odds, as logistic regression formally assumes. Perform the following steps to complete the exercise:

> **NOTE**
>
> Before beginning step 1 of this exercise, make sure that you have imported the necessary libraries. You can refer to the following notebook for the prerequisite steps: https://packt.link/gtpF9.

1.  Confirm you still have access to the variables from *Exercise 3.02, Visualizing the Relationship between the Features and Response Variable*, in your notebook by reviewing the DataFrame of the average value of the response variable for different values of **PAY_1** with this code:

```
group_by_pay_mean_y
```

The output should be as follows:

| group_by_pay_mean_y | |
| --- | --- |
| | **default payment next month** |
| **PAY_1** | |
| -2 | 0.131664 |
| -1 | 0.170002 |
| 0 | 0.128295 |
| 1 | 0.336400 |
| 2 | 0.694701 |
| 3 | 0.773973 |
| 4 | 0.682540 |
| 5 | 0.434783 |
| 6 | 0.545455 |
| 7 | 0.777778 |
| 8 | 0.588235 |

**Figure 3.27: Rates of default within groups of PAY_1 values as probabilities of default**

2.  Extract the mean values of the response variable from these groups and put them in a variable, **p**, representing the probability of default:

```
p = group_by_pay_mean_y['default payment next month'].values
```

3. Create a probability, **q**, of not defaulting. Since there are only two possible outcomes in this binary problem, and probabilities of all outcomes always sum to 1, it is easy to calculate **q**. Also print the values of **p** and **q** to confirm:

```
q = 1-p
print(p)
print(q)
```

The output should be as follows:

```
[0.13166397 0.17000198 0.12829525 0.33639988 0.69470143 0.7739726
 0.68253968 0.43478261 0.54545455 0.77777778 0.58823529]
[0.86833603 0.82999802 0.87170475 0.66360012 0.30529857 0.2260274
 0.31746032 0.56521739 0.45454545 0.22222222 0.41176471]
```

Figure 3.28: Calculating q from p

4. Calculate the odds ratio from **p** and **q**, as well as the log odds, using the natural logarithm function from NumPy:

```
odds_ratio = p/q
log_odds = np.log(odds_ratio)
log_odds
```

The output should look like this:

```
array([0.15162791, 0.20482215, 0.14717742, 0.50693161, 2.27548209,
       3.42424242, 2.15      , 0.76923077, 1.2       , 3.5       ,
       1.42857143])
```

```
array([-1.88632574, -1.58561322, -1.91611649, -0.67937918,  0.82219194,
        1.23088026,  0.76546784, -0.26236426,  0.18232156,  1.25276297,
        0.35667494])
```

Figure 3.29: Odds ratio and log odds

5. In order to plot the log odds against the values of the feature, we can get the feature values from the index of the DataFrame containing **groupby/mean**. You can show the index like this:

```
group_by_pay_mean_y.index
```

This should produce the following output:

```
Int64Index([-2, -1, 0, 1, 2, 3, 4, 5, 6, 7, 8], dtype='int64',
name='PAY_1')
```

6. Create a similar plot to what we have already done, to show the log odds against the values of the feature. Here is the code:

```
plt.plot(group_by_pay_mean_y.index, log_odds, '-x')
plt.ylabel('Log odds of default')
plt.xlabel('Values of PAY_1')
```

The plot should look like this:

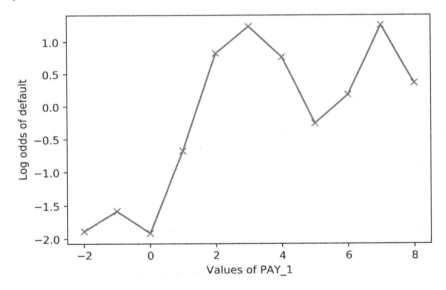

**Figure 3.30: Log odds of default for values of PAY_1**

We can see in this plot that the relationship between the log odds of the response variable and the **PAY_1** feature is not all that different from the relationship between the rate of default and this feature that we plotted in *Exercise 3.02, Visualizing the Relationship between the Features and Response Variable*. For this reason, if the "rate of default" is a simpler concept for you to communicate to the business partner, it may be preferable. However, in terms of understanding the workings of logistic regression, this plot shows exactly what is assumed to be linear.

## Is a straight-line fit a good model for this data?

It certainly seems like a "line of best fit" drawn on this plot would go up from left to right. At the same time, this data doesn't seem like it would result in a truly linear process. One way to look at this data is that the values -2, -1, and 0 seem like they lie in a different regime of log odds than the others. **PAY_1 = 1** is sort of intermediate, and the rest are mostly larger. It may be that engineered features based on this variable, or different ways of encoding the categories represented by -2, -1, and 0, would be more effective for modeling. Keep this in mind as we proceed to model this data with logistic regression and then other approaches later in the book.

# FROM LOGISTIC REGRESSION COEFFICIENTS TO PREDICTIONS USING SIGMOID

Before the next exercise, let's take a look at how the coefficients for logistic regression are used to calculate predicted probabilities, and ultimately make predictions for the class of the response variable.

Recall that logistic regression predicts the probability of class membership, according to the sigmoid equation. In the case of two features with an intercept, the equation is as follows:

$$p = \frac{1}{1 + e^{-(\theta_0 + \theta_1 X_1 + \theta_2 X_2)}}$$

**Figure 3.31: Sigmoid function to predict the probability of class membership for two features**

When you call the **.fit** method of a logistic regression model object in scikit-learn using the training data, the $\theta_0$, $\theta_1$, and $\theta_2$ parameters (intercept and coefficients) are estimated from this labeled training data. Effectively, scikit-learn figures out how to choose values for $\theta_0$, $\theta_1$, and $\theta_2$, so that it will classify as many training data points correctly as possible. We'll gain some insight into how this process works in the next chapter.

When you call **.predict**, scikit-learn calculates predicted probabilities according to the fitted parameter values and the sigmoid equation. A given sample will then be classified as positive if $p \geq 0.5$, and negative otherwise.

We know that the plot of the sigmoid equation looks like the following, which we can connect to the equation in *Figure 3.31* by making the substitution $X = \theta_0 + \theta_1 X_1 + \theta_2 X_2$:

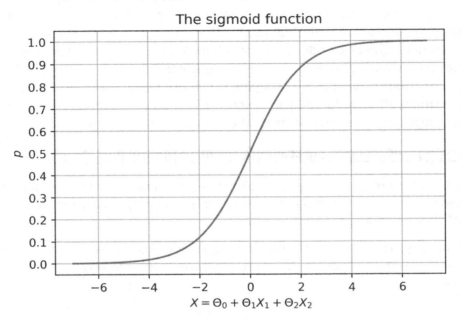

Figure 3.32: Predictions and true classes plotted together

Notice here that if $X = \theta_0 + \theta_1 X_1 + \theta_2 X_2 \geq 0$ on the x axis, then the predicted probability would be $p \geq 0.5$ on the y axis and the sample would be classified as positive. Otherwise, $p < 0.5$ and the sample would be classified as negative. We can use this observation to calculate a linear condition for positive prediction, in terms of the $X_1$ and $X_2$ features, using the coefficients and intercept. Solving the inequality for positive prediction, $X = \theta_0 + \theta_1 X_1 + \theta_2 X_2 \geq 0$, for $X_2$, we can obtain a linear inequality similar to a linear equation in $y = mx + b$ form: $X_2 \geq -(\theta_1/\theta_2)X_1 - (\theta_0/\theta_2)$.

This will help to see the linear decision boundary of logistic regression in the $X_1$-$X_2$ **feature space** in the following exercise.

We have now learned, from a theoretical and mathematical perspective, why logistic regression is considered a linear model. We also examined a single feature and considered whether the assumption of linearity was appropriate. It is also important to understand the assumption of linearity, in terms of how flexible and powerful we can expect logistic regression to be. We explore this in the following exercise.

## EXERCISE 3.05: LINEAR DECISION BOUNDARY OF LOGISTIC REGRESSION

In this exercise, we illustrate the concept of a **decision boundary** for a binary classification problem. We use synthetic data to create a clear example of how the decision boundary of logistic regression looks in comparison to the training samples. We start by generating two features, $X_1$ and $X_2$, at random. Since there are two features, we can say that the data for this problem is two-dimensional. This makes it easy to visualize. The concepts we illustrate here generalize to cases of more than two features, such as the real-world datasets you're likely to see in your work; however, the decision boundary is harder to visualize in higher-dimensional spaces.

Perform the following steps to complete the exercise:

> **NOTE**
>
> Before beginning step 1 of this exercise, make sure that you have imported the necessary libraries. You can refer to the following notebook for the prerequisite steps: https://packt.link/35ge1.

1. Generate the features using the following code:

```
from numpy.random import default_rng
rg = default_rng(4)
X_1_pos = rg.uniform(low=1, high=7, size=(20,1))
print(X_1_pos[0:3])
X_1_neg = rg.uniform(low=3, high=10, size=(20,1))
print(X_1_neg[0:3])
X_2_pos = rg.uniform(low=1, high=7, size=(20,1))
print(X_2_pos[0:3])
X_2_neg = rg.uniform(low=3, high=10, size=(20,1))
print(X_2_neg[0:3])
```

You don't need to worry too much about why we selected the values we did; the plotting we do later should make it clear. Notice, however, that we have assigned the true class at the same time, by defining here which points (**$X_1$**, **$X_2$**) will be in the positive and negative classes. The result of this is that we have 20 samples each in the positive and negative classes, for a total of 40 samples, and that we have two features for each sample. We show the first three values of each feature for both the positive and negative classes.

The output should be the following:

```
[[6.65833663]
 [4.06796532]
 [6.85746223]]
[[7.93405322]
 [9.59962575]
 [7.65960192]]
[[5.15531227]
 [5.6237829 ]
 [2.14473103]]
[[6.49784918]
 [9.69185251]
 [9.32236912]]
```

**Figure 3.33: Generating synthetic data for a binary classification problem**

2.  Plot this data, coloring the positive samples as red squares and the negative samples as blue *x*'s. The plotting code is as follows:

```
plt.scatter(X_1_pos, X_2_pos, color='red', marker='s')
plt.scatter(X_1_neg, X_2_neg, color='blue', marker='x')
plt.xlabel(,$X_1$')
plt.ylabel(,$X_2$')
plt.legend(['Positive class', 'Negative class'])
```

The result should look like this:

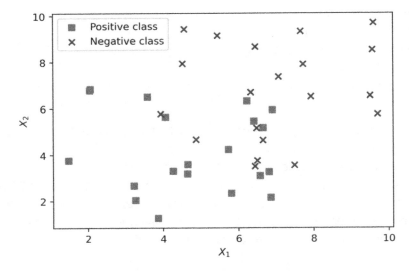

**Figure 3.34: Generating synthetic data for a binary classification problem**

In order to use our synthetic features with scikit-learn, we need to assemble them into a matrix. We use NumPy's **block** function for this, to create a 40 by 2 matrix. There will be 40 rows because there are 40 total samples, and 2 columns because there are 2 features. We will arrange things so that the features for the positive samples come in the first 20 rows and those for the negative samples after that.

3.  Create a 40 by 2 matrix and then show the shape and the first 3 rows:

```
X = np.block([[X_1_pos, X_2_pos], [X_1_neg, X_2_neg]])
print(X.shape)
print(X[0:3])
```

The output should be as follows:

```
(40, 2)
[[6.65833663 5.15531227]
 [4.06796532 5.6237829  ]
 [6.85746223 2.14473103]]
```

We also need a response variable to go with these features. We know how we defined them, but we need an array of **y** values to let scikit-learn know.

4.  Create a vertical stack (**vstack**) of 20 ones and then 20 zeros to match our arrangement of the features and reshape to the way that scikit-learn expects. Here is the code:

```
y = np.vstack((np.ones((20,1)), np.zeros((20,1)))).reshape(40,)
print(y[0:5])
print(y[-5:])
```

You will obtain the following output:

```
[1. 1. 1. 1. 1.]
[0. 0. 0. 0. 0.]
```

At this point, we are ready to fit a logistic regression model to this data with scikit-learn. We will use all of the data as training data and examine how well a linear model is able to fit the data. The next few steps should be familiar from your work in earlier chapters on how to instantiate a model class and fit the model.

5.  First, import the model class using the following code:

```
from sklearn.linear_model import LogisticRegression
```

6. Now instantiate, indicating the **liblinear** solver, and show the model object using the following code:

```
example_lr = LogisticRegression(solver='liblinear')
example_lr
```

The output should be as follows:

```
LogisticRegression(solver='liblinear')
```

We'll discuss some of the different solvers available for logistic regression in scikit-learn in *Chapter 4, The Bias-Variance Trade-Off*, but for now we'll use this one.

7. Now train the model on the synthetic data:

```
example_lr.fit(X, y)
```

**How do the predictions from our fitted model look?**

We first need to obtain these predictions, by using the trained model's **.predict** method on the same samples we used for model training. Then, in order to add these predictions to the plot, we will create two lists of indices to use with the arrays, according to whether the prediction is 1 or 0. See whether you can understand how we've used a list comprehension, including an **if** statement, to accomplish this.

8. Use this code to get predictions and separate them into indices of positive and negative class predictions. Show the indices of positive class predictions as a check:

```
y_pred = example_lr.predict(X)
positive_indices = [counter for counter in range(len(y_pred))
                    if y_pred[counter]==1]
negative_indices = [counter for counter in range(len(y_pred))
                    if y_pred[counter]==0]
positive_indices
```

The output should be as follows:

```
[2, 3, 4, 5, 6, 7, 9, 11, 13, 15, 16, 17, 18, 19, 26, 34, 36]
```

From the indices of positive predictions, we can already tell that not every sample in the training data was classified correctly: the positive samples were the first 20 samples, but there are indices outside of that range here. You may have already guessed that a linear decision boundary would not be able to perfectly classify this data, based on examining it. Now let's put these predictions on the plot, in the form of squares and circles around each data point, colored according to positive and negative predictions, respectively: red for positive and blue for negative.

You can compare the color and shape of the inner symbols, the true labels of the data, to those of the outer symbols (predictions), to see which points were classified correctly or incorrectly.

9.  Here is the plotting code:

```
plt.scatter(X_1_pos, X_2_pos, color='red', marker='s')
plt.scatter(X_1_neg, X_2_neg, color='blue', marker='x')
plt.scatter(X[positive_indices,0], X[positive_indices,1],
            s=150, marker='s',
            edgecolors='red', facecolors='none')
plt.scatter(X[negative_indices,0], X[negative_indices,1],
            s=150, marker='o',
            edgecolors='blue', facecolors='none')
plt.xlabel('$X_1$')
plt.ylabel('$X_2$')
plt.legend(['Positive class', 'Negative class',\
            'Positive predictions', 'Negative predictions'])
```

The plot should appear as follows:

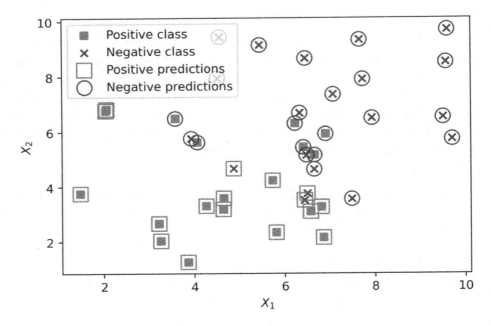

**Figure 3.35: Predictions and true classes plotted together**

From the plot, it's apparent that the classifier struggles with data points that are close to where you may imagine the linear decision boundary to be; some of these may end up on the wrong side of that boundary. How might we figure out, and visualize, the actual location of the decision boundary? From the previous section, we know we can obtain the decision boundary of a logistic regression, in two-dimensional feature space, using the inequality $X_2 \geq -(\theta_1/\theta_2)X_1 - (\theta_0/\theta_2)$. Since we've fitted the model here, we can retrieve the $\theta_1$ and $\theta_2$ coefficients, as well as the $\theta_0$ intercept, to plug into this equation and create the plot.

10. Use this code to get the coefficients from the fitted model and print them:

```
theta_1 = example_lr.coef_[0][0]
theta_2 = example_lr.coef_[0][1]
print(theta_1, theta_2)
```

The output should look like this:

```
-0.16472042583006558 -0.25675185949979507
```

11. Use this code to get the intercept:

```
theta_0 = example_lr.intercept_
```

Now use the coefficients and intercept to define the linear decision boundary. This captures the dividing line of the inequality, $X_2 \geq -(\theta_1/\theta_2)X_1 - (\theta_0/\theta_2)$:

```
X_1_decision_boundary = np.array([0, 10])
X_2_decision_boundary = -(theta_1/theta_2)*X_1_decision_boundary\
                        - (theta_0/theta_2)
```

To summarize the last few steps, after using the **.coef_** and **.intercept_** methods to retrieve the $\theta_1$ and $\theta_2$ model coefficients and the $\theta_0$ intercept, we then used these to create a line defined by two points, according to the equation we described for the decision boundary.

12. Plot the decision boundary using the following code, with some adjustments to assign the correct labels for the legend, and to move the legend to a location (**loc**) outside a plot that is getting crowded:

```
pos_true = plt.scatter(X_1_pos, X_2_pos,
                       color='red', marker='s',
                       label='Positive class')
neg_true = plt.scatter(X_1_neg, X_2_neg,
                       color='blue', marker='x',
                       label='Negative class')
pos_pred = plt.scatter(X[positive_indices,0],
                       X[positive_indices,1],
                       s=150, marker='s',
                       edgecolors='red', facecolors='none',
                       label='Positive predictions')
neg_pred = plt.scatter(X[negative_indices,0],
                       X[negative_indices,1],
                       s=150, marker='o',
                       edgecolors='blue', facecolors='none',
                       label='Negative predictions')
dec = plt.plot(X_1_decision_boundary, X_2_decision_boundary,
               'k-', label='Decision boundary')
plt.xlabel('$X_1$')
plt.ylabel('$X_2$')
plt.legend(loc=[0.25, 1.05])
```

You will obtain the following plot:

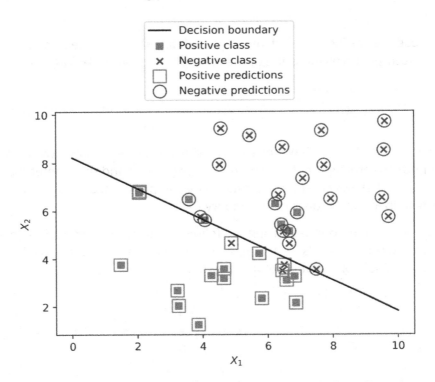

Figure 3.36: True classes, predicted classes, and the decision boundary
of a logistic regression

**How does the location of the decision boundary compare with where you thought it would be?**

**Can you see how a linear decision boundary will never perfectly classify this data?**

As a way around this, we could create **engineered features** from existing features here, such as polynomials or interactions, to allow for more complex, non-linear decision boundaries in a logistic regression. Or, we could use non-linear models such as random forest, which can also accomplish this, as we'll see later.

As a final note here, this example was easily visualized in two dimensions since there are only two features. In general, the decision boundary can be described by a **hyperplane**, which is the generalization of a straight line to multi-dimensional spaces. However, the restrictive nature of the linear decision boundary is still a factor for hyperplanes.

## ACTIVITY 3.01: FITTING A LOGISTIC REGRESSION MODEL AND DIRECTLY USING THE COEFFICIENTS

In this activity, we're going to train a logistic regression model on the two most important features we discovered in univariate feature exploration, as well as learning how to manually implement logistic regression using coefficients from the fitted model. This will show you how you could use logistic regression in a computing environment where scikit-learn may not be available, but the mathematical functions necessary to compute the sigmoid function are. On successful completion of the activity, you should observe that the calculated ROC AUC values using scikit-learn predictions and those obtained from manual predictions should be the same: approximately 0.63.

Perform the following steps to complete the activity:

1. Create a train/test split (80/20) with **PAY_1** and **LIMIT_BAL** as features.

2. Import **LogisticRegression**, with the default options, but set the solver to **'liblinear'**.

3. Train on the training data and obtain predicted classes, as well as class probabilities, using the test data.

4. Pull out the coefficients and intercept from the trained model and manually calculate predicted probabilities. You'll need to add a column of ones to your features, to multiply by the intercept.

5. Using a threshold of **0.5**, manually calculate predicted classes. Compare this to the class predictions outputted by scikit-learn.

6. Calculate the ROC AUC using both scikit-learn's predicted probabilities and your manually predicted probabilities, and compare them.

> **NOTE**
>
> The Jupyter notebook containing the code for this activity can be found here: https://packt.link/4FHec. This notebook contains only the Python code and corresponding outputs. The complete step-wise solution can be found on page 377.

## SUMMARY

In this chapter, we have learned how to explore features one at a time, using univariate feature selection methods including Pearson correlation and an ANOVA F-test. While looking at features in this way does not always tell the whole story, since you are potentially missing out on important interactions between features, it is often a helpful step. Understanding the relationships between the most predictive features and the response variable, and creating effective visualizations around them, is a great way to communicate your findings to your client. We used customized plots, such as overlapping histograms created with Matplotlib, to create visualizations of the most important features.

Then we began an in-depth description of how logistic regression works, exploring such topics as the sigmoid function, log odds, and the linear decision boundary. While logistic regression is one of the simplest classification models, and often is not as powerful as other methods, it is one of the most widely used and is the basis for more sophisticated models such as deep neural networks for classification. So, a detailed understanding of logistic regression can serve you well as you explore more advanced topics in machine learning. And, in some cases, a simple logistic regression may be all that's needed. All other things considered, the simplest model that satisfies the requirements is probably the best model.

If you master the materials in this and the next chapter, you will be well prepared to use logistic regression in your work. In the next chapter, we'll build on the fundamentals we learned here, to see how coefficients are estimated for a logistic regression, as well as how logistic regression can be used effectively with large numbers of features and can also be used for feature selection.

# 4

# THE BIAS-VARIANCE TRADE-OFF

## OVERVIEW

In this chapter, we'll cover the remaining elements of logistic regression, including what happens when you call `.fit` to train the model, and the statistical assumptions you should be aware of when using this modeling technique. You will learn how to use L1 and L2 regularization with logistic regression to prevent overfitting and how to use the practice of cross-validation to decide the regularization strength. After reading this chapter, you will be able to use logistic regression in your work and employ regularization in the model fitting process to take advantage of the bias-variance trade-off and improve model performance on unseen data.

# INTRODUCTION

In this chapter, we will introduce the remaining details of logistic regression left over from the previous chapter. In addition to being able to use scikit-learn to fit logistic regression models, you will gain insight into the gradient descent procedure, which is similar to the processes that are used "under the hood" (invisible to the user) to accomplish model fitting in scikit-learn. Finally, we'll complete our discussion of the logistic regression model by familiarizing ourselves with the formal statistical assumptions of this method.

We begin our exploration of the foundational machine learning concepts of overfitting, underfitting, and the bias-variance trade-off by examining how the logistic regression model can be extended to address the overfitting problem. After reviewing the mathematical details of the regularization methods that are used to alleviate overfitting, you will learn a useful practice for tuning the hyperparameters of regularization: cross-validation. Through the methods of regularization and some simple feature engineering, you will gain an understanding of how to improve both overfitted and underfitted models.

Although we are focusing on logistic regression in this chapter, the concepts of overfitting, underfitting, regularization, and the bias-variance trade-off are relevant to nearly all supervised modeling techniques in machine learning.

# ESTIMATING THE COEFFICIENTS AND INTERCEPTS OF LOGISTIC REGRESSION

In the previous chapter, we learned that the coefficients of a logistic regression model (each of which goes with a particular feature), as well as the intercept, are determined using the training data when the `.fit` method is called on a logistic regression model in scikit-learn. These numbers are called the **parameters** of the model, and the process of finding the best values for them is called parameter **estimation**. Once the parameters are found, the logistic regression model is essentially a finished product: with just these numbers, we can use a logistic regression model in any environment where we can perform common mathematical functions.

It is clear that the process of parameter estimation is important, since this is how we can make a predictive model from our data. So, how does parameter estimation work? To understand this, the first step is to familiarize ourselves with the concept of a **cost function**. A cost function is a way of telling how far away the model predictions are from perfectly describing the data. The larger the difference between the model predictions and the actual data, then the larger the "cost" returned by the cost function.

This is a straightforward concept for regression problems: the difference between predictions and true values can be used for the cost, after going through a transformation (such as absolute value or squaring) to make the value of the cost positive, and then averaging this over all the training samples.

For classification problems, especially in fitting logistic regression models, a typical cost function is the **log-loss** function, also called cross-entropy loss. This is the cost function that scikit-learn uses, in a modified form, to fit logistic regression:

$$\log loss = \frac{1}{n}\sum_{i=1}^{n} -\left(y_i \log(p_i) + (1 - y_i)\log(1 - p_i)\right)$$

**Figure 4.1: The log-loss function**

Here, there are $n$ training samples, $y_i$ is the true label (0 or 1) of the $i^{th}$ sample, $p_i$ is the predicted probability that the label of the $i^{th}$ sample equals 1, and log is the natural logarithm. The summation notation (that is, the uppercase Greek letter, sigma) over all the training samples and division by $n$ serve to take the average of this cost function over all training samples. With this in mind, take a look at the following graph of the natural logarithm function and consider what the interpretation of this cost function is:

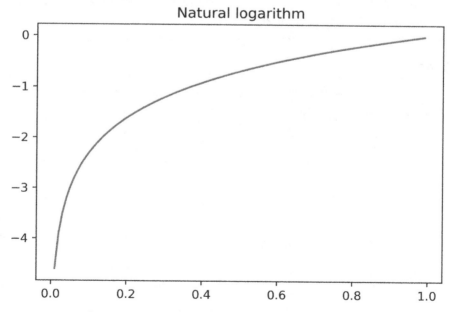

**Figure 4.2: Natural logarithm on the interval (0, 1)**

To see how the log-loss cost function works, consider its value for a sample where the true label is 1, which is $y = 1$ in this case, so the second part of the cost function, $(1 - y_i)log(1 - p_i)$, will be exactly equal to 0 and will not affect the value. Then the value of the cost function is $-y_i log(p_i) = -log(p_i)$ since $y_i = 1$. So, the cost for this sample is simply the negative of the natural logarithm of the predicted probability. Now since the true label for the sample is 1, consider how the cost function should behave. We expect that for predicted probabilities that are close to 1, the cost function will be small, representing a small error for predictions that are closer to the true value. For predictions that are closer to 0, it will be larger, since the cost function is supposed to take on larger values the more "wrong" the prediction is.

From the graph of the natural logarithm in *Figure 4.2* we can see that for values of $p$ that are closer to 0, the natural logarithm takes on increasingly negative values. This means the cost function will take on increasingly positive values, so that the cost of classifying a positive sample with a very low probability is relatively high, as it should be. Conversely, if the predicted probability is closer to 1, then the graph indicates the cost will be closer to 0 – again, this is as expected for a prediction that is "more correct." Therefore, the cost function behaves as expected for a positive sample. A similar observation can be made for samples where the true label is 0.

Now we understand how the log-loss cost function works for logistic regression. But what does this have to do with how the coefficients and the intercept are determined? We will learn in the next section.

> **NOTE**
>
> The code for generating the plots presented in this section can be found here: https://packt.link/NeF8P.

# GRADIENT DESCENT TO FIND OPTIMAL PARAMETER VALUES

The problem of finding the parameter values (coefficients and intercept) for a logistic regression model using a log-loss cost boils down to a problem of **optimization**: we would like to find the set of parameters that results in the **minimum** cost, since costs are higher for worse predictions. In other words, we want the set of parameters that is the "least wrong" on average over all of the training samples. This process is done for you automatically by the `.fit` method of the logistic regression model in scikit-learn. There are different solution techniques for finding the set of parameters with the lowest cost, and you can choose which one you would like to use with the **solver** keyword when you are instantiating the model class. All of these methods work somewhat differently. However, they are all based on the concept of **gradient descent**.

The gradient descent process starts with an **initial guess**. The choice of the initial guess is not that important for logistic regression and you don't need to make it manually; this is handled by the **solver** keyword. However, for more advanced machine learning algorithms such as deep neural networks, selection of the initial guesses for parameters requires more attention.

For the sake of illustration, we will consider a problem where there is only one parameter to estimate. We'll look at the value of a hypothetical cost function ($y = f(x)$ $= x^2 - 2x$) and devise a gradient descent procedure to find the value of the parameter, $x$, for which the cost, $y$, is the lowest. Here, we choose some $x$ values, create a function that returns the value of the cost function, and look at the value of the cost function over this range of parameters.

The code to do this is as follows:

```
X_poly = np.linspace(-3,5,81)
print(X_poly[:5], '...', X_poly[-5:])
```

Here is the output of the print statement:

```
[-3.  -2.9 -2.8 -2.7 -2.6] ... [4.6 4.7 4.8 4.9 5. ]
```

The remaining code snippet is as follows:

```
def cost_function(X):
    return X * (X-2)
y_poly = cost_function(X_poly)
plt.plot(X_poly, y_poly)
plt.xlabel('Parameter value')
plt.ylabel('Cost function')
plt.title('Error surface')
```

The resulting plot should appear as follows:

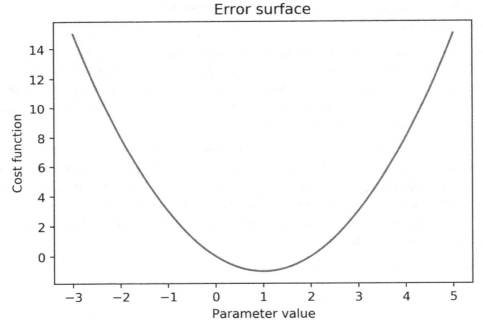

Figure 4.3: A cost function plot

> **NOTE**
>
> In the preceding code snippets, we assume that you would have imported the necessary libraries. You can refer to the following notebook for the complete code for the chapter including the import statement for the preceding snippets: https://packt.link/A4VyF.

Looking at the **error surface** in *Figure 4.3*, which is the plot of the cost function over a range of parameter values, it's pretty evident what parameter value will result in the lowest value of the cost function: *x = 1*. In fact, with some calculus, you could easily confirm this by setting the derivative to zero and then solving for *x*, confirming that *x = 1* is the minimum. However, generally speaking, it is not always feasible to solve the problem so simply. In cases where it is necessary to use gradient descent, we don't always know how the entire error surface looks. Rather, after we've chosen the initial guess for the parameter, all we're able to know is the direction of the error surface in the immediate vicinity of that point.

**Gradient descent** is an iterative algorithm; starting from the initial guess, we try to find a new guess that lowers the cost function and continue with this until we've found a good solution. We are trying to move "downhill" on the error surface, but we only know which direction to move in and how far to move in that direction, based on the shape of the error surface in the immediate neighborhood of our current guess. In mathematical terms, we only know the value of the **derivative** (which is called the **gradient** in more than one dimension) at the parameter value of the current guess. If you have not studied calculus, you can think of the gradient as telling you which direction is downhill, and how steep the hill is from where you're standing. We use this information to "take a step" in the direction of decreasing error. How big a step we decide to take depends on the **learning rate**. Since the gradient declines toward the direction of decreasing error, we want to take a step in the direction that is the negative of the gradient.

These notions can be formalized in the following equation. To get to the new guess, $x_{new}$, from the current guess, $x_{old}$, where $f'(x_{old})$ is the derivative (that is, the gradient) of the cost function at the current guess:

$$x_{new} = x_{old} - f'(x_{old}) \times learning\ rate$$

Figure 4.4: Equation to obtain the new guess from the current guess

In the following graph, we can see the results of starting a gradient descent procedure from *x = 4.5*, with a learning rate of 0.75, and then optimizing *x* to attain the lowest value of the cost function:

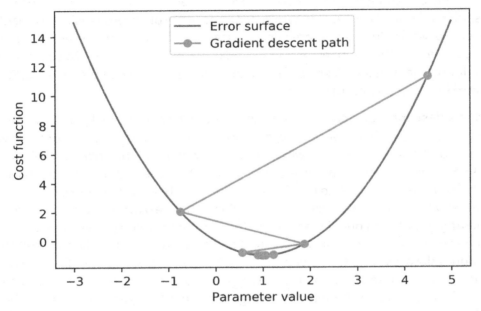

**Figure 4.5: The gradient descent path**

Gradient descent also works in higher-dimensional spaces; in other words, with more than one parameter. However, you can only visualize up to a two-dimensional error surface (that is, two parameters at a time on a three-dimensional plot) on a single graph.

Having described the workings of gradient descent, let's perform an exercise to implement the gradient descent algorithm, expanding on the example of this section.

> **NOTE**
>
> The code for generating the plots presented in this section can be found here: https://packt.link/NeF8P. If you're reading the print version of this book, you can download and browse the color versions of some of the images in this chapter by visiting the following link: https://packt.link/FAXBM

## EXERCISE 4.01: USING GRADIENT DESCENT TO MINIMIZE A COST FUNCTION

In this exercise, our task is to find the best set of parameters in order to minimize the following hypothetical cost function: $y = f(x) = x^2 - 2x$. To do this, we will employ gradient descent, which was described in the preceding section. Perform the following steps to complete the exercise:

> **NOTE**
>
> Before you begin this exercise, please make sure you have executed the prerequisite steps of importing the necessary libraries and loading the cleaned dataframe. These steps along with the code for this exercise can be found at https://packt.link/NeF8P.

1. Create a function that returns the value of the cost function and look at the value of the cost function over a range of parameters. You can use the following code to do this (note that this repeats code from the preceding section):

```
X_poly = np.linspace(-3,5,81)
print(X_poly[:5], '...', X_poly[-5:])
def cost_function(X):
    return X * (X-2)
y_poly = cost_function(X_poly)
plt.plot(X_poly, y_poly)
plt.xlabel('Parameter value')
plt.ylabel('Cost function')
plt.title('Error surface')
```

You will obtain the following plot of the cost function:

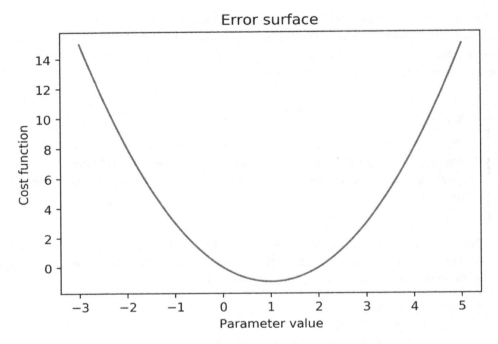

**Figure 4.6: A cost function plot**

2.  Create a function for the value of the gradient. This is the analytical derivative of the cost function. Use this function to evaluate the gradient at the point *x = 4.5*, and then use this in combination with the learning rate to find the next step of the gradient descent process:

```
def gradient(X):
    return (2*X) - 2
x_start = 4.5
learning_rate = 0.75
x_next = x_start - gradient(x_start)*learning_rate
x_next
```

> **NOTE**
>
> It doesn't matter if you haven't studied calculus and don't understand this part; you can just take it as a given that this is the function for the gradient. In some applications, it's not actually possible to calculate an analytical derivative, so this may need to be numerically approximated.

After running the cell with **x_next**, you will obtain the following output:

```
-0.75
```

This is the next gradient descent step after *x = 4.5*.

3. Plot the gradient descent path, from the starting point to the next point, using the following code:

```
plt.plot(X_poly, y_poly)
plt.plot([x_start, x_next],
         [cost_function(x_start), cost_function(x_next)],
         '-o')
plt.xlabel('Parameter value')
plt.ylabel('Cost function')
plt.legend(['Error surface', 'Gradient descent path'])
```

You will obtain the following output:

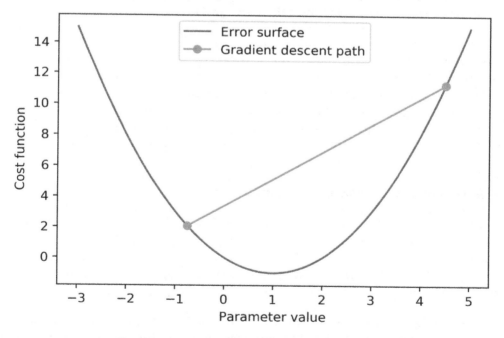

Figure 4.7: The first gradient descent path step

Here, it appears as though we've taken a step in the right direction. However, it's clear that we've overshot where we want to be. It may be that our learning rate is too large, and consequently, we are taking steps that are too big. While tuning the learning rate will be a good way to converge toward an optimal solution more quickly, in this example, we can just continue illustrating the remainder of the process. Here, it looks like we may need to take a few more steps. In practice, gradient descent continues until the size of the steps become very small, or the change in the cost function becomes very small (you can specify how small by using the **tol** argument in the scikit-learn logistic regression), indicating that we're close enough to a good solution – that is, a **local minimum** of the cost function. For this example, we'll just take a total of 14 steps, or **iterations**, beyond the initial guess (note that you can also set the maximum number of iterations in scikit-learn with **max_iter**).

4. Perform 14 iterations to converge toward the local minimum of the cost function by using the following code snippet (note that **iterations = 15**, but the endpoint is not included in the call to **range()**):

```
iterations = 15
x_path = np.empty(iterations,)
x_path[0] = x_start
for iteration_count in range(1,iterations):
    derivative = gradient(x_path[iteration_count-1])
    x_path[iteration_count] = x_path[iteration_count-1] \
                            - (derivative*learning_rate)
x_path
```

You will obtain the following output:

```
array([ 4.5       , -0.75      ,  1.875     ,  0.5625    ,  1.21875
,
        0.890625  ,  1.0546875 ,  0.97265625,  1.01367188,
0.99316406,
        1.00341797,  0.99829102,  1.00085449,  0.99957275,
1.00021362])
```

This **for** loop stores the successive estimates in the **x_path** array, using the current estimate to calculate the derivative and find the next estimate. From the resulting values of the gradient descent process, it looks like we've gotten very close (**1.00021362**) to the optimal solution of 1.

5.  Plot the gradient descent path using the following code:

```
plt.plot(X_poly, y_poly)
plt.plot(x_path, cost_function(x_path), '-o')
plt.xlabel('Parameter value')
plt.ylabel('Cost function')
plt.legend(['Error surface', 'Gradient descent path'])
```

You will obtain the following output:

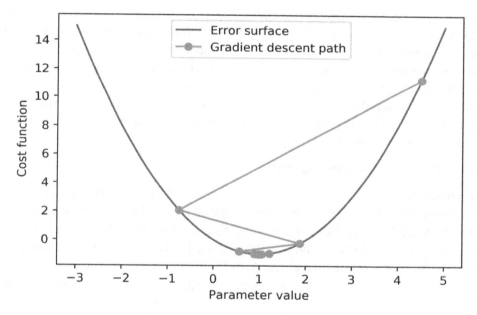

Figure 4.8: The gradient descent path

We encourage you to repeat the previous procedure with different learning rates in order to see how they affect the gradient descent path. With the right learning rate, it's possible to converge on a highly accurate solution very quickly. While the choice of learning rate can be important in different machine learning applications, for logistic regression, the problem is usually pretty easy to solve and you don't need to select a learning rate in scikit-learn.

As you experimented with different learning rates, did you notice what happened when the learning rate was greater than one? In this case, the step that we take in the direction of the decreasing error is too large and we actually wind up with a higher error. This problem can compound itself and actually lead the gradient descent process away from the region of minimum error. On the other hand, if the step size is too small, it can take a very long time to find the desired solution.

# ASSUMPTIONS OF LOGISTIC REGRESSION

Since it is a classical statistical model, similar to the F-test and Pearson correlation we already examined, logistic regression makes certain assumptions about the data. While it's not necessary to follow every one of these assumptions in the strictest possible sense, it's good to be aware of them. That way, if a logistic regression model is not performing very well, you can try to investigate and figure out why, using your knowledge of the ideal situation that logistic regression is intended for. You may find slightly different lists of the specific assumptions from different resources. However, those that are listed here are widely accepted.

## Features Are Linear in the Log Odds

We learned about this assumption in the previous chapter, *Chapter 3, Details of Logistic Regression and Feature Exploration*. Logistic regression is a linear model, so it will only work well as long as the features are effective at describing a linear trend in the log odds. In particular, logistic regression won't capture interactions, polynomial features, or the discretization of features, on its own. You can, however, specify all of these as "new features" – even though they may be engineered from existing features.

Remember from the previous chapter that the most important feature from univariate feature exploration, **PAY_1**, was not found to be linear in the log odds.

## No Multicollinearity of Features

Multicollinearity means that features are correlated with each other. The worst violation of this assumption is when features are perfectly correlated with each other, such as one feature being identical to another, or when one feature equals another multiplied by a constant. We can investigate the correlation of features using the correlation plot that we're already familiar with from univariate feature selection. Here is the correlation plot from the previous chapter:

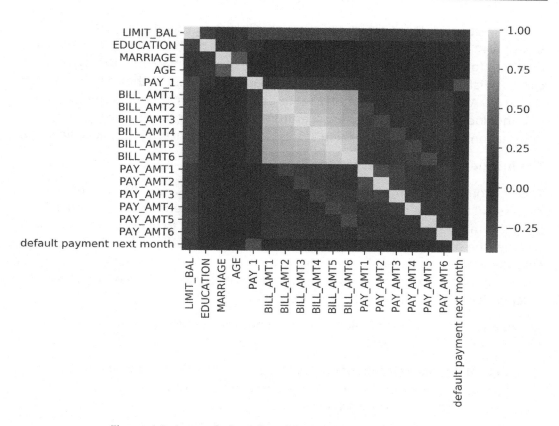

**Figure 4.9: A correlation plot of features and the response**

We can see from the correlation plot what perfect correlation looks like: since every feature and the response variable has a correlation of 1 with itself, we can see that a correlation of 1 is a light, cream color. From the color bar, which doesn't include -1, we know there are no correlations with that value.

> **NOTE**
>
> The Jupyter notebook containing the code and the corresponding plots presented in this section can be found here: https://packt.link/UOEMp.

The clearest examples of correlated predictors in our case study data are the **BILL_AMT** features. It makes intuitive sense that bills might be similar from month to month for a given account. For instance, there may be an account that typically carries a balance of zero, or an account that has a large balance that is taking a while to pay off. Are any of the **BILL_AMT** features perfectly correlated? From *Figure 4.9*, it does not look like it. So, while these features may not contribute much independent information, we won't remove them at this point out of concern for multicollinearity.

### The Independence of Observations

This is a common assumption in classical statistical models, including linear regression. Here, the observations (or samples) are assumed to be independent. Does this make sense with the case study data? We'd want to confirm with our client whether the same individual can hold multiple credit accounts across the dataset and consider what to do depending on how common it was. Let's assume we've been told that in our data each credit account belongs to a unique person, so we may assume independence of observations in this respect.

Across different domains of data, some common violations of independence of observations are as follows:

- **Spatial autocorrelation** of observations; for example, in natural phenomena such as soil types, where observations that are geographically close to each other may be similar to each other.

- **Temporal autocorrelation** of observations, which may occur in time series data. Observations at the current point in time are usually assumed to be correlated to the most recent point(s) in time.

However, these issues are not relevant to our case study data.

### No Outliers

Outliers are observations where the value of the feature(s) or response are very far from most of the data or are different in some other way. A more appropriate term for an outlier observation of a feature value is a high leverage point, as the term "outlier" is usually applied to the response variable. However, in our binary classification problem, it's not possible to have an outlier value of the response variable, since it can only take on the values 0 and 1. In practice, you may see both of these terms used to refer to features.

To see why these kinds of points can have an adverse effect on linear models in general, take a look at this synthetic linear data with 100 points and the line of best fit that results from linear regression:

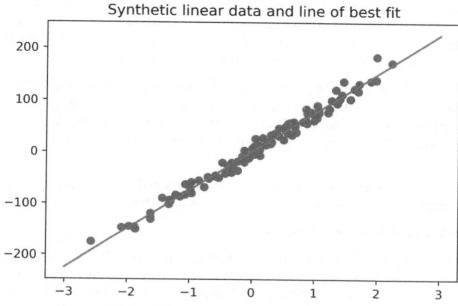

Figure 4.10: "Well-behaved" linear data and a regression fit

Here, the model intuitively appears to be a good fit for the data. However, what if an outlier feature value is added? To illustrate this, we add a point with an x value that is very different from most of the observations and a y value that is in a similar range to the other observations. We then show the resulting regression line:

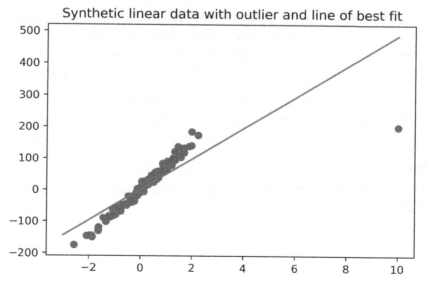

Figure 4.11: A plot showing what happens when an outlier is included

Due to the presence of a single high leverage point, the regression model fit for all the data is no longer a very good representation of much of the data. This shows the potential effect of just a single data point on linear models, especially if that point doesn't appear to follow the same trend as the rest of the data.

There are methods for dealing with outliers. But a more fundamental question to ask is "Is data like this realistic?". If the data doesn't seem right, it is a good idea to ask the client whether the outliers are believable. If not, they should be excluded. However, if they do represent valid data, then non-linear models or other methods should be used.

With our case study data, we did not observe outliers in the histograms that we plotted during feature exploration. Therefore, we don't have this concern.

**How Many Features Should You Include?**

This is not so much an assumption as it is guidance on model building. There is no clear-cut law that states how many features to include in a logistic regression model. However, a common rule of thumb is the "rule of 10," which states that for every 10 occurrences of the rarest outcome class, 1 feature may be added to the model. So, for example, in a binary logistic regression problem with 100 samples, if the class balance has 20% positive outcomes and 80% negative outcomes, then there are only 20 positive outcomes in total, and so only 2 features should be used in the model. A "rule of 20" has also been suggested, which would be a more stringent limit on the number of features to include (1 feature in our example).

Another point to consider in the case of binary features, such as those that result from one-hot encoding, is how many samples will have a positive value for that feature. If the feature is very imbalanced, in other words, with very few samples containing either a 1 or a 0, it may not make sense to include it in the model.

For the case study data, we are fortunate to have a relatively large number of samples and relatively balanced features, so these are not concerns.

> **NOTE**
>
> The code for generating the plots presented in this section can be found here: https://packt.link/SnX3y.

# THE MOTIVATION FOR REGULARIZATION: THE BIAS-VARIANCE TRADE-OFF

We can extend the basic logistic regression model that we have learned about by using a powerful concept known as **shrinkage** or **regularization**. In fact, every logistic regression that you have fit so far in scikit-learn has used some amount of regularization. That is because it is a default option in the logistic regression model object. However, until now, we have ignored it.

As you learn about these concepts in greater depth, you will also become familiar with a few foundational concepts in machine learning: **overfitting**, **underfitting**, and the **bias-variance trade-off**. A model is said to overfit the training data if the performance of the model on the training data (for example, the ROC AUC) is substantially better than the performance on a held-out test set. In other words, good performance on the training set does not generalize to the unseen test set. We started to discuss these concepts in *Chapter 2, Introduction to Scikit-Learn and Model Evaluation*, when we distinguished between model training and test scores.

When a model is overfitted to the training data, it is said to have high **variance**. In other words, whatever variability exists in the training data, the model has learned this very well – in fact, too well. This will be reflected in a high model training score. However, when such a model is used to make predictions on new and unseen data, the performance is lower. Overfitting is more likely in the following circumstances:

- There are a large number of features available in relation to the number of samples. In particular, there may be so many possible features that it is cumbersome to directly inspect all of them, like we were able to do with the case study data.

- A complex model, that is, more complex than logistic regression, is used. These include models such as gradient boosting ensembles or neural networks.

Under these circumstances, the model has an opportunity develop more complex **hypotheses** about the relationships between features and the response variable in the training data during model fitting, making overfitting more likely.

In contrast, if a model is not fitting the training data very well, this is known as underfitting, and the model is said to have high **bias**.

We can examine the differences between underfitting, overfitting, and the ideal that sits in between, by fitting polynomial models on some hypothetical data:

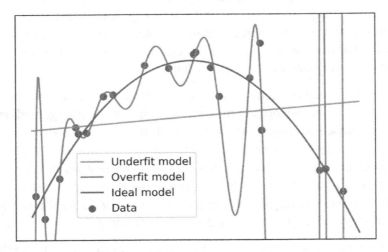

**Figure 4.12: Quadratic data with underfit, overfit, and ideal models**

In *Figure 4.12*, we can see that including too few features, in this case, a linear model of *y* with just two features, a slope and an intercept, is clearly not a good representation of the data. This is known as an underfit model. However, if we include too many features, that is, many high-degree polynomial terms, such as $x^2$, $x^3$, $x^4$,... $x^{10}$, we can fit the training data almost perfectly. However, this is not necessarily a good thing. When we look at the results of the overfitted model in between the training data points, where new predictions may need to be made, we can see that the model is unstable and may not provide reliable predictions for data that was not in the training set. We can tell this just based on an intuitive understanding of the relationship between the features and the response variable, which we can get from visualizing the data.

> **NOTE**
>
> The code for generating the plots presented in this section can be found here: https://packt.link/SnX3y.

The synthetic data for this example was generated by a second-degree (that is, quadratic) polynomial. Knowing this, we could easily find the ideal model by fitting a second-degree polynomial to the training data, as shown in *Figure 4.12*.

In general, however, we won't know what the ideal model formulation is ahead of time. For this reason, we need to compare training and test scores to assess whether a model may be overfitting or underfitting.

In some cases, it may be desirable to introduce some bias into the model training process, especially if this decreases overfitting and increases model performance on new, unseen data. In this way, it may be possible to leverage the bias-variance trade-off to improve a model. We can use **regularization** methods to accomplish this. Additionally, we may also be able to use these methods for **variable selection** as part of the modeling process. Using a predictive model to select variables is an alternative to the univariate feature selection methods that we've already explored. We begin to experiment with these concepts in the following exercise.

## EXERCISE 4.02: GENERATING AND MODELING SYNTHETIC CLASSIFICATION DATA

In this exercise, we'll observe overfitting in practice by using a synthetic dataset. Consider yourself in the situation of having been given a binary classification dataset with many candidate features (200), where you don't have time to look through all of them individually. It's possible that some of these features are highly correlated or related in some other way. However, with this many variables, it can be difficult to effectively explore all of them. Additionally, the dataset has relatively few samples: only 1,000. We are going to generate this challenging dataset by using a feature of scikit-learn that allows you to create synthetic datasets for making conceptual explorations such as this. Perform the following steps to complete the exercise:

> **NOTE**
>
> Before you begin this exercise, please make sure you have executed the prerequisite steps of importing the necessary libraries. These steps along with the code for this exercise can be found at https://packt.link/mIMsT.

1. Import the **make_classification**, **train_test_split**, **LogisticRegression**, and **roc_auc_score** classes using the following code:

```
from sklearn.datasets import make_classification
from sklearn.model_selection import train_test_split
from sklearn.linear_model import LogisticRegression
from sklearn.metrics import roc_auc_score
```

Notice that we've imported several familiar classes from scikit-learn, in addition to a new one that we haven't seen before: **make_classification**. This class does just what its name indicates – it makes data for a classification problem. Using the various keyword arguments, you can specify how many samples and features to include, and how many classes the response variable will have. There is also a range of other options that effectively control how "easy" the problem will be to solve.

> **NOTE**
>
> For more information, refer to https://scikit-learn.org/stable/modules/generated/sklearn.datasets.make_classification.html. Suffice to say that we've selected options here that make a reasonably easy-to-solve problem, with some curveballs thrown in. In other words, we expect high model performance, but we'll have to work a little bit to get it.

2. Generate a dataset with two variables, **x_synthetic** and **y_synthetic**. **x_synthetic** has the 200 candidate features, and **y_synthetic** the response variable, each for 1,000 samples. Use the following code:

```
X_synthetic, y_synthetic = make_classification(
    n_samples=1000, n_features=200,
    n_informative=3, n_redundant=10,
    n_repeated=0, n_classes=2,
    n_clusters_per_class=2,
    weights=None, flip_y=0.01,
    class_sep=0.8, hypercube=True,
    shift=0.0, scale=1.0,
    shuffle=True, random_state=24)
```

3. Examine the shape of the dataset and the class fraction of the response variable using the following code:

```
print(X_synthetic.shape, y_synthetic.shape)
print(np.mean(y_synthetic))
```

You will obtain the following output:

```
(1000, 200) (1000,)
0.501
```

After checking the shape of the output, note that we've generated an almost perfectly balanced dataset: close to a 50/50 class balance. It is also important to note that we've generated all the features so that they have the same **shift** and **scale** – that is, a mean of 0 with a standard deviation of 1. Making sure that the features are on the same scale, or have roughly the same range of values, is a key point for using regularization methods – and we'll see why later. If the features in a raw dataset are on widely different scales, it is advisable to normalize them so that they are on the same scale. Scikit-learn has the functionality to make this easy, which we'll learn about in the activity at the end of this chapter.

4.  Plot the first few features as histograms to show that the range of values is the same using the following code:

```
for plot_index in range(4):
    plt.subplot(2, 2, plot_index+1)
    plt.hist(X_synthetic[:, plot_index])
    plt.title('Histogram for feature {}'.format(plot_index+1))
plt.tight_layout()
```

You will obtain the following output:

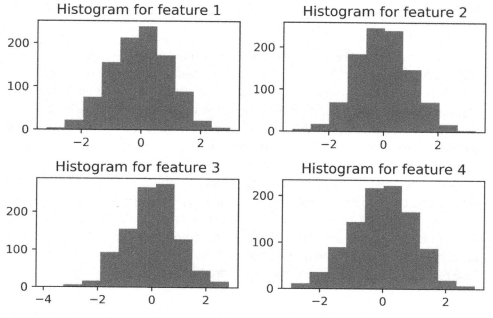

Figure 4.13: Histograms for the first 4 of 200 synthetic features

Because we generated this dataset, we don't need to directly examine all 200 features to make sure that they're on the same scale. So, what are the possible concerns with this dataset? The data is balanced in terms of the class fractions of the response variable, so we don't need to undersample, oversample, or use other methods that are helpful for imbalanced data. What about relationships among the features themselves, and the features and response variable? There are a lot of these relationships and it is a challenge to investigate them all directly. Based on our rule of thumb (that is, 1 feature allowed for every 10 samples of the rarest class), 200 features is too many. We have 500 observations in the rarest class, so by that rule, we shouldn't have more than 50 features. It's possible that with so many features, the model training procedure will overfit. We will now start to learn how to use options in the scikit-learn logistic regression to prevent this.

5. Split the data into training and test sets using an 80/20 split, and then instantiate a logistic regression model object using the following code:

```
X_syn_train, X_syn_test, y_syn_train, y_syn_test = \
train_test_split(X_synthetic, y_synthetic,\
                 test_size=0.2, random_state=24)
lr_syn = LogisticRegression(solver='liblinear', penalty='l1',
                            C=1000, random_state=1)

lr_syn.fit(X_syn_train, y_syn_train)
```

Notice here that we are specifying some new options in the logistic regression model, which, so far, we have not paid attention to. First, we specify the **penalty** argument to be **l1**. This means we are going to use **L1 regularization**, which is also known as **lasso regularization**. We'll discuss the mathematical definition of this shortly. Second, notice that we have set the **C** parameter to be equal to 1,000. **C** is the "inverse of regularization strength," according to the scikit-learn documentation (https://scikit-learn.org/stable/modules/generated/sklearn.linear_model.LogisticRegression.html). This means that higher values of **C** correspond to less regularization. By choosing a relatively large number, such as 1,000, we are using relatively little regularization. The default value of **C** is 1. So, we are not really using much regularization here, rather, we are simply becoming familiar with the options to do so. Finally, we are using the **liblinear** solver, which we have used in the past.

Although we happen to be using scaled data here (all features have a mean of 0 and standard deviation of 1), it's worth noting at this point that among the various options we have available for solvers, **liblinear** is "robust to unscaled data." Also note that **liblinear** is one of only two solver options that support the L1 penalty – the other option being **saga**.

> **NOTE**
>
> You can find out more information on available solvers at https://scikit-learn. org/stable/modules/linear_model.html#logistic-regression.

6.  Fit the logistic regression model on the training data using the following code:

```
lr_syn.fit(X_syn_train, y_syn_train)
```

Here is the output:

```
LogisticRegression(C=1000, penalty='l1', random_state=1, \
                   solver='liblinear')
```

7.  Calculate the training score using this code by first getting predicted probabilities and then obtaining the ROC AUC:

```
y_syn_train_predict_proba = lr_syn.predict_proba(X_syn_train)
roc_auc_score(y_syn_train, y_syn_train_predict_proba[:,1])
```

The output should be as follows:

```
0.9420000000000001
```

8.  Calculate the test score similar to how the training score was obtained:

```
y_syn_test_predict_proba = lr_syn.predict_proba(X_syn_test)
roc_auc_score(y_syn_test, y_syn_test_predict_proba[:,1])
```

The output should be as follows:

```
0.8075807580758075
```

From these results, it's apparent that the logistic regression model has overfit the data. That is, the ROC AUC score on the training data is substantially higher than that of the test data.

## LASSO (L1) AND RIDGE (L2) REGULARIZATION

Before applying regularization to a logistic regression model, let's take a moment to understand what regularization is and how it works. The two ways of regularizing logistic regression models in scikit-learn are called **lasso** (also known as **L1** regularization) and **ridge** (also known as **L2** regularization). When instantiating the model object from the scikit-learn class, you can choose `penalty = 'l1'` or `'l2'`. These are called "penalties" because the effect of regularization is to add a penalty, or a cost, for having larger values of the coefficients in a fitted logistic regression model.

As we've already learned, coefficients in a logistic regression model describe the relationship between the log odds of the response and each of the features. Therefore, if a coefficient value is particularly large, then a small change in that feature will have a large effect on the prediction. When a model is being fit and is learning the relationship between features and the response variable, the model can start to learn the noise in the data. We saw this previously in *Figure 4.12*: if there are many features available when fitting a model, and there are no guardrails on the values that their coefficients can take, then the model fitting process may try to discover relationships between the features and the response variable that won't generalize to new data. In this way, the model becomes tuned to the unpredictable, random noise that accompanies real-world, imperfect data. Unfortunately, this only serves to increase the model's skill at predicting the training data, which is not our ultimate goal. Therefore, we should seek to root out such spurious relationships from the model.

Lasso and ridge regularization use different mathematical formulations to accomplish this goal. These methods work by making changes to the cost function that is used for model fitting, which we introduced previously as the log-loss function. Lasso regularization uses what is called the **1-norm** (hence the term L1):

$$\log loss \ with \ lasso \ penalty = \sum_{j=1}^{m} |\sigma_j| + \frac{c}{n} \sum_{i=1}^{n} - (y_i \log(p_i) + (1 - y_i)\log (1 - p_i))$$

**Figure 4.14: Log-loss equation with lasso penalty**

The 1-norm, which is the first term in the equation in *Figure 4.14*, is just the sum of the absolute values of the coefficients of the *m* different features. The absolute value is used because having a coefficient that's large in either the positive or negative directions can contribute to overfitting. So, what else is different about this cost function compared to the log-loss function that we saw earlier? Well, now there is a *C* factor that is multiplied by the fraction in front of the sum of the log-loss function.

This is the "inverse of regularization strength," as described in the scikit-learn documentation (https://scikit-learn.org/stable/modules/generated/sklearn.linear_model.LogisticRegression.html). Since this factor is in front of the term of the cost function that calculates the prediction error, as opposed to the term that does regularization, then making it larger makes the prediction error more important in the cost function, while regularization is made less important. In short, *larger values of C lead to less regularization* in the scikit-learn implementation.

L2, or ridge regularization, is similar to L1, except that instead of the sum of absolute values of coefficients, ridge uses the sum of their squares, called the **2-norm**:

$$\log loss\ with\ ridge\ penalty = \sum_{j=1}^{m} \sigma_j^2 + \frac{C}{n}\sum_{i=1}^{n} -(y_i \log(p_i) + (1 - y_i)\log(1 - p_i))$$

Figure 4.15: Log-loss equation with ridge penalty

Note that if you look at the cost functions for logistic regression in the scikit-learn documentation, the specific form is different than what is used here, but the overall idea is similar. Additionally, after you become comfortable with the concepts of lasso and ridge penalties, you should be aware that there is an additional regularization method called **elastic-net**, which is a combination lasso and ridge.

## Why Are There Two Different Formulations of Regularization?

It may be that one or the other will provide better out-of-sample performance, so you may wish to test them both. There is another key difference in these methods: the L1 penalty also performs feature selection, in addition to regularization. It does this by setting some coefficient values to exactly zero during the regularization process, effectively removing features from the model. L2 regularization makes the coefficient values smaller but does not completely eliminate them. Not all solver options in scikit-learn support both L1 and L2 regularization, so you will need to select an appropriate solver for the regularization technique you want to use.

> **NOTE**
>
> The mathematical details of why L1 regularization removes features but L2 doesn't are beyond the scope of this book. However, for a more thorough explanation of this topic and further reading in general, we recommend the very readable (and free) resource, *An Introduction to Statistical Learning by Gareth James*, et al. In particular, see *page 222* of the corrected 7th printing, for a helpful graphic on the difference between L1 and L2 regularization.

## Intercepts and Regularization

We have not discussed intercepts very much, other than to note that we have been estimating them with our linear models, along with the coefficients that go with each feature. So, should you use an intercept? The answer is probably yes, until you've developed an advanced understanding of linear models and are certain that in a specific case you should not. However, such cases do exist, for example, in a linear regression where the features and the response variable have all been normalized to have a mean of zero.

Intercepts don't go with any particular feature. Therefore, it doesn't make much sense to regularize them, as they shouldn't contribute to overfitting. Notice that in the regularization penalty term for L1, the summation starts with $j = 1$, and similarly for L2, we have skipped $\sigma_0$, which is the intercept term.

This is the ideal situation: not regularizing the intercept. However, some of the solvers in scikit-learn, such as **liblinear**, actually do regularize the intercept. There is an **intercept_scaling** option that you can supply to the model class to counteract this effect. We have not illustrated this here as, although it is theoretically incorrect, regularizing the intercept often does not have much effect on the model's predictive quality in practice.

## Scaling and Regularization

As noted in the previous exercise, it is best practice to **scale** the data so that all the features have roughly the same range of values before using regularization. This is because the coefficients are all going to be subject to the same penalty in the cost function. If the range of values for a particular feature, such as **LIMIT_BAL** in our dataset, is much larger than other features, such as **PAY_1**, it may, in fact, be desirable to have a larger value for the coefficient of **PAY_1** and a smaller value for that of **LIMIT_BAL** in order to put their effects on the same scale in the linear combination of features and coefficients that are used for model prediction. Normalizing all the features before using regularization avoids complications such as this that arise simply from differences in scale.

In fact, scaling your data may also be necessary, depending on which solver you are using. The different variations on the gradient descent process available in scikit-learn may or may not be able to work effectively with unscaled data.

## The Importance of Selecting the Right Solver

As we've come to learn, the different solvers available for logistic regression in scikit-learn have different behaviors regarding the following:

- Whether they support both L1 and L2 regularization

- How they treat the intercept during regularization

- How they deal with unscaled data

> **NOTE**
>
> There are other differences as well. A helpful table comparing these and other traits is available at https://scikit-learn.org/stable/modules/linear_model.html#logistic-regression. You can use this table to decide which solver is appropriate for your problem.

To summarize this section, we have learned the mathematical foundations of lasso and ridge regularization. *These methods work by shrinking the coefficient values toward 0, and in the case of the lasso, setting some coefficients to exactly 0 and thus performing feature selection.* You can imagine that in our example of overfitting in *Figure 4.12*, if the complex, overfitted model had some coefficients shrunk toward 0, it would look more like the ideal model, which has fewer coefficients.

Here is a plot of a regularized regression model, using the same high-degree polynomial features as the overfitted model, but with a ridge penalty:

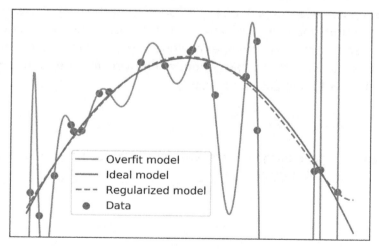

**Figure 4.16: An overfit model and regularized model using the same features**

The regularized model looks similar to the ideal model, demonstrating the ability of regularization to correct overfitting. Note, however, that the regularized model should not be recommended for extrapolation. Here, we can see that the regularized model starts to increase toward the right side of *Figure 4.16*. This increase should be viewed with suspicion, as there is nothing in the training data that makes it clear that this would be expected. This is an example of the general view that the *extrapolation of model predictions outside the range of training data is not recommended*. However, it is clear from *Figure 4.16* that even if we didn't have knowledge of the model that was used to generate this synthetic data (as we typically don't have knowledge of the data-generating process in real-world predictive modeling work), we can still use regularization to reduce the effect of overfitting when a large number of candidate features are available.

**Model and Feature Selection**

L1 regularization is one way to use a model, such as logistic regression, to perform feature selection. Other methods include forward or backward **stepwise selection** from the pool of candidate features. Here is the high-level idea behind these methods: in the case of **forward selection**, features are added to the model one at a time, and the out-of-sample performance is observed along the way. At each iteration, the addition of all possible features from the candidate pool is considered, and the one resulting in the greatest increase in the out-of-sample performance is chosen. When adding additional features ceases to improve the model's performance, no more features need to be added from the candidates. In the case of **backward selection**, you first start with all the features in the model and determine which one you should remove: the one resulting in the smallest decrease in the out-of-sample performance. You can continue removing features in this way until the performance begins to decrease appreciably.

> **NOTE**
>
> The code for generating the plots presented in this section can be found here: https://packt.link/aUBMb.

# CROSS-VALIDATION: CHOOSING THE REGULARIZATION PARAMETER

By now, you may suspect that we could use regularization in order to decrease the overfitting we observed when we tried to model the synthetic data in *Exercise 4.02, Generating and Modeling Synthetic Classification Data*. The question is, how do we choose the regularization parameter, *C*? *C* is an example of a model **hyperparameter**. Hyperparameters are different from the parameters that are estimated when a model is trained, such as the coefficients and the intercept of a logistic regression. Rather than being estimated by an automated procedure like the parameters are, hyperparameters are input directly by the user as keyword arguments, typically when instantiating the model class. So, how do we know what values to choose?

Hyperparameters are more difficult to estimate than parameters. This is because it is up to the data scientist to determine what the best value is, as opposed to letting an optimization algorithm find it. However, it is possible to programmatically choose hyperparameter values, which could be viewed as an optimization procedure in its own right. Practically speaking, in the case of the regularization parameter *C*, this is most commonly done by fitting the model on one set of data with a particular value of *C*, determining model training performance, and then assessing the out-of-sample performance on another set of data.

We are already familiar with the concept of using model training and test sets. However, there is a key difference here; for instance, what would happen if we were to use the test set multiple times in order to see the effect of different values of *C*?

It may occur to you that after the first time you use the unseen test set to assess the out-of-sample performance for a particular value of *C*, it is no longer an "unseen" test set. While only the training data was used for estimating the model parameters (that is, the coefficients and the intercept), now the test data is being used to estimate the hyperparameter *C*. Effectively, the test data has now become additional training data in the sense that it is being used to find a good value for the hyperparameter.

For this reason, it is common to divide the data into three parts: a training set, a test set, and a **validation set**. The validation set serves multiple purposes:

### Estimating Hyperparameters

The validation set can be repeatedly used to assess the out-of-sample performance with different hyperparameter values to select hyperparameters.

## A Comparison of Different Models

In addition to finding hyperparameter values for a model, the validation set can be used to estimate the out-of-sample performance of different models; for example, if we wanted to compare logistic regression to random forest.

> **NOTE**
>
> **Data Management Best Practices**
>
> As a data scientist, it's up to you to figure out how to divide up your data for different predictive modeling tasks. In the ideal case, you should reserve a portion of your data for the very end of the process, after you've already selected model hyperparameters and also selected the best model. This **unseen test set** is reserved for the last step, when it can be used to assess the endpoint of your model-building efforts, to see how the final model generalizes to new unseen data. When reserving the test set, it is good practice to make sure that the features and responses have similar characteristics to the rest of the data. In other words, the class fraction should be the same, and the distribution of features should be similar. This way, the test data should be representative of the data you built the model with.

While model validation is a good practice, it raises the question of whether the particular split we choose for the training, validation, and test data has any effect on the outcomes that we are tracking. For example, perhaps the relationship between the features and the response variable is slightly different in the unseen test set that we have reserved, or in the validation set, versus the training set. It is likely impossible to eliminate all such variability, but we can use the method of **cross-validation** to avoid placing too much faith in one particular split of the data.

Scikit-learn provides convenient functions to facilitate cross-validation analyses. These functions play a similar role to **train_test_split**, which we have already been using, although the default behavior is somewhat different. Let's get familiar with them now. First, import these two classes:

```
from sklearn.model_selection import StratifiedKFold
from sklearn.model_selection import KFold
```

Similar to **train_test_split**, we need to specify what proportion of the dataset we would like to use for training versus testing. However, with cross-validation (specifically the **k-fold cross-validation** that was implemented in the classes we just imported), rather than specifying a proportion directly, we simply indicate how many folds we would like – that is, the "**k folds**." The idea here is that the data will be divided into **k** equal proportions. For example, if we specify 4 folds, then each fold will have 25% of the data. These folds will be the test data in four separate instances of model training, while the remaining 75% from each fold will be used to train the model. In this procedure, each data point gets used as training data a total of *k - 1* times, and as test data only once.

When instantiating the class, we indicate the number of folds, whether or not to shuffle the data before splitting, and a random seed if we want repeatable results across different runs:

```
n_folds = 4
k_folds = KFold(n_splits=n_folds, shuffle=False)
```

Here, we've instantiated an object with four folds and no shuffling. The way in which we use the object that is returned, which we've called **k_folds**, is by passing the features and response data that we wish to use for cross-validation, to the **.split** method of this object. This outputs an **iterator**, which means that we can loop through the output to get the different splits of training and test data. If we took the training data from our synthetic classification problem, **X_syn_train** and **y_syn_train**, we could loop through the splits like this:

```
for train_index, test_index in k_folds_iterator.split(X_syn_train,
                                                       y_syn_train):
```

The iterator will return the row indices of **X_syn_train** and **y_syn_train**, which we can use to index the data. Inside this **for** loop, we can write code to use these indices to select data for repeatedly training and testing a model object with different subsets of the data. In this way, we can get a robust indication of the out-of-sample performance when using one particular hyperparameter value, and then repeat the whole process using another hyperparameter value. Consequently, the cross-validation loop may sit **nested** inside an outer loop over different hyperparameter values. We'll illustrate this in the following exercise.

First though, what do these splits look like? If we were to simply plot the indices from **train_index** and **test_index** as different colors, we would get something that looks like this:

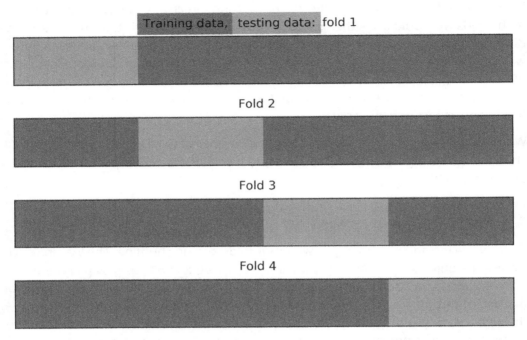

**Figure 4.17: Training/test splits for k-folds with four folds and no shuffling**

Here, we see that with the options we've indicated for the **KFold** class, the procedure has simply taken the first 25% of the data, according to the order of rows, as the first test fold, then the next 25% of data for the second fold, and so on. But what if we wanted stratified folds? In other words, what if we wanted to ensure that the class fractions of the response variable were equal in every fold? While **train_test_split** allows this option as a keyword argument, there is a separate **StratifiedKFold** class that implements this for cross-validation. We can illustrate how the stratified splits will appear as follows:

```
k_folds = StratifiedKFold(n_splits=n_folds, shuffle=False)
```

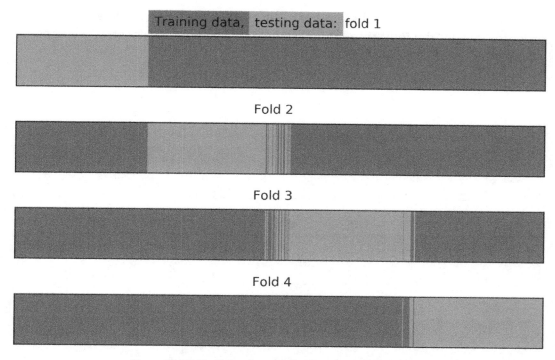

Training data, testing data: fold 1

Fold 2

Fold 3

Fold 4

**Figure 4.18: Training/test splits for stratified k-folds**

In *Figure 4.18*, we can see that there has been some amount of "shuffling" between the different folds. The procedure has moved samples between folds as necessary to ensure that the class fractions in each fold are equal.

Now, what if we want to shuffle the data to choose samples from throughout the range of indices for each test fold? First, why might we want to do this? Well, with the synthetic data that we've created for our problem, we can be certain that the data is in no particular order. However, in many real-world situations, the data we receive may be sorted in some way.

For instance, perhaps the rows of the data have been ordered by the date an account was created, or by some other logic. Therefore, it can be a good idea to shuffle the data before splitting. This way, any traits that might have been used for sorting can be expected to be consistent throughout the folds. Otherwise, the data in different folds may have different characteristics, possibly leading to different relationships between features and response.

This can lead to a situation where model performance is uneven between the folds. In order to "mix up" the folds throughout all the row indices of a dataset, all we need to do is set the **shuffle** parameter to **True**:

```
k_folds = StratifiedKFold(n_splits=n_folds, shuffle=True,
                          random_state=1)
```

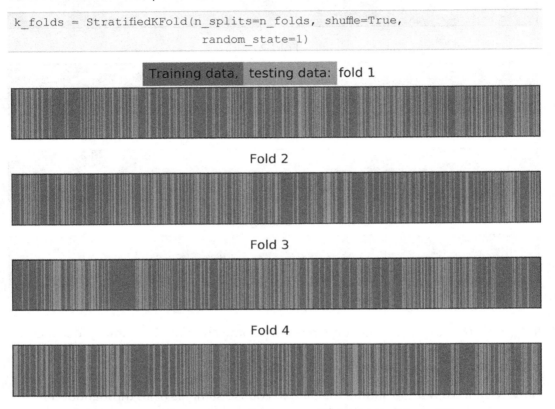

Figure 4.19: Training/test splits for stratified k-folds with shuffling

With shuffling, the test folds are spread out randomly, and fairly evenly, across the indices of the input data.

K-fold cross-validation is a widely used method in data science. However, the choice of how many folds to use depends on the particular dataset at hand. Using a smaller number of folds means that the amount of training data in each fold will be relatively small. Therefore, this increases the chances that the model will underfit, as models generally work better when trained on more data. It's a good idea to try a few different numbers of folds and see how the mean and the variability of the k-fold test score changes. Common numbers of folds can range anywhere from 4 or 5 to 10.

In the event of a very small dataset, it may be necessary to use as much data as possible for training in the cross-validation folds. In this scenario, you can use a method called **leave-one-out cross-validation** (**LOOCV**). In LOOCV, the test set for each fold consists of a single sample. In other words, there will be as many folds as there are samples in the training data. For each iteration, the model is trained on all but one sample, and a prediction is made for that sample. The accuracy, or other performance metric, can then be constructed using these predictions.

Other concerns that relate to the creation of a test set, such as choosing an out-of-time test set for problems where observations from the past must be used to predict future events, also apply to cross-validation.

In *Exercise 4.02, Generating and Modeling Synthetic Classification Data*, we saw that fitting a logistic regression on our training data led to overfitting. Indeed, the test score (*ROC AUC = 0.81*) was substantially lower than the training score (*ROC AUC = 0.94*). We had essentially used very little or no regularization by setting the regularization parameter *C* to a relatively large value (1,000). Now we will see what happens when we vary *C* through a wide range of values.

> **NOTE**
>
> The code for generating the plots presented in this section can be found here: https://packt.link/37Zks.

# EXERCISE 4.03: REDUCING OVERFITTING ON THE SYNTHETIC DATA CLASSIFICATION PROBLEM

This exercise is a continuation of *Exercise 4.02, Generating and Modeling Synthetic Classification Data*. Here, we will use a cross-validation procedure in order to find a good value for the hyperparameter *C*. We will do this by using only the training data, reserving the test data for after model building is complete. Be prepared – this is a long exercise – but it will illustrate a general procedure that you will be able to use with many different kinds of machine learning models, so it is worth the time spent here. Perform the following steps to complete the exercise:

> **NOTE**
>
> Before you begin this exercise, you need to execute some prerequisite steps that can be found in the following notebook along with the code for this exercise: https://packt.link/JqbsW.

1. Vary the value of the regularization parameter, *C*, to range from *C = 1000* to *C = 0.001*. You can use the following snippets to do this.

   First, define exponents, which will be powers of 10, as follows:

   ```
   C_val_exponents = np.linspace(3,-3,13)
   C_val_exponents
   ```

   Here is the output of the preceding code:

   ```
   array([ 3. ,  2.5,  2. ,  1.5,  1. ,  0.5,  0. , -0.5, -1. , -1.5,
   -2. , -2.5, -3. ])
   ```

   Now, vary *C* by the powers of 10, as follows:

   ```
   C_vals = np.float(10)**C_val_exponents
   C_vals
   ```

   Here is the output of the preceding code:

   ```
   array([1.00000000e+03, 3.16227766e+02, 1.00000000e+02,
   3.16227766e+01,
           1.00000000e+01, 3.16227766e+00, 1.00000000e+00, 3.16227766e-
   01,
           1.00000000e-01, 3.16227766e-02, 1.00000000e-02, 3.16227766e-
   03,
           1.00000000e-03])
   ```

It's generally a good idea to vary the regularization parameter by powers of 10, or by using a similar strategy, as training models can take a substantial amount of time, especially when using k-fold cross-validation. This gives you a good idea of how a wide range of $C$ values impacts the bias-variance trade-off, without needing to train a very large number of models. In addition to the integer powers of 10, we also include points on the $\log_{10}$ scale that are about halfway between. If it seems like there is some interesting behavior in between these relatively widely spaced values, you can add more granular values for $C$ in a smaller part of the range of possible values.

2.  Import the **roc_curve** class:

```
from sklearn.metrics import roc_curve
```

We'll continue to use the ROC AUC score for assessing, training, and testing performance. Now that we have several values of $C$ to try and several folds (in this case four) for the cross-validation, we will want to store the training and test scores for each fold and for each value of $C$.

3.  Define a function that takes the **k_folds** cross-validation splitter, the array of $C$ values (**C_vals**), the model object (**model**), and the features and response variable (**X** and **Y**, respectively) as inputs, to explore different amounts of regularization with k-fold cross-validation. Use the following code:

```
def cross_val_C_search(k_folds, C_vals, model, X, Y):
```

> **NOTE**
>
> The function we started in this step will return the ROC AUCs and ROC curve data. The return block will be written during a later step in the exercise. For now, you can simply write the preceding code as is, because we will be defining **k_folds**, **C_vals**, **model**, **X**, and **Y** as we progress in the exercise.

4.  Within this function block, create a NumPy array to hold model performance data, with dimensions **n_folds** by **len(C_vals)**:

```
n_folds = k_folds.n_splits
cv_train_roc_auc = np.empty((n_folds, len(C_vals)))
cv_test_roc_auc = np.empty((n_folds, len(C_vals)))
```

Next, we'll store the arrays of true and false positive rates and thresholds that go along with each of the test ROC AUC scores in a **list of lists**.

> **NOTE**
>
> This is a convenient way to store all this model performance information, as a list in Python can contain any kind of data, including another list. Here, each item of the inner lists in the **list of lists** will be a tuple holding the arrays of TPR, FPR, and the thresholds for each of the folds, for each of the C values. Tuples are an ordered collection data type in Python, similar to lists, but unlike lists they are immutable: the items in a tuple can't be changed after the tuple is created. When a function returns multiple values, like the roc_curve function of scikit-learn, these values can be output to a single variable, which will be a tuple of those values. This way of storing results should be more obvious when we access these arrays later in order to examine them.

5. Create a list of empty lists using **[[]]** and **\*len(C_vals)** as follows:

```
cv_test_roc = [[]]*len(C_vals)
```

Using **\*len(C_vals)** indicates that there should be a list of tuples of metrics (TPR, FPR, thresholds) for each value of C.

We have learned how to loop through the different folds for cross-validation in the preceding section. What we need to do now is write an outer loop in which we will nest the cross-validation loop.

6. Create an outer loop for training and testing each of the k-folds for each value of C:

```
for c_val_counter in range(len(C_vals)):
    #Set the C value for the model object
    model.C = C_vals[c_val_counter]
    #Count folds for each value of C
    fold_counter = 0
```

We can reuse the same model object that we have already, and simply set a new value of C within each run of the loop. Inside the loop of C values, we run the cross-validation loop. We begin by yielding the training and test data row indices for each split.

7. Obtain the training and test indices for each fold:

```
for train_index, test_index in k_folds.split(X, Y):
```

8. Index the features and response variable to obtain the training and test data for this fold using the following code:

```
X_cv_train, X_cv_test = X[train_index], X[test_index]
y_cv_train, y_cv_test = Y[train_index], Y[test_index]
```

The training data for the current fold is then used to train the model.

9. Fit the model on the training data, as follows:

```
model.fit(X_cv_train, y_cv_train)
```

This will effectively "reset" the model from whatever the previous coefficients and intercept were to reflect the training on this new data.

The training and test ROC AUC scores are then obtained, as well as the arrays of TPRs, FPRs, and thresholds that go along with the test data.

10. Obtain the training ROC AUC score:

```
y_cv_train_predict_proba = model.predict_proba(X_cv_train)
cv_train_roc_auc[fold_counter, c_val_counter] = \
roc_auc_score(y_cv_train, y_cv_train_predict_proba[:,1])
```

11. Obtain the test ROC AUC score:

```
y_cv_test_predict_proba = model.predict_proba(X_cv_test)
cv_test_roc_auc[fold_counter, c_val_counter] = \
roc_auc_score(y_cv_test, y_cv_test_predict_proba[:,1])
```

12. Obtain the test ROC curves for each fold using the following code:

```
this_fold_roc = roc_curve(y_cv_test, y_cv_test_predict_proba[:,1])
cv_test_roc[c_val_counter].append(this_fold_roc)
```

We will use a fold counter to keep track of the folds that are incremented, and once outside the cross-validation loop, we print a status update to standard output. Whenever performing long computational procedures, it's a good idea to periodically print the status of the job so that you can monitor its progress and confirm that things are still working correctly. This cross-validation procedure will likely take only a few seconds on your laptop, but for longer jobs this can be especially reassuring.

13. Increment the fold counter using the following code:

```
fold_counter += 1
```

14. Write the following code to indicate the progress of execution for each value of *C*:

```
print('Done with C = {}'.format(lr_syn.C))
```

15. Write the code to return the ROC AUCs and ROC curve data and finish the function:

```
return cv_train_roc_auc, cv_test_roc_auc, cv_test_roc
```

Note that we will continue to use the split into four folds that we illustrated previously, but you are encouraged to try this procedure with different numbers of folds to compare the effect.

We have covered a lot of material in the preceding steps. You may want to take a few moments to review this with your classmates in order to make sure that you understand each part. Running the function is comparatively simple. That is the beauty of a well-designed function – all the complicated parts get abstracted away, allowing you to concentrate on usage.

16. Run the function we've designed to examine cross-validation performance, with the *C* values that we previously defined, and by using the model and data we were working with in the previous exercise. Use the following code:

```
cv_train_roc_auc, cv_test_roc_auc, cv_test_roc = \
cross_val_C_search(k_folds, C_vals, lr_syn, X_syn_train, y_syn_train)
```

When you run this code, you should see the following output populate below the code cell as the cross-validation is completed for each value of *C*:

```
Done with C = 1000.0
Done with C = 316.22776601683796
Done with C = 100.0
Done with C = 31.622776601683793
Done with C = 10.0
Done with C = 3.1622776601683795
Done with C = 1.0
Done with C = 0.31622776601683794
Done with C = 0.1
```

```
Done with C = 0.03162277660168379
Done with C = 0.01
Done with C = 0.0031622776601683794
Done with C = 0.001
```

So, what do the results of the cross-validation look like? There are a few ways to examine this. It is useful to look at the performance of each fold individually, so that you can see how variable the results are.

This tells you how different subsets of your data perform as test sets, leading to a general idea of the range of performance you can expect from the unseen test set. What we're interested in here is whether or not we are able to use regularization to alleviate the overfitting that we saw. We know that using $C = 1,000$ led to overfitting – we know this from comparing the training and test scores. But what about the other $C$ values that we've tried? A good way to visualize this will be to plot the training and test scores on the *y-axis* and the values of $C$ on the *x-axis*.

17. Loop over each of the folds to view their results individually by using the following code:

```
for this_fold in range(k_folds.n_splits):
    plt.plot(C_val_exponents, cv_train_roc_auc[this_fold], '-o',\
             color=cmap(this_fold),\
             label='Training fold {}'.format(this_fold+1))
    plt.plot(C_val_exponents, cv_test_roc_auc[this_fold], '-x',\
             color=cmap(this_fold),\
             label='Testing fold {}'.format(this_fold+1))
plt.ylabel('ROC AUC')
plt.xlabel('log$_{10}$(C)')
plt.legend(loc = [1.1, 0.2])
plt.title('Cross validation scores for each fold')
```

You will obtain the following output:

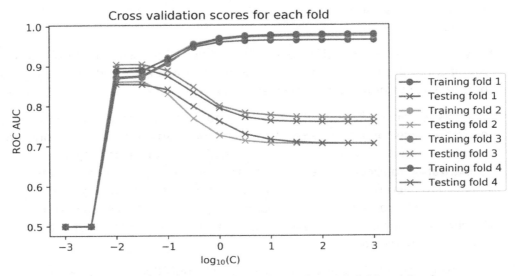

Figure 4.20: The training and test scores for each fold and C-value

We can see that for each fold of the cross-validation, as *C* decreases, the training performance also decreases. However, at the same time, the test performance increases. For some folds and values of *C*, the test ROC AUC score actually exceeds that of the training data, while for others, these two metrics simply come closer together. In all cases, we can say that the *C* values of $10^{-1.5}$ and $10^{-2}$ appear to have a similar test performance, which is substantially higher than the test performance of *C* = $10^3$. So, it appears that regularization has successfully addressed our overfitting problem.

But what about the lower values of *C*? For values that are lower than $10^{-2}$, the ROC AUC metric suddenly drops to 0.5. As you know, this value means that the classification model is essentially useless, performing no better than a coin flip. You are encouraged to check on this later when exploring how regularization affects the coefficient values; however, this is what happens when so much L1 regularization is applied that all model coefficients shrink to 0. Obviously, such models are not useful to us, as they encode no information about the relationship between the features and response variable.

Looking at the training and test performance of each k-fold split is helpful for gaining insights into the variability of model performance that may be expected when the model is scored on new, unseen data. But in order to summarize the results of the k-folds procedure, a common approach is to average the performance metric over the folds, for each value of the hyperparameter being considered. We'll perform this in the next step.

18. Plot the mean of training and test ROC AUC scores for each *C* value using the following code:

```
plt.plot(C_val_exponents, np.mean(cv_train_roc_auc, axis=0), \
         '-o', label='Average training score')
plt.plot(C_val_exponents, np.mean(cv_test_roc_auc, axis=0), \
         '-x', label='Average testing score')
plt.ylabel('ROC AUC')
plt.xlabel('log$_{10}$(C)')
plt.legend()
plt.title('Cross validation scores averaged over all folds')
```

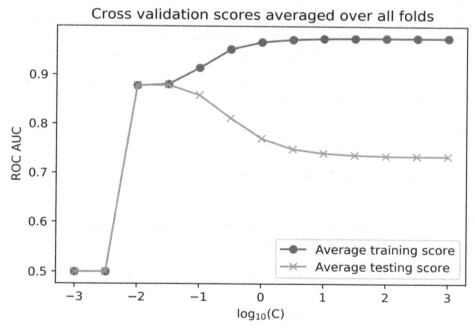

**Figure 4.21: The average training and test scores across cross-validation folds**

From this plot, it's clear that $C = 10^{-1.5}$ and $10^{-2}$ are the best values of $C$. There is little or no overfitting here, as the average training and test scores are nearly the same. You could search a finer grid of $C$ values (that is $C = 10^{-1.1}$, $10^{-1.2}$, and so on) in order to more precisely locate a $C$ value. However, from our graph, we can see that either $C = 10^{-1.5}$ or $C = 10^{-2}$ will likely be good solutions. We will move forward with $C = 10^{-1.5}$.

Examining the summary metric of ROC AUC is a good way to get a quick idea of how models will perform. However, for any real-world business application, you will often need to choose a specific threshold, which goes along with specific true and false positive rates. These will be needed to use the classifier to make the required "yes" or "no" decision, which, in our case study, is a prediction of whether an account will default. For this reason, it is useful to look at the ROC curves across the different folds of the cross-validation. To facilitate this, the preceding function has been designed to return the true and false positive rates, and thresholds, for each test fold and value of $C$, in the **cv_test_roc** list of lists. First, we need to find the index of the outer list that corresponds to the $C$ value that we've chosen, $10^{-1.5}$.

To accomplish this, we could simply look at our list of $C$ values and count by hand, but it's safer to do this programmatically by finding the index of the non-zero element of a Boolean array, as is shown in the next step.

19. Use a Boolean array to find the index where $C = 10^{-1.5}$ and convert it to an integer data type with the following code:

```
best_C_val_bool = C_val_exponents == -1.5
best_C_val_bool.astype(int)
```

Here is the output of the preceding code:

```
array([0, 0, 0, 0, 0, 0, 0, 0, 0, 1, 0, 0, 0])
```

20. Convert the integer version of the Boolean array into a single integer index using the **nonzero** function with this code:

```
best_C_val_ix = np.nonzero(best_C_val_bool.astype(int)) best_C_val_
ix[0][0]
```

Here is the output of the preceding code:

```
9
```

We have now successfully located the $C$ value that we wish to use.

21. Access the true and false positive rates in order to plot the ROC curves for each fold:

```
for this_fold in range(k_folds_n_splits):
    fpr = cv_test_roc[best_C_val_ix[0][0]][this_fold][0]
    tpr = cv_test_roc[best_C_val_ix[0][0]][this_fold][1]
    plt.plot(fpr, tpr, label='Fold {}'.format(this_fold+1))
plt.xlabel('False positive rate')
plt.ylabel('True positive rate')
plt.title('ROC curves for each fold at C = $10^{-1.5}$')
plt.legend()
```

You will obtain the following output:

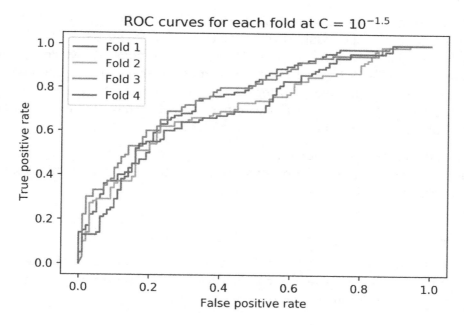

Figure 4.22: ROC curves for each fold

It appears that there is a fair amount of variability in the ROC curves. For example, if, for some reason, we want to limit the false positive rate to 40%, then from the plot it appears that we may be able to achieve a true positive rate of anywhere from approximately 60% to 80%. You can find the exact values by examining the arrays that we have plotted. This gives you an idea of how much variability in performance can be expected when deploying the model on new data. Generally, the more training data that is available, then the less variability there will be between the folds of cross-validation, so this could also be a sign that it would be a good idea to collect additional data, especially if the variability between training folds seems unacceptably high. You also may wish to try different numbers of folds with this procedure so as to see the effect on the variability of results between folds.

While normally we would try other models on our synthetic data problem, such as a random forest or support vector machine, if we imagine that in cross-validation, logistic regression proved to be the best model, we would decide to make this our final choice. When the final model is selected, all the training data can be used to fit the model, using the hyperparameters chosen with cross-validation. It's best to use as much data as possible in model fitting, as models typically work better when trained on more data.

22. Train the logistic regression on all the training data from our synthetic problem and compare the training and test scores, using the held-out test set as shown in the following steps.

> **NOTE**
>
> This is the final step in the model selection process. You should only use the unseen test set after your choice of model and hyperparameters are considered finished, otherwise it will not be "unseen."

23. Set the *C* value and train the model on all the training data with this code:

```
lr_syn.C = 10**(-1.5)
lr_syn.fit(X_syn_train, y_syn_train)
```

Here is the output of the preceding code:

```
LogisticRegression(C=0.03162277660168379, penalty='l1', \
                random_state=1, solver='liblinear'))
```

24. Obtain predicted probabilities and the ROC AUC score for the training data with this code:

```
y_syn_train_predict_proba = lr_syn.predict_proba(X_syn_train)
roc_auc_score(y_syn_train, y_syn_train_predict_proba[:,1])
```

Here is the output of the preceding code:

```
0.8802812499999999
```

25. Obtain predicted probabilities and the ROC AUC score for the test data with this code:

```
y_syn_test_predict_proba = lr_syn.predict_proba(X_syn_test)
roc_auc_score(y_syn_test, y_syn_test_predict_proba[:,1])
```

Here is the output of the preceding code:

```
0.8847884788478848
```

Here, we can see that by using regularization, the model training and test scores are similar, indicating that the overfitting problem has been greatly reduced. The training score is lower since we have introduced bias into the model at the expense of variance. However, this is OK, since the test score, which is the most important part, is higher. The out-of-sample test score is what matters for predictive capability. You are encouraged to check that these training and test scores are similar to those from the cross-validation procedure by printing the values from the arrays that we plotted previously; you should find that they are.

> **NOTE**
>
> In a real-world project, before delivering this model to your client for production use, you may wish to train the model on all the data that you were given, including the unseen test set. This follows the idea that the more data a model has seen, the better it is likely to perform in practice. However, some practitioners prefer to only use models that have been tested, meaning you would deliver the model trained only on the training data, not including the test set.

We know that L1 regularization works by decreasing the magnitude (that is, absolute value) of coefficients of the logistic regression. It can also set some coefficients to zero, therefore performing feature selection. In the next step, we will determine how many coefficients were set to zero.

26. Access the coefficients of the trained model and determine how many do not equal zero (**!= 0**) with this code:

```
sum((lr_syn.coef_ != 0)[0])
```

The output should be as follows:

```
2
```

This code takes the sum of a Boolean array indicating the locations of non-zero coefficients, so it shows how many coefficients in the model did not get set to zero by L1 regularization. Only 2 of the 200 features were selected!

27. Examine the value of the intercept using this code:

```
lr_syn.intercept_
```

The output should be as follows:

```
array([0.])
```

This shows that the intercept was regularized to 0.

In this exercise, we accomplished several goals. We used the k-fold cross-validation procedure to tune the regularization hyperparameter. We saw the power of regularization for reducing overfitting, and in the case of L1 regularization in logistic regression, selecting features.

Many machine learning algorithms offer some type of feature selection capability. Many also require the tuning of hyperparameters. The function here that loops over hyperparameters, and performs cross-validation, is a powerful concept that generalizes to other models. Scikit-learn offers functionality to make this process easier; in particular, the **sklearn.model_selection.GridSearchCV** procedure, which applies cross-validation to a grid search over hyperparameters. A **grid search** can be helpful when there are multiple hyperparameters to tune, by looking at all combinations of the ranges of different hyperparameters that you specify. A **randomized grid search** can speed up this process by randomly choosing a smaller number of combinations when an exhaustive grid search would take too long. Once you are comfortable with the concepts illustrated here, you are encouraged to streamline your workflow with convenient functions like these.

## OPTIONS FOR LOGISTIC REGRESSION IN SCIKIT-LEARN

We have used and discussed most of the options that you may supply to scikit-learn when instantiating or tuning the hyperparameters of a **LogisticRegression** model class. Here, we list them all and provide some general advice on their usage:

| Parameter | Possible values | Notes and advice for choosing |
|---|---|---|
| penalty | string, '11', '12', 'elasticnet', or 'none' | L1 (lasso) or L2 (ridge) regularization of coefficients. L1 performs feature selection, while L2 does not. Elastic-net is a blend of L1 and L2. The best overall model performance should be assessed by trying all options. |
| dual | bool, True, or False | This has to do with the optimization algorithm used to find coefficients. The documentation says *"only implemented for l2 penalty with liblinear solver. Prefer dual=False when n_samples > n_features."* |
| tol | float (decimal number) | Determines the size of the change in values for the optimization algorithm to stop. This is one way to control how long the optimization runs for, and how close to the ideal value the solution is. |
| c | float | The regularization parameter for L1 or L2 penalties. Smaller values mean more regularization. This needs to be determined using a validation set, or cross-validation. |
| fit_intercept | Bool | Whether or not an intercept term should be estimated. Unless you are sure you don't need an intercept, it's probably best to have one. |
| intercept_scaling | float | Can be used to avoid regularizing the intercept, an undesirable practice, when using the liblinear solver. |
| class_weight | Dictionary-specify weight for each class, 'balanced' string, or None | Whether or not to weight different classes during the model training process. Otherwise all samples will be considered equally important when fitting the model. Can be useful for imbalanced datasets: try using 'balanced' in this case. |
| random_state | int | Seed for a random number generator used by certain solver algorithms. |
| solver | string ('newton-cg', 'lbfgs', 'liblinear', 'sag', 'saga') | Select the type of optimization algorithm used to estimate the model parameters. See earlier discussion in this chapter or the documentation for the relative strengths and weaknesses of different solvers. |
| max_iter | int | The maximum number of iterations for the solution algorithm, which controls how close to the ideal parameters the solution is. If you get a warning that the solution algorithm did not converge, you can try increasing this. |
| multi_class | string ('ovr', 'multinomial', 'auto') | Various strategies for multiclass classification, beyond the scope of this book. |
| verbose | int | Controls the nature of the output to the terminal, during the optimization procedure. |
| warm_start | bool | If re-using the same model object for multiple training iterations, whether or not to use the previous solution as the starting point for the next optimization procedure. |
| n_jobs | int or None | Number of processers to use for parallel processing, in the case of 'ovr' multiclass classification. |
| l1_ratio | float | A parameter controlling the relative contributions of L1 and L2 regularization when using the elastic-net penalty. |

**Figure 4.23: A complete list of options for the logistic regression model in scikit-learn**

If you are in doubt regarding which option to use for logistic regression, we recommend you consult the scikit-learn documentation for further guidance (https://scikit-learn.org/stable/modules/linear_model.html#logistic-regression). Some options, such as the regularization parameter $C$, or the choice of a penalty for regularization, will need to be explored through the cross-validation process. Here, as with many choices to be made in data science, there is no universal approach that will apply to all datasets. The best way to see which options to use with a given dataset is to try several of them and see which gives the best out-of-sample performance. Cross-validation offers you a robust way to do this.

## SCALING DATA, PIPELINES, AND INTERACTION FEATURES IN SCIKIT-LEARN

### Scaling Data

Compared to the synthetic data we were just working with, the case study data is relatively large. If we want to use L1 regularization, then according to the official documentation ([https://scikit-learn.org/stable/modules/linear_model.html#logistic-regression](https://scikit-learn.org/stable/modules/linear_model.html#logistic-regression)), we ought to use the **saga** solver. However, this solver is not robust to unscaled datasets. Hence, we need to be sure to scale the data. This is also a good idea whenever doing regularization, so all the features are on the same scale and are equally penalized by the regularization process. A simple way to make sure that all the features have the same scale is to put them all through the transformation of subtracting the minimum and dividing by the range from minimum to maximum. This transforms each feature so that it will have a minimum of 0 and a maximum of 1. To instantiate the **MinMaxScaler** scaler that does this, we can use the following code:

```
from sklearn.preprocessing import MinMaxScaler
min_max_sc = MinMaxScaler()
```

### Pipelines

Previously, we used a logistic regression model in the cross-validation loop. However, now that we're scaling data, what new considerations are there? The scaling is effectively "learned" from the minimum and maximum values of the training data. After this, a logistic regression model would be trained on data scaled by the extremes of the model training data. However, we won't know the minimum and maximum values of the new, unseen data. So, following the philosophy of making cross-validation an effective indicator of model performance on unseen data, we need to use the minimum and maximum values of the training data in each cross-validation fold in order to scale the test data in that fold, before making predictions on the test data. Scikit-learn has the functionality to facilitate the combination of several training and test steps for situations such as this: the **Pipeline**. Our pipeline will consist of two steps: the scaler and the logistic regression model. These can both be fit on the training data and then used to make predictions on the test data. The process of fitting a pipeline is executed as a single step in the code, so all the parts of the pipeline are fit at once in this sense. Here is how a **Pipeline** is instantiated:

```
from sklearn.pipeline import Pipeline
scale_lr_pipeline = Pipeline(steps=[('scaler', min_max_sc), \
                                    ('model', lr)])
```

**Interaction Features**

Considering the case study data, do you think a logistic regression model with all possible features would be overfit or underfit? You can think about this from the perspective of rules of thumb, such as the "rule of 10," and the number of features (17) versus samples (26,664) that we have. Alternatively, you can consider all the work we've done so far with this data. For instance, we've had a chance to visualize all the features and ensure they make sense. Since there are relatively few features, and we have relatively high confidence that they are high quality because of our data exploration work, we are in a different situation than with the synthetic data exercises in this chapter, where we had a large number of features about which we knew relatively little. So, it may be that overfitting will be less of an issue with our case study at this point, and the benefits of regularization may not be significant.

In fact, it may be that we will underfit the model using only the 17 features that came with the data. One strategy to deal with this is to engineer new features. Some simple feature engineering techniques we've discussed include interaction and polynomial features. Polynomials may not make sense given the way in which some of the data has been encoded; for example, $-1^2 = 1$, which may not be sensible for **PAY_1**. However, we may wish to try creating interaction features to capture the relationships between features. **PolynomialFeatures** can be used to create interaction features only, without polynomial features. The example code is as follows:

```
make_interactions = PolynomialFeatures(degree=2, \
                                       interaction_only=True, \
                                       include_bias=False)
```

Here, **degree** represents the degree of the polynomial features, **interaction_only** takes a Boolean value (setting it to **True** indicates that only interaction features will be created), and so does **include_bias**, which adds an intercept to the model (the default value is **False**, which is correct here as the logistic regression model will add an intercept).

## ACTIVITY 4.01: CROSS-VALIDATION AND FEATURE ENGINEERING WITH THE CASE STUDY DATA

In this activity, we'll apply the knowledge of cross-validation and regularization that we've learned in this chapter to the case study data. We'll perform basic feature engineering. In order to estimate parameters for the regularized logistic regression model for the case study data, which is larger in size than the synthetic data that we've worked with, we'll use the **saga** solver. In order to use this solver, and for the purpose of regularization, we'll need to **scale** our data as part of the modeling process, leading us to the use of **Pipeline** class in scikit-learn. Once you have completed the activity, you should obtain an improved cross-validation test performance with the use of interaction features, as shown in the following diagram:

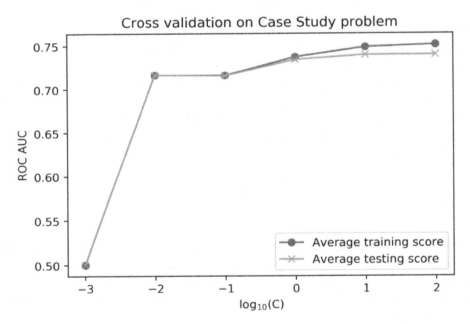

Figure 4.24: Improved model test performance

Perform the following steps to complete the activity:

1.  Select the features from the DataFrame of the case study data.

    You can use the list of feature names that we've already created in this chapter, but be sure not to include the response variable, which would be a very good (but entirely inappropriate) feature!

2.  Make a training/test split using a random seed of 24.

We'll use this going forward and reserve this test data as the unseen test set. By specifying the random seed, we can easily create separate notebooks with other modeling approaches using the same training data.

3. Instantiate **MinMaxScaler** to scale the data.

4. Instantiate a logistic regression model with the **saga** solver, L1 penalty, and set **max_iter** to **1000** as we want the solver to have enough iterations to find a good solution.

5. Import the **Pipeline** class and create a pipeline with the scaler and the logistic regression model, using the names **'scaler'** and **'model'** for the steps, respectively.

6. Use the **get_params** and **set_params** methods to see how to view the parameters from each stage of the pipeline and change them.

7. Create a smaller range of $C$ values to test with cross-validation, as these models will take longer to train and test with more data than our previous exercise; we recommend $C = [10^2, 10, 1, 10^{-1}, 10^{-2}, 10^{-3}]$.

8. Make a new version of the **cross_val_C_search** function called **cross_val_C_search_pipe**. Instead of the **model** argument, this function will take a **pipeline** argument. The changes inside the function will be to set the $C$ value using **set_params(model__C = <value you want to test>)** on the pipeline, replacing the model with the pipeline for the **fit** and **predict_proba** methods, and accessing the $C$ value using **pipeline.get_params()['model__C']** for the printed status update.

9. Run this function as in the previous exercise, but using the new range of $C$ values, the pipeline you created, and the features and response variable from the training split of the case study data.

   You may see warnings here, or in later steps, regarding the non-convergence of the solver; you could experiment with the **tol** or **max_iter** options to try and achieve convergence, although the results you obtain with **max_iter = 1000** are likely to be sufficient.

10. Plot the average training and test ROC AUC across folds for each $C$ value.

11. Create interaction features for the case study data and confirm that the number of new features makes sense.

12. Repeat the cross-validation procedure and observe the model performance when using interaction features.

Note that this will take substantially more time, due to the larger number of features, but it will probably take less than 10 minutes. So, does the average cross-validation test performance improve with the interaction features? Is regularization useful?

> **NOTE**
>
> The Jupyter notebook containing the Python code for this activity can be found at https://packt.link/ohGgX. Detailed step-wise solution to this activity can be found on page 380.

## SUMMARY

In this chapter, we introduced the final details of logistic regression and continued to understand how to use scikit-learn to fit logistic regression models. We gained more visibility into how the model fitting process works by learning about the concept of a cost function, which is minimized by the gradient descent procedure to estimate parameters during model fitting.

We also learned of the need for regularization by introducing the concepts of underfitting and overfitting. In order to reduce overfitting, we saw how to adjust the cost function to regularize the coefficients of a logistic regression model using an L1 or L2 penalty. We used cross-validation to select the amount of regularization by tuning the regularization hyperparameter. To reduce underfitting, we saw how to do some simple feature engineering with interaction features for the case study data.

We are now familiar with some of the most important concepts in machine learning. We have, so far, only used a very basic classification model: logistic regression. However, as you increase your toolbox of models that you know how to use, you will find that the concepts of overfitting and underfitting, the bias-variance trade-off, and hyperparameter tuning will come up again and again. These ideas, as well as convenient scikit-learn implementations of the cross-validation functions that we wrote in this chapter, will help us through our exploration of more advanced prediction methods.

In the next chapter, we will learn about decision trees, an entirely different type of predictive model than logistic regression, and the random forests that are based on them. However, we will use the same concepts that we learned here, cross-validation and hyperparameter search, to tune these models.

# 5

# DECISION TREES AND RANDOM FORESTS

## OVERVIEW

In this chapter, we'll shift our focus to another type of machine learning model that has taken data science by storm in recent years: tree-based models. In this chapter, after learning about trees individually, you'll then learn how models made up of many trees, called random forests, can improve the overfitting associated with individual trees. After reading this chapter, you will be able to train decision trees for machine learning purposes, visualize trained decision trees, and train random forests and visualize the results.

# INTRODUCTION

In the last two chapters, we have gained a thorough understanding of the workings of logistic regression. We have also gotten a lot of experience with using the scikit-learn package in Python to create logistic regression models.

In this chapter, we will introduce a powerful type of predictive model that takes a completely different approach from the logistic regression model: **decision trees**. Decision trees and the models based on them are some of the most performant models available today for general machine learning applications. The concept of using a tree process to make decisions is simple, and therefore, decision tree models are easy to interpret. However, a common criticism of decision trees is that they overfit to the training data. In order to remedy this issue, researchers have developed **ensemble methods**, such as **random forests**, that combine many decision trees to work together and make better predictions than any individual tree could.

We will see that decision trees and random forests can improve the quality of the predictive modeling of the case study data beyond what we have achieved so far with logistic regression.

# DECISION TREES

**Decision trees** and the machine learning models that are based on them, in particular, **random forests** and **gradient boosted trees**, are fundamentally different types of models than Generalized Linear Models (GLMs), such as logistic regression. GLMs are rooted in the theories of classical statistics, which have a long history. The mathematics behind linear regression was originally developed at the beginning of the 19th century, by Legendre and Gauss. Because of this, the normal distribution is also known as the Gaussian distribution.

In contrast, while the idea of using a tree process to make decisions is relatively simple, the popularity of decision trees as mathematical models has come about more recently. The mathematical procedures that we currently use for formulating decision trees in the context of predictive modeling were published in the 1980s. The reason for this more recent development is that the methods used to grow decision trees rely on computational power – that is, the ability to crunch a lot of numbers quickly. We take such capabilities for granted nowadays, but they weren't widely available until more recently in the history of mathematics.

So, what is meant by a decision tree? We can illustrate the basic concept using a practical example. Imagine that you are considering whether or not to venture outdoors on a certain day. The only information you will base your decision on involves the weather and, in particular, whether the sun is shining and how warm it is. If it is sunny, your tolerance for cool temperatures is increased, and you will go outside if the temperature is at least 10 °C.

However, if it's cloudy, you require somewhat warmer temperatures and will only go outside if the temperature is 15 °C or more. Your decision-making process could be represented by the following tree:

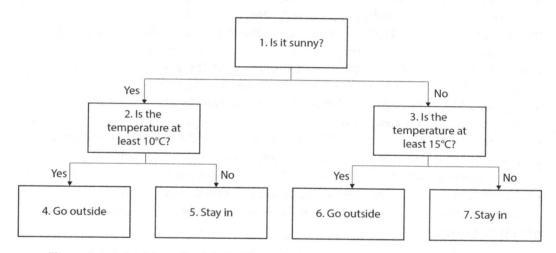

**Figure 5.1: A decision tree for deciding whether to go outside given the weather**

As you can see, decision trees have an intuitive structure and mimic the way that logical decisions might be made by humans. Therefore, they are a highly **interpretable** type of mathematical model, which can be a particularly desirable property depending on the audience. For example, the client for a data science project may be especially interested in a clear understanding of how a model works. Decision trees are a good way of delivering on this requirement, as long as their performance is sufficient.

# THE TERMINOLOGY OF DECISION TREES AND CONNECTIONS TO MACHINE LEARNING

Looking at the tree in *Figure 5.1*, we can begin to become familiar with some of the terminology of decision trees. Because there are two levels of decisions being made, based on cloud conditions at the first level and temperature at the second level, we say that this decision tree has a **depth** of two. Here, both **nodes** at the second level are temperature-based decisions, but the kinds of decisions could be different within a level; for example, we could base our decision on whether or not it was raining if it was not sunny.

In the context of machine learning, the quantities that are used to make decisions at the nodes (in other words, to **split** the nodes) are the features. The features in the example in *Figure 5.1* are a binary categorical feature for whether it's sunny, and a continuous feature for temperature. While we have only illustrated each feature being used once in a given branch of the tree, the same feature could be used multiple times in a branch. For example, we may choose to go outside on a sunny day with a temperature of at least 10 °C, but not if it were more than 40 °C – that's too hot! In this case, node 4 of *Figure 5.1* would be split on the condition "Is the temperature greater than 40 °C?" where "stay in" is the outcome if the answer is "yes," but "go outside" is the outcome if the answer is "no," meaning that the temperature is between 10 °C and 40 °C. Decision trees are therefore able to capture non-linear effects of the features, as opposed to a linear relationship that might assume that the hotter it was, the more likely we would be to go outside, regardless of how hot it was.

Consider the way that trees are typically represented, such as in *Figure 5.1*. The branches grow downward based on the binary decisions that can split the nodes into two more nodes. These binary decisions can be thought of as "if, then" rules. In other words, if a certain condition is met, do this, otherwise, do something else. The decision being made in our example tree is analogous to the concept of the response variable in machine learning. If we made a decision tree for the case study problem of credit default, the decisions would instead be predictions of the binary response values, which are "this account defaults" or "this account doesn't default." A tree that answers a binary yes/no type of question is a **classification tree**. However, decision trees are quite versatile and can also be used for multiclass classification and regression.

The terminal nodes at the bottom of the tree are called **leaves**, or leaf nodes. In our example, the leaves are the final decisions as to whether to go outside or stay in. There are four leaves on our tree, although you can imagine that if the tree only had a depth of one, where we made our decision based only on cloud conditions, there would be two leaves; and nodes 2 and 3 in *Figure 5.1* would be leaf nodes with "go outside" and "stay in" as the decisions, respectively.

In our example, every node at every level before the final level is split. This is not strictly necessary as you may go outside on any sunny day, regardless of the temperature. In this case, node 2 will not be split, so this branch of the tree will end on the first level with a "yes" decision. Your decision on cloudy days, however, may involve temperature, meaning this branch can extend to a further level. In the case that every node before the final level is split, consider how quickly the number of leaves grows with the number of levels.

For example, what would happen if we grew the decision tree in *Figure 5.1* down through an additional level, perhaps with a wind speed feature, to factor in wind chill for the four combinations of cloud conditions and temperature. Each of the four nodes that are now leaves, nodes numbered from four to seven in *Figure 5.1*, would be split into two more leaf nodes, based on wind speed in each case. Then, there would be *4 × 2 = 8* leaf nodes. In general, it should be clear that in a tree with n levels, where every node before the final level is split, there will be *2n* leaf nodes. This is important to bear in mind as **maximum depth** is one of the hyperparameters that you can set for a decision tree classifier in scikit-learn. We'll now explore this in the following exercise.

## EXERCISE 5.01: A DECISION TREE IN SCIKIT-LEARN

In this exercise, we will use the case study data to grow a decision tree, where we specify the maximum depth. We'll also use some handy functionality to visualize the decision tree, in the form of the `graphviz` package. Perform the following steps to complete the exercise:

> **NOTE**
>
> The Jupyter notebook for this exercise can be found at https://packt.link/
> IUt7d. Before you begin the exercise, please ensure that you have followed
> the instructions in the *Preface* regarding setting up your environment and
> importing the necessary libraries.

1. Load several of the packages that we've been using, and an additional one, **graphviz**, so that we can visualize decision trees:

```
import numpy as np #numerical computation
import pandas as pd #data wrangling
import matplotlib.pyplot as plt #plotting package
#Next line helps with rendering plots
%matplotlib inline
import matplotlib as mpl #add'l plotting functionality
mpl.rcParams['figure.dpi'] = 400 #high res figures
import graphviz #to visualize decision trees
```

2. Load the cleaned case study data:

```
df = pd.read_csv('../Data/Chapter_1_cleaned_data.csv')
```

> **NOTE**
>
> The location of the cleaned data may differ depending on where you saved it.

3. Get a list of column names of the DataFrame:

```
features_response = df.columns.tolist()
```

4. Make a list of columns to remove that aren't features or the response variable:

```
items_to_remove = ['ID', 'SEX', 'PAY_2', 'PAY_3',\
                   'PAY_4', 'PAY_5', 'PAY_6',\
                   'EDUCATION_CAT', 'graduate school',\
                   'high school', 'none',\
                   'others', 'university']
```

5. Use a list comprehension to remove these column names from our list of features and the response variable:

```
features_response = [item for item in features_response if item not
in items_to_remove]
features_response
```

This should output the list of features and the response variable:

```
['LIMIT_BAL',
 'EDUCATION',
 'MARRIAGE',
```

```
'AGE',
'PAY_1',
'BILL_AMT1',
'BILL_AMT2',
'BILL_AMT3',
'BILL_AMT4',
'BILL_AMT5',
'BILL_AMT6',
'PAY_AMT1',
'PAY_AMT2',
'PAY_AMT3',
'PAY_AMT4',
'PAY_AMT5',
'PAY_AMT6',
'default payment next month']
```

Now the list of features is prepared. Next, we will make some imports from scikit-learn. We want to make a train/test split, which we are already familiar with. We also want to import the decision tree functionality.

6. Run this code to make imports from scikit-learn:

```
from sklearn.model_selection import train_test_split
from sklearn import tree
```

The **tree** library of scikit-learn contains decision tree-related classes.

7. Split the data into training and testing sets using the same random seed that we have used throughout the book:

```
X_train, X_test, y_train, y_test = \
train_test_split(df[features_response[:-1]].values,
                 df['default payment next month'].values,
                 test_size=0.2, random_state=24)
```

Here, we use all but the last element of the list to get the names of the features, but not the response variable: **features_response[:-1]**. We use this to select columns from the DataFrame, and then retrieve their values using the **.values** method. We also do something similar for the response variable, but specify the column name directly. In making the train/test split, we've used the same random seed as in previous work, as well as the same split size. This way, we can directly compare the work we will do in this chapter with previous results. Also, we continue to reserve the same "unseen test set" from the model development process.

Now we are ready to instantiate the decision tree class.

8. Instantiate the decision tree class by setting the **max_depth** parameter to **2**:

```
dt = tree.DecisionTreeClassifier(max_depth=2)
```

We have used the **DecisionTreeClassifier** class because we have a classification problem. Since we specified **max_depth=2**, when we grow the decision tree using the case study data, the tree will grow to a depth of at most **2**. Let's now train this model.

9. Use this code to fit the decision tree model and grow the tree:

```
dt.fit(X_train, y_train)
```

This should display the following output:

```
DecisionTreeClassifier(max_depth=2)
```

Now that we have fit this decision tree model, we can use the **graphviz** package to display a graphical representation of the tree.

10. Export the trained model in a format that can be read by the **graphviz** package using this code:

```
dot_data = tree.export_graphviz(dt,
                                out_file=None,
                                filled=True,
                                rounded=True,
                                feature_names=\
                                features_response[:-1],
                                proportion=True,
                                class_names=[
                                'Not defaulted', 'Defaulted'])
```

Here, we've provided a number of options for the **.export_graphviz** method. First, we need to say which trained model we'd like to graph, which is **dt**. Next, we say we don't want an output file: **out_file=None**. Instead, we provide the **dot_data** variable to hold the output of this method. The rest of the options are set as follows:

**filled=True**: Each node will be filled with a color.

**rounded=True**: The nodes will appear with rounded edges as opposed to rectangles.

**feature_names=features_response[:-1]**: The names of the features from our list will be used as opposed to generic names such as **X[0]**.

**proportion=True**: The proportion of training samples in each node will be displayed (we'll discuss this more later).

**class_names=['Not defaulted', 'Defaulted']**: The name of the predicted class will be displayed for each node.

What is the output of this method?

If you examine the contents of **dot_data**, you will see that it is a long text string. The **graphviz** package can interpret this text string to create a visualization.

11. Use the **.Source** method of the **graphviz** package to create an image from **dot_data** and display it:

```
graph = graphviz.Source(dot_data)
graph
```

The output should look like this:

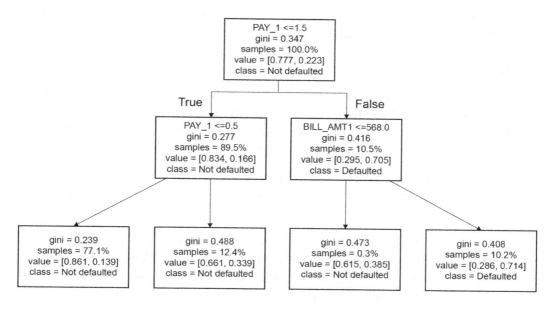

**Figure 5.2: A decision tree plot from graphviz**

The graphical representation of the decision tree in *Figure 5.2* should be rendered directly in your Jupyter notebook.

> **NOTE**
>
> Alternatively, you could save the output of `.export_graphviz` to disk by providing a file path to the `out_file` keyword argument. To turn this output file into an image file, for example, a `.png` file that you could use in a presentation, you could run this code at the command line, substituting in the filenames as appropriate: `$ dot -Tpng <exported_file_name> -o <image_file_name_you_want>.png`.
>
> For further details on the options relating to `.export_graphviz`, you should consult the scikit-learn documentation (https://scikit-learn.org/stable/modules/generated/sklearn.tree.export_graphviz.html).

The visualization in *Figure 5.2* contains a lot of information about how the decision tree was trained, and how it can be used to make predictions. We will discuss the training process in more detail later, but suffice to say that training a decision tree works by starting with all the training samples in the initial node at the top of the tree, and then splitting these into two groups based on a **threshold** in one of the features. The cut point is represented by the inequality `PAY_1 <= 1.5` in the first node.

All the samples where the value of the `PAY_1` feature is less than or equal to the cut point of `1.5` will be represented as **True** under this Boolean condition. As shown in *Figure 5.2*, these samples get sorted into the left side of the tree, following the arrow that says **True** next to it.

As you can see in the graph, each node that is split contains the splitting criteria on the first line of text. The next line relates to `gini`, which we will discuss shortly.

The following line contains information about the proportion of samples in each node. In the top node, we are starting with all the samples (`samples = 100.0%`). Following the first split, 89.5% of the samples get sorted into the node on the left, while the remaining 10.5% go into the node on the right. This information is shown directly in the visualization and reflects how the training data was used to create the tree. Let's confirm this by examining the training data.

12. To confirm the proportion of training samples where the **PAY_1** feature is less than or equal to **1.5**, first identify the index of this feature in the list of **features_response[:-1]** feature names:

```
features_response[:-1].index('PAY_1')
```

This code should output the following:

```
4
```

13. Now, observe the shape of the training data:

```
X_train.shape
```

This should give you the following output:

```
(21331, 17)
```

To confirm the fraction of samples following the first split of the decision tree, we need to know the proportion of samples, where the **PAY_1** feature meets the Boolean condition, that was used to make this split. To do this, we can use the index of the **PAY_1** feature in the training data, corresponding to the index in the list of feature names, and the number of samples in the training data, which is the number of rows we observed from **.shape**.

14. Use this code to confirm the proportion of samples after the first split of the decision tree:

```
(X_train[:,4] <= 1.5).sum()/X_train.shape[0]
```

The output should be as follows:

```
0.8946134733486475
```

By applying a logical condition to the column of the training data corresponding to the **PAY_1** feature, and then taking the sum of this, we calculated the number of samples meeting this condition. Then, by dividing by the total number of samples, we converted this to a proportion. We can see that the proportion we directly calculated from the training data is equal to the proportion displayed in the left node following the first split in *Figure 5.2*.

Following the first split, the samples contained in each of the two nodes on the first level are split again. As further splits are made beyond the first split, smaller and smaller proportions of the training data will be assigned to any given node in the subsequent levels of a branch, as can be seen in *Figure 5.2*.

Now we want to interpret the remaining lines of text in the nodes in *Figure 5.2*. The lines starting with **value** give the class fractions of the response variable for the samples contained in each node. For example, in the top node, we see **value = [0.777, 0.223]**. These are simply the class fractions for the overall training set, which you can confirm in the following step.

15. Calculate the class fraction in the training set with this code:

```
y_train.mean()
```

The output should be as follows:

```
0.223102526838873
```

This is equal to the second member of the pair of numbers following **value** in the top node; the first number is simply one minus this, in other words, the fraction of negative training samples. In each subsequent node, the class fractions of the samples that are contained in that node are displayed. The class fractions are also how the nodes are colored: those with a higher proportion of the negative class than the positive class are orange, with darker orange signifying higher proportions, while those with a higher proportion of the positive class have a similar scheme using a blue color.

Finally, the line starting with **class** indicates how the decision tree would make predictions from a given node, if that node were a leaf node. Decision trees for classification make predictions by determining which leaf node a sample will be sorted into, given the values of the features, and then predicting the class of the majority of the training samples in that leaf node. This strategy means that the tree structure and the class proportions in the leaf nodes are pieces of information that are needed to make a prediction.

For example, if we've made no splits and we are forced to make a prediction knowing nothing but the class fractions for the overall training data, we will simply choose the majority class. Since most people don't default, the class on the top node is **Not defaulted**. However, the class fractions in the nodes of deeper levels are different, leading to different predictions. How does scikit-learn decide the structure of the tree? We'll discuss the training process in the following section.

**Importance of max_depth**

Recall that the only hyperparameter we specified in this exercise was **max_depth**, that is, the maximum depth to which the decision tree can be grown during the model training process. It turns out that this is one of the most important hyperparameters. Without placing a limit on the depth, the tree will be grown until one of the other limitations, specified by other hyperparameters, takes effect. This can lead to very deep trees, with very many nodes. For example, consider how many leaf nodes there could be in a tree with a depth of 20. This would be *220* leaf nodes, which is over 1 million! Do we even have 1 million training samples to sort into all these nodes? In this case, we do not. It would clearly be impossible to grow such a tree, with every node before the final level being split, using this training data. However, if we remove the **max_depth** limit and rerun the model training of this exercise, observe the effect:

Figure 5.3: A portion of the decision tree grown with no maximum depth

Here, we have shown a portion of the decision tree that is grown with the default options, which include **max_depth=None**, meaning no limit in terms of the depth of the tree. The entire tree is about twice as wide as the portion shown here. There are so many nodes that they only appear as very small orange or blue patches; the exact interpretation of each node is not important as we are just trying to illustrate how large trees can potentially be. It should be clear that without hyperparameters to govern the tree-growing process, extremely large and complex trees may result.

# TRAINING DECISION TREES: NODE IMPURITY

At this point, you should have an understanding of how a decision tree makes predictions using features, and the class fractions of training samples in the leaf nodes. Now, we will learn how decision trees are trained. The training process involves selecting features to split nodes on, and the thresholds at which to make splits, for example **PAY_1 <= 1.5** for the first split in the tree of the previous exercise. Computationally, this means the samples in each node must be sorted on the values of each feature to consider a split for, and splits between each successive pair of sorted feature values are considered. All features may be considered, or only a subset as we will learn about shortly.

**How Are the Splits Decided during the Training Process?**

Given that the method of prediction is to take the majority class of a leaf node, it makes sense that we'd like to find leaf nodes that are primarily from one class or the other; choosing the majority class will be a more accurate prediction, the closer a node is to containing just one class. In the perfect case, the training data can be split so that every leaf node contains entirely positive or entirely negative samples. Then, we will have a high level of confidence that a new sample, once sorted into one of these nodes, will be either positive or negative. In practice, this rarely, if ever, happens. However, this illustrates the goal of training decision trees – that is, to make splits so that the next two nodes after the split have a higher **purity**, or, in other words, are closer to containing either only positive or only negative samples.

In practice, decision trees are actually trained using the inverse of purity, or **node impurity**. This is some measure of how far the node is from having 100% of the training samples belonging to one class and is analogous to the concept of a cost function, which signifies how far a given solution is from a theoretical perfect solution. The most intuitive concept of node impurity is the **misclassification rate**. Adopting a widely used notation (for example, https://scikit-learn.org/stable/modules/tree.html) for the proportion of samples in each node belonging to a certain class, we can define $p_{mk}$ as the proportion of samples belonging to the $k^{th}$ class in the $m^{th}$ node. In a binary classification problem, there are only two classes: $k = 0$ and $k = 1$. For a given node $m$, the misclassification rate is simply the proportion of the less common class in that node, since all these samples will be misclassified when the majority class in that node is taken as the prediction.

Let's visualize the misclassification rate as a way to start thinking about how decision trees are trained. Programmatically, we consider possible class fractions, $p_{m0}$, between 0.01 and 0.99 of the negative class, $k = 0$, in a node, $m$, using NumPy's `linspace` function:

```
pm0 = np.linspace(0.01,0.99,99)
pm1 = 1 - pm0
```

Then, the fraction of the positive class for this node is one minus $p_{m0}$:

$$p_{m1} = 1 - p_{m0}$$

**Figure 5.4: Equation for calculating the positive class fraction for node m0**

Now, the misclassification rate for this node will be whatever the smaller class fraction is, between $p_{m0}$ and $p_{m1}$. We can find the smaller of the corresponding elements between two arrays with the same shape in NumPy by using the **minimum** function:

```
misclassification_rate = np.minimum(pm0, pm1)
```

What does the misclassification rate look like plotted against the possible class fractions of the negative class?

We can plot this using the following code:

```
mpl.rcParams['figure.dpi'] = 400
plt.plot(pm0, misclassification_rate,
        label='Misclassification rate')
plt.xlabel('$p_{m0}$')
plt.legend()
```

You should obtain this graph:

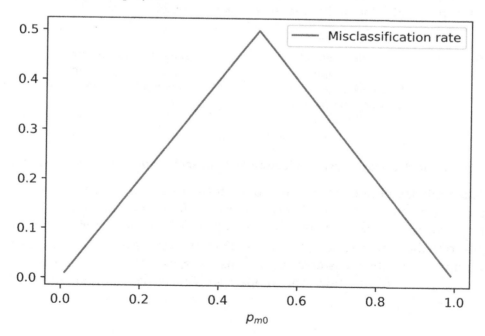

Figure 5.5: The misclassification rate for a node

Now, it's clear that the closer the class fraction of the negative class, $p_{m0}$, is to 0 or 1, the lower the misclassification rate will be. How is this information used when growing decision trees? Consider the process that might be followed.

Every time a node is split when growing a decision tree, two new nodes are created. Since the prediction from either of these new nodes is simply the majority class, an important goal will be to reduce the misclassification rate. Therefore, we will want to find a feature, from all the possible features, and a value of this feature at which to make a cut point, so that the misclassification rate in the two new nodes will be as low as possible when averaging over all the classes. This is very close to the actual process that is used to train decision trees.

Continuing for the moment with the idea of minimizing the misclassification rate, the decision tree training algorithm goes about node splitting by considering all the features, although the algorithm may possibly only consider a randomly selected subset if you set the **max_features** hyperparameter to anything less than the total number of features. We'll discuss possible reasons for doing this later. In either case, the algorithm then considers each possible threshold for every candidate feature and chooses the one that results in the lowest impurity, calculated as the average impurity across the two possible new nodes, weighted by the number of samples in each node. The node splitting process is shown in *Figure 5.6*. This process is repeated until a stopping criterion of the tree, such as **max_depth**, is reached:

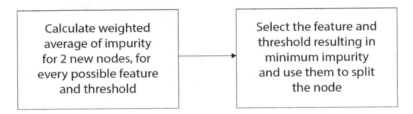

**Figure 5.6: How to select a feature and threshold in order to split a node**

While the misclassification rate is an intuitive measure of impurity, it happens that there are better measures that can be used to find splits during the model training process. The two options that are available in scikit-learn for the impurity calculation, which you can specify with the **criterion** keyword argument, are the **Gini impurity** and the **cross-entropy** options. Here, we will describe these options mathematically and show how they compare with the misclassification rate.

Gini impurity is calculated for a node $m$ using the following formula:

$$Gini = \sum_k p_{mk}(1 - p_{mk})$$

**Figure 5.7: Equation for calculating Gini impurity**

Here, the summation is taken over all classes. In the case of a binary classification problem, there are only two classes, and we can write this programmatically as follows:

```
gini = (pm0*(1-pm0)) + (pm1*(1-pm1))
```

Cross-entropy is calculated using this formula:

$$cross\ entropy = -\sum_k p_{mk} \log(p_{mk})$$

**Figure 5.8: Equation for calculating cross-entropy**

Using this code, we can calculate the cross-entropy:

```
cross_ent = -1*((pm0*np.log(pm0)) + (pm1*np.log(pm1)))
```

In order to add Gini impurity and cross-entropy to our plot of misclassification rate and see how they compare, we just need to include the following lines of code after we plot the misclassification rate:

```
mpl.rcParams['figure.dpi'] = 400
plt.plot(pm0, misclassification_rate,\
        label='Misclassification rate')
plt.plot(pm0, gini, label='Gini impurity')
plt.plot(pm0, cross_ent, label='Cross entropy')
plt.xlabel('$p_{m0}$')
plt.legend()
```

The final plot should appear as follows:

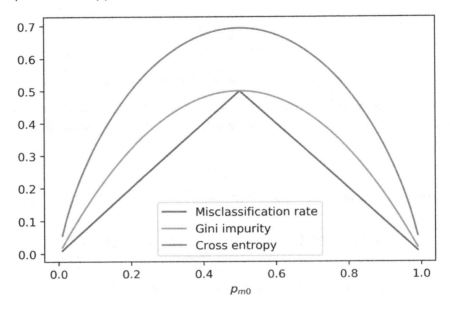

**Figure 5.9: The misclassification rate, Gini impurity, and cross-entropy**

> **NOTE**
>
> If you're reading the print version of this book, you can download and browse the color versions of some of the images in this chapter by visiting the following link:
>
> https://packt.link/mQ4Xn

Like the misclassification rate, both the Gini impurity and cross-entropy are highest when the class fractions are equal at 0.5, and they decrease as the node becomes purer – in other words, when they contain a higher proportion of just one of the classes. However, the Gini impurity is somewhat steeper than the misclassification rate in certain regions of the class fraction, which enables it to more effectively find the best split. Cross-entropy looks even steeper. So, which one is better for your work? This is the kind of question that does not have a concrete answer across all datasets. You should consider both impurity metrics in a cross-validation search for hyperparameters in order to determine the appropriate one. Note that in scikit-learn, Gini impurity can be specified with the **`criterion`** argument using the **`'gini'`** string, while cross-entropy is just referred to as **`'entropy'`**.

## FEATURES USED FOR THE FIRST SPLITS: CONNECTIONS TO UNIVARIATE FEATURE SELECTION AND INTERACTIONS

We can begin to get an impression of how important various features are to decision tree models, based on the small tree shown in *Figure 5.2*. Notice that **PAY_1** was the feature chosen for the first split. This means that it was the best feature in terms of decreasing node impurity on the node containing all of the training samples. Recall our experience with univariate feature selection in *Chapter 3, Details of Logistic Regression and Feature Exploration*, where **PAY_1** was the top-selected feature from the F-test. So, the appearance of this feature in the first split of the decision tree makes sense given our previous analysis.

In the second level of the tree, there is another split on **PAY_1**, as well as a split on **BILL_AMT_1**. **BILL_AMT_1** was not listed among the top features in univariate feature selection. However, it may be that there is an important interaction between **BILL_AMT_1** and **PAY_1**, which would not be found up by univariate methods. In particular, from the splits chosen by the decision tree, it seems that those accounts with both a value of 2 or greater for **PAY_1**, and a **BILL_AMT_1** of greater than 568, are especially at risk of default. This combined effect of **PAY_1** and **BILL_AMT_1** is an interaction and may also be why we were able to improve logistic regression performance by including interaction terms in the activity of the previous chapter.

## TRAINING DECISION TREES: A GREEDY ALGORITHM

There is no guarantee that a decision tree trained by the process described previously will be the best possible decision tree for finding leaf nodes with the lowest impurity. This is because the algorithm used to train decision trees is what is called a greedy algorithm. In this context, this means that at each opportunity to split a node, the algorithm is looking for the best possible split at that point in time, without any regard for the fact that the opportunities for later splits are being affected.

For example, consider the following hypothetical scenario: the best initial split for the training data of the case study involves **PAY_1**, as we've seen in *Figure 5.2*. But what if we instead split on **BILL_AMT_1**, and then make subsequent splits on **PAY_1** in the next level? Even though the initial split on **BILL_AMT_1** is not the best one available at first, it is possible that the end result will be better if the tree is grown this way. The algorithm has no way of finding solutions like this if they exist, since it only considers the best possible split at each node and not possible future splits.

The reason why we still use greedy tree-growing algorithms is that it takes substantially longer to consider all possible splits in a way that enables the truly optimal tree to be found. Despite this shortcoming of the decision tree training process, there are methods that you can use to reduce the possible harmful effects of the greedy algorithm. Instead of searching for the best split at each node, the **splitter** keyword argument to the decision tree class can be set to **random** in order to choose a random feature to make a split on. However, the default is **best**, which searches all features for the best split. Another option, which we've already discussed, is to limit the number of features that will be searched at each splitting opportunity using the **max_features** keyword. Finally, you can also use ensembles of decision trees, such as random forests, which we will describe shortly. Note that all these options, in addition to possibly avoiding the ill-effects of the greedy algorithm, are also options for addressing the overfitting that decision trees are often criticized for.

## TRAINING DECISION TREES: DIFFERENT STOPPING CRITERIA AND OTHER OPTIONS

We have already reviewed using the **max_depth** parameter as a limit to how deep a tree will grow. However, there are several other options available in scikit-learn as well. These are mainly related to how many samples are present in a leaf node, or how much the impurity can be decreased by further splitting nodes. As discussed previously, you may be limited by the size of your dataset in terms of how deep you can grow a tree. And it may not make sense to grow trees deeper, especially if the splitting process is no longer finding nodes with substantially higher purity.

We summarize all of the keyword arguments that you can supply to the **DecisionTreeClassifier** class in scikit-learn here:

| Parameter | Possible values | Notes |
|---|---|---|
| criterion | string, 'gini', or 'entropy' | The formula used to calculate node impurity. |
| splitter | string, 'best', or 'random' | Whether to search among all candidate features when making a split, or to choose one at random. |
| max_depth | int or None | Stopping criterion. None means there is no limit to the maximum depth for growing the tree, although the tree may be stopped for reasons specified in other hyperparameters. An integer means stop growing the tree after that many levels. |
| min_samples_split | int or float | Stopping criterion. If an integer, then a node must have at least this many samples in order to be split. If a float, it is the fraction of the total number of samples that must be in a node to split it. |
| min_samples_leaf | int or float | Stopping criterion. Similar to min_samples_split, but this refers to the number of samples that will be in the nodes following the split. Refers to a node at any depth. |
| min_weight_fraction_leaf | Float | Similar to min_samples_leaf, but uses the weight fraction of samples instead of the fraction of samples. Useful only if sample weighting has been specified with the class_weight parameter. |
| max_features | int, float, string: 'auto', 'sqrt', 'log2', or None | Strategy for how many features to consider when trying to split a node. If None, all the features are considered. If an int or float, that number or fraction of features are considered. 'auto' and 'sqrt' both use the square root of the number of features, and 'log2' uses the base 2 logarithm. If the number here is less than the total number of features, a random selection of features is taken. However, more than this number of features may be considered if none of the random selection satisfies other criteria such as min_impurity_decrease. |
| random_state | int or None | If an integer is supplied, this will seed the random number generator for repeatable results between runs of the same code. |
| max_leaf_nodes | int or None | Stopping criterion. The maximum number of leaf nodes if an integer is supplied, or no limit for None. |
| min_impurity_decrease | Float | Stopping criterion. If larger than 0, the required decrease in impurity to split a node. This means the tree only keeps growing if the nodes are getting purer. |
| min_impurity_split | Float | Stopping criterion, but being phased out. Use min_impurity_decrease instead. |
| class_weight | dict, list of dict, 'balanced', or None | If the response variable has imbalanced classes, 'balanced' will weight samples similar to logistic regression. Here, this would be used to calculate the weighted average of node impurity. A dictionary can be used to manually supply class weights. A list of dictionaries can be used for multi-output problems, which is when there are multiple response variables (beyond the scope of this book). None does no sample weighting. |
| ccp_alpha | Non-negative float | Related to a process called pruning, which means removing nodes after the tree is grown. |

**Figure 5.10: The complete list of options for the decision tree classifier in scikit-learn**

# USING DECISION TREES: ADVANTAGES AND PREDICTED PROBABILITIES

While decision trees are simple in concept, they have several practical advantages.

## No Need to Scale Features

Consider the reasons why we needed to scale features for logistic regression. One reason is that, for some of the solution algorithms based on gradient descent, it is necessary that the features are on the same scale in order to quickly find a minimum of the cost function. Another is that when we are using L1 or L2 regularization to penalize coefficients, all the features must be on the same scale so that they are penalized equally. With decision trees, the node splitting algorithm considers each feature individually and, therefore, it doesn't matter whether the features are on the same scale.

## Non-Linear Relationships and Interactions

Because each successive split in a decision tree is performed on a subset of the training samples resulting from the previous split(s), decision trees can describe complex non-linear relationships of a single feature, as well as interactions between features. Consider our discussion previously in the *Features Used for the First Splits: Connections to Univariate Feature Selection and Interactions* section. Also, as a hypothetical example with synthetic data, consider the following dataset for classification:

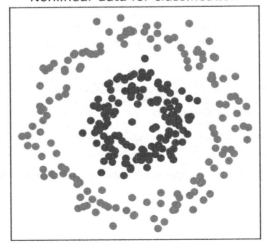

Nonlinear data for classification

Figure 5.11: An example classification dataset, with the classes shown in red and blue (if reading in black and white, please refer to the GitHub repository for a color version of this figure; the blue dots are on the inside circle)

We know from *Chapter 3, Details of Logistic Regression and Feature Exploration*, that logistic regression has a linear decision boundary. So, how do you think logistic regression would cope with a dataset like that shown in *Figure 5.11*? Where would you draw a line to separate the blue and red classes? It should be clear that without engineering additional features, a logistic regression is not likely to be a good classifier for this data. Now think about the set of "if, then" rules of a decision tree, which could be used with the features represented on the *x* and *y* axes of *Figure 5.11*. Do you think a decision tree will be effective with this data?

Here, we plot in the background the predicted probabilities of class membership using red and blue, for both of these models:

Figure 5.12: Decision tree and logistic regression predictions

In *Figure 5.12*, the predicted probabilities for both models are colored so that darker red corresponds to a higher predicted probability for the red class, and darker blue for the blue class. We can see that the decision tree can isolate the blue class in the middle of the circle of red points. This is because, by using thresholds for the *x* and *y* coordinates in the node-splitting process, a decision tree can mathematically model the fact that the location of the blue and red classes depends on both the *x* and *y* coordinates together (interactions), and that the likelihood of either class is not a linearly increasing or decreasing function of *x* or *y* (non-linearities). Consequently, the decision tree approach is able to get most classifications right.

> **NOTE**
>
> The code to generate *Figures 5.11* and *5.12* can be found in the reference notebook: https://packt.link/9W4WN.

However, the logistic regression has a linear decision boundary, which will be the straight line between the lightest blue and red patches in the background. The logistic regression decision boundary goes right through the middle of the data and doesn't provide a useful classifier. This shows the power of decision trees "out of the box," without the need for engineering non-linear or interaction features.

**Predicted Probabilities**

We know that logistic regression produces probabilities as raw output. However, a decision tree makes predictions based on the majority class of the leaf nodes. So, where would predicted probabilities come from, like those shown in *Figure 5.12*? In fact, decision trees do offer the `.predict_proba` method in scikit-learn to calculate predicted probabilities. The probability is based on the proportion of the majority class in the leaf node used for a given prediction. If 75% of the samples in a leaf node belonged to the positive class, for example, the prediction for that node would be the positive class and the predicted probability will be 0.75. The predicted probabilities from decision trees are not considered to be as statistically rigorous as those from generalized linear models, but they are still commonly used to measure the performance of models by methods that depend on varying the threshold for classification, such as the ROC curve or the precision-recall curve.

> **NOTE**
>
> We are focusing here on decision trees for classification because of the nature of the case study. However, decision trees can also be used for regression, making them a versatile method. The tree-growing process is similar for regression as it is for classification, except that instead of seeking to reduce node impurity, a regression tree seeks to minimize other metrics such as the **Mean Squared Error (MSE)** or **Mean Absolute Error (MAE)** of the predictions, where the prediction for a node may be the average or median of the samples in the node, respectively.

# A MORE CONVENIENT APPROACH TO CROSS-VALIDATION

In *Chapter 4, The Bias-Variance Trade-Off*, we gained a deep understanding of cross-validation by writing our own function to do it, using the **KFold** class to generate the training and testing indices. This was helpful to get a thorough understanding of how the process works. However, scikit-learn offers a convenient class that can do more of the heavy lifting for us: **GridSearchCV**. **GridSearchCV** can take as input a model that we want to find optimal hyperparameters for, such as a decision tree or a logistic regression, and a "grid" of hyperparameters that we want to perform cross-validation over. For example, in a logistic regression, we may want to get the average cross-validation score over all the folds for different values of the regularization parameter, **C**. With decision trees, we may want to explore different depths of trees.

You can also search multiple parameters at once, for example, if we wanted to try different depths of trees and different numbers of **max_features** to consider at each node split.

**GridSearchCV** does what is called an exhaustive grid search over all the possible combinations of parameters that we supply. This means that if we supplied five different values for each of the two hyperparameters, the cross-validation procedure would be run 5 x 5 = 25 times. If you are searching many values of many hyperparameters, the number of cross-validation runs can grow very quickly. In these cases, you may wish to use **RandomizedSearchCV**, which searches a random subset of hyperparameter combinations from the universe of all possibilities in the grid you supply.

**GridSearchCV** can speed up your work by streamlining the cross-validation process. You should be familiar with the concepts of cross-validation from the previous chapter, so we proceed directly to listing all the options available for **GridSearchCV**.

In the following exercise, we will get hands-on practice using **GridSearchCV** with the case study data, in order to search hyperparameters for a decision tree classifier. Here are the options for **GridSearchCV**:

| Parameter | Possible values | Notes |
| --- | --- | --- |
| Estimator | estimator object | This is a model object that you have instantiated from a model class. The hyperparameters will be updated as GridSearchCV does its work. |
| param_grid | dict or list of dict (dictionaries) | The dictionary has parameter names as keys and lists of parameters values as values. These are the hyperparameter values for which you want to search all possible combinations. To do multiple grid searches, supply a list of dictionaries. |
| Scoring | String, callable, list, tuple, or dict | This represents the model assessment metric(s) you want to use to measure training and testing performance across the folds, for example, 'roc_auc'. |
| n_jobs | int or None | The number of processing jobs to run in parallel. It may speed up cross-validation to run parallel jobs, but it is good to experiment to be sure. |
| pre_dispatch | int or string | The number of jobs or a formula for the number of jobs to dispatch. Relevant for parallel processing using **n_jobs**. |
| Cv | int, cross-validation generator, or iterable | If supplying an integer, this is the number of folds to use for cross-validation. |
| Refit | bool or string | After doing the cross-validation, the "best" hyperparameters according to the metric specified in scoring can be used directly with the fitted GridSearchCV object to make predictions. If refit=True, the model will be refit to all of the data (not just one of the folds) using the best hyperparameters. Use the **string** argument in case multiple metrics are specified, to indicate which one to use in order to choose the best hyperparameters. |
| Verbose | int | Controls how much output you will see from the cross-validation procedure. |
| error_score | 'raise' or numeric | What to do if an error happens during model fitting. |
| return_train_score | bool | Whether or not to compute and return training scores on the folds. It is not required for selecting the best hyperparameters based on testing fold scores, and for some datasets and models, this can take substantially more time. However, it does give insights into possible overfitting. |

**Figure 5.13: The options for GridSearchCV**

In the following exercise, we'll make use of the **standard error of the mean** to create error bars. We'll average the model performance metric across the testing folds, and the error bars will help us visualize how variable model performance is across the folds.

The standard error of the mean is also known as the standard deviation of the sampling distribution of the sample mean. That is a long name, but the concept isn't too complicated. The idea behind this is that the population of model performance metrics that we wish to make error bars for represents one possible way of sampling a theoretical, larger population of similar samples, for example if more data were available and we used it to have more testing folds. If we could take repeated samples from the larger population, each of these sampling events would result in a slightly different mean (the sample mean). Constructing a distribution of these means (the sampling distribution of the sample mean) from repeated sampling events would allow us to know the variance of this sampling distribution, which would be useful as a measure of uncertainty in the sample mean. It turns out this variance (let's call it $\sigma_{\overline{X}}^2$, where $\overline{X}$ indicates this is the variance of the sample mean) depends on the number of observations in our sample (n): it is inversely proportional to sample size, but also directly proportional to the variance of the larger, unobserved population ($\sigma^2$): $\sigma_{\overline{X}}^2 = \frac{\sigma^2}{n}$. If you're working with standard deviation of the sample mean, simply take the square root of both sides: $\sigma_{\overline{X}} = \frac{\sigma}{\sqrt{n}}$. While we don't know the true value of $\sigma^2$ since we don't observe the theoretical population, we can estimate it with the variance of the population of testing folds that we do observe.

This is a key concept in statistics called the **Central Limit Theorem**.

## EXERCISE 5.02: FINDING OPTIMAL HYPERPARAMETERS FOR A DECISION TREE

In this exercise, we will use **GridSearchCV** to tune the hyperparameters for a decision tree model. You will learn about a convenient way of searching different hyperparameters with scikit-learn. Perform the following steps to complete the exercise:

> **NOTE**
>
> Before you begin this exercise, you need import the necessary packages and load the cleaned dataframe. You can refer to the following Jupyter notebook for the prerequisite steps: https://packt.link/SKuoB.

1. Import the **GridSearchCV** class with this code:

```
from sklearn.model_selection import GridSearchCV
```

The next step is to define the hyperparameters that we want to search using cross-validation. We will find the best maximum depth of tree, using the **max_depth** parameter. Deeper trees have more node splits, which partition the training set into smaller and smaller subspaces using the features. While we don't know the best maximum depth ahead of time, it is helpful to consider some limiting cases when considering the range of parameters to use for the grid search.

We know that one is the minimum depth, consisting of a tree with just one split. As for the largest depth, you can consider how many samples you have in your training data, or, more appropriately in this case, how many samples will be in the training fold for each split of the cross-validation. We will perform a 4-fold cross-validation like we did in the previous chapter. So, how many samples will be in each training fold, and how does this relate to the depth of the tree?

2. Find the number of samples in the training data using this code:

```
X_train.shape
```

The output should be as follows:

```
(21331, 17)
```

With 21,331 training samples and 4-fold cross-validation, there will be three-fourths of the samples, or about 16,000 samples, in each training fold.

### What Does This Mean for How Deep We May Wish to Grow Our Tree?

A theoretical limitation is that we need at least one sample in each leaf. From our discussion regarding how the depth of the tree relates to the number of leaves, we know a tree that splits at every node before the last level, with n levels, has *2n* leaf nodes. Therefore, a tree with L leaf nodes has a depth of approximately *log2(L)*. In the limiting case, if we grow the tree deep enough so that every leaf node has one training sample for a given fold, the depth will be *log2(16,000)* ≈ 14. So, 14 is the theoretical limit to the depth of a tree that we could grow in this case.

Practically speaking, you will probably not want to grow a tree this deep, as the rules used to generate the decision tree will be very specific to the training data and the model is likely to be overfit. However, this gives you an idea of the range of values we may wish to consider for the **max_depth** hyperparameter. We will explore a range of depths from 1 up to 12.

3. Define a dictionary with the key being the hyperparameter name and the value being the list of values of this hyperparameter that we want to search in cross-validation:

```
params = {'max_depth':[1, 2, 4, 6, 8, 10, 12]}
```

In this case, we are only searching one hyperparameter. However, you could define a dictionary with multiple key-value pairs to search over multiple hyperparameters simultaneously.

4. If you are running all the exercises for this chapter in a single notebook, you can reuse the decision tree object, **dt**, from earlier. If not, you need to create a decision tree object for the hyperparameter search:

```
dt = tree.DecisionTreeClassifier()
```

Now we want to instantiate the **GridSearchCV** class.

5. Instantiate the **GridSearchCV** class using these options:

```
cv = GridSearchCV(dt, param_grid=params, scoring='roc_auc',
                  n_jobs=None, refit=True, cv=4, verbose=1,
                  pre_dispatch=None, error_score=np.nan,
                  return_train_score=True)
```

Note here that we use the ROC AUC metric (**scoring='roc_auc'**), that we do 4-fold cross-validation **(cv=4)**, and that we calculate training scores (**return_train_score=True**) to assess the bias-variance trade-off.

Once the cross-validation object is defined, we can simply use the **.fit** method on it as we would with a model object. This encapsulates essentially all the functionality of the cross-validation loop we wrote in the previous chapter.

6. Perform 4-fold cross-validation to search for the optimal maximum depth using this code:

```
cv.fit(X_train, y_train)
```

The output should be as follows:

```
Fitting 4 folds for each of 7 candidates, totalling 28 fits

[Parallel(n_jobs=1)]: Using backend SequentialBackend with 1 concurrent workers.
[Parallel(n_jobs=1)]: Done   28 out of   28 | elapsed:    3.2s finished

GridSearchCV(cv=4, estimator=DecisionTreeClassifier(),
             param_grid={'max_depth': [1, 2, 4, 6, 8, 10, 12]},
             pre_dispatch=None, return_train_score=True, scoring='roc_auc',
             verbose=1)
```

Figure 5.14: The cross-validation fitting output

All the options that we specified are printed as output. Additionally, there is some output information regarding how many cross-validation fits were performed. We had 4 folds and 7 hyperparameters, meaning 4 x 7 = 28 fits are performed. The amount of time this took is also displayed. You can control how much output you get from this procedure with the **verbose** keyword argument; larger numbers mean more output.

Now it's time to examine the results of the cross-validation procedure. Among the methods that are available on the fitted **GridSearchCV** object is **.cv_results_**. This is a dictionary containing the names of results as keys and the results themselves as values. For example, the **mean_test_score** key holds the average testing score across the folds for each of the seven hyperparameters. You could directly examine this output by running **cv.cv_results_** in a code cell. However, this is not easy to read. Dictionaries with this kind of structure can be used immediately in the creation of a pandas DataFrame, which makes looking at the results a little easier.

7. Run the following code to create and examine a pandas DataFrame of cross-validation results:

```
cv_results_df = pd.DataFrame(cv.cv_results_)
cv_results_df
```

The output should look like this:

| | mean_fit_time | std_fit_time | mean_score_time | std_score_time | param_max_depth | params | split0_test_score |
|---|---|---|---|---|---|---|---|
| 0 | 0.023161 | 0.002917 | 0.002712 | 0.000827 | 1 | {'max_depth': 1} | 0.639514 |
| 1 | 0.040478 | 0.005298 | 0.003616 | 0.001432 | 2 | {'max_depth': 2} | 0.695134 |
| 2 | 0.062975 | 0.001703 | 0.002196 | 0.000017 | 4 | {'max_depth': 4} | 0.732720 |
| 3 | 0.094926 | 0.005329 | 0.002393 | 0.000150 | 6 | {'max_depth': 6} | 0.743836 |
| 4 | 0.123850 | 0.008124 | 0.003107 | 0.000768 | 8 | {'max_depth': 8} | 0.727948 |
| 5 | 0.142454 | 0.001005 | 0.002620 | 0.000221 | 10 | {'max_depth': 10} | 0.709049 |
| 6 | 0.178841 | 0.016180 | 0.002716 | 0.000238 | 12 | {'max_depth': 12} | 0.675597 |

**Figure 5.15: First several columns of the cross-validation results DataFrame**

The DataFrame has one row for each combination of hyperparameters in the grid. Since we are only searching one hyperparameter here, there is one row for each of the seven values that we searched for. You can see a lot of output for each row, such as the mean and standard deviation of the time in seconds that each of the four folds took for both training (fitting) and testing (scoring). The hyperparameter values that were searched are also shown. In *Figure 5.16*, we can see the ROC AUC score for the testing data of the first fold (index 0). What are the rest of the columns in the results DataFrame?

8. View the names of the remaining columns in the results DataFrame using this code:

```
cv_results_df.columns
```

The output should be as follows:

```
Index(['mean_fit_time', 'std_fit_time',\
       'mean_score_time', 'std_score_time',\
       'param_max_depth', 'params',\
       'split0_test_score', 'split1_test_score',\
       'split2_test_score', 'split3_test_score',\
       'mean_test_score', 'std_test_score',\
       'rank_test_score', 'split0_train_score',\
```

```
                'split1_train_score', 'split2_train_score',\
                'split3_train_score', 'mean_train_score',\
                'std_train_score'],
           dtype='object')
```

The columns in the cross-validation results DataFrame include the testing scores for each fold, their average and standard deviation, and the same information for the training scores.

Generally speaking, the "best" combination of hyperparameters is that with the highest average testing score. This is an estimation of how well the model, fitted using these hyperparameters, could perform when scored on new data. Let's make a plot showing how the average testing score varies with the **max_depth** hyperparameter. We will also show the average training scores on the same plot, to see how bias and variance change as we allow deeper and more complex trees to be grown during model fitting.

We include the standard errors of the 4-fold training and testing scores as error bars, using the Matplotlib **errorbar** function. This gives you an indication of how variable the scores are across the folds.

9. Execute the following code to create an error bar plot of training and testing scores for each value of **max_depth** that was examined in cross-validation:

```
ax = plt.axes()
ax.errorbar(cv_results_df['param_max_depth'],
            cv_results_df['mean_train_score'],
            yerr=cv_results_df['std_train_score']/np.sqrt(4),
            label='Mean $\pm$ 1 SE training scores')
ax.errorbar(cv_results_df['param_max_depth'],
            cv_results_df['mean_test_score'],
            yerr=cv_results_df['std_test_score']/np.sqrt(4),
            label='Mean $\pm$ 1 SE testing scores')
ax.legend()
plt.xlabel('max_depth')
plt.ylabel('ROC AUC')
```

The plot should appear as follows:

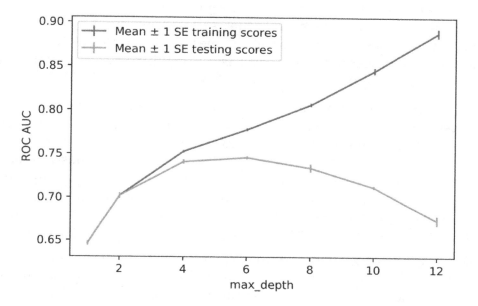

**Figure 5.16: An error bar plot of training and testing scores across the four folds**

Note that standard errors are calculated as the standard deviation divided by the square root of the number of folds. The standard errors of the training and testing scores are shown as vertical lines at each value of **max_depth** that was tried; the distance above and below the average score is 1 standard error. Whenever making error bar plots, it's best to ensure that the units of the error measurement are the same as the units of the *y* axis. In this case they are, since standard error has the same units as the underlying data, as opposed to variance, for example, which has squared units.

The error bars indicate how variable the scores are across folds. If there were a large amount of variation across the folds, it would indicate that the nature of the data across the folds was different in a way that affected the ability of our model to describe it. This could be concerning because it would indicate that we may not have enough data to train a model that would reliably perform on new data. However, in our case here, there is not much variability between the folds, so this is not an issue.

What about the general trends of the training and testing scores across the different values of `max_depth`? We can see that as we grow deeper and deeper trees, the model fits the training data better and better. As noted previously, if we grew trees deep enough so that each leaf node had just one training sample, we would create a model that is very specific to the training data. In fact, it would fit the training data perfectly. We could say that such a model had extremely high **variance**.

But this performance on the training set does not necessarily translate over to the testing set. In *Figure 5.16* it's apparent that increasing `max_depth` only increases testing scores up to a point, after which deeper trees in fact have lower testing performance. This is another example of how we can leverage the **bias-variance trade-off** to create a better predictive model – similar to how we used a regularized logistic regression. Shallower trees have more **bias**, since they are not fitting the training data as well. But this is fine because if we accept some bias, we will have better performance on the testing data, which is the metric we ultimately care about.

In this case, we would select `max_depth` = 6. You could also perform a more thorough search by trying every integer between 2 and 12, instead of going by 2s, as we've done here. In general, it is a good idea to perform as thorough a search of parameter space as you can, up to the limits of the computational time that you have. In this case, it would lead to the same result.

**Comparison between Models**

At this point, we've calculated a 4-fold cross-validation of several different machine learning models on the case study data. So, how are we doing? What's our best so far? In the last chapter, we got an average testing ROC AUC of 0.718 with logistic regression, and 0.740 by engineering interaction features in a logistic regression. Here, with a decision tree, we can achieve 0.745. So, we are making gains in model performance. Now, let's, explore another type of model, based on decision tress, to see whether we can push performance even higher.

# RANDOM FORESTS: ENSEMBLES OF DECISION TREES

As we saw in the previous exercise, decision trees are prone to overfitting. This is one of the principal criticisms of their usage, despite the fact that they are highly interpretable. We were able to limit this overfitting, to an extent, however, by limiting the maximum depth to which the tree could be grown.

Building on the concepts of decision trees, machine learning researchers have leveraged multiple trees as the basis for more complex procedures, resulting in some of the most powerful and widely used predictive models. In this chapter, we will focus on random forests of decision trees. Random forests are examples of what are called ensemble models, because they are formed by combining other, simpler models. By combining the predictions of many models, it is possible to improve upon the deficiencies of any given one of them. This is sometimes called combining many weak learners to make a strong learner.

Once you understand decision trees, the concept behind random forests is fairly simple. That is because random forests are just ensembles of many decision trees; all the models in this kind of ensemble have the same mathematical form. So, how many decision tree models will be included in a random forest? This is one of the hyperparameters, **n_estimators**, that needs to be specified when building a random forest model. Generally speaking, the more trees, the better. As the number of trees increases, the variance of the overall ensemble will decrease. This should result in the random forest model having better generalization to new data, which will be reflected in increased testing scores. However, there will be a point of diminishing returns after which increasing the number of trees does not result in a substantial improvement in model performance.

So, how do random forests reduce the high variance (overfitting) issue that affects decision trees? The answer to this question lies in what is different about the different trees in the forest. There are two main ways in which the trees are different, one of which we are already familiar with:

- The number of features considered at each split

- The training samples used to grow different trees

**The Number of Features Considered at Each Split**

We are already familiar with this option from the **DecisionTreeClassifier** class: **max_features**. In our previous usage of this class, we left **max_features** at its default value of **None**, which meant that all features were considered at each split. By using all the features to fit the training data, overfitting is possible. By limiting the number of features considered at each split, some of the decision trees in a random forest will potentially find better splits. This is because, although they are still greedily searching for the best split, they are doing it with a limited selection of features. This may make certain splits possible later in the tree that may not have been found if all features were being searched at each split.

There is a **max_features** option in the **RandomForestClassifier** class in scikit-learn just as there is for the **DecisionTreeClassifier** class and the options are similar. However, for the random forest, the default setting is **'auto'**, which means the algorithm will only search a random selection of the square root of the number of possible features at each split, for example, a random selection of √9 = 3 features from a total of 9 possible features. Because each tree in the forest will likely choose different random selections of features to split as the trees are being grown, the trees in the forest will not be the same.

## The Samples Used to Grow Different Trees

The other way that the trees in a random forest differ from each other is that they are usually grown with different training samples. To do this, a statistical procedure known as bootstrapping is used, which means generating new synthetic datasets from the original data. The synthetic datasets are created by randomly selecting samples from the original dataset using replacement. Here, "replacement" means that if we select a certain sample, we will continue to consider it for selection, that is, it is "replaced" in the original dataset after we've sampled it. The number of samples in the synthetic datasets are the same as those in the original dataset, but some samples may be repeated because of replacement, while others may not be present at all.

The procedure of using random sampling to create synthetic datasets, and training models on them separately, is called bagging, which is short for bootstrapped aggregation. Bagging can, in fact, be used with any machine learning model, not just decision trees, and scikit-learn offers functionality to do this for both classification (**BaggingClassifier**) and regression (**BaggingRegressor**) problems. In the case of random forest, bagging is turned on by default and the **bootstrap** option is set to **True**. But if you want all the trees in the forest to be grown using all of the training data, you can set this option to **False**.

Now you should have a good understanding of what a random forest is. As you can see, if you are already familiar with decision trees, understanding random forests does not involve much additional knowledge. A reflection of this fact is that the hyperparameters available for the **RandomForestClassifier** class in scikit-learn are mostly the same as those for the **DecisionTreeClassifier** class.

In addition to **n_estimators** and **bootstrap**, which we discussed previously, there are only two new options beyond what's available for decision trees:

- **oob_score**, a **bool**: This option controls whether or not to calculate an **Out Of Bag (OOB)** score for each tree. This can be thought of as a testing score, where the samples that were not selected by the bagging procedure to grow a given tree are used to assess the model performance of that tree. Here, use **True** to calculate the OOB score or **False** (the default) not to.

- **warm_start**, a **bool**: This is **False** by default – if you set this to **True**, then reusing the same random forest model object will cause additional trees to be added to the already generated forest.

- **max_samples**, an **int** or **float**: Controls how many samples are used to train each tree in the forest, when using the bootstrapping procedure. The default is to use the same number as the original dataset.

**Other Kinds of Ensemble Models**

Random forest, as we now know, is an example of a bagging ensemble. Another kind of ensemble is a **boosting** ensemble. The general idea of boosting is to use successive new models of the same type and to train them on the errors of previous models. This way, successive models learn where earlier models didn't do well and correct these errors. Boosting has enjoyed successful application with decision trees and is available in scikit-learn and another popular Python package called XGBoost. We will discuss boosting in the next chapter.

**Stacking** ensembles are a somewhat more advanced kind of ensemble, where the different models (estimators) within the ensemble do not need to be of the same type as they do in bagging and boosting. For example, you could build a stacking ensemble with a random forest and a logistic regression. The predictions of the different members of the ensemble are combined for a final prediction using yet another model (the **stacker**), which considers the predictions of the **stacked** models as features.

# RANDOM FOREST: PREDICTIONS AND INTERPRETABILITY

Since a random forest is just a collection of decision trees, somehow the predictions of all those trees must be combined to create the prediction of the random forest.

After model training, classification trees will take an input sample and produce a predicted class, for example, whether or not a credit account in our case study problem will default. One intuitive approach to combining the predictions of these trees into the ultimate prediction of the forest is to take a majority vote. That is, whatever the most common prediction of all the trees is becomes the prediction of the forest, for a given sample. This was the approach taken in the publication first describing random forests (https://scikit-learn.org/stable/modules/ensemble.html#forest). However, scikit-learn uses a somewhat different approach: adding up the predicted probabilities for each class and then choosing the one with the highest probability sum. This captures more information from each tree than just the predicted class.

## Interpretability of Random Forests

One of the main advantages of decision trees is that it is straightforward to see how any individual prediction is made. You can trace the decision path for any sample through the series of "if, then" rules used to make a prediction and know exactly how it came to have that prediction. By contrast, imagine that you have a random forest consisting of 1,000 trees. This would mean there are 1,000 sets of rules like this, which are much harder to communicate to human beings than one set of rules!

That being said, there are various methods that can be used to understand how random forests make predictions. A simple way to interpret how a random forest works, and which is available in scikit-learn, is to observe the **feature importances**. Feature importances of a random forest are a measure of how useful each of the features was when growing the trees in the forest. This usefulness is measured by a combination of the fraction of training samples that were split using each feature, and the decrease in node impurity that resulted.

Because of the feature importance calculation, which can be used to rank features by how impactful they are within the random forest model, random forests can also be used for feature selection.

# EXERCISE 5.03: FITTING A RANDOM FOREST

In this exercise, we will extend our efforts with decision trees by using the random forest model with cross-validation on the training data from the case study. We will observe the effect of increasing the number of trees in the forest and examine the feature importance that can be calculated using a random forest model. Perform the following steps to complete the exercise:

> **NOTE**
>
> The Jupyter notebook for this exercise can be found at https://packt.link/
> VSz2T. This notebook contains the prerequisite steps of importing the
> necessary libraries and loading the cleaned dataframe. Please execute
> these steps before you begin this exercise.

1. Import the random forest classifier model class as follows:

```
from sklearn.ensemble import RandomForestClassifier
```

2. Instantiate the class using these options:

```
rf = RandomForestClassifier(n_estimators=10,\
                            criterion='gini',\
                            max_depth=3,\
                            min_samples_split=2,\
                            min_samples_leaf=1,\
                            min_weight_fraction_leaf=0.0,\
                            max_features='auto',\
                            max_leaf_nodes=None,\
                            min_impurity_decrease=0.0,\
                            min_impurity_split=None,\
                            bootstrap=True,\
                            oob_score=False,\
                            n_jobs=None,
                            random_state=4,\
                            verbose=0,\
                            warm_start=False,\
                            class_weight=None)
```

For this exercise, we'll use mainly the default options. However, note that we will set **max_depth** = 3. Here, we are only going to explore the effect of using different numbers of trees, which we will illustrate with relatively shallow trees for the sake of shorter runtimes. To find the best model performance, we'd typically try more trees and deeper depths of trees.

We also set **random_state** for consistent results across runs.

3. Create a parameter grid for this exercise in order to search the numbers of trees, ranging from 10 to 100 by 10s:

```
rf_params_ex = {'n_estimators':list(range(10,110,10))}
```

We use Python's **range()** function to create an iterator for the integer values we want, and then convert them to a list using **list()**.

4. Instantiate a grid search cross-validation object for the random forest model using the parameter grid from the previous step. Otherwise, you can use the same options that were used for the cross-validation of the decision tree:

```
cv_rf_ex = GridSearchCV(rf, param_grid=rf_params_ex,
                        scoring='roc_auc', n_jobs=None,
                        refit=True, cv=4, verbose=1,
                        pre_dispatch=None, error_score=np.nan,
                        return_train_score=True)
```

5. Fit the cross-validation object as follows:

```
cv_rf_ex.fit(X_train, y_train)
```

The fitting procedure should output the following:

```
Fitting 4 folds for each of 10 candidates, totalling 40 fits

[Parallel(n_jobs=1)]: Using backend SequentialBackend with 1 concurrent workers.
[Parallel(n_jobs=1)]: Done  40 out of  40 | elapsed:   25.2s finished

GridSearchCV(cv=4,
             estimator=RandomForestClassifier(max_depth=3, n_estimators=10,
                                              random_state=4),
             param_grid={'n_estimators': [10, 20, 30, 40, 50, 60, 70, 80, 90,
                                          100]},
             pre_dispatch=None, return_train_score=True, scoring='roc_auc',
             verbose=1)
```

Figure 5.17: The output from the cross-validation of the random forest
across different numbers of trees

You may have noticed that, although we are only cross-validating over 10 hyperparameter values, comparable to the 7 values that we examined for the decision tree in the previous exercise, this cross-validation took noticeably longer. Consider how many trees we are growing in this case. For the last hyperparameter, **n_estimators = 100**, we have grown a total of 400 trees across all the cross-validation splits.

How long has model fitting taken across the various numbers of trees that we just tried? What gains in terms of cross-validation testing performance have we made by using more trees? These are good things to examine using plots. First, we'll pull the cross-validation results out into a pandas DataFrame, as we've done before.

6. Put the cross-validation results into a pandas DataFrame:

```
cv_rf_ex_results_df = pd.DataFrame(cv_rf_ex.cv_results_)
```

You can examine the whole DataFrame in the accompanying Jupyter notebook. Here, we move directly to creating plots of the quantities of interest. We'll make a line plot, with symbols, of the mean fit time across the folds for each hyperparameter, contained in the **mean_fit_time** column, as well as an error bar plot of testing scores, which we've already done for decision trees. Both plots will be against the number of trees on the *x* axis.

7. Create two subplots of the mean training time and mean testing scores with standard error:

```
fig, axs = plt.subplots(nrows=1, ncols=2, figsize=(6, 3))
axs[0].plot(cv_rf_ex_results_df['param_n_estimators'],
            cv_rf_ex_results_df['mean_fit_time'],
            '-o')
axs[0].set_xlabel('Number of trees')
axs[0].set_ylabel('Mean fit time (seconds)')
axs[1].errorbar(cv_rf_ex_results_df['param_n_estimators'],
            cv_rf_ex_results_df['mean_test_score'],
            yerr=cv_rf_ex_results_df['std_test_score']/
np.sqrt(4))
axs[1].set_xlabel('Number of trees')
axs[1].set_ylabel('Mean testing ROC AUC $\pm$ 1 SE ')
plt.tight_layout()
```

Here, we've used **plt.subplots** to create two axes at once, within a figure, in a one-row-by-two-column configuration. We then access the axes objects by indexing the array of **axs** axes returned from this operation in order to create plots.

The output should look similar to this plot:

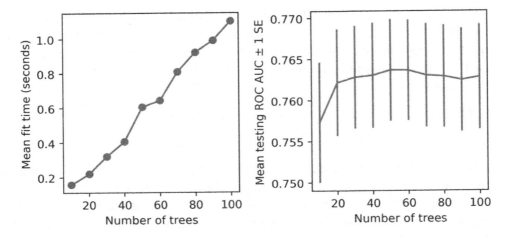

Figure 5.18: The mean fitting time and testing scores for different numbers of trees in the forest

> **NOTE**
>
> Your results may differ due to the differences in the platform or if you set a different random seed.

There are several things to note regarding these visualizations. First of all, we can see that by using a random forest, we have increased model performance on the cross-validation testing folds above that of any of our previous efforts. While we haven't made an attempt to tune the random forest hyperparameters to achieve the best model performance we can, this is a promising result and indicates that a random forest will be a valuable addition to our modeling efforts.

However, along with these higher model testing scores, notice that there is also more variability between the folds than what we saw with the decision tree; this variability is visible as larger standard errors in model testing scores across the folds. While this indicates that there is a wider range in model performance that might be expected from using this model, you are encouraged to examine the model testing scores of the folds directly in the pandas DataFrame in the Jupyter notebook. You should see that even the lowest score from an individual fold is still higher than the average testing score from the decision tree, indicating that it will be better to use a random forest.

So, what about the other questions that we set out to explore with this visualization? We are interested in seeing how long it takes to fit random forest models with various numbers of trees, and what the gains in model performance are from using more trees. The subplot on the left of *Figure 5.18* shows that there is a fairly linear increase in training time as more trees are added to the forest. This is probably to be expected; we are simply adding to the amount of computation to be done in the training procedure by adding more trees.

But is this additional computational time worth it in terms of increased model performance? The subplot on the right of *Figure 5.18* shows that beyond about 20 trees, it's not clear that adding more trees reliably improves testing performance. While the model with 50 trees has the highest score, the fact that adding more trees actually decreases the testing score somewhat indicates that the gain in ROC AUC for 50 trees may just be due to randomness, as adding more trees theoretically should increase model performance. Based on this reasoning, if we were limited to **max_depth = 3**, we may choose a forest of 20 or perhaps 50 trees and proceed. However, we will explore the parameter space more fully in the activity at the end of this chapter.

Finally, note that we have not shown the training ROC AUC metrics here. If you were to plot these or look them up in the results DataFrame, you'd see that the training scores are higher than the testing scores, indicating that some amount of overfitting is happening. While this may be the case, it's still true that the cross-validation testing scores for this random forest model are higher than those that we've observed for any other model. Based on this result, we would likely choose the random forest model at this point.

For a few additional insights into what we can access using our fitted cross-validation object, let's take a look at the best hyperparameters and feature importance.

8. Use this code to see the best hyperparameters from cross-validation:

```
cv_rf_ex.best_params_
```

This should be the output:

```
{'n_estimators': 50}
```

Here, best just means the hyperparameters that resulted in the highest average model testing score.

9. Run this code to create a DataFrame of the feature names and importances, and then show a horizontal bar plot sorted by importance:

```
feat_imp_df = pd.DataFrame({
    'Importance':cv_rf_ex.best_estimator_.feature_importances_
    },
    index=features_response[:-1])
feat_imp_df.sort_values('Importance', ascending=True).plot.barh()
```

The plot should look like this:

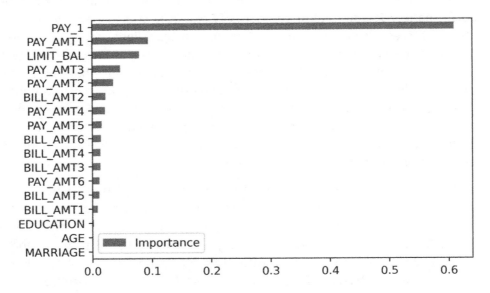

Figure 5.19: Feature importance from a random forest

In this code, we've created a dictionary with feature importances and used this along with the feature names as an index to create a DataFrame. The feature importances came from the **best_estimator_** method of the fitted cross-validation object, so it refers to the model with the highest average testing score (in other words, the model with 50 trees). This is a way to access the random forest model object, which was trained on all the training data, using the best hyperparameters found by the cross-validation grid search. **feature_importances_** is a method that can be used on fitted random forest models.

After accessing all these attributes, we plot them on a horizontal bar chart, which is a convenient way to look at feature importances. Notice that the top five most important features from the random forest are the same as the top five chosen by an ANOVA F-test in *Chapter 3, Details of Logistic Regression and Feature Exploration*, although they are in a somewhat different order. This is good confirmation between the different methods.

## CHECKERBOARD GRAPH

Before moving on to the activity, we illustrate a visualization technique in Matplotlib. Plotting a two-dimensional grid with colored squares or other shapes on it can be useful when you want to show three dimensions of data. Here, color illustrates the third dimension. For example, you may want to visualize model testing scores over a grid of two hyperparameters, as we'll do in *Activity 5.01, Cross-Validation Grid Search with Random Forest*.

The first step in the process is to create grids of *x* and *y* coordinates. The NumPy **meshgrid** function can be used to do this. This function takes one-dimensional arrays of *x* and *y* coordinates and creates the mesh grid with all the possible pairs from both. The points in the mesh grid will be the corners of each square on the checkerboard plot. Here is how the code looks for a 4 x 4 grid of colored patches. Since we are specifying the corners, we require a 5 x 5 grid of points. We also show the arrays of the *x* and *y* coordinates:

```
xx_example, yy_example = np.meshgrid(range(5), range(5))
print(xx_example)
print(yy_example)
```

The output is as follows:

```
[[0 1 2 3 4]
 [0 1 2 3 4]
 [0 1 2 3 4]
 [0 1 2 3 4]
 [0 1 2 3 4]]
[[0 0 0 0 0]
 [1 1 1 1 1]
 [2 2 2 2 2]
 [3 3 3 3 3]
 [4 4 4 4 4]]
```

The grid of data to plot on this mesh should have a 4 x 4 shape. We make a one-dimensional array of integers between 1 and 16, and reshape it to a two-dimensional, 4 x 4 grid:

```
z_example = np.arange(1,17).reshape(4,4)
z_example
```

This outputs the following:

```
array([[ 1,  2,  3,  4],
       [ 5,  6,  7,  8],
       [ 9, 10, 11, 12],
       [13, 14, 15, 16]])
```

We can plot the **z_example** data on the **xx_example, yy_example** mesh grid with the following code. Notice that we use **pcolormesh** to make the plot with the **jet** colormap, which gives a rainbow color scale. We add a **colorbar**, which needs to be passed the **pcolor_ex** object returned by **pcolormesh** as an argument, so the interpretation of the color scale is clear:

```
ax = plt.axes()
pcolor_ex = ax.pcolormesh(xx_example, yy_example, z_example,
                          cmap=plt.cm.jet)
plt.colorbar(pcolor_ex, label='Color scale')
ax.set_xlabel('X coordinate')
ax.set_ylabel('Y coordinate')
```

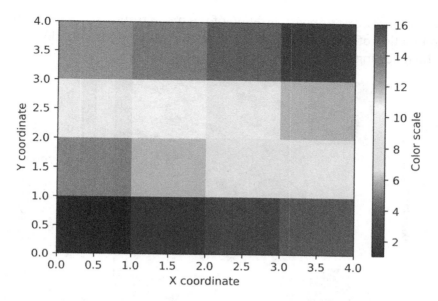

Figure 5.20: A pcolormesh plot of consecutive integers

# ACTIVITY 5.01: CROSS-VALIDATION GRID SEARCH WITH RANDOM FOREST

In this activity, you will conduct a grid search over the number of trees in the forest (**n_estimators**) and the maximum depth of a tree (**max_depth**) for a random forest model on the case study data. You will then create a visualization showing the average testing score for the grid of hyperparameters that you searched over. Perform the following steps to complete the activity:

1.  Create a dictionary representing the grid for the **max_depth** and **n_ estimators** hyperparameters that will be searched. Include depths of 3, 6, 9, and 12, and 10, 50, 100, and 200 trees. Leave the other hyperparameters at their defaults.

2.  Instantiate a **GridSearchCV** object using the same options that we have had previously in this chapter, but with the dictionary of hyperparameters created in step 1 here. Set **verbose=2** to see the output for each fit performed. You can reuse the same random forest model object, **rf**, that we have been using or create a new one.

3.  Fit the **GridSearchCV** object on the training data.

4.  Put the results of the grid search in a pandas DataFrame.

5. Create a **pcolormesh** visualization of the mean testing score for each combination of hyperparameters. You should obtain a visualization similar to the following:

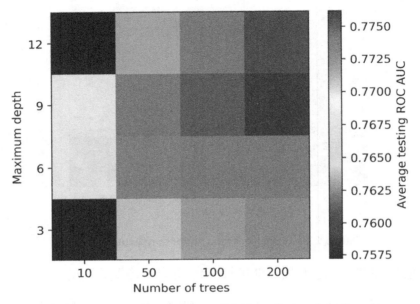

Figure 5.21: Results of cross-validation of a random forest over a grid with two hyperparameters

6. Conclude which set of hyperparameters to use.

> **NOTE**
>
> The Jupyter notebook containing the Python code for this activity can be found at https://packt.link/D0OBc. Detailed step-wise solution to this activity can be found on page 386.

# SUMMARY

In this chapter, we've learned how to use decision trees and the ensemble models called random forests that are made up of many decision trees. Using these simply conceived models, we were able to make better predictions than we could with logistic regression, judging by the cross-validation ROC AUC score. This is often the case for many real-world problems. Decision trees are robust to a lot of the potential issues that can prevent logistic regression models from good performance, such as non-linear relationships between features and the response variable, and the presence of complicated interactions among features.

Although a single decision tree is prone to overfitting, the random forest ensemble method has been shown to reduce this high-variance issue. Random forests are built by training many trees. The decreased variance of the ensemble of trees is achieved by increasing the bias of the individual trees in the forest, by only training them on a portion of the available training set (bootstrapped aggregation or bagging), and by only considering a reduced number of features at each node split.

Now that we have tried several different machine learning approaches to modeling the case study data, we found that some work better than others; for example, a random forest with tuned hyperparameters provides the highest average cross-validation ROC AUC score of 0.776, as we saw in *Activity 5, Cross-Validation Grid Search with Random Forest*.

In the next chapter, we'll learn about another type of ensemble method, called gradient boosting, which is often used in conjunction with decision trees. Gradient boosting has yielded some of the best performance of all machine learning models for binary classification use cases. We'll also learn a powerful method for explaining and interpreting the predictions of gradient boosted ensembles of trees, using **SHapely Additive exPlanation** (**SHAP**) values.

# 6

# GRADIENT BOOSTING, XGBOOST, AND SHAP VALUES

## OVERVIEW

After reading this chapter, you will be able to describe the concept of gradient boosting, the fundamental idea underlying the XGBoost package. You will then train XGBoost models on synthetic data, while learning about early stopping as well as several XGBoost hyperparameters along the way. In addition to using a similar method to grow trees as we have previously (by setting `max_depth`), you'll also discover a new way of growing trees that is offered by XGBoost: loss-guided tree growing. After learning about XGBoost, you'll then be introduced to a new and powerful way of explaining model predictions, called **SHAP** (**SHapley Additive exPlanations**). You will see how SHAP values can be used to provide individualized explanations for model predictions from any dataset, not just the training data, and also understand the additive property of SHAP values.

# INTRODUCTION

As we saw in the previous chapter, decision trees and ensemble models based on them provide powerful methods for creating machine learning models. While random forests have been around for decades, recent work on a different kind of tree ensemble, gradient boosted trees, has resulted in state-of-the-art models that have come to dominate the landscape of predictive modeling with tabular data, or data that is organized into a structured table, similar to the case study data. The two main packages used by machine learning data scientists today to create the most accurate predictive models with tabular data are XGBoost and LightGBM. In this chapter, we'll become familiar with XGBoost using a synthetic dataset, and then apply it to the case study data in the activity.

> **NOTE**
>
> Perhaps some of the best motivation for using XGBoost comes from the paper describing this machine learning system, in the context of Kaggle, a popular online forum for machine learning competitions:
>
> "Among the 29 challenge-winning solutions published on Kaggle's blog during 2015, 17 solutions used XGBoost. Among these solutions, eight solely used XGBoost to train the model, while most others combined XGBoost with neural nets in ensembles. For comparison, the second most popular method, deep neural nets, was used in 11 solutions " (Chen and Guestrin, 2016, https://dl.acm.org/doi/abs/10.1145/2939672.2939785).

As we'll see, XGBoost ties together a few of the different ideas we've discussed so far, including decision trees and ensemble modeling as well as gradient descent.

In addition to more performant models, recent machine learning research has yielded more detailed ways to explain the predictions of models. Rather than relying on interpretations that only represent the model training set in aggregate, such as logistic regression coefficients or the feature importances of a random forest, a new package called SHAP allows us to interpret model predictions individually, and for any dataset we want, such as validation or test data. This can be very helpful in enabling us, as data scientists, as well as our business partners, to understand the workings of a model at a granular level, even for new data.

# GRADIENT BOOSTING AND XGBOOST

## WHAT IS BOOSTING?

**Boosting** is a procedure for creating ensembles of many machine learning models, or **estimators**, similar to the bagging concept that underlies the random forest model. Like bagging, while boosting can be used with any kind of machine learning model, it is commonly used to build ensembles of decision trees. A key difference from bagging is that in boosting, each new estimator added to the ensemble depends on all the estimators added before it. Because the boosting procedure proceeds in sequential stages, and the predictions of ensemble members are added up to calculate the overall ensemble prediction, it is also called **stagewise additive modeling**. The difference between bagging and boosting can be visualized as in *Figure 6.1*:

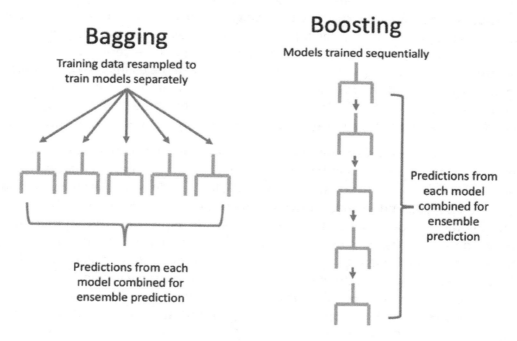

Figure 6.1: Bagging versus boosting

While bagging trains many estimators using different random samples of the training data, boosting trains new estimators using information about which samples were incorrectly classified by the previous estimators in the ensemble. By focusing new estimators on these samples, the goal is that the overall ensemble will have better performance across the whole training dataset. **AdaBoost**, a precursor to **XGBoost**, accomplished this goal by giving more weight to incorrectly classified samples as new estimators in the ensemble are trained.

# GRADIENT BOOSTING AND XGBOOST

XGBoost is a modeling procedure and Python package that is one of the most popular machine learning methods in use today, due to its superior performance in many domains, from business to the natural sciences. XGBoost has also proven to be one of the most successful tools in machine learning competitions. We will not discuss all the details of how XGBoost is implemented, but rather get a high-level idea of how it works and look at some of the most important hyperparameters. For further details, the interested reader should refer to the publication *XGBoost: A Scalable Tree Boosting System*, by Tianqi Chen and Carlos Guestrin ([https://dl.acm.org/doi/abs/10.1145/2939672.2939785](https://dl.acm.org/doi/abs/10.1145/2939672.2939785)).

The XGBoost implementation of the gradient boosting procedure is a stagewise additive model similar to AdaBoost. However, instead of directly giving more weight to misclassified samples during model training, XGBoost uses a procedure similar in nature to gradient descent. Recall from *Chapter 4, The Bias Variance Trade-off*, that optimization with gradient descent uses information about the derivative of a **loss function** (another name for the cost function) to update the estimated coefficients when training a logistic regression model. The derivative of the loss function contains information about which direction and how much to adjust the coefficient estimates at each iteration of the procedure, so as to reduce the level of error in the predictions.

XGBoost applies the gradient descent idea to stagewise additive modeling, using information about the gradient (another word for derivative) of a loss function to train new decision trees to add to the ensemble. In fact, XGBoost takes things a step further than gradient descent as described in *Chapter 4, The Bias-Variance Trade-Off*, and uses information about both the first and second derivatives. The approach of training decision trees using error gradients is an alternative to the node impurity idea introduced in *Chapter 5, Decision Trees and Random Forests*. Conceptually, XGBoost trains new trees with the goal of moving the ensemble prediction in the direction of decreasing error. How big a step to take in that direction is controlled by the `learning_rate` hyperparameter, analogous to `learning_rate` in *Exercise 4.01 Using Gradient Descent to Minimize a Cost Function*, from *Chapter 4, The Bias Variance Trade-off*.

At this point, we should have enough knowledge about how XGBoost works to start getting our hands dirty and using it. To illustrate XGBoost, we'll create a synthetic dataset for binary classification, with scikit-learn's **make_classification** function. This dataset will have 5,000 samples and 40 features. The rest of the options here control how challenging a classification task this will be, and you should consult the scikit-learn documentation to better understand them. Of particular interest is the fact that we'll have multiple clusters (**n_clusters_per_class**), meaning there will be several regions of points in multidimensional feature space that belong to a certain class, similar to the cluster shown in the last chapter in *Figure 5.3*. A tree-based model should be able to identify these clusters. Also, we are specifying that there are only 3 informative features out of a total of 40 (**n_informative**), as well as 2 redundant features (**n_redundant**) that will contain the same information as the informative ones. So, all told, only 5 out of the 40 features should be useful in making predictions, and of those, all the information is encoded in 3 of them.

If you want to follow along with the examples in this chapter on your computer, please refer to the Jupyter notebook at https://packt.link/L5oS7:

```
from sklearn.datasets import make_classification
X, y = make_classification(n_samples=5000, n_features=40,\
                           n_informative=3, n_redundant=2,\
                           n_repeated=0, n_classes=2,\
                           n_clusters_per_class=3,\
                           weights=None, flip_y=0.05,\
                           class_sep=0.1, hypercube=True,\
                           shift=0.0,scale=1.0, shuffle=True,\
                           random_state=2)
```

Note that the class fraction of the response variable **y** is about 50%:

```
y.mean()
```

This should output the following:

```
0.4986
```

Instead of using cross-validation, in this chapter, we will split this synthetic dataset just once into a training and validation set. However, the concepts we introduce here could be extended to the cross-validation scenario. We'll split this synthetic data into 80% for training and 20% for validation. In a real-world data problem, we would also want to have a test set reserved for later use in evaluating the final model, but we'll forego this here:

```
from sklearn.model_selection import train_test_split
X_train, X_val, y_train, y_val = \
train_test_split(X, y, test_size=0.2, random_state=24)
```

Now that we've prepared the data for modeling, we need to instantiate an object of the **XGBClassifier** class. Note that we will now be using the XGBoost package, and not scikit-learn, to develop a predictive model. However, XGBoost has an API (application programming interface) that was designed to be similar to that of scikit-learn, so using this class should be intuitive. The **XGBClassifier** class can be used to create a model object with **fit** and **predict** methods and other familiar functionality, and we can specify model hyperparameters when instantiating the class. We'll specify just a few hyperparameters here, which we've already discussed: **n_estimators** is the number of boosting rounds to use for the model (in other words, the number of stages for the stagewise additive modeling procedure), **objective** is the loss function that will be used to calculate gradients, and **learning_rate** controls how much each new estimator adds to the ensemble, or, in essence, how far of a step to take to decrease prediction error. The remaining hyperparameters are related to how much output we want to see during model training (**verbosity**) and the soon-to-be-deprecated **label_encoder** option, which XGBoost developers recommend setting to **False**:

```
xgb_model_1 = xgb.XGBClassifier(n_estimators=1000,\
                                verbosity=1,\
                                use_label_encoder=False,\
                                objective='binary:logistic',\
                                learning_rate=0.3)
```

The hyperparameter values we've indicated specify that:

- We will have 1,000 estimators, or boosting rounds. We'll discuss in more detail shortly how many rounds are needed; the default value is 100.

- We are familiar with the objective function (also known as the cost function) for binary logistic regression from *Chapter 4, The Bias-Variance Trade-Off*. XGBoost also offers a wide variety of objective functions for a range of tasks, including classification and regression.

- The learning rate is set to **0.3**, which is the default. Different values can be explored via hyperparameter search procedures, which we'll demonstrate.

> **NOTE**
>
> It is recommended to install XGBoost and SHAP using an Anaconda environment as demonstrated in the *Preface.* If you install different versions than those indicated, your results may be different than shown here.

Now that we have a model object and some training data, we are ready to fit the model. This looks similar to how it did in scikit-learn:

```
%%time
xgb_model_1.fit(X_train, y_train, \
                eval_metric="auc", \
                verbose=True)
```

Here, we are tracking how long the fitting procedure takes using the **%%time** "cell magic" in the Jupyter notebook. We need to supply the features **X_train** features and the response variable **y_train** of the training data. We also supply **eval_metric** and set the verbosity, which we'll explain shortly. Executing this cell should give output similar to this:

```
CPU times: user 52.5 s, sys: 986 ms, total: 53.4 s
Wall time: 17.5 s
Out[7]:
XGBClassifier(base_score=0.5, booster='gbtree', \
              colsample_bylevel=1, colsample_bynode=1, \
              colsample_bytree=1, gamma=0, gpu_id=-1, \
              importance_type='gain', interaction_constraints='', \
              learning_rate=0.3, max_delta_step=0, max_depth=6, \
              min_child_weight=1, missing=nan, \
              monotone_constraints='()', n_estimators=1000, \
              n_jobs=4, num_parallel_tree=1, random_state=0, \
              reg_alpha=0, reg_lambda=1, scale_pos_weight=1, \
              subsample=1, tree_method='exact', \
              use_label_encoder=False, validate_parameters=1, \
              verbosity=1)
```

The output tells us that this cell took 17.5 seconds to execute, called the "wall time," or the elapsed time on a clock that might be on your wall. The CPU times are longer than this because XGBoost efficiently uses multiple processors simultaneously. XGBoost also prints out all the hyperparameters, including the ones we set and the others that were left at their defaults.

Now, to examine the performance of this fitted model, we'll evaluate the area under the ROC curve on the validation set. First, we need to obtain the predicted probabilities:

```
val_set_pred_proba = xgb_model_1.predict_proba(X_val)[:,1]
from sklearn.metrics import roc_auc_score
roc_auc_score(y_val, val_set_pred_proba)
```

The output of this cell should be as follows:

```
0.7773798710782294
```

This indicates an ROC AUC of about 0.78. This will be our model performance baseline, using nearly default options for XGBoost.

# XGBOOST HYPERPARAMETERS

### EARLY STOPPING

When training ensembles of decision trees with XGBoost, there are many options available for reducing overfitting and leveraging the bias-variance trade-off. **Early stopping** is a simple one of these and can help provide an automated answer to the question "How many boosting rounds are needed?". It's important to note that early stopping relies on having a separate validation set of data, aside from the training set. However, this validation set will actually be used during the model training process, so it does not qualify as "unseen" data that was held out from model training, similar to how we used validation sets in cross-validation to select model hyperparameters in *Chapter 4, The Bias-Variance Trade-Off*.

When XGBoost is training successive decision trees to reduce error on the training set, it's possible that adding more and more trees to the ensemble will provide increasingly better fits to the training data, but start to cause lower performance on held-out data. To avoid this, we can use a validation set, also called an evaluation set or **eval_set** by XGBoost. The evaluation set will be supplied as a list of tuples of features and their corresponding response variables. Whichever tuple comes last in this list will be the one that is used for early stopping. We want this to be the validation set since the training data will be used to fit the model and can't provide an estimate of out-of-sample generalization:

```
eval_set = [(X_train, y_train), (X_val, y_val)]
```

Now we can fit the model again, but this time we supply the **eval_set** keyword argument with the evaluation set we just created. At this point, the **eval_metric** of **auc** becomes important. This means that after each boosting round, before training another decision tree, the area under the ROC curve will be evaluated on all the datasets supplied with **eval_set**. Since we'll indicate **verbosity=True**, we'll get output printed below the cell with the ROC AUC for both the training set and the validation set. This provides a nice live look at how model performance changes on the training and validation data as more boosting rounds are trained.

Since, in predictive modeling, we're primarily interested in how a model performs on new and unseen data, we would like to stop training additional boosting rounds when it becomes clear that they are not improving model performance on out-of-sample data. The **early_stopping_rounds=30** argument indicates that once 30 boosting rounds have been completed without any additional improvement in the ROC AUC on the validation set, XGBoost should stop model training. Once model training is complete, the final fitted model will only have as many ensemble members as needed to get the highest model performance on the validation set. This means that the last 30 members of the ensemble will be discarded, since they didn't provide any increase in validation set performance. Let's now fit this model and watch the progress:

```
%%time
xgb_model_1.fit(X_train, y_train, eval_set=eval_set,\
                eval_metric='auc',\
                verbose=True, early_stopping_rounds=30)
```

The output should look something like this:

```
[0]  validation_0-auc:0.80412    validation_1-auc:0.75223
[1]  validation_0-auc:0.84422    validation_1-auc:0.79207
[2]  validation_0-auc:0.85920    validation_1-auc:0.79278
[3]  validation_0-auc:0.86616    validation_1-auc:0.79517
[4]  validation_0-auc:0.88261    validation_1-auc:0.79659
[5]  validation_0-auc:0.88605    validation_1-auc:0.80061
[6]  validation_0-auc:0.89226    validation_1-auc:0.80224
[7]  validation_0-auc:0.89826    validation_1-auc:0.80305
[8]  validation_0-auc:0.90559    validation_1-auc:0.80095
[9]  validation_0-auc:0.91954    validation_1-auc:0.79685
[10] validation_0-auc:0.92113    validation_1-auc:0.79608
...
[33] validation_0-auc:0.99169    validation_1-auc:0.78323
[34] validation_0-auc:0.99278    validation_1-auc:0.78261
[35] validation_0-auc:0.99329    validation_1-auc:0.78139
[36] validation_0-auc:0.99344    validation_1-auc:0.77994
CPU times: user 2.65 s, sys: 136 ms, total: 2.78 s
Wall time: 2.36 s
...
```

Notice that this took much less time than the previous fit. This is because, due to early stopping, we only trained 37 rounds of boosting (notice boosting rounds are zero indexed). This means that the boosting procedure only needed 8 rounds to achieve the best validation score, as opposed to the 1,000 we tried previously! You can access the number of boosting rounds needed to reach the optimal validation set score, as well as that score, with the **booster** attribute of the model object. This attribute presents a lower-level interface to the model than the scikit-learn API we have been using:

```
xgb_model_1.get_booster().attributes()
```

The output should look like this, confirming the number of iterations and best validation score:

```
{'best_iteration': '7', 'best_score': '0.80305'}
```

From the training procedure, we can also see the ROC AUC after each round for both the training data, **validation_0-auc**, and the validation data, **validation_1-auc**, which provide insights into overfitting as the boosting procedure progresses. Here we can see that the validation score increased up to round 8, after which it started to decrease, indicating that further boosting would likely produce an undesirably overfitted model. However, the training score continued to increase up to the point the procedure was terminated, showing how powerfully XGBoost is able to fit the training data.

We can further confirm that the fitted model object only represents seven rounds of boosting, and check validation set performance, by manually calculating the ROC AUC as we did previously:

```
val_set_pred_proba_2 = xgb_model_1.predict_proba(X_val)[:,1]
roc_auc_score(y_val, val_set_pred_proba_2)
```

This should output the following:

```
0.8030501882609966
```

This matches the highest validation score achieved after seven rounds of boosting. So, with one simple tweak to the model training procedure, by using a validation set and early stopping, we were able to improve model performance on the validation set from about 0.78 to 0.80, a substantial increase. This shows the importance of early stopping in boosting.

One natural question to ask here is "How did we know that 30 rounds for early stopping would be enough?". You can experiment with this number, as with any hyperparameter, and different values may be appropriate for different datasets. You can look to see how the validation score changes with each boosting round to get an idea for this. Sometimes, the validation score can increase and decrease in a jumpy way from round to round, so it's a good idea to have enough rounds to make sure you've found the maximum, and boosted through any temporary decreases.

## TUNING THE LEARNING RATE

The learning rate is also referred to as **eta** in the XGBoost documentation, as well as **step size shrinkage**. This hyperparameter controls how much of a contribution each new estimator will make to the ensemble prediction. If you increase the learning rate, you may reach the optimal model, defined as having the highest performance on the validation set, faster. However, there is the danger that setting it too high will result in boosting steps that are too large. In this case, the gradient boosting procedure may not converge on the optimal model, due to similar issues to those discussed in *Exercise 4.01, Using Gradient Descent to Minimize a Cost Function,* from *Chapter 4, The Bias Variance Trade-off,* regarding large learning rates in gradient descent. Let's explore how the learning rate affects model performance on our synthetic data.

The learning rate is a number between zero and 1 (inclusive of endpoints, although a learning rate of zero is not useful). We make an array of 25 evenly spaced numbers between 0.01 and 1 for the learning rates we'll test:

```
learning_rates = np.linspace(start=0.01, stop=1, num=25)
```

Now we set up a **for** loop to train a model for each learning rate and save the validation scores in an array. We'll also track the number of boosting rounds that it takes to reach the best iteration. The next several code blocks should be run together as one cell in a Jupyter notebook. We start by measuring how long this will take, creating empty lists to store results, and opening the **for** loop:

```
%%time
val_aucs = []
best_iters = []
for learning_rate in learning_rates:
```

At each loop iteration, the **learning_rate** variable will hold successive elements of the **learning_rates** array. Once inside the loop, the first step is to update the hyperparameters of the model object with the new learning rate. This is accomplished using the **set_params** method, which we supply with a double asterisk **\*\*** and a dictionary mapping hyperparameter names to values. The **\*\*** function call syntax in Python allows us to supply an arbitrary number of keyword arguments, also called **kwargs**, as a dictionary. In this case, we are only changing one keyword argument, so the dictionary only has one item:

```
xgb_model_1.set_params(**{'learning_rate':learning_rate})
```

Now that we've set the new learning rate on the model object, we train the model using early stopping as before:

```
xgb_model_1.fit(X_train, y_train, eval_set=eval_set,\
                eval_metric='auc',\
                verbose=False, early_stopping_rounds=30)
```

After fitting, we obtain the predicted probabilities for the validation set and then use them to calculate the validation ROC AUC. This is added to our list of results using the **append** method:

```
val_set_pred_proba_2 = xgb_model_1.predict_proba(X_val)[:,1]
val_aucs.append(roc_auc_score(y_val, val_set_pred_proba_2))
```

Finally, we also capture the number of rounds required for each learning rate:

```
best_iters.append(
    int(xgb_model_1.get_booster().\
                    attributes()['best_iteration']))
```

The previous five code snippets should all be run together in one cell. The output should be similar to this:

```
CPU times: user 1min 23s, sys: 526 ms, total: 1min 24s
Wall time: 22.2 s
```

Now that we have our results from this hyperparameter search, we can visualize validation set performance and the number of iterations. Since these two metrics are on different scales, we'll want to create a dual *y* axis plot. pandas makes this easy, so first we'll put all the data into a data frame:

```
learning_rate_df = \
pd.DataFrame({'Learning rate':learning_rates,\
             'Validation AUC':val_aucs,\
             'Best iteration':best_iters})
```

Now we can visualize performance and the number of iterations for different learning rates like this, noting that:

- We set the index (**set_index**) so that the learning rate is plotted on the *x* axis, and the other columns on the *y* axis.

- The **secondary_y** keyword argument indicates which column to plot on the right-hand *y* axis.

- The **style** argument allows us to specify different line styles for each column plotted. **-o** is a solid line with dots, while **--o** is a dashed line with dots:

```
mpl.rcParams['figure.dpi'] = 400
learning_rate_df.set_index('Learning rate')\
    .plot(secondary_y='Best iteration', style=['-o', '--o'])
```

The resulting plot should look like this:

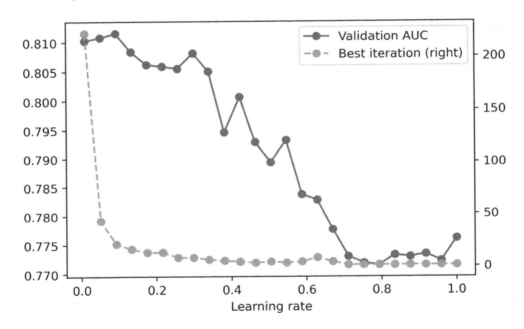

**Figure 6.2: XGBoost model performance on a validation set, with the number of boosting rounds until best iteration, for different learning rates**

Overall, it appears that smaller learning rates result in better model performance for this synthetic data. By using a learning rate smaller than the default of 0.3, the best performance we can obtain can be seen as follows:

```
max(val_aucs)
```

The output is as follows:

```
0.8115309360232714
```

By adjusting the learning rate, we were able to increase the validation AUC from about 0.80 to 0.81, indicating the benefits of using an appropriate learning rate.

In general, smaller learning rates will usually result in better model performance, although they will require a larger number of boosting rounds, since the contribution of each round is smaller. This will translate into more time required for model training. We can see this in the plot of the number of rounds needed to reach the best iteration in *Figure 6.2*. In this case, it looks like good performance can be attained with fewer than 50 rounds, and the model training time is not that long for this data in any case. For larger datasets, training time may be longer. Depending on how much computational time you have, decreasing the learning rate and training more rounds can be an effective way to increase model performance.

When exploring smaller learning rates, be sure to set the **n_estimators** hyperparameter large enough to allow the training process to find the optimal model, ideally in conjunction with early stopping.

## OTHER IMPORTANT HYPERPARAMETERS IN XGBOOST

We've seen that overfitting in XGBoost can be compensated for by using different learning rates, as well as early stopping. What are some of the other hyperparameters that may be relevant? XGBoost has many hyperparameters and we won't list them all here. You're encouraged to consult the documentation (https://xgboost.readthedocs.io/en/latest/parameter.html) for a full list.

In the following exercise, we'll do a grid search over ranges of six hyperparameters, including the learning rate. We will also include **max_depth**, which should be familiar from *Chapter 5*, *Decision Trees and Random Forests*, and controls the depth to which trees in the ensemble are grown. Aside from these, we will also consider the following:

- **gamma** limits the complexity of trees in the ensemble by only allowing a node to be split if the reduction in the loss function value is greater than a certain amount.

- **min_child_weight** also controls the complexity of trees by only splitting nodes if they have at least a certain amount of "sample weight." If all samples have equal weight (as they do for our exercise), this equates to the minimum number of training samples in a node. This is similar to **min_weight_fraction_leaf** and **min_samples_leaf** for decision trees in scikit-learn.

- **`colsample_bytree`** is a randomly selected fraction of features that will be used to grow each tree in the ensemble. This is similar to the **`max_features`** parameter in scikit-learn (which does the selection at a node level as opposed to the tree level here). XGBoost also makes **`colsample_bylevel`** and **`colsample_bynode`** available to do the feature sampling at each level of each tree, and each node, respectively.

- **`subsample`** controls what fraction of samples from the training data is randomly selected prior to growing a new tree for the ensemble. This is similar to the **`bootstrap`** option for random forests in scikit-learn. Both this and the **`colsample`** parameters limit the information available during model training, increasing the bias of the individual ensemble members, but hopefully also reducing the variance of the overall ensemble and improving out-of-sample model performance.

As you can see, gradient boosted trees in XGBoost implement several concepts that are familiar from decision trees and random forests. Now, let's explore how these hyperparameters affect model performance.

## EXERCISE 6.01: RANDOMIZED GRID SEARCH FOR TUNING XGBOOST HYPERPARAMETERS

In this exercise, we'll use a randomized grid search to explore the space of six hyperparameters. A randomized grid search is a good option when you have many values of many hyperparameters you'd like to search over. We'll look at six hyperparameters here. If, for example, there were five values for each of these that we'd like to test, we'd need $5^6$ = 15,625 searches. Even if each model fit only took a second, we'd still need several hours to exhaustively search all possible combinations. A randomized grid search can achieve satisfactory results by only searching a random sample of all these combinations. Here, we'll show how to do this using scikit-learn and XGBoost.

The first step in a randomized grid search is to specify the range of values you'd like to sample from, for each hyperparameter. This can be done by either supplying a list of values, or a distribution object to sample from. In the case of discrete hyperparameters such as **`max_depth`**, where there are only a few possible values, it makes sense to specify them as a list. On the other hand, for continuous hyperparameters, such as **`subsample`**, that can vary anywhere on the interval (0, 1], we don't need to specify a list of values. Rather, we can ask that the grid search randomly sample values in a uniform way over this interval. We will use a uniform distribution to sample several of the hyperparameters we consider:

> **NOTE**
>
> The Jupyter notebook for this exercise can be found at https://packt.link/TOXso.

1. Import the **uniform** distribution class from **scipy** and specify ranges for all hyperparameters to be searched, using a dictionary. **uniform** can take two arguments, **loc** and **scale**, specifying the lower bound of the interval to sample from and the width of the interval, respectively:

```
from scipy.stats import uniform
param_grid = {'max_depth':[2,3,4,5,6,7],
              'gamma':uniform(loc=0.0, scale=3),
              'min_child_weight':list(range(1,151)),
              'colsample_bytree':uniform(loc=0.1, scale=0.9),
              'subsample':uniform(loc=0.5, scale=0.5),
              'learning_rate':uniform(loc=0.01, scale=0.5)}
```

Here, we've selected parameter ranges based on experimentation and experience. For example with subsample, the XGBoost documentation recommends choosing values of at least 0.5, so we've indicated **uniform(loc=0.5, scale=0.5)**, which means sampling from the interval [0.5, 1].

2. Now that we've indicated which distributions to sample from, we need to do the sampling. scikit-learn offers the **ParameterSampler** class, which will randomly sample the **param_grid** parameters supplied and return as many samples as requested (**n_iter**). We also set **RandomState** for repeatable results across different runs of the notebook:

```
from sklearn.model_selection import ParameterSampler
rng = np.random.RandomState(0)
n_iter=1000
param_list = list(ParameterSampler(param_grid, n_iter=n_iter,
                                   random_state=rng))
```

We have returned the results in a list of dictionaries of specific parameter values, corresponding to locations in the 6-dimensional hyperparameter space.

Note that in this exercise, we are iterating through 1,000 hyperparameter combinations, which will likely take over 5 minutes. You may wish to decrease this number for faster results.

3.  Examine the first item of **param_list**:

```
param_list[0]
```

This should return a combination of six parameter values, from the distributions indicated:

```
{'colsample_bytree': 0.5939321535345923,
 'gamma': 2.1455680991172583,
 'learning_rate': 0.31138168803582195,
 'max_depth': 5,
 'min_child_weight': 104,
 'subsample': 0.7118273996694524}
```

4.  Observe how you can set multiple XGBoost hyperparameters simultaneously with a dictionary, using the ** syntax. First create a new XGBoost classifier object for this exercise.

```
xgb_model_2 = xgb.XGBClassifier(
    n_estimators=1000,
    verbosity=1,
    use_label_encoder=False,
    objective='binary:logistic')
xgb_model_2.set_params(**param_list[0])
```

The output should show the indicated hyperparameters being set:

```
XGBClassifier(base_score=0.5, booster='gbtree',\
              colsample_bylevel=1, colsample_bynode=1,\
              colsample_bytree=0.5939321535345923,\
              gamma=2.1455680991172583, gpu_id=-1,\
              importance_type='gain',interaction_constraints='',\
              learning_rate=0.31138168803582195,\
              max_delta_step=0, max_depth=5,\
              min_child_weight=104, missing=nan,\
              monotone_constraints='()', n_estimators=1000,\
              n_jobs=4, num_parallel_tree=1,\
              random_state=0, reg_alpha=0, reg_lambda=1,\
```

```
                    scale_pos_weight=1, subsample=0.7118273996694524,\
                    tree_method='exact', use_label_encoder=False,\
                    validate_parameters=1, verbosity=1)
```

We will use this procedure in a loop to look at all hyperparameter values.

5. The next several steps will be contained in one cell inside a **for** loop. First, measure the time it will take to do this, create an empty list to save validation AUCs, and then start a counter:

```
%%time
val_aucs = []
counter = 1
```

6. Open the **for** loop, set the hyperparameters, and fit the XGBoost model, similar to the preceding example of tuning the learning rate:

```
for params in param_list:
    #Set hyperparameters and fit model
    xgb_model_2.set_params(**params)
    xgb_model_2.fit(X_train, y_train, eval_set=eval_set,\
                    eval_metric='auc',\
                    verbose=False, early_stopping_rounds=30)
```

7. Within the **for** loop, get the predicted probability and validation set AUC:

```
    #Get predicted probabilities and save validation ROC AUC
    val_set_pred_proba = xgb_model_2.predict_proba(X_val)[:,1]
    val_aucs.append(roc_auc_score(y_val, val_set_pred_proba))
```

8. Since this procedure will take a few minutes, it's nice to print the progress to the Jupyter notebook output. We use the Python remainder syntax, %, to print a message every 50 iterations, in other words, when the remainder of **counter** divided by 50 equals zero. Finally, we increment the counter:

```
    #Print progress
    if counter % 50 == 0:
        print('Done with {counter} of {n_iter}'.format(
            counter=counter, n_iter=n_iter))
    counter += 1
```

9. Assembling steps 5-8 in one cell and running the for loop should give output like this:

```
Done with 50 of 1000
Done with 100 of 1000
...
Done with 950 of 1000
Done with 1000 of 1000
CPU times: user 24min 20s, sys: 18.9 s, total: 24min 39s
Wall time: 6min 27s
```

10. Now that we have all the results from our hyperparameter exploration, we need to examine them. We can easily put all the hyperparameter combinations in a data frame, since they are organized as a list of dictionaries. Do this and look at the first few rows:

```
xgb_param_search_df = pd.DataFrame(param_list)
xgb_param_search_df.head()
```

The output should look like this:

| | colsample_bytree | gamma | learning_rate | max_depth | min_child_weight | subsample |
|---|---|---|---|---|---|---|
| 0 | 0.593932 | 2.145568 | 0.311382 | 5 | 104 | 0.711827 |
| 1 | 0.681305 | 1.312762 | 0.455887 | 2 | 141 | 0.691721 |
| 2 | 0.812553 | 1.586685 | 0.294022 | 7 | 26 | 0.535518 |
| 3 | 0.178416 | 0.060655 | 0.426310 | 2 | 83 | 0.736804 |
| 4 | 0.820820 | 1.561432 | 0.349440 | 2 | 10 | 0.768687 |

Figure 6.3: Hyperparameter combinations from a randomized grid search

11. We can also add the validation set ROC AUCs to the data frame and see what the maximum is:

```
xgb_param_search_df['Validation ROC AUC'] = val_aucs
max_auc = xgb_param_search_df['Validation ROC AUC'].max()
max_auc
```

The output should be as follows:

```
0.8151220995602575
```

The result of searching over the hyperparameter space is that the validation set AUC is about 0.815. This is larger than the 0.812 we obtained with early stopping and searching over learning rates (*Figure 6.3*), although not much. This means that, for this data, the default hyperparameters (aside from the learning rate) were sufficient to achieve pretty good performance. While we didn't improve performance much with the hyperparameter search, it is instructive to see how the changing values of the hyperparameters affect model performance. We'll examine the marginal distributions of AUCs with respect to each parameter individually in the following steps. This means that we'll look at how the AUCs change as one hyperparameter at a time changes, keeping in mind the fact that the other hyperparameters are also changing in our grid search results.

12. Set up a grid of six subplots for plotting performance against each hyperparameter using the following code, which also adjusts the figure resolution and starts a counter we'll use to loop through the subplots:

```
mpl.rcParams['figure.dpi'] = 400
fig, axs = plt.subplots(3,2,figsize=(8,6))
counter = 0
```

13. Open a **for** loop to iterate through the hyperparameter names, which are the columns of the data frame, not including the last column. Access the axes objects by flattening the 3 x 2 array returned by **subplot** and indexing it with **counter**. For each hyperparameter, use the **plot.scatter** method of the data frame to make a scatter plot on the appropriate axis. The *x* axis will show the hyperparameter, the *y* axis the validation AUC, and the other options help us get black circular markers with white face colors (interiors):

```
for col in xgb_param_search_df.columns[:-1]:
    this_ax = axs.flatten()[counter]
    xgb_param_search_df.plot.scatter(x=col,\
                            y='Validation ROC AUC',\
                            ax=this_ax, marker='o',\
                            color='w',\
                            edgecolor='k',\
                            linewidth=0.5)
```

14. The data frame's **plot** method will automatically create *x* and *y* axis labels. However, since the *y* axis label will be the same for all of these plots, we only need to include it in the first one. So we set all the others to an empty string, `' '`, and increment the counter:

```
if counter > 0:
    this_ax.set_ylabel('')
counter += 1
```

Since we will be plotting marginal distributions, as we look at how validation AUC changes with a given hyperparameter, all the other hyperparameters are also changing. This means that the relationship may be noisy. To get an idea of the overall trend, we are also going to create line plots with the average value of the validation AUC in each decile of the hyperparameter. Deciles organize data into bins based on whether the values fall into the bottom 10%, the next 10%, and so on, up to the top 10%. pandas offers a function called **qcut**, which cuts a Series into quantiles (a quantile is one of a group of equal-size bins, for example one of the deciles in the case of 10 bins), returning another series of the quantiles, as well as the endpoints of the quantile bins, which you can think of as histogram edges.

15. Use pandas **qcut** to generate a series of deciles (10 quantiles) for each hyperparameter (except **max_depth**), returning the bin edges (there will be 11 of these for 10 quantiles) and dropping bin edges as needed if there are not enough unique values to divide into 10 quantiles (**duplicates='drop'**). Create a list of points halfway between each pair of bin edges for plotting:

```
if col != 'max_depth':
    out, bins = pd.qcut(xgb_param_search_df[col], q=10,\
                        retbins=True, duplicates='drop')
    half_points = [(bins[ix] + bins[ix+1])/2
                    for ix in range(len(bins)-1)]
```

16. For **max_depth**, since there are only six unique values, we can use these values directly in a similar way to the deciles:

```
else:
    out = xgb_param_search_df[col]
    half_points = np.sort(xgb_param_search_df[col].unique())
```

17. Create a temporary data frame by copying the hyperparameter search data frame, create a new column with the Series of deciles, and use this to find the average value of the validation AUC within each hyperparameter decile:

```
tmp_df = xgb_param_search_df.copy()
tmp_df['param_decile'] = out
mean_df = tmp_df.groupby('param_decile').agg(
    {'Validation ROC AUC':'mean'})
```

18. We can visualize results with a dashed line plot of the decile averages of validation AUC within each grouping, on the same axis as each scatter plot. Close the **for** loop and clean up the subplot formatting with **plt.tight_layout()**:

```
this_ax.plot(half_points, \
             mean_df.values, \
             color='k', \
             linestyle='--')
plt.tight_layout()
```

After running the **for** loop, the resulting image should look like this:

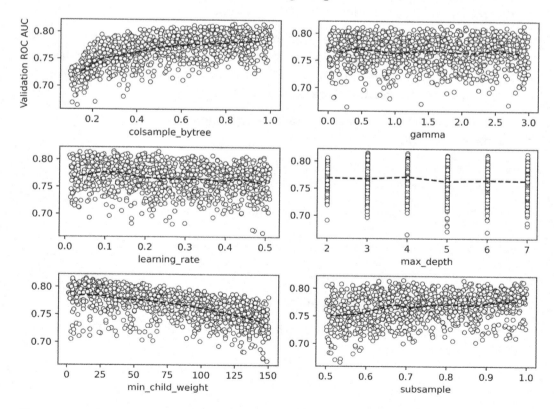

**Figure 6.4: Validation AUCs plotted against each hyperparameter, along with the average values within hyperparameter deciles**

While we noted that the hyperparameter search in this exercise did not result in a substantial increase in validation AUC over previous efforts in this chapter, the plots in *Figure 6.4* can still show us how XGBoost hyperparameters affect model performance for this particular dataset. One way that XGBoost combats overfitting is by limiting the data available when growing trees, either by randomly selecting only a fraction of the features available to each tree (**colsample_bytree**), or a fraction of the training samples (**subsample**). However, for this synthetic data, it appears the model performs best when using 100% of the features and samples for each tree; less than this and model performance steadily degrades. Another way to control overfitting is to limit the complexity of trees in the ensemble, by controlling their **max_depth**, the minimum number of training samples in the leaves (**min_child_weight**), or the minimum reduction in the value of the loss function reduction required to split a node (**gamma**). Neither **max_depth** nor **gamma** appear to have much effect on model performance in our example here, while limiting the number of samples in the leaves appears to be detrimental.

It appears that in this case, the gradient boosting procedure is robust enough on its own to achieve good model performance, without any additional tricks required to reduce overfitting. Similar to what we observed above, however, having a smaller **learning_rate** is beneficial.

19. We can show the optimal hyperparameter combination and the corresponding validation set AUC as follows:

```
max_ix = xgb_param_search_df['Validation ROC AUC'] == max_auc
xgb_param_search_df[max_ix]
```

This should return a row of the data frame similar to this:

| | colsample_bytree | gamma | learning_rate | max_depth | min_child_weight | subsample | Validation ROC AUC |
|---|---|---|---|---|---|---|---|
| **308** | 0.83627 | 1.843039 | 0.120745 | 3 | 14 | 0.692646 | 0.815122 |

Figure 6.5: Optimal hyperparameter combination and validation set AUC

The validation set AUC is similar to what we achieved above (*step 10*) by tuning only the learning rate.

# ANOTHER WAY OF GROWING TREES: XGBOOST'S GROW_POLICY

In addition to limiting the maximum depth of trees using a **max_depth** hyperparameter, there is another paradigm for controlling tree growth: finding the node where a split would result in the greatest reduction in the loss function, and splitting this node, regardless of how deep it will make the tree. This may result in a tree with one or two very deep branches, while the other branches may not have grown very far. XGBoost offers a hyperparameter called **grow_policy**, and setting this to **lossguide** results in this kind of tree growth, while the **depthwise** option is the default and grows trees to an indicated **max_depth**, as we've done in *Chapter 5, Decision Trees and Random Forests*, and so far in this chapter. The **lossguide** grow policy is a newer option in XGBoost and mimics the behavior of LightGBM, another popular gradient boosting package.

To use the **lossguide** policy, it is necessary to set another hyperparameter we haven't discussed yet, **tree_method**, which must be set to **hist** or **gpu-hist**. Without going into too much detail, the **hist** method will use a faster way of searching for splits. Instead of looking between every sequential pair of sorted feature values for the training samples in a node, the **hist** method builds a histogram, and only considers splits on the edges of the histogram. So, for example, if there are 100 samples in a node, their feature values may be binned into 10 groups, meaning there are only 9 possible splits to consider instead of 99.

We can instantiate an XGBoost model for the **lossguide** grow policy as follows, using a learning rate of **0.1** based on intuition from our hyperparameter exploration in the previous exercise:

```
xgb_model_3 = xgb.XGBClassifier(
    n_estimators=1000,
    max_depth=0,
    learning_rate=0.1,
    verbosity=1,
    objective='binary:logistic',
    use_label_encoder=False,
    n_jobs=-1,
    tree_method='hist',
    grow_policy='lossguide')
```

Notice here that we've set **max_depth=0**, since this hyperparameter is not relevant for the **lossguide** policy. Instead, we are going to set a hyperparameter called **max_leaves**, which simply controls the maximum number of leaves in the trees that will be grown. We'll do a hyperparameter search of values ranging from 5 to 100 leaves:

```
max_leaves_values = list(range(5,105,5))
print(max_leaves_values[:5])
print(max_leaves_values[-5:])
```

This should output the following:

```
[5, 10, 15, 20, 25]
[80, 85, 90, 95, 100]
```

Now we are ready to repeatedly fit and validate the model across this range of hyperparameter values, similar to what we've done previously:

```
%%time
val_aucs = []
for max_leaves in max_leaves_values:
    #Set parameter and fit model
    xgb_model_3.set_params(**{'max_leaves':max_leaves})
    xgb_model_3.fit(X_train, y_train, eval_set=eval_set,\
                    eval_metric='auc', verbose=False,\
                    early_stopping_rounds=30)

    #Get validation score
    val_set_pred_proba = xgb_model_3.predict_proba(X_val)[:,1]
    val_aucs.append(roc_auc_score(y_val, val_set_pred_proba))
```

The output will include the wall time for all of these fits, which was about 24 seconds in testing. Now let's put the results in a data frame:

```
max_leaves_df = \
pd.DataFrame({'Max leaves':max_leaves_values,
              'Validation AUC':val_aucs})
```

We can visualize how the validation AUC changes with the maximum number of leaves, similar to our visualization of the learning rate:

```
mpl.rcParams['figure.dpi'] = 400
max_leaves_df.set_index('Max leaves').plot()
```

This will result in a plot like this:

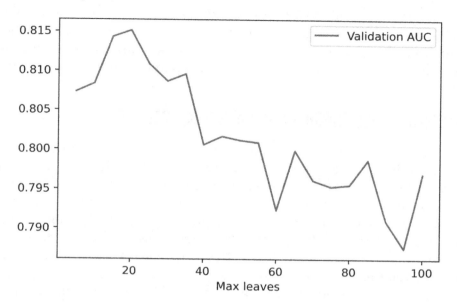

Figure 6.6: Validation AUC against the max_leaves hyperparameter

Smaller values of **max_leaves** will limit the complexity of the trees grown for the ensemble, which will ideally increase bias, but also decrease variance for improved out-of-sample performance. We can see this in a higher validation set AUC when the trees are limited to 15 or 20 leaves. What is the maximum validation set AUC?

```
max_auc = max_leaves_df['Validation AUC'].max()
max_auc
```

This should output the following:

```
0.8151200989120475
```

Let's confirm that this maximum validation AUC occurs at **max_leaves=20**, as indicated in *Figure 6.6*:

```
max_ix = max_leaves_df['Validation AUC'] == max_auc
max_leaves_df[max_ix]
```

This should return a row of the data frame:

| | Max leaves | Validation AUC |
|---|---|---|
| **3** | 20 | 0.81512 |

Figure 6.7: Optimal max_leaves

By using the **lossguide** grow policy, we can achieve performance at least as good as anything else we've tried so far. One key advantage of the **lossguide** policy is that, for larger datasets, it can result in training times that are faster than the **depthwise** policy, especially for smaller values of **max_leaves**. While the dataset here is small enough that this is not of practical importance, this speed may be desirable in other applications.

## EXPLAINING MODEL PREDICTIONS WITH SHAP VALUES

Along with cutting-edge modeling techniques such as XGBoost, the practice of explaining model predictions has undergone substantial development in recent years. So far, we've learned that logistic regression coefficients, or feature importances from random forests, can provide insight into the reasons for model predictions. A more powerful technique for explaining model predictions was described in a 2017 paper, *A Unified Approach to Interpreting Model Predictions*, by Scott Lundberg and Su-In Lee (https://arxiv.org/abs/1705.07874). This technique is known as **SHAP** (**SHapley Additive exPlanations**) as it is based on earlier work by mathematician Lloyd Shapley. Shapely developed an area of game theory to understand how coalitions of players can contribute to the overall outcome of a game. Recent machine learning research into model explanation leveraged this concept to consider how groups or coalitions of features in a predictive model contribute to the output model prediction. By considering the contribution of different groups of features, the SHAP method can isolate the effect of individual features.

> **NOTE**
>
> At the time of writing, the SHAP library used in *Chapter 6, Gradient Boosting, XGBoost, and SHAP Values*, is not compatible with Python 3.9. Hence, if you are using Python 3.9 as your base environment, we suggest that you set up a Python 3.8 environment as described in the *Preface*.

Some notable aspects of using SHAP values to explain model predictions include:

- SHAP values can be used to make **individualized** explanations of model predictions; in other words, the prediction of a single sample, in terms of the contribution of each feature, can be understood using SHAP. This is in contrast to the feature importance method of explaining random forests that we've already seen, which only considers the average importance of a feature across the model training set.

- SHAP values are calculated relative to a background dataset. By default, this is the training data, although other datasets can be supplied.

- SHAP values are additive, meaning that for the prediction of an individual sample, the SHAP values can be added up to recover the value of the prediction, for example, a predicted probability.

There are different implementations of the SHAP method for various types of models and here we will focus on SHAP for trees (Lundberg et al., 2019, https://arxiv.org/abs/1802.03888) to get insights into XGBoost model predictions on our validation set of synthetic data. First, let's refit **xgb_model_3** from the previous section with the optimal number of **max_leaves**, 20:

```
%%time
xgb_model_3.set_params(**{'max_leaves':20})
xgb_model_3.fit(X_train, y_train,\
                eval_set=eval_set,\
                eval_metric='auc',
                verbose=False,\
                early_stopping_rounds=30)
```

Now we're ready to start calculating SHAP values for the validation dataset. There are 40 features and 1,000 samples here:

```
X_val.shape
```

This should output the following:

```
(1000, 40)
```

To automatically label the plots we can make with the **shap** package, we'll put the validation set features in a data frame with column names. We'll use a list comprehension to make generic feature names, for example, "Feature 0, Feature 1, ..." and create the data frame as follows:

```
feature_names = ['Feature {number}'.format(number=number)
                 for number in range(X_val.shape[1])]
X_val_df = pd.DataFrame(data=X_val, columns=feature_names)
X_val_df.head()
```

The **dataframe** head should look like this:

| | Feature 0 | Feature 1 | Feature 2 | Feature 3 | Feature 4 | Feature 5 | Feature 6 | Feature 7 | Feature 8 | Feature 9 | ... |
|---|---|---|---|---|---|---|---|---|---|---|---|
| 0 | 1.852885 | -2.170293 | 1.057288 | 0.441873 | -0.803131 | -0.025139 | -0.037143 | 0.037565 | 1.163995 | 0.678410 | ... |
| 1 | -0.818316 | -1.126948 | 0.647810 | 0.092433 | -1.030356 | 0.754323 | -0.351566 | -0.523476 | 1.144878 | 0.219172 | ... |
| 2 | 0.020271 | -0.758004 | -1.136195 | 0.473366 | 1.291465 | 0.890423 | -2.217706 | -2.030749 | 1.768624 | -2.106202 | ... |
| 3 | -0.271543 | -0.366639 | -1.139614 | -0.753586 | 1.427853 | 1.249856 | 0.060528 | -0.374193 | 0.047770 | 0.640638 | ... |
| 4 | -0.549078 | 0.494648 | -1.266778 | -0.292728 | 1.459779 | 0.497898 | -0.618724 | -1.225373 | 0.171507 | 0.833027 | ... |

**Figure 6.8: Data frame of the validation features**

With the trained model, **xgb_model_3**, and the data frame of validation features, we're ready to create an **explainer** interface. The SHAP package has various kinds of explainers and we'll use the one specifically for tree models:

```
explainer = shap.explainers.Tree(xgb_model_3, data=X_val_df)
```

This has created an explainer using the model validation data as the background dataset. Now we are ready to use the explainer to obtain SHAP values. The SHAP package makes this very simple. All we need to do is pass in the dataset we want explanations for:

```
shap_values = explainer(X_val_df)
```

That's all there is to it! What is this variable, **shap_values**, that has been created? If you examine the contents of the **shap_values** variable directly, you will see that it contains three attributes. The first is **values**, which contains the SHAP values. Let's examine the shape:

```
shap_values.values.shape
```

This should return the following:

```
(1000, 40)
```

Because SHAPs provide individualized explanations, there is a row for each of the 1,000 samples in the validation set. There are 40 columns because we have 40 features and SHAP values tell us the contribution of each feature to the prediction for each sample. **shap_values** also contains a **base_values** attribute, which is the naïve prediction before any feature contributions are considered, also defined as the average prediction across the entire dataset. There is one of these for each sample (1,000). Finally, there is also a **data** attribute, which contains the feature values. All of this information can be combined in various ways to explain model predictions.

Thankfully, not only does the **shap** package provide fast and convenient methods for calculating SHAP values, but it also provides a rich suite of visualization techniques. One of the most popular is a SHAP summary plot, which visualizes the contribution of each feature to each sample. Let's create this plot and then understand what is being shown. Please note that most interesting SHAP visualizations use color, so if you're reading in black and white, please refer to the GitHub repository for color figures:

```
mpl.rcParams['figure.dpi'] = 75
shap.summary_plot(shap_values.values, X_val_df)
```

This should produce the following:

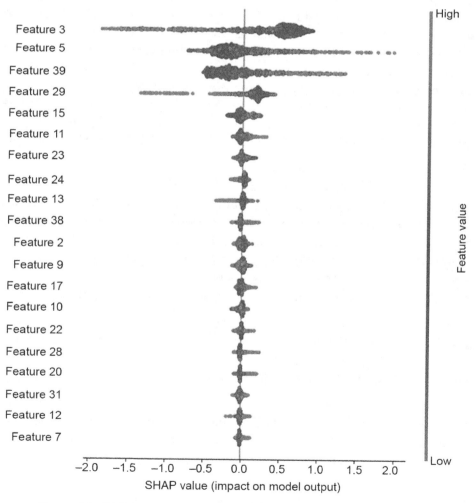

Figure 6.9: SHAP summary plot for the synthetic data validation set

> **NOTE**
>
> If you're reading the print version of this book, you can download and browse the color versions of some of the images in this chapter by visiting the following link: https://packt.link/ZFiYH

*Figure 6.9* contains a lot of information to help us explain the model. The summary plot may contain up to 40,000 plotted points, one for each of the 40 features and each of the 1,000 validation samples (although only the first 20 features are shown by default). Let's start by understanding the *x* axis. The SHAP value indicates the additive contribution of each feature value to the prediction for a sample. SHAP values are shown here relative to the expected values, which are the **base_values** described earlier. So if a given feature has a small impact on the prediction for a given sample, it will not tend to move the prediction very far from the expected value, and the SHAP value will be close to zero. However if a feature has a large effect, which, in the case of our binary classification problem, means that the predicted probability will be pushed closer to 0 or 1, the SHAP value will be further from 0. Negative SHAP values indicate a feature moving the prediction closer to 0, and positive SHAP values indicate closer to 1.

Note that the SHAP values shown in *Figure 6.9* cannot be directly interpreted as predicted probabilities. By default, SHAP values for the XGBoost binary classification model with the **binary:logistic** objective function are calculated and plotted using the log-odds representation of probability, which was introduced in *Chapter 3, Details of Logistic Regression and Feature Exploration* in the *Why Is Logistic Regression Considered a Linear Model?* section. This means that they can be added and subtracted, or in other words, we can perform linear transformations on them.

What about the color of the dots in *Figure 6.9*? These represent the values of the features for each sample, with red meaning a higher value and blue lower. So, for example, we can see in the fourth row of the plot that the lowest SHAP values come from high feature values (red dots) for Feature 29.

The vertical arrangement of the dots, in other words, the width of the band of dots for each feature, indicates how many dots there are at that location on the *x* axis. If there are many samples, the band of dots will be wider.

The vertical arrangement of features in the diagram is based on feature importance. The most important features, in other words, those with the largest average effect (mean absolute SHAP value) on model predictions, are placed at the top of the list.

While the summary plot in *Figure 6.9* is a great way to look at all of the most important features and their SHAP values at once, it may not reveal some interesting relationships. For example, the most important feature, Feature 3, appears to have a large clump of purple dots (middle of the range of feature values) that have positive SHAP values, while the negative SHAP values for this feature may result from high or low feature values.

What is going on here? Often, when the effects of features seem unclear from a SHAP summary plot, the tree-based model we are using is capturing interaction effects between features. To gain additional insight into individual features and their interactions with others, we can use a SHAP scatter plot. Firstly, let's make a simple scatter plot of the SHAP values of Feature 3. Note that we can index the **shap_ values** object in a similar way to a data frame:

```
shap.plots.scatter(shap_values[:,'Feature 3'])
```

This should produce the following plot:

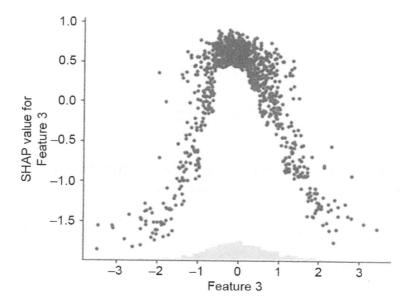

**Figure 6.10: Scatter plot of SHAP values for Feature 3**

From *Figure 6.10*, we can tell pretty much the same information that we could from the summary plot of *Figure 6.9*: feature values in the middle of the range have high SHAP values, while those at the extremes are lower. However, the **scatter** method also allows us to color the points of the scatter plot by another feature value, so we can see whether there are interactions between the features. We'll color points by the second most important feature, Feature 5:

```
shap.plots.scatter(shap_values[:,'Feature 3'],
                   color=shap_values[:,'Feature 5'])
```

The resulting plot should look like this:

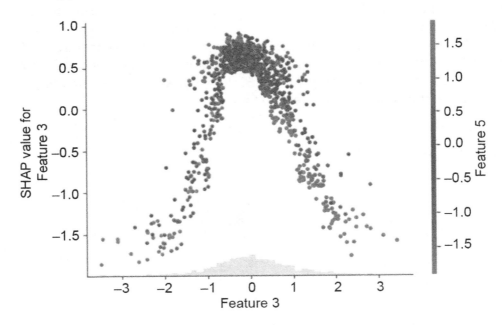

Figure 6.11: Scatter plot of SHAP values for Feature 3, colored by feature values of Feature 5. Arrows A and B indicated interesting interaction effects between these features

*Figure 6.11* shows an interesting interaction between Feature 3 and Feature 5. When samples are in the middle of the range of feature values for Feature 3, in other words, at the top of the hump shape in *Figure 6.11*, the color of dots appears to get more red going from the bottom to the top of the cluster of dots here (arrow A). This means that for feature values in the middle of the Feature 3 range, as the value of Feature 5 increases, so does the SHAP value for Feature 3. We can also see that as feature values of Feature 3 increase along the *x* axis from the middle toward the top of the range, this relationship reverses to where higher feature values for Feature 5 begin to correspond to lower SHAP values for Feature 3 (arrow B). So the interaction with Feature 5 appears to have a substantial impact on the SHAP values for Feature 3.

The complex relationships depicted in *Figure 6.11* show how increasing a feature value may lead to either increasing or decreasing SHAP values when interaction effects are present. The specific reasons for the patterns in *Figure 6.11* relate to the creation of the synthetic dataset we are modeling, where we specified multiple clusters in the feature space. As discussed in *Chapter 5, Decision Trees and Random Forests*, in the *Using Decision Trees: Advantages and Predicted Probabilities* section, tree-based models such as XGBoost are able to effectively model clusters of points in multi-dimensional feature space that belong to a certain class. SHAP explanations can help us to understand how the model is making these representations.

Here, we've used synthetic data, and the features have no real-world interpretation, so we can't assign any meaning to interactions we observe. However, with real-world data, detailed exploration with SHAP values and interactions can provide insight into how a model is representing complex relationships between attributes of customers or users, for example. SHAP values are also useful since they can provide explanations relative to any background dataset. While logistic regression coefficients and feature importances of random forests are determined entirely by the model training data, SHAP values can be calculated for any background dataset; so far in this chapter, we've been using the validation data. This provides an opportunity, when predicted models are deployed in a production environment, to understand how new predictions are being made. If the SHAP values for new predictions are very different from those of model training and test data, this may indicate that the nature of incoming data has changed, and it may be time to consider developing a new model. We'll consider these practical aspects of using models in the real world in the final chapter.

# EXERCISE 6.02: PLOTTING SHAP INTERACTIONS, FEATURE IMPORTANCE, AND RECONSTRUCTING PREDICTED PROBABILITIES FROM SHAP VALUES

In this exercise, you'll become more familiar with using SHAP values to provide visibility into the workings of a model. First, we'll take an alternate look at the interaction between Features 3 and 5, and then use SHAP values to calculate feature importances similar to what we did with a random forest model in *Chapter 5, Decision Trees and Random Forests*. Finally, we'll see how model outputs can be obtained from SHAP values, taking advantage of their additive property:

> **NOTE**
>
> The Jupyter notebook for this exercise can be found at https://packt.link/JcMoA.

1. Given the preliminary steps accomplished in this section already, we can take another look at the interaction between Features 3 and 5, the two most important features of the synthetic dataset. Use the following code to make an alternate version of *Figure 6.11*, except this time, look at the SHAP values of Feature 5, colored by those of Feature 3:

```
shap.plots.scatter(shap_values[:,'Feature 5'],
                   color=shap_values[:,'Feature 3'])
```

The resulting plot should look like this:

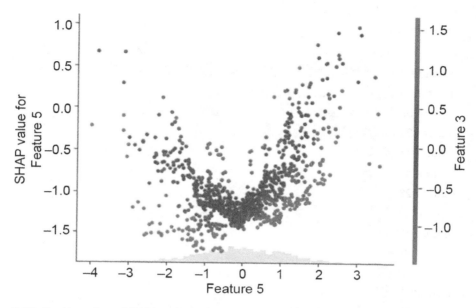

**Figure 6.12: Scatter plot of SHAP values for Feature 5, colored by feature values of Feature 3**

As opposed to *Figure 6.11*, here we are seeing the SHAP values of Feature 5. In general, from the scatter plot, we can see that SHAP values tend to increase as feature values increase for Feature 5. However there are certainly counterexamples to that general trend, as well as an interesting interaction with Feature 3: for a given value of Feature 5, which can be thought of as a vertical slice from the image, the color of the dots can either become more red, going from the bottom to the top, for negative feature values, or less red for positive feature values. This means that for a given value of Feature 5, its SHAP value depends on the value of Feature 3. This is a further illustration of the interesting interaction between Features 3 and 5. In a real project, which plot you would choose to show depends on what kind of story you want to tell with the data, relating to what real-world quantities Features 3 and 5 might represent.

2. Create a feature importance bar plot using the following code:

```
mpl.rcParams['figure.dpi'] = 75
shap.summary_plot(shap_values.values, X_val, plot_type='bar')
```

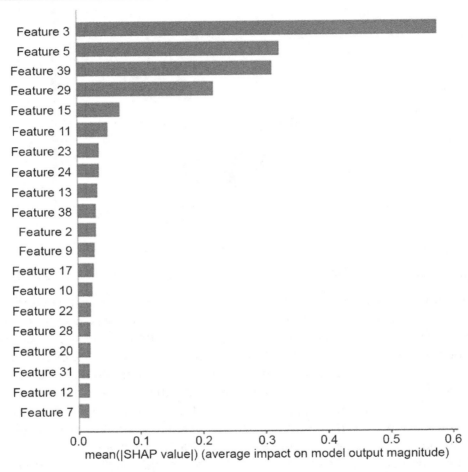

Figure 6.13: Feature importance bar plot using SHAP values

The feature importance bar plot gives a visual presentation of information similar to that obtained in *Exercise 5.03, Fitting a Random Forest,* in *Chapter 5, Decision Trees and Random Forests*, with a random forest: this is a single number for each feature, representing how important it is overall for a dataset.

Do these results make sense? Recall that we created this synthetic data with three informative features and two redundant ones. In *Figure 6.13*, it appears that there are four features that are substantially more important than all the others, so perhaps one of the redundant features was created in such a way that XGBoost selected it for splitting nodes fairly often, but the other redundant feature was not used as much.

Compared to the feature importances we found in *Chapter 5*, *Decision Trees and Random Forests*, the ones here are a bit different. The feature importances we can obtain from scikit-learn for a random forest model are calculated using the decrease in node impurity due to the feature as well as the fraction of training samples split by the feature. By contrast, feature importances using SHAP values are calculated as follows: first, the absolute value of all the SHAP values (**shap_values.values**) is taken, then an average of all the samples is taken for each feature, as implied by the *x* axis label. The interested reader can confirm this by calculating these metrics directly from **shap_values**.

Now that we've familiarized ourselves with a range of uses of SHAP values, let's see how their additive property allows the reconstruction of predicted probabilities.

3. SHAP values are calculated relative to the expected value, or base value, of a model. This can be interpreted as the average prediction over all samples in the background dataset. However, the prediction will be in units of log-odds as opposed to probability, as mentioned earlier, to support additivity. The expected value of a model can be accessed from the explainer object as follows:

```
explainer.expected_value
```

The output should look like this:

```
-0.30949621941894295
```

This information isn't particularly useful on its own. However, it gives us the baseline from which we can reconstruct predicted probabilities.

4. Recall that the shape of the SHAP values matrix is the number of samples by the number of features. In our exercise with the validation data, here that would be 1,000 by 40. To add up all the SHAP values for each sample, we therefore want to take a sum over the column axis (**axis=1**). This adds all the feature contributions, effectively providing the offset from the expected value. If we add the expected value to this, we then have the following predictions:

```
shap_sum = shap_values.values.sum(axis=1) + explainer.expected_value
shap_sum.shape
```

This should return the following:

```
(1000,)
```

Indicating we now have a single number for each sample. However, these predictions are in log-odds space. To transform them to probability space, we need to apply the logistic function introduced in *Chapter 3, Details of Logistic Regression and Feature Exploration*.

5. Apply the logistic transformation to log-odds predictions like this:

```
shap_sum_prob = 1 / (1 + np.exp(-1 * shap_sum))
```

Now we'd like to compare the predicted probabilities obtained from SHAP values with direct model output for confirmation.

6. Obtain predicted probabilities for the model validation set and check the shape with this code:

```
y_pred_proba = xgb_model_3.predict_proba(X_val)[:,1]
y_pred_proba.shape
```

The output should be as follows:

```
(1000,)
```

This is the same shape as our SHAP-derived predictions, as expected.

7. Put the model output and sums of SHAP values together in a data frame for side-by-side comparison, and spot check a random selection of five rows:

```
df_check = pd.DataFrame(
    {'SHAP sum':shap_sum_prob,
     'Predicted probability':y_pred_proba})
df_check.sample(5, random_state=1)
```

The output should confirm that the two methods have identical results:

| | SHAP sum | Predicted probability |
|---|---|---|
| **507** | 0.497260 | 0.497260 |
| **818** | 0.466160 | 0.466160 |
| **452** | 0.881343 | 0.881343 |
| **368** | 0.145347 | 0.145347 |
| **242** | 0.481065 | 0.481065 |

**Figure 6.14: Comparison of SHAP-derived predicted probabilities and those obtained directly from XGBoost**

The spot check indicates that these five samples have identical values. While the values may not be precisely equal due to rounding errors of machine arithmetic, you could use NumPy's **allclose** function to ensure they're the same within a user-configurable amount of rounding error.

8. Ensure that the SHAP-derived probabilities and model output probabilities are all very close to each other like this:

```
np.allclose(df_check['SHAP sum'],\
            df_check['Predicted probability'])
```

The output should be as follows:

```
True
```

This indicates that all elements of both columns are equal within rounding error. **allclose** is useful for when rounding errors are present and exact equality (testable with **np.array_equal**) would not hold.

By now, you should be getting an impression of the power of SHAP values to help understand machine learning models. The sample-specific, individualized nature of SHAP values opens up the possibility of very detailed analyses, which could help answer a wide variety of potential questions from business stakeholders such as "How would the model make predictions for people like this?" or "Why did the model make this prediction for this specific person"? Now that we're familiar with XGBoost and SHAP values, two state-of-the-art machine learning techniques, we return to the case study data to apply them.

# MISSING DATA

As a final note on the use of both XGBoost and SHAP, one valuable trait of both packages is their ability to handle missing values. Recall that in *Chapter 1, Data Exploration and Cleaning*, we found that some samples in the case study data had missing values for the **PAY_1** feature. So far, our approach has been to simply remove these samples from the dataset when building models. This is because, without specifically addressing the missing values in some way, the machine learning models implemented by scikit-learn cannot work with the data. Ignoring them is one approach, although this may not be satisfactory as it involves throwing data away. If it's a very small fraction of the data, this may be fine; however, in general, it's good to be able to know how to deal with missing values.

There are several approaches for imputing missing values of features, such as filling them in with the mean or mode of the non-missing values of that feature, or a randomly selected value from the non-missing values. You can also build a model outputting the feature in question as the response variable, with all the other features acting as features for this new model, and then predict the missing feature values. These approaches were explored in the first edition of this book (https://packt.link/oLb6C). However, since XGBoost typically performs at least as well as other machine learning models for binary classification tasks with tabular data like we're using here, and handles missing values, we'll forego more in-depth exploration of imputing missing values and let XGBoost do the work for us.

How does XGBoost handle missing data? At every opportunity to split a node, XGBoost considers only the non-missing feature values. If a feature with missing values is chosen to make a split, the samples with missing values for that feature are then sent down the optimal path to one of the child nodes, in terms of minimizing the loss function.

## SAVING PYTHON VARIABLES TO A FILE

In the activity for this chapter, to write to and read from files we'll use a new python statement (**with**) and the **pickle** package. **with** statements make it easier to work with files since they both open and close the file, instead of the user needing to do this separately. You can use code snippets like this to save variables to a file:

```
with open('filename.pkl', 'wb') as f:
    pickle.dump([var_1, var_2], f)
```

where **filename.pkl** is your chosen file path, **'wb'** indicates the file is open for writing in a binary format, and **pickle.dump** saves a list of variables **var_1** and **var_2** to the file. To open this file and load these variables, possibly into a separate Jupyter Notebook, the code is similar but now the file needs to be opened for reading in a binary format (**'rb'**):

```
with open('filename.pkl', 'rb') as f:
    var_1, var_2 = pickle.load(f)
```

## ACTIVITY 6.01: MODELING THE CASE STUDY DATA WITH XGBOOST AND EXPLAINING THE MODEL WITH SHAP

In this activity, we'll take what we've learned in this chapter with a synthetic dataset and apply it to the case study data. We'll see how an XGBoost model performs on a validation set and explain the model predictions using SHAP values. We have prepared the dataset for this activity by replacing the samples that had missing values for the **PAY_1** feature, that we had previously ignored, while maintaining the same train/test split for the samples with no missing values. You can see how the data was prepared in the Appendix to the notebook for this activity.

> **NOTE**
>
> The Jupyter notebook containing the solution as well as the appendix can be found here: https://packt.link/YFb4r.

1. Load the case study data that has been prepared for this exercise. The file path is **../../Data/Activity_6_01_data.pkl** and the variables are: **features_response, X_train_all, y_train_all, X_test_all, y_test_all**.

2. Define a validation set to train XGBoost with early stopping.

3. Instantiate an XGBoost model. Use the **lossguide** grow policy to enable the examination of validation set performance for several values of **max_leaves**.

4. Create a list of values of **max_leaves** from 5 to 200, counting by 5's.

5. Create the evaluation set for early stopping.

6. Loop through hyperparameter values and create a list of validation ROC AUCs, using the same technique as in *Exercise 6.01: Randomized Grid Search for Tuning XGBoost Hyperparameters*.

7. Create a data frame of the hyperparameter search results and plot the validation AUC against `max_leaves`.

8. Observe the number of `max_leaves` corresponding to the highest ROC AUC on the validation set.

9. Refit the XGBoost model with the optimal hyperparameter. So that we can examine SHAP values for the validation set, make a data frame of this data.

10. Create a SHAP explainer for our new model using the validation data as the background dataset, obtain the SHAP values, and make a summary plot.

11. Make a scatter plot of `LIMIT_BAL` SHAP values, colored by the feature with the strongest interaction.

12. Save the trained model along with the training and test data to a file.

> **NOTE**
>
> The solution to this activity can be found on page 392.

# SUMMARY

In this chapter, we've learned some of the most cutting-edge techniques for building machine learning models with tabular data. While other types of data, such as image or text data, warrant exploration with different types of models such as neural networks, many standard business applications leverage tabular data. XGBoost and SHAP are some of the most advanced and popular tools you can use to build and understand models with this kind of data. Having gained familiarity and practical experience using these tools with synthetic data, in the following activity, we return to the dataset for the case study and see how we can use XGBoost to model it, including the samples with missing feature values, and use SHAP values to understand the model.

# 7

# TEST SET ANALYSIS, FINANCIAL INSIGHTS, AND DELIVERY TO THE CLIENT

## OVERVIEW

This chapter presents several techniques for analyzing a model test set for deriving insights into likely model performance in the future. These techniques include the same model performance metrics we've already calculated, such as the ROC AUC, as well as new kinds of visualizations, such as the sloping of default risk by bins of predicted probability and the calibration of predicted probability. After reading this chapter, you will be able to bridge the gap between the theoretical metrics of machine learning and the financial metrics of the business world. You will be able to identify key insights while estimating the financial impact of a model and provide guidance to the client on how to realize this impact. We close with a discussion of the key elements to consider when delivering and deploying a model, such as the format of delivery and ways to monitor the model as it is being used.

# INTRODUCTION

In the previous chapter, we used XGBoost to push model performance even higher than all our previous efforts and learned how to explain model predictions using SHAP values. Now, we will consider model building to be complete and address the remaining issues that need attention before delivering the model to the client. The key elements of this chapter are analysis of the test set, including financial analysis, and things to consider when delivering a model to a client who wants to use it in the real world.

We look at the test set to get an idea of how well the model will perform in the future. By calculating metrics we already know, like the ROC AUC, but now on the test set, we can gain confidence that our model will be useful for new data. We'll also learn some intuitive ways to visualize the power of the model for grouping customers into different levels of risk of default, such as a decile chart.

Your client will likely appreciate the efforts you made in creating a more accurate model or one with a higher ROC AUC. However, they will definitely appreciate understanding how much money the model can help them earn or save and will probably be happy to receive specific guidance on how to maximize the model's potential for this. A financial analysis of the test set can simulate different scenarios of model-based strategies and help the client pick one that works for them.

After completing the financial analysis, we will wrap up by discussing how to deliver a model for use by the client and how to monitor its performance over time.

# REVIEW OF MODELING RESULTS

In order to develop a binary classification model to meet the business requirements of our client, we have now tried several modeling techniques with varying degrees of success. In the end, we'd like to choose the model with the best performance to do further analyses on and present to our client. However, it is also good to communicate the other options we explored, demonstrating a thoroughly researched project.

Here, we review the different models that we tried for the case study problem, the hyperparameters that we needed to tune, and the results from cross-validation, or the validation set in the case of XGBoost. We only include the work we did using all possible features, not the earlier exploratory models where we used only one or two features:

| Model | Location in book | Tuned hyperparameters | Validation ROC AUC |
|---|---|---|---|
| Logistic regression with L1 regularization | Chapter 4, The Bias-Variance Trade-Off, Activity 4.01, Cross-Validation and Feature Engineering with the Case Study Data | Regularization parameter C | 0.719 |
| Logistic regression with L1 regularization and interaction features | Chapter 4, The Bias-Variance Trade-Off, Activity 4.01, Cross-Validation and Feature Engineering with the Case Study Data | Regularization parameter C | 0.739 |
| Decision tree | Chapter 5, Decision Trees, Exercise 5.02, Finding Optimal Hyperparameters for a Decision Tree | Maximum depth | 0.746 |
| Random forest | Chapter 5, Decision Trees, Activity 5.01, Cross-Validation Grid Search with Random Forest | Maximum depth and number of trees | 0.776 |
| XGBoost | Chapter 6, Gradient Boosting, SHAP Values (SHapley Additive exPlanations), and Dealing with Missing Data, Activity 6.01, Modeling the Case Study Data with XGBoost and Explaining the Model with SHAP | Maximum leaves | 0.779 |

**Figure 7.1: Summary of modeling activities with case study data**

When presenting results to the client, you should be prepared to interpret them for business partners at all levels of technical familiarity, including those with very little technical background. For example, business partners may not understand the derivation of the ROC AUC measure; however, this is an important concept since it's the main performance metric we used to assess models. You may need to explain that it's a metric that can vary between 0.5 and 1 and give intuitive explanations for these limits: 0.5 is no better than a coin flip and 1 is perfection, which is essentially unattainable.

Our results are somewhere in between, getting close to 0.78 with the best model we developed. While the ROC AUC of a given model may not necessarily be meaningful by itself, *Figure 7.1* shows that we've tried several methods and have achieved improved performance above our initial attempts. In the end, for a business application like the case study, abstract model performance metrics like the ROC AUC should be accompanied by a financial analysis if possible. We will explore this later in this chapter.

> **NOTE: ON INTERPRETING THE ROC AUC**
>
> An interesting interpretation of the ROC AUC score is the probability that for two samples, one with a positive outcome and one with a negative outcome, the positive sample will have a higher predicted probability than the negative sample. In other words, for all possible pairs of positive and negative samples in the dataset being assessed, the proportion of pairs where the positive sample has a higher model prediction than the negative sample is equivalent to the ROC AUC.

From *Figure 7.1*, we can see that for the case study, our efforts in creating more **complex models**, either by engineering new features to add to a simple logistic regression or by creating an ensemble of decision trees, yielded better model performance. In particular, the random forest and XGBoost models perform similarly, although these validation scores are technically not directly comparable since in the case of random forest we excluded missing values and used 4-fold cross-validation, while for XGBoost the missing values were included and there was just one validation set that was used for early stopping. However, *Figure 7.1* provides an indication that either XGBoost or random forest would probably be the best choice. We'll move forward here with the XGBoost model.

Now that we've decided which model we'll deliver, it's good to consider additional things we could have tried in the model development process. These concepts won't be explored in this book, but you may wish to experiment with them on your own.

## FEATURE ENGINEERING

Another way to increase model performance that we touched on briefly is **feature engineering**. While we used scikit-learn's automated feature engineering capabilities to make interaction features, you can also manually engineer features from existing features. For example, a credit account that is using a large percentage of its credit limit may be considered particularly risky. We have information in our features about the credit limit, and also the amounts of past bills. In fact, the most important feature in the XGBoost model we trained in *Activity 6.01, Modeling the Case Study Data with XGBoost and Explaining the Model with SHAP* was the credit limit feature `LIMIT_BAL`. The feature with the strongest interaction with this was the bill amount from two months ago. Although XGBoost can find interactions like this and model them to some extent, we could also engineer a new feature: the ratio of past monthly billed amounts to the credit limit, assuming the billed amount is the account's balance. This measure of **credit utilization** may be a stronger feature, and result in better model performance when calculated in this way, than having the credit limit and monthly billed amounts available to the model separately.

Feature engineering may take the form of manipulating existing features to make new ones, as in the previous example, or it may involve bringing in entirely new data sources and creating features with them.

The inspiration for new features may come from domain knowledge: it can be very helpful to have a conversation with your business partner about what they think good features might be, especially if they have more domain knowledge than you for the application you're on. Examining the interactions of existing features can also be a way to hypothesize new features, such as how we saw an interaction that seems related to credit utilization in *Activity 6.01, Modeling the Case Study Data with XGBoost and Explaining the Model with SHAP*.

## ENSEMBLING MULTIPLE MODELS

In choosing the final model to deliver for the case study project, it would probably be fine to deliver either random forest or XGBoost. Another commonly used approach in machine learning is to **ensemble** together multiple models. This means combining the predictions of different models, similar to how random forest and XGBoost combine many decision trees. But in this case, the way to combine model predictions is up to the data scientist. A simple way to create an ensemble of models is to take the average of their predictions.

Ensembling is often done when there are multiple models, perhaps different kinds of models or models trained with different features that all have good performance. In our case, it may be that using the average prediction from the random forest and XGBoost would have better performance than either model on its own. To explore this, we could compare performance on a validation set, for example, the one used for early stopping in XGBoost.

## DIFFERENT MODELING TECHNIQUES

Depending on how much time you have for a project and your expertise in different modeling techniques, you will want to try as many methods as possible. More advanced methods, such as neural networks for classification, may yield improved performance on this problem. We encourage you to continue your studies and learn how to use these models. However, for tabular data such as what we have for the case study, XGBoost is a good de facto choice and will likely provide excellent performance, if not the best performance of all methods.

## BALANCING CLASSES

Note that we did not address the class imbalance in the response variable. You are encouraged to try fitting models with the **class_weight='balanced'** option in scikit-learn or using the **scale_pos_weight** hyperparameter in XGBoost, to see the effect.

While these would be interesting avenues for further model development, for the purposes of this book, we are done with model building at this point. We'll move forward to examine XGBoost model performance on the test set.

# MODEL PERFORMANCE ON THE TEST SET

We already have some idea of the out-of-sample performance of the XGBoost model, from the validation set. However, the validation set was used in model fitting, via early stopping. The most rigorous estimate of expected future performance we can make should be created with data that was not used at all for model fitting. This was the reason for reserving a test dataset from the model building process.

You may notice that we did examine the test set to some extent already, for example, in the first chapter when assessing data quality and doing data cleaning. The gold standard for predictive modeling is to set aside a test set at the very beginning of a project and not examine it at all until the model is finished. This is the easiest way to make sure that none of the knowledge from the test set has "leaked" into the training set during model development. When this happens, it opens up the possibility that the test set is no longer a realistic representation of future, unknown data. However, it is sometimes convenient to explore and clean all of the data together, as we've done. If the test data has the same quality issues as the rest of the data, then there would be no leakage. It is most important to make sure you're not looking at the test set when you decide which features to use, fit various models, and compare their performance.

We begin the test set examination by loading the trained model from *Activity 6.01, Modeling the Case Study Data with XGBoost and Explaining the Model with SHAP* along with the training and test data and feature names, using Python's **pickle**:

```
with open('../../Data/xgb_model_w_data.pkl', 'rb') as f:
    features_response, X_train_all, y_train_all, X_test_all,\
    y_test_all, xgb_model_4 = pickle.load(f)
```

With these variables loaded in the notebook, we can make predictions for the test set and analyze them. First obtain the predicted probabilities for the test set:

```
test_set_pred_proba = xgb_model_4.predict_proba(X_test_all)[:,1]
```

Now import the ROC AUC calculation routine from scikit-learn, use it to calculate this metric for the test set, and display it:

```
from sklearn.metrics import roc_auc_score
test_auc = roc_auc_score(y_test_all, test_set_pred_proba)
test_auc
```

The result should be as follows:

```
0.7735528979671706
```

The ROC AUC of 0.774 on the test set is a bit lower than the 0.779 we saw on the validation set for the XGBoost model; however, it is not very different. Since the model fitting process optimized the model for performance on the validation set, it's not totally surprising to see somewhat lower performance on new data. Overall, the testing performance is in line with expectations and we can consider this model successfully tested in terms of the ROC AUC metric.

While we won't do this here, a final step before delivering a trained model might be to fit it on all of the available data, including the unseen test set. This could be done by concatenating the training and testing data features (**X_train_all**, **X_test_all**) and labels (**y_train_all**, **y_test_all**), and using them to fit a new model, perhaps by defining a new validation set for early stopping or using the current test set for that purpose. This approach is motivated by the idea that machine learning models generally perform better when trained on more data. The downside is that since there would be no unseen test set in these circumstances, the final model could be considered to be untested.

Data scientists have varying opinions on which approach to use: only using the unseen test set for model assessment versus using as much data as possible, including the test set, to train the final model once all previous steps in the process are completed. One consideration is whether or not a model would benefit from being trained on more data. This could be determined by constructing a **learning curve**. Although we won't illustrate this here, the concept behind a learning curve is to train a model on successively increasing amounts of data and calculating the validation score on the same validation set. For example, if you had 10,000 training samples, you might set aside 500 as a validation set and then train a model on the first 1,000 samples, then the first 2,000 samples, and so on, up to all 9,500 samples that aren't in the validation set. If training on more data consistently increases the validation score even up to the point of using all available data, this is a sign that training on more data than you have in the training set would be beneficial. However, if model performance starts to level off at some point and it doesn't seem like additional data would create a more performant model, you may not need to do this. Learning curves can provide guidance on which approach to take with the test set, as well as whether more data is needed in a project generally.

For the purposes of the case study, we'll assume that we wouldn't realize any benefit from refitting the model using the test set. So, our main concerns now are presenting the model to the client, helping them design a strategy to use it to meet their business goals, and providing guidance on how the model's performance can be monitored as time goes on.

## DISTRIBUTION OF PREDICTED PROBABILITY AND DECILE CHART

The ROC AUC metric is helpful because it provides a single number that summarizes model performance on a dataset. However, it's also insightful to look at model performance for different subsets of the population. One way to break up the population into subsets is to use the model predictions themselves. Using the test set, we can visualize the predicted probabilities with a histogram:

```
mpl.rcParams['figure.dpi'] = 400
plt.hist(test_set_pred_proba, bins=50)
plt.xlabel('Predicted probability')
plt.ylabel('Number of samples')
```

This code should produce the following plot:

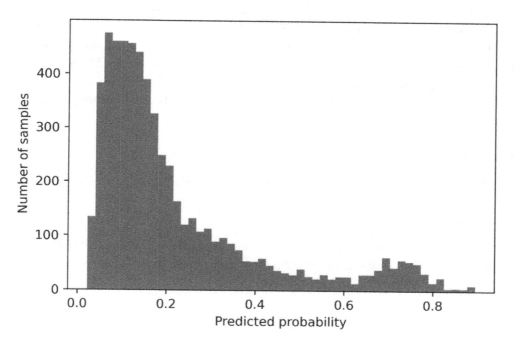

Figure 7.2: Distribution of predicted probabilities for the test set

The histogram of predicted probabilities for the test set shows that most predictions are clustered in the range **[0, 0.2]**. In other words, most borrowers have between a 0 and 20% chance of default, according to the model. However, there appears to be a small cluster of borrowers with a higher risk, centered near 0.7.

A visually intuitive way to examine model performance for different regions of predicted default risk is to create a decile chart, which groups borrowers together based on the decile of predicted probability. Within each decile, we can compute the true default rate. We would expect to see a steady increase in the default rate from the lowest prediction deciles to the highest.

We can compute deciles like we did in *Exercise 6.01, Randomized Grid Search for Tuning XGBoost Hyperparameters*, using pandas' **qcut**:

```
deciles, decile_bin_edges = pd.qcut(x=test_set_pred_proba,\
                                    q=10,\
                                    retbins=True)
```

Here we are splitting the predicted probabilities for the test set, supplied with the **x** keyword argument. We want to split them into 10 equal-sized bins, with the bottom 10% of predicted probabilities in the first bin, and so on, so we indicate we want **q=10** quantiles. However, you can split into any number of bins you want, such as 20 (ventiles) or 5 (quintiles). Since we indicate **retbins=True**, the bin edges are returned in the **decile_bin_edges** variable, while the series of decile labels is in **deciles**. We can examine the 11 bin edges needed to create 10 bins:

```
decile_bin_edges
```

That should produce this:

```
array([0.02213463, 0.06000734, 0.08155108, 0.10424594, 0.12708404,
       0.15019046, 0.18111563, 0.23032923, 0.32210371, 0.52585585,
       0.89491451])
```

In order to make use of the **decile** series, we can combine it with the true labels for the test set, and the predicted probabilities, into a DataFrame:

```
test_set_df = pd.DataFrame({'Predicted probability':test_set_pred_proba,\
                            'Prediction decile':deciles,\
                            'Outcome':y_test_all})
test_set_df.head()
```

The first few rows of the DataFrame should look like this:

| | Predicted probability | Prediction decile | Outcome |
|---|---|---|---|
| 0 | 0.544556 | (0.526, 0.895] | 0 |
| 1 | 0.621311 | (0.526, 0.895] | 0 |
| 2 | 0.049883 | (0.0211, 0.06] | 0 |
| 3 | 0.890924 | (0.526, 0.895] | 1 |
| 4 | 0.272326 | (0.23, 0.322] | 0 |

**Figure 7.3: DataFrame with predicted probabilities and deciles**

In the DataFrame, we can see that each sample is labeled with a decile bin, indicated using the edges of the bin that contains the predicted probability. The outcome shows the true label. What we want to show in our decile chart is the true default rate within the decile bins. For this, we can use pandas' **groupby** capabilities. First, we create a **groupby** object, by grouping our DataFrame on the **decile** column:

```
test_set_gr = test_set_df.groupby('Prediction decile')
```

The **groupby** object can be aggregated by other columns. In particular, here we're interested in the default rate within decile bins, which is the mean of the **outcome** variable. We also calculate a count of the data in each bin. Since quantiles, such as deciles, group the population into equal-sized bins, we expect the counts to be the same or similar:

```
gr_df = test_set_gr.agg({'Outcome':['count', 'mean']})
```

Examine our grouped DataFrame, **gr_df**:

| Prediction decile | Outcome | |
|---|---|---|
| | count | mean |
| (0.0211, 0.06] | 594 | 0.045455 |
| (0.06, 0.0816] | 594 | 0.070707 |
| (0.0816, 0.104] | 594 | 0.099327 |
| (0.104, 0.127] | 593 | 0.112985 |
| (0.127, 0.15] | 594 | 0.116162 |
| (0.15, 0.181] | 594 | 0.171717 |
| (0.181, 0.23] | 593 | 0.195616 |
| (0.23, 0.322] | 594 | 0.282828 |
| (0.322, 0.526] | 594 | 0.392256 |
| (0.526, 0.895] | 594 | 0.676768 |

**Figure 7.4: Default rate in deciles of predicted probability on the test set**

In *Figure 7.4*, we can see that indeed the counts are nearly equal in all bins. We also can tell that the true default rate increases with the decile, as we hope and expect since we know our model has good performance. Before visualizing the data, it's worth noting that this DataFrame has a special kind of column index called a **multiindex**. Notice that there are two lines of text describing the columns, a top-level index that only contains one label **Outcome** and a second-level index with the labels **count** and **mean**. Accessing data in DataFrames that have a multiindex is a little more complicated than for the DataFrames we've worked with previously. We can display the column index as follows:

```
gr_df.columns
```

That should produce the following result:

```
MultiIndex([('Outcome', 'count'),
            ('Outcome',  'mean')],
           )
```

Here we can see that to access a column from a multiindex, we need to use tuples that specify each level of the index, for example, **gr_df[('Outcome','count')]**. While here the MultiIndex isn't really necessary since we've only done an aggregation of one column (**Outcome**), it can come in handy when there are aggregations on multiple columns.

Now we'd like to create a visualization, showing how the model predictions do a good job of binning borrowers into groups with consistently increasing default risk. We're going to show the counts in each bin, as well as the default risk in each bin. Because these columns are on different scales, with counts in the hundreds and risk between 0 and 1, we should use a dual y-axis plot. In order to have more control over plot appearance, we'll create this plot using Matplotlib functions instead of doing it through pandas. First, we create the plot of sample size in each bin, labeling the y-axis ticks with the same color as the plot for clarity. Please see the notebook on GitHub if you're reading in black and white, as color is important for this plot. This code snippet should be run in the same cell as the next one. Here we create a set of axes, then add a plot to it along with some formatting and annotation:

```
ax_1 = plt.axes()
color_1 = 'tab:blue'
gr_df[('Outcome', 'count')].plot.bar(ax=ax_1, color=color_1)
ax_1.set_ylabel('Count of observations', color=color_1)
ax_1.tick_params(axis='y', labelcolor=color_1)
ax_1.tick_params(axis='x', labelrotation = 45)
```

Notice that we're creating a **bar** plot for the sample sizes. We'd like to add a line plot to this, showing the default rate in each bin on a right-hand y-axis but the same x-axis as the existing plot. Matplotlib makes a method called **twinx** available for this purpose, which can be called on an **axes** object to return a new axes object sharing the same x-axis. We take similar steps to then plot the default rate and annotate:

```
ax_2 = ax_1.twinx()
color_2 = 'tab:red'
gr_df[('Outcome', 'mean')].plot(ax=ax_2, color=color_2)
ax_2.set_ylabel('Default rate', color=color_2)
ax_2.tick_params(axis='y', labelcolor=color_2)
```

After running the preceding two snippets in a code cell, the following plot should appear:

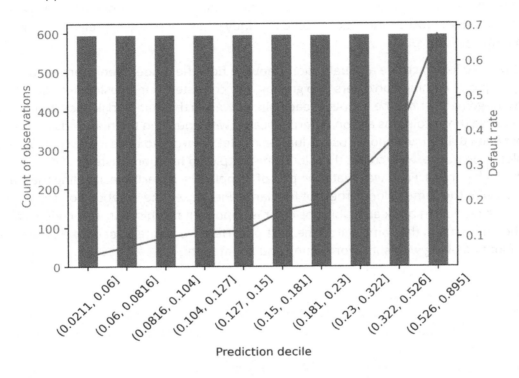

Figure 7.5: Default rate according to model prediction decile

*Figure 7.5* contains the same information as displayed in the DataFrame in *Figure 7.4*, but in a nicer presentation. It's clear that default risk increases with each decile, where the riskiest 10% of borrowers have a default rate close to 70%, but the least risky are below 10%. When a model is able to effectively distinguish groups of borrowers with consistently increasing default risk, the model is said to **slope** the population being examined. Notice also that the default rate is relatively flat across the lowest 5 to 7 deciles, likely because these observations are mostly clustered in the range [0, 0.2] of predicted risk, as seen in the histogram in *Figure 7.2*.

Splitting the test set into equal-population deciles is one way to examine model performance, in terms of sloping default risk. However, a client may be interested in looking at default rate by different groups, such as equal interval bins (for example, binning together all observations in the prediction ranges [0, 0.2), [0.2, 0.4), and so on, regardless of sample size in each bin), or some other way. You'll explore how to easily do this in pandas in the following exercise.

In the following exercise, we'll make use of a couple of statistical concepts to help create error bars, including the **standard error of the mean**, which we learned about previously, and the **normal approximation to the binomial distribution**.

We know from *Chapter 5, Decision Trees and Random Forests* that we can estimate the variance of the sample mean as $\sigma_{\bar{X}}^2 = \frac{\sigma^2}{n}$, where *n* is the sample size and $\sigma^2$ is the unobserved variance of a theoretical larger population. While we don't know $\sigma^2$, it can be estimated by the variance of the sample we observed. For binary variables, the sample variance can be calculated as *p(1-p)*, where *p* is the proportion of successes, or defaults for the case study. Given the formula for the variance of the sample mean above, we can plug in the observed variance, then take the square root to get the standard error of the mean: $\sqrt{\frac{p(1-p)}{n}}$. This formula is also known as the normal approximation to the binomial distribution in some contexts. We'll use it below to create error bars on an equal-interval chart of default rates for different model prediction bins. For more details on these concepts, you are encouraged to consult a statistics textbook.

## EXERCISE 7.01: EQUAL-INTERVAL CHART

In this exercise, you will make a similar chart to that shown in *Figure 7.5*; however, instead of splitting the test set into equal-population deciles of predicted probability, you'll use equal intervals of predicted probability. Specifying the intervals could be helpful if a business partner wants to think about potential model-based strategies using certain score ranges. You can use pandas **cut** to create equal-interval binnings, or custom binnings using an array of bin edges, similar to how you used **qcut** to create quantile labels:

> **NOTE**
>
> You can find the Jupyter notebook for this exercise at https://packt.link/4Ev3n.

1. Create the series of equal-interval labels, for 5 bins, using the following code:

```
equal_intervals, equal_interval_bin_edges = \
    pd.cut(x=test_set_pred_proba, \
        bins=5,\
        retbins=True)
```

Notice that this is similar to the call to **qcut**, except here with **cut** we can say how many equal-interval bins we want by supplying an integer to the **bins** argument. You could also supply an array for this argument to specify the bin edges, for custom bins.

2. Examine the equal-interval bin edges with this code:

```
equal_interval_bin_edges
```

The result should be as follows:

```
array([0.02126185, 0.1966906 , 0.37124658, 0.54580256, 0.72035853,
       0.89491451])
```

You can confirm that these bin edges have equal intervals between them by subtracting the subarray going from the first to the next-to-last item, from the subarray starting with the second, and going to the end.

3. Check the intervals between bin edges like this:

```
equal_interval_bin_edges[1:] - equal_interval_bin_edges[:-1]
```

The result should be this:

```
array([0.17542876, 0.17455598, 0.17455598, 0.17455598, 0.17455598])
```

You can see that the distance between the bin edges is roughly equal. The first bin edge is a bit smaller than the minimum predicted probability, as you can confirm for yourself.

In order to create a similar plot to *Figure 7.5*, first we need to put the bin labels together with the response variable in a DataFrame, as we did previously with decile labels. We also put the predicted probabilities in the DataFrame for reference.

4. Make a DataFrame of predicted probabilities, bin labels, and the response variable for the test set like this:

```
test_set_bins_df =\
pd.DataFrame({'Predicted probability':test_set_pred_proba,\
             'Prediction bin':equal_intervals,\
             'Outcome':y_test_all})
test_set_bins_df.head()
```

The result should look as follows:

| | Predicted probability | Prediction bin | Outcome |
|---|---|---|---|
| 0 | 0.544556 | (0.371, 0.546] | 0 |
| 1 | 0.621311 | (0.546, 0.72] | 0 |
| 2 | 0.049883 | (0.0213, 0.197] | 0 |
| 3 | 0.890924 | (0.72, 0.895] | 1 |
| 4 | 0.272326 | (0.197, 0.371] | 0 |

Figure 7.6: DataFrame with equal-interval bins

We can use this DataFrame to group by the bin labels, then get the metrics we are interested in: aggregations that represent the default rate and the number of samples in each bin.

5. Group by the bin label and calculate the default rate and sample count within bins with this code:

```
test_set_equal_gr = test_set_bins_df.groupby('Prediction bin')
gr_eq_df = test_set_equal_gr.agg({'Outcome':['count', 'mean']})
gr_eq_df
```

The resulting DataFrame should appear like this:

| | Outcome | |
|---|---|---|
| | count | mean |
| Prediction bin | | |
| (0.0213, 0.197] | 3778 | 0.108788 |
| (0.197, 0.371] | 1207 | 0.257664 |
| (0.371, 0.546] | 389 | 0.465296 |
| (0.546, 0.72] | 312 | 0.608974 |
| (0.72, 0.895] | 252 | 0.761905 |

Figure 7.7: Grouped data for five equal-interval bins

Notice that here, unlike with quantiles, there are a different number of samples in each bin. The default rate appears to increase across bins in a consistent manner. Let's plot this DataFrame to create a similar visualization to *Figure 7.5*.

Before creating this visualization, in order to consider that the estimates of default rate may be less robust for higher predicted probabilities, due to decreased sample size in these ranges, we'll calculate the standard error of the default rates.

6.  Calculate the standard errors of the default rates within bins using this code:

```
p = gr_eq_df[('Outcome', 'mean')].values
n = gr_eq_df[('Outcome', 'count')].values
std_err = np.sqrt(p * (1-p) / n)
std_err
```

The result should appear as follows:

```
array([0.00506582, 0.01258848, 0.02528987, 0.02762643, 0.02683029])
```

Notice that for the bins with higher score ranges and fewer samples, the standard error is larger. It will be helpful to visualize these standard errors with the default rates.

7.  Use this code to create an equal-interval plot of default rate and sample size. The code is very similar to that needed for *Figure 7.5*, except here we include error bars on the default rate plot using the **yerr** keyword and the results from the previous step:

```
ax_1 = plt.axes()
color_1 = 'tab:blue'
gr_eq_df[('Outcome', 'count')].plot.bar(ax=ax_1, color=color_1)
ax_1.set_ylabel('Count of observations', color=color_1)
ax_1.tick_params(axis='y', labelcolor=color_1)
ax_1.tick_params(axis='x', labelrotation = 45)

ax_2 = ax_1.twinx()
color_2 = 'tab:red'
```

```
gr_eq_df[('Outcome', 'mean')].plot(ax=ax_2, color=color_2,
                                    yerr=std_err)
ax_2.set_ylabel('Default rate', color=color_2)
ax_2.tick_params(axis='y', labelcolor=color_2)
```

The result should appear like this:

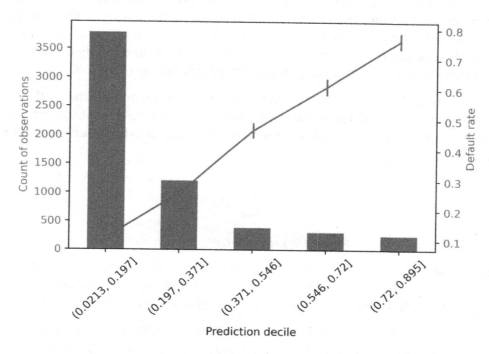

Figure 7.8: Plot of default rate and sample count for equal-interval bins

We can see in *Figure 7.8* that the number of samples is pretty different among the different bins, in contrast to the quantile approach. While there are relatively few samples in the higher score bins, leading to a larger standard error, the error bars on the plot of default rate are still small compared to the overall trend of an increasing default rate from lower to higher score bins, so we can be confident in this trend.

## CALIBRATION OF PREDICTED PROBABILITIES

One interesting feature of *Figure 7.8* is that the line plot of default rates increases by roughly the same amount from bin to bin. Contrast this to the decile plot in *Figure 7.5*, where the default rate increases slowly at first and then more rapidly. Notice also that the default rate appears to be roughly the midpoint of the edges of predicted probability for each bin. This implies that the default rate is similar to the average model prediction in each bin. In other words, not only does our model appear to effectively rank borrowers from low to high risk of default, as quantified by the ROC AUC, but it also appears to accurately predict the probability of default.

Measuring how closely predicted probabilities match actual probabilities is the goal of **calibrating probabilities**. A standard measure for probability calibration follows from the concepts discussed above and is called **expected calibration error (ECE)**, defined as

$$ECE = \sum_{i=1}^{N} F_i |o_i - e_i|$$

**Figure 7.9: Expected Calibration Error**

where the index *i* ranges from 1 to the number of bins (*N*), $F_i$ is the fraction of all samples falling in bin *i*, $o_i$ is the fraction of samples in bin *i* that are positive (that is, for the case study, defaulters), and $e_i$ is the average of predicted probabilities within bin *i*.

We can calculate the ECE for the predicted probabilities within decile bins of the test set using a DataFrame very similar to that shown in *Figure 7.4*, needed to create the decile chart. The only addition we need is the mean predicted probability in each bin. Create such a DataFrame as follows:

```
cal_df = test_set_gr.agg({'Outcome':['count', 'mean'],\
                          'Predicted probability':'mean'})
cal_df
```

The output DataFrame should look like this:

| Prediction decile | Outcome count | Outcome mean | Predicted probability mean |
|---|---|---|---|
| (0.0211, 0.06] | 594 | 0.045455 | 0.046931 |
| (0.06, 0.0816] | 594 | 0.070707 | 0.070745 |
| (0.0816, 0.104] | 594 | 0.099327 | 0.093163 |
| (0.104, 0.127] | 593 | 0.112985 | 0.115823 |
| (0.127, 0.15] | 594 | 0.116162 | 0.138657 |
| (0.15, 0.181] | 594 | 0.171717 | 0.165012 |
| (0.181, 0.23] | 593 | 0.195616 | 0.203106 |
| (0.23, 0.322] | 594 | 0.282828 | 0.273172 |
| (0.322, 0.526] | 594 | 0.392256 | 0.400159 |
| (0.526, 0.895] | 594 | 0.676768 | 0.693437 |

Figure 7.10: DataFrame for calculating the ECE metric

For convenience, let's define a variable for **F**, which is the fraction of samples in each bin. This is the counts in each bin from the above DataFrame divided by the total number of samples, taken from the shape of the response variable for the test set:

```
F = cal_df[('Outcome', 'count')].values/y_test_all.shape[0]
F
```

The output should be this:

```
array([0.10003368, 0.10003368, 0.10003368, 0.09986527, 0.10003368,
       0.10003368, 0.09986527, 0.10003368, 0.10003368, 0.10003368])
```

So, each bin has about 10% of the samples. This is expected, of course, since the bins were created using a quantile approach. However, for other binnings, the sample sizes in the bins may not be equal. Now let's implement the formula for ECE in code to calculate this metric:

```
ECE = np.sum(
    F
    * np.abs(
        cal_df[('Outcome', 'mean')]
        - cal_df[('Predicted probability', 'mean')]))
ECE
```

The output should be this:

```
0.008144502190176022
```

This number represents the ECE for our final model, on the test set. By itself, the number isn't all that meaningful. However, metrics like this can be monitored over time, after the model has been put in production and is being used in the real world. If the ECE starts to increase, this is a sign that the model is becoming less calibrated and may need to be retrained, for example, or have a calibration procedure applied to the outputs.

A more intuitive way to examine the calibration of our predicted probabilities for the test set is to plot the ingredients needed for ECE, in particular the true default rate of the response variable, against the average of model predictions in each bin. To this we add a 1-1 line, which represents perfect calibration, as a point of reference:

```
ax = plt.axes()
ax.plot([0, 0.8], [0, 0.8], 'k--', linewidth=1,
        label='Perfect calibration')
ax.plot(cal_df[('Outcome', 'mean')],\
        cal_df[('Predicted probability', 'mean')],\
        marker='x',\
        label='Model calibration on test set')
ax.set_xlabel('True default rate in bin')
ax.set_ylabel('Average model prediction in bin')
ax.legend()
```

The resulting plot should look like this:

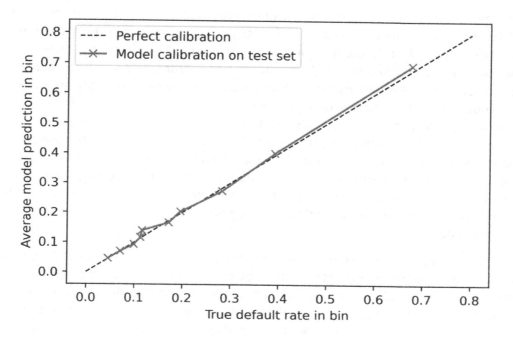

**Figure 7.11: Calibration plot for predicted probabilities**

*Figure 7.11* shows that model-predicted probabilities are very close to the true default rates, so the model appears to be well calibrated. For additional insight, you can try adding error bars to this plot yourself as an exercise. Also note that scikit-learn makes a function available to calculate the information needed to create *Figure 7.11*: `sklearn.calibration.calibration_curve`. However, this function does not return the sample size in each bin.

One additional point to be aware of for probability calibration is that some methods for dealing with class imbalance, such as oversampling or undersampling, change the class fraction in the training dataset, which will affect the predicted probabilities and likely make them less accurate. This may not be that important though, compared to the ability of the model to rank borrowers on their risk of default, as measured by the ROC AUC, depending on the needs of the client.

# FINANCIAL ANALYSIS

The model performance metrics we have calculated so far were based on abstract measures that could be applied to analyze any classification model: how accurate a model is, how skillful a model is at identifying true positives relative to false positives at different thresholds (ROC AUC), the correctness of positive predictions (precision), or intuitive measures such as sloping risk. These metrics are important for understanding the basic workings of a model and are widely used within the machine learning community, so it's important to understand them. However, for the application of a model to business use cases, we can't always directly use such performance metrics to create a strategy for how to use the model to guide business decisions or figure out how much value a model is expected to create. To go the extra mile and connect the mathematical world of predicted probabilities and thresholds to the business world of costs and benefits, a financial analysis of some kind is usually needed.

In order to help the client with this analysis, the data scientist needs to understand what kinds of decisions and actions might be taken, based on predictions made by the model. This should be the topic of a conversation with the client, preferably early on in the project life cycle. We have left it until the end of the book so that we could establish a baseline understanding of what predictive modeling is and how it works. However, learning the business context around model usage at the beginning of a project allows you to set goals for model performance in terms of the creation of value, which you can track throughout a project as we tracked the ROC AUC of the different models we built. Translating model performance metrics into financial terms is the topic of this section.

For a binary classification model such as that of the case study, here are a few questions that the data scientist needs to know the answers to, in order to help the client figure out how to use the model:

- What kinds of decisions does the client want to use the model to help them make?

- How can the predicted probabilities of a binary classification model be used to help make these decisions?

- Are they yes/no decisions? If so, then choosing a single threshold of predicted probability will be sufficient.

- Are there more than two levels of activity that will be decided on, based on model results? If so, then choosing two or more thresholds, to sort predictions into low, medium, and high risk, for example, may be the solution. For instance, predicted probabilities below 0.5 may be considered low risk, those between 0.5 and 0.75 medium risk, and those above 0.75 high risk.

- What are the costs of taking all the different courses of action that are available, based on model guidance?

- What are the potential benefits to be gained from successful actions taken as a result of model guidance?

## FINANCIAL CONVERSATION WITH THE CLIENT

We ask the case study client about the points outlined above and learn the following: for credit accounts that are at a high risk of default, the client is designing a new program to provide individualized counseling for the account holder, to encourage them to pay their bill on time or provide alternative payment options if that will not be possible. Credit counseling is performed by trained customer service representatives who work in a call center. The cost per counseling session is NT$7,500 and the expected success rate of a session is 70%, meaning that on average 70% of the recipients of phone calls offering counseling will pay their bill on time, or make alternative arrangements that are acceptable to the creditor. The potential benefits of successful counseling are that the amount of an account's monthly bill will be realized as savings, if it was going to default but instead didn't, as a result of the counseling. Currently, the monthly bills for accounts that default are reported as losses.

After having the preceding conversation with the client, we have the materials we need to make a financial analysis. The client would like us to help them decide which members to contact and offer credit counseling to. If we can help them narrow down the list of people who will be contacted for counseling, we can help save them money by avoiding unnecessary and expensive contacts. The clients' limited resources for counseling will be more appropriately spent on accounts that are at higher risk of default. This should create greater savings due to prevented defaults. Additionally, the client lets us know that our analysis can help them request a budget for the counseling program, if we can give them an idea of how many counseling sessions it would be worthwhile to offer.

As we proceed to the financial analysis, we see that the decision that the model will help the client make, on an account by account basis, is a yes/no decision: whether to offer counseling to the holder of a given account. Therefore, our analysis should focus on finding an appropriate threshold of predicted probability, by which we may divide our accounts into two groups: higher-risk accounts that will receive counseling and lower-risk ones that won't.

## EXERCISE 7.02: CHARACTERIZING COSTS AND SAVINGS

The connection between model output and business decisions the client will make comes down to selecting a threshold for the predicted probabilities. Therefore, in this exercise, we will characterize the expected costs of the counseling program, in terms of costs of offering individual counseling sessions, as well as the expected savings, in terms of prevented defaults, at a range of thresholds. There will be different costs and savings at each threshold, because each threshold is expected to result in a different number of positive predictions, as well as a different number of true positives within these. The first step is to create an array of potential thresholds. We will use 0 through 1, going by an increment of 0.01. Perform the following steps to complete the exercise:

> **NOTE**
>
> The Jupyter notebook for this exercise can be found here: https://packt.link/yiMEr. Additional steps to prepare data for this exercise, based on previous results in this chapter, have been added to the notebook. Please make sure you execute the prerequisite steps as presented in the notebook before you perform this exercise.

1. Create a range of thresholds to calculate expected costs and benefits of counseling with this code:

```
thresholds = np.linspace(0, 1, 101)
```

This creates 101 linearly spaced points between 0 and 1, inclusive.

Now, we need to know the potential savings of a prevented default. To calculate this precisely, we would need to know the next month's monthly bill. However, the client has informed us that this will not be available at the time they need to create the list of account holders to be contacted. Therefore, in order to estimate the potential savings, we will use the most recent monthly bill.

We will use the testing data to create this analysis, as this provides a simulation of how the model will be used after we deliver it to the client: on new accounts that weren't used for model training.

2.  Confirm the index of the testing data features array that corresponds to the most recent month's bill:

```
features_response[5]
```

The output should be this:

```
'BILL_AMT1'
```

The index 5 is for the most recent months' bill, which we'll use later.

3.  Store the cost of counseling in a variable to use for analysis:

```
cost_per_counseling = 7500
```

We also know from the client that the counseling program isn't 100% effective. We should take this into account in our analysis.

4.  Store the effectiveness rate the client gave us for use in analysis:

```
effectiveness = 0.70
```

Now, we will calculate costs and savings for each of the thresholds. We'll step through each calculation and explain it, but for now, we need to create empty arrays to hold the results for each threshold.

5.  Create empty arrays to store analysis results. We'll explain what each one will hold in the following steps:

```
n_pos_pred = np.empty_like(thresholds)
total_cost = np.empty_like(thresholds)
n_true_pos = np.empty_like(thresholds)
total_savings = np.empty_like(thresholds)
```

These create empty arrays with the same number of elements as there are thresholds in our analysis. We will loop through each threshold value to fill these arrays.

6. Make a **counter** variable and open a **for** loop to go through thresholds:

```
counter = 0
for threshold in thresholds:
```

For each threshold, there will a different number of positive predictions, according to how many predicted probabilities are above that threshold. These correspond to accounts that are predicted to default. Each account that is predicted to default will receive a counseling phone call, which has a cost associated with it. So, this is the first part of the cost calculation.

7. Determine which accounts get positive predictions at this threshold:

```
pos_pred = test_set_pred_proba > threshold
```

**pos_pred** is a Boolean array. The sum of **pos_pred** indicates the number of predicted defaults at this threshold.

8. Calculate the number of positive predictions for the given threshold:

```
n_pos_pred[counter] = sum(pos_pred)
```

9. Calculate the total cost of counseling for the given threshold:

```
total_cost[counter] \
    = n_pos_pred[counter] * cost_per_counseling
```

Now that we have characterized the possible costs of the counseling program, at each threshold, we need to see what the projected savings are. Savings are obtained when counseling is offered to the right account holders: those who would otherwise default. In terms of the classification problem, these are positive predictions, where the true value of the response variable is also positive – in other words, true positives.

10. Determine which accounts are true positives, based on the array of positive predictions and the response variable:

```
true_pos = pos_pred & y_test_all.astype(bool)
```

11. Calculate the number of true positives as the sum of the true positive array:

```
n_true_pos[counter] = sum(true_pos)
```

The savings we can get from successfully counseling account holders who would otherwise default depends on the savings per prevented default, as well as the effectiveness rate of counseling. We won't be able to prevent every default.

12. Calculate the anticipated savings at each threshold using the number of true positives, the savings due to prevented default (estimated using last month's bill), and the effectiveness rate of counseling:

```
total_savings[counter] = np.sum(
    true_pos.astype(int)
    * X_test_all[:,5]
    * effectiveness
    )
```

13. Increment the counter:

```
counter += 1
```

*Steps 5* through *13* should be run as a **for** loop in one cell in the Jupyter Notebook. Afterward, the net savings for each threshold can be calculated as the savings minus the cost.

14. Calculate the net savings for all the thresholds by subtracting the savings and cost arrays:

```
net_savings = total_savings - total_cost
```

Now, we're in a position to visualize how much money we might help our client save by providing counseling to the appropriate account holders. Let's visualize this.

15. Plot the net savings against the thresholds as follows:

```
mpl.rcParams['figure.dpi'] = 400
plt.plot(thresholds, net_savings)
plt.xlabel('Threshold')
plt.ylabel('Net savings (NT$)')
plt.xticks(np.linspace(0,1,11))
plt.grid(True)
```

The resulting plot should look like this:

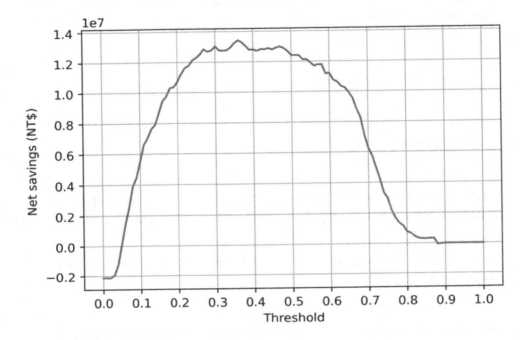

**Figure 7.12: Plot of net savings versus thresholds**

The plot indicates that the choice of threshold is important. While it will be possible to create net savings at many different values of the threshold, it looks like the highest net savings will be generated by setting the threshold somewhere in the range of about 0.25 to 0.5.

Let's confirm the optimal threshold for creating the greatest savings and see how much the savings are.

16. Find the index of the largest element of the net savings array using NumPy's **argmax**:

```
max_savings_ix = np.argmax(net_savings)
```

17. Display the threshold that results in the greatest net savings:

```
thresholds[max_savings_ix]
```

The output should be as follows:

```
0.36
```

18. Display the greatest possible net savings:

```
net_savings[max_savings_ix]
```

The output should be as follows:

```
13415710.0
```

We see that the greatest net savings occurs at a threshold of 0.36. The amount of net savings realized at this threshold is over NT$13 million, for this testing dataset of accounts. These savings would need to be scaled by the number of accounts served by the client, to estimate the total possible savings, assuming the data we are working with is representative of all these accounts.

Note, however, that the savings are about the same up to a threshold of about 0.5, as seen in *Figure 7.12*.

As the threshold increases, we are "raising the bar" for how risky a client must be, in order for us to contact them and offer counseling. Increasing the threshold from 0.36 to 0.5 means we would be only contacting riskier clients whose probability is > 0.5. This means contacting fewer clients, reducing the upfront cost of the program. *Figure 7.12* indicates that we may be still able to create roughly the same amount of net savings, by contacting fewer people. While the net effect is the same, the initial expenditure on counseling will be smaller. This may be desirable to the client. We explore this concept further in the following activity.

## ACTIVITY 7.01: DERIVING FINANCIAL INSIGHTS

The raw materials of the financial analysis are completed. However, in this activity, your aim is to generate some additional insights from these results, to provide the client with more context around how the predictive model we built can generate value for them. In particular, we have looked at results for the testing set we reserved from model building. The client may have more accounts than those they supplied to us, that are representative of their business. You should report to them results that could be easily scaled to however big their business is, in terms of the number of accounts.

We can also help them understand how much this program will cost; while the net savings are an important number to consider, the client will have to fund the counseling program before any of these savings will be realized. Finally, we will link the financial analysis back to standard machine learning model performance metrics.

Once you complete the activity, you should be able to communicate the initial cost of the counseling program to the client, as well as obtain plots of precision and recall such as this:

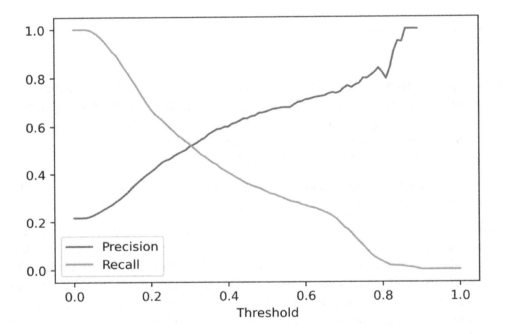

Figure 7.13: Expected precision-recall curve

This curve will be useful in interpreting the value created by the model at different thresholds.

Perform the following steps to complete the activity:

> **NOTE**
>
> The Jupyter notebook containing the code for this activity can be found here: https://packt.link/2kTVB. Additional steps to prepare data for this activity, based on previous results in this chapter, have been added to the notebook. Please execute the perquisite steps as presented in the notebook before you attempt this activity.

1. Using the testing set, calculate the cost of all defaults if there were no counseling program.

2. Calculate by what percent the cost of defaults can be decreased by the counseling program.

3. Calculate the net savings per account at the optimal threshold, considering all accounts it might be possible to counsel, in other words relative to the whole test set.

4. Plot the net savings per account against the cost of counseling per account for each threshold.

5. Plot the fraction of accounts predicted as positive (this is called the "flag rate") at each threshold.

6. Plot a precision-recall curve for the testing data.

7. Plot precision and recall separately on the *y*-axis against threshold on the *x*-axis.

> **NOTE**
>
> The solution to this activity can be found on page 399.

# FINAL THOUGHTS ON DELIVERING A PREDICTIVE MODEL TO THE CLIENT

We have now completed the modeling activities and also created a financial analysis to indicate to the client how they can use the model. While we have completed the essential intellectual contributions that are the data scientist's responsibility, it is necessary to agree with the client on the form in which all these contributions will be delivered.

A key contribution is the predictive capability embodied in the trained model. Assuming the client can work with the trained model object we created with XGBoost, this model could be saved to disk as we've done and sent to the client. Then, the client would be able to use it within their workflow. This pathway to model delivery may require the data scientist to work with engineers in the client's organization, to deploy the model within the client's infrastructure.

Alternatively, it may be necessary to express the model as a mathematical equation (for example, using logistic regression coefficients) or a set of if-then statements (as in decision trees or random forest) that the client could use to implement the predictive capability in SQL. While expressing random forests in SQL code is cumbersome due to the possibility of having many trees with many levels, there are software packages that will create this representation for you from a trained scikit-learn model (for example, https://pypi.org/project/SKompiler/).

> **NOTE: CLOUD PLATFORMS FOR MODEL DEVELOPMENT AND DEPLOYMENT**
>
> In this book, we used scikit-learn and the XGBoost package to build predictive models locally on our computers. Recently, cloud platforms such as **Amazon Web Services** (**AWS**) have made machine learning capabilities available through offerings such as Amazon SageMaker. SageMaker includes a version of XGBoost, which you can use to train models with similar syntax to what we've done here. Subtle differences may exist in the implementation of model training between the methods shown in this book and the Amazon distribution of SageMaker, and you are encouraged to check your work every step of the way to make sure your results are as intended. For example, fitting an XGBoost model using early stopping may require additional steps in SageMaker to ensure the trained model uses the best iteration for predictions, as opposed to the last iteration when training stopped.
>
> Cloud platforms such as AWS are attractive because they may greatly simplify the process of integrating a trained machine learning model into a client's technical stack, which in many cases may already be built on a cloud platform.

Before using the model to make predictions, the client would need to *ensure that the data was prepared in the same way it was for the model building we have done.* For example, the removal of samples with values of **0** for all the features and the cleaning of the **EDUCATION** and **MARRIAGE** features would have to be done in the same way we demonstrated earlier in this chapter. Alternatively, there are other possible ways to deliver model predictions, such as an arrangement where the client delivers features to the data scientist and receives the predictions back.

Another important consideration for the discussion of deliverables is: *what format should the predictions be delivered in?* A typical delivery format for predictions from a binary classification model, such as that we've created for the case study, is to rank accounts by their predicted probability of default. The predicted probability should be supplied along with the account ID and whatever other columns the client would like. This way, when the call center is working their way through the list of account holders to offer counseling to, they can contact those at highest risk for default first and proceed to lower-priority account holders as time and resources allow. The client should be informed of which threshold to use for predicted probabilities, to result in the highest net savings. This threshold would represent the stopping point on the list of account holders to contact if it is ranked on the predicted probability of default.

## MODEL MONITORING

Depending on how long the client has engaged the data scientist for, it is always beneficial to monitor the performance of the model over time, as it is being used. Does predictive capability remain the same or degrade over time? When assessing this for the case study, it would be  important to keep in mind that if account holders are receiving counseling, their probability of default would be expected to be lower than the predicted probability indicates, due to the intended effects of the new counseling program. For this reason, and to test the effectiveness of the counseling program, it is good practice to reserve a randomly chosen portion of account holders who will not receive any counseling, regardless of credit default risk. This group would be known as the **control group** and should be small compared to the rest of the population who receives counseling, but large enough to draw statistically significant inferences from.

While it's beyond the scope of this book to go into details about how to design and use a control group, suffice to say here that model predictive capability could be assessed on the control group since they have received no counseling, similar to the population of accounts the model was trained on. Another benefit of a control group is that the rate of default, and financial loss due to defaults, can be compared to those accounts that received the model-guided counseling program. If the program is working as intended, the accounts receiving counseling should have a lower rate of default and a smaller financial loss due to default. The control group can provide evidence that the program is, in fact, working.

> **NOTE: ADVANCED MODELING TECHNIQUE FOR SELECTIVE TREATMENTS—UPLIFT MODELING**
>
> When a business is considering selectively offering a costly treatment to its customers, such as the counseling program of the case study, a technique known as uplift modeling should be considered. Uplift modeling seeks to determine, on an individual basis, how effective treatments are. We made a blanket assumption that phone counseling treatment is 70% effective across customers on average. However, it may be that the effectiveness varies by customer; some customers are more receptive and others less so. For more information on uplift modeling, see https://www.steveklosterman.com/uplift-modeling/.

A relatively simple way to monitor a model implementation is to see if the distribution of model predictions is changing over time, as compared to the population used for model training. We plotted the histogram of predicted probabilities for the test set in *Figure 7.2*. If the shape of the histogram of predicted probabilities changes substantially, it may be a sign that the features have changed, or that the relationship between the features and response has changed and the model may need to be re-trained or rebuilt. To quantify changes in distributions, the interested reader is encouraged to consult a statistics resource to learn about the chi-squared goodness-of-fit test or the Kolmogorov-Smirnov test. Changing distributions of model predictions may also become evident if the proportion of accounts predicted to default, according to a chosen threshold, changes in a noticeable way.

All the other model assessment metrics presented in this chapter and throughout the book can also be good ways to monitor model performance in production: decile and equal-interval charts, calibration, ROC AUC, and others.

## ETHICS IN PREDICTIVE MODELING

The question of whether a model makes fair predictions has received increased attention as machine learning has expanded in scope to touch most modern businesses. Fairness may be assessed on the basis of whether a model is equally skillful at making predictions for members of different protected classes, for example, different gender groups.

In this book, we took the approach of removing gender from being considered as a feature for the model. However, it may be that other features can effectively serve as a proxy for gender, so that a model may wind up producing biased results for different gender groups, even though gender was not used as a feature. One simple way to screen for the possibility of such bias is to check if any of the features used in the model have a particularly high association with a protected class, for example, by using a t-test. If so, it may be better to remove these features from the model.

How to determine whether a model is fair, and if not, what to do about it, is the subject of active research. You are encouraged to become familiar with efforts such as AI Fairness 360 (https://aif360.mybluemix.net/) that are making tools available to improve fairness in machine learning. Before embarking on work related to fairness, it's important to understand from the client what the definition of fairness is, as this may vary by geographic region due to different laws in different countries, as well as the specific policies of the client's organization.

## SUMMARY

In this chapter, you learned several analysis techniques to provide insight into model performance, such as decile and equal-interval charts of default rate by model prediction bin, as well as how to investigate the quality of model calibration. It's good to derive these insights, as well as calculate metrics such as the ROC AUC, using the model test set, since this is intended to represent how the model might perform in the real world on new data.

We also saw how to go about conducting a financial analysis of model performance. While we left this to the end of the book, an understanding of the costs and savings going along with the decisions to be guided by the model should be understood from the beginning of a typical project. These allow the data scientist to work toward a tangible goal in terms of increased profit or savings. A key step in this process, for binary classification models, is to choose a threshold of predicted probability at which to declare a positive prediction, so that the profits or savings due to model-guided decision making are maximized.

Finally, we considered tasks related to delivering and monitoring the model, including the idea of establishing a control group to monitor model performance and test the effectiveness of any programs guided by model output. The structure of control groups and model monitoring strategies will be different from project to project, so you will need to determine the appropriate course of action in each new case. To further your knowledge of using models in the real world, you are encouraged to continue studying topics such as experimental design, cloud platforms such as AWS that can be used to train and deploy models, and issues with fairness in predictive modeling.

You have now completed the project and are ready to deliver your findings to the client. Along with trained models saved to disk, or other data products or services you may provide to the client, you will probably also want to create a presentation, typically a slide show, detailing your progress. Contents of such presentations usually include a problem statement, results of data exploration and cleaning, a comparison of the performance of different models you built, model explanations such as SHAP values, and the financial analysis which shows how valuable your work is. As you craft presentations of your work, it's usually better to *tell your story with pictures as opposed to a lot of text*. We've demonstrated many visualization techniques throughout the book that you can use to do this, and you should continue to explore ways to depict data and modeling results.

Always be sure to ask the client which specific things they may want to have in a presentation and be sure to answer all their questions. When a client sees that you can create value for them in an understandable way, you have succeeded.

# APPENDIX

# CHAPTER 01: DATA EXPLORATION AND CLEANING

## ACTIVITY 1.01: EXPLORING THE REMAINING FINANCIAL FEATURES IN THE DATASET

**Solution:**

Before beginning, set up your environment and load in the cleaned dataset as follows:

```
import pandas as pd
import matplotlib.pyplot as plt #import plotting package
#render plotting automatically
%matplotlib inline
import matplotlib as mpl #additional plotting functionality
mpl.rcParams['figure.dpi'] = 400 #high resolution figures
mpl.rcParams['font.size'] = 4 #font size for figures
from scipy import stats
import numpy as np
df = pd.read_csv('../../Data/Chapter_1_cleaned_data.csv')
```

1. Create lists of feature names for the remaining financial features.

   These fall into two groups, so we will make lists of feature names as before, to facilitate analyzing them together. You can do this with the following code:

```
bill_feats = ['BILL_AMT1', 'BILL_AMT2', 'BILL_AMT3', \
              'BILL_AMT4', 'BILL_AMT5', 'BILL_AMT6']
pay_amt_feats = ['PAY_AMT1', 'PAY_AMT2', 'PAY_AMT3', \
                 'PAY_AMT4', 'PAY_AMT5', 'PAY_AMT6']
```

2. Use **.describe()** to examine statistical summaries of the bill amount features. Reflect on what you see. Does it make sense?

   Use the following code to view the summary:

```
df[bill_feats].describe()
```

The output should appear as follows:

```
df[bill_feats].describe()
```

|  | BILL_AMT1 | BILL_AMT2 | BILL_AMT3 | BILL_AMT4 | BILL_AMT5 | BILL_AMT6 |
|---|---|---|---|---|---|---|
| count | 26664.000000 | 26664.000000 | 26664.000000 | 26664.000000 | 26664.000000 | 26664.000000 |
| mean | 51405.730723 | 49300.001500 | 47026.340047 | 43338.894539 | 40338.136701 | 38889.872337 |
| std | 73633.687106 | 70934.549534 | 68705.359524 | 64275.250740 | 60705.944083 | 59432.541657 |
| min | -165580.000000 | -69777.000000 | -157264.000000 | -170000.000000 | -81334.000000 | -339603.000000 |
| 25% | 3580.000000 | 2999.750000 | 2627.250000 | 2341.750000 | 1745.000000 | 1256.000000 |
| 50% | 22361.000000 | 21150.000000 | 20079.500000 | 19037.000000 | 18066.000000 | 17005.000000 |
| 75% | 67649.750000 | 64395.500000 | 60360.000000 | 54727.500000 | 50290.500000 | 49253.750000 |
| max | 746814.000000 | 671563.000000 | 855086.000000 | 706864.000000 | 823540.000000 | 699944.000000 |

Figure 1.47: Statistical description of bill amounts for the past 6 months

We see that the average monthly bill is roughly 40,000 to 50,000 NT dollars. You are encouraged to examine the conversion rate to your local currency. For example, 1 US dollar ~= 30 NT dollars. Do the conversion and ask yourself, is this a reasonable monthly payment? We should also confirm this with the client, but it seems reasonable.

We also notice there are some negative bill amounts. This seems reasonable because of the possible overpayment of the previous month's bill, perhaps in anticipation of a purchase that would show up on the current month's bill. A scenario like this would leave that account with a negative balance, in the sense of a credit to the account holder.

3. Visualize the bill amount features using a 2 by 3 grid of histogram plots using the following code:

```
df[bill_feats].hist(bins=20, layout=(2,3))
```

The graph should look like this:

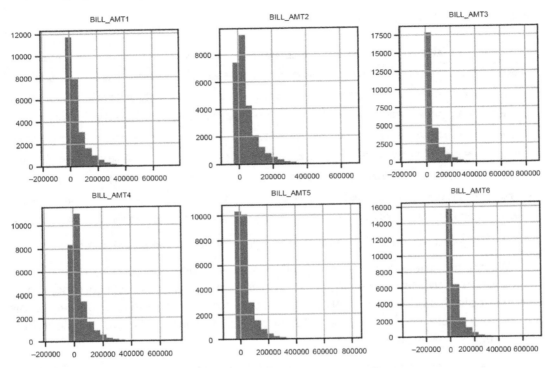

**Figure 1.48: Histograms of bill amounts**

The histogram plots in *Figure 1.48* make sense in several respects. Most accounts have relatively small bills. There is a steady decrease in the number of accounts as the amount of the bill increases. It also appears that the distribution of billed amounts is roughly similar month to month, so we don't notice any data inconsistency issues as we did with the payment status features. This feature appears to pass our data quality inspection. Now, we'll move on to the final set of features.

4. Use the `.describe()` method to obtain a summary of the payment amount features using the following code:

```
df[pay_amt_feats].describe()
```

The output should appear thus:

```
df[pay_amt_feats].describe()
```

| | PAY_AMT1 | PAY_AMT2 | PAY_AMT3 | PAY_AMT4 | PAY_AMT5 | PAY_AMT6 |
|---|---|---|---|---|---|---|
| count | 26664.000000 | 2.666400e+04 | 26664.000000 | 26664.000000 | 26664.000000 | 26664.000000 |
| mean | 5704.085771 | 5.881110e+03 | 5259.514964 | 4887.048717 | 4843.729973 | 5257.843047 |
| std | 16699.398632 | 2.121431e+04 | 17265.439561 | 15956.349371 | 15311.721795 | 17635.468185 |
| min | 0.000000 | 0.000000e+00 | 0.000000 | 0.000000 | 0.000000 | 0.000000 |
| 25% | 1000.000000 | 8.020000e+02 | 390.000000 | 294.750000 | 242.750000 | 111.000000 |
| 50% | 2114.500000 | 2.007000e+03 | 1822.000000 | 1500.000000 | 1500.000000 | 1500.000000 |
| 75% | 5027.000000 | 5.000000e+03 | 4556.250000 | 4050.500000 | 4082.750000 | 4015.000000 |
| max | 873552.000000 | 1.227082e+06 | 889043.000000 | 621000.000000 | 426529.000000 | 528666.000000 |

Figure 1.49: Statistical description of bill payment amounts for the past 6 months

The average payment amounts are about an order of magnitude (power of 10) lower than the average bill amounts we summarized earlier in the activity. This means that the "average case" is an account that is not paying off its entire balance from month to month. This makes sense in light of our exploration of the **PAY_1** feature, for which the most prevalent value was 0 (the account made at least the minimum payment but did not pay off the whole balance). There are no negative payments, which also seems right.

5. Plot a histogram of the bill payment features similar to the bill amount features, but also apply some rotation to the x-axis labels with the **xrot** keyword argument so that they don't overlap. Use the **xrot=\<angle\>** keyword argument to rotate the x-axis labels by a given angle in degrees using the following code:

```
df[pay_amt_feats].hist(layout=(2,3), xrot=30)
```

In our case, we found that 30 degrees of rotation worked well. The plot should look like this:

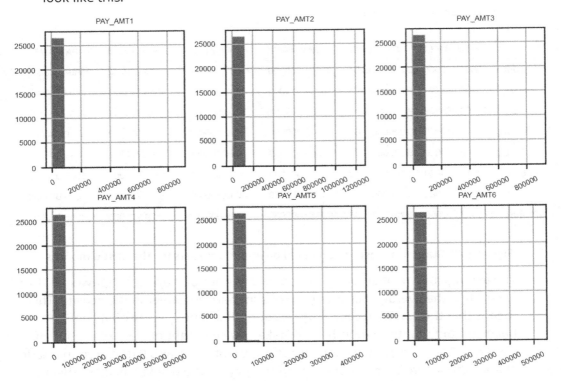

**Figure 1.50: Histograms of raw payment amount data**

A quick glance at this figure indicates that this is not a very informative graphic; there is only one bin in most of the histograms that is of a noticeable height. This is not an effective way to visualize this data. It appears that the monthly payment amounts are mainly in a bin that includes 0. How many are in fact 0?

6.  Use a Boolean mask to see how much of the payment amount data is exactly equal to 0 using the following code: Do this with the following code:

```
pay_zero_mask = df[pay_amt_feats] == 0
pay_zero_mask.sum()
```

The output should look like this:

```
PAY_AMT1    4656
PAY_AMT2    4833
PAY_AMT3    5293
PAY_AMT4    5697
PAY_AMT5    5981
PAY_AMT6    6373
dtype: int64
```

Figure 1.51: Counts of bill payments equal to 0

**Does this data make sense given the histogram in the previous step?**

The first line here creates a new DataFrame called **pay_zero_mask**, which is a DataFrame of **True** and **False** values according to whether the payment amount is equal to 0. The second line takes the column sums of this DataFrame, interpreting **True** as 1 and **False** as 0, so the column sums indicate how many accounts have a value of 0 for each feature.

We see that a substantial portion, roughly around 20-25% of accounts, have a bill payment equal to 0 in any given month. However, most bill payments are above 0. So, why can't we see them in the histogram? This is due to the **range** of values for bill payments relative to the values of the majority of the bill payments.

In the statistical summary, we can see that the maximum bill payment in a month is typically 2 orders of magnitude (100 times) larger than the average bill payment. It seems likely there are only a small number of these very large bill payments. But, because of the way the histogram is created, using equal-sized bins, nearly all the data is lumped into the smallest bin, and the larger bins are nearly invisible because they have so few accounts. We need a strategy to effectively visualize this data.

7. Ignoring the payments of 0 using the mask you created in the previous step, use pandas' `.apply()` and NumPy's **`np.log10()`** method to plot histograms of logarithmic transformations of the non-zero payments. You can use `.apply()` to apply any function, including **`log10`**, to all the elements of a DataFrame. Use the following code for this:

```
df[pay_amt_feats][~pay_zero_mask].apply(np.log10)\
                                 .hist(layout=(2,3))
```

This is a relatively advanced use of pandas, so don't worry if you couldn't figure it out by yourself. However, it's good to start to get an impression of how you can do a lot in pandas with relatively little code.

The output should be as follows:

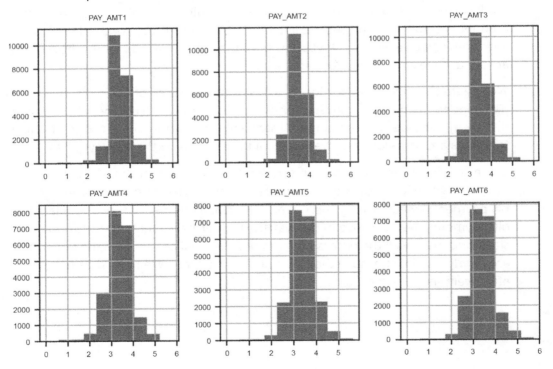

Figure 1.52: Base-10 logs of non-zero bill payment amounts

While we could have tried to create variable-width bins for better visualization of the payment amounts, a more convenient approach that is often used to visualize, and sometimes even model, data that has a few values on a much different scale than most of the values is a logarithmic transformation, or **log transform**. We used a base-10 log transform. Roughly speaking, this transform tells us the number of zeros in a value. In other words, a balance of at least 1 million dollars, but less than 10 million, would have a log transform of at least 6 but less than 7, because 106 = 1,000,000 (and conversely log10(1,000,000) = 6) while 107 = 10,000,000.

To apply this transformation to our data, first, we needed to mask out the zero payments, because **log10(0)** is undefined (another common approach in this case is to add a very small number to all values, such as 0.01, so there are no zeros). We did this with the Python logical **not** operator ~ and the zero mask we created already. Then we used the pandas **.apply()** method, which applies any function we like to the data we have selected. In this case, we wished to apply a base-10 logarithm, calculated by **np.log10**. Finally, we made histograms of these values.

The result is a more effective data visualization: the values are spread in a more informative way across the histogram bins. We can see that the most commonly occurring bill payments are in the range of thousands (**log10(1,000) = 3**), which matches what we observed for the mean bill payment in the statistical summary. There are some pretty small bill payments, and also a few pretty large ones. Overall, the distribution of bill payments appears pretty consistent from month to month, so we don't see any potential issues with this data.

# CHAPTER 02: INTRODUCTION TO SCIKIT-LEARN AND MODEL EVALUATION

## ACTIVITY 2.01: PERFORMING LOGISTIC REGRESSION WITH A NEW FEATURE AND CREATING A PRECISION-RECALL CURVE

**Solution:**

1. Use scikit-learn's **train_test_split** to make a new set of training and test data. This time, instead of **EDUCATION**, use **LIMIT_BAL**, the account's credit limit, as the feature.

   Execute the following code to do this:

```
X_train_2, X_test_2, y_train_2, y_test_2 = train_test_split\
                          (df['LIMIT_BAL']\
                          .values\
                          .reshape(-1,1),\
                          df['default'\
                              'payment next'\
                              'month'].values,\
                          test_size=0.2,\
                          random_state=24))
```

   Notice here we create new training and test splits, with new variable names.

2. Train a logistic regression model using the training data from your split.

   The following code does this:

```
example_lr.fit(X_train_2, y_train_2)
```

   You can reuse the same model object you used earlier, **example_lr**, if you're running the whole chapter in a single notebook. You can **re-train** this object to learn the relationship between this new feature and the response. You could even try a different train/test split, if you wanted to, without creating a new model object. The existing model object has been updated **in-place** in these scenarios.

3. Create the array of predicted probabilities for the test data.

   Here is the code for this step:

   ```
   y_test_2_pred_proba = example_lr.predict_proba(X_test_2)
   ```

4. Calculate the ROC AUC using the predicted probabilities and the true labels of the test data. Compare this to the ROC AUC from using the **EDUCATION** feature.

   Run this code for this step:

   ```
   metrics.roc_auc_score(y_test_2, y_test_2_pred_proba[:,1])
   ```

   The output is as follows:

   ```
   0.6201990844642832
   ```

   Notice that we index the predicted probabilities array in order to get the predicted probability of the positive class from the second column. How does this compare to the ROC AUC from the **EDUCATION** logistic regression? The AUC is higher. This may be because now we are using a feature that has something to do with an account's financial status (credit limit), to predict something else related to the account's financial status (whether or not it will default), instead of using something less directly related to finances.

5. Plot the ROC curve.

   Here is the code to do this; it's similar to the code we used in the previous exercise:

   ```
   fpr_2, tpr_2, thresholds_2 = metrics.roc_curve\
                               (y_test_2, \
                               y_test_2_pred_proba[:,1])
   plt.plot(fpr_2, tpr_2, '*-')
   plt.plot([0, 1], [0, 1], 'r--')
   plt.legend(['Logistic regression', 'Random chance'])
   plt.xlabel('FPR')
   plt.ylabel('TPR')
   plt.title('ROC curve for logistic regression with '\
           'LIMIT_BAL feature')
   ```

The plot should appear as follows:

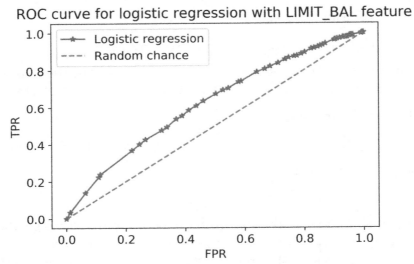

**Figure 2.30: ROC curve for the LIMIT_BAL logistic regression**

This looks a little closer to an ROC curve that we'd like to see: it's a bit further from the random chance line than the model using only **EDUCATION**. Also notice that the variation in pairs of true and false positive rates is a little smoother over the range of thresholds, reflective of the larger number of distinct values of the **LIMIT_BAL** feature.

6.  Calculate the data for the precision-recall curve on the test data using scikit-learn's functionality.

    Precision is often considered in tandem with recall. We can use **precision_recall_curve** in **sklearn.metrics** to automatically vary the threshold and calculate pairs of precision and recall values at each threshold value. Here is the code to retrieve these values, which is similar to **roc_curve**:

```
precision, recall, thresh_3 = metrics.precision_recall_curve\
                              (y_test_2,\
                               y_test_2_pred_proba[:,1])
```

7. Plot the precision-recall curve using matplotlib: we can do this with the following code.

   Note that we put recall on the **x**-axis and precision on the **y**-axis, and we set the axes' limits to the range [0, 1]:

```
plt.plot(recall, precision, '-x')
plt.xlabel('Recall')
plt.ylabel('Precision')
plt.title('Precision and recall for the logistic'\
          'regression 'with LIMIT_BAL')
plt.xlim([0, 1])
plt.ylim([0, 1])
```

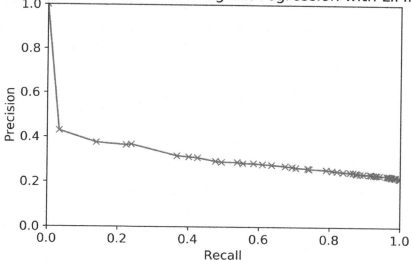

Figure 2.31: Plot of the precision-recall curve

8. Use scikit-learn to calculate the area under the precision-recall curve.

   Here is the code for this:

```
metrics.auc(recall, precision)
```

You will obtain the following output:

```
0.31566964427378624
```

We saw that the precision-recall curve shows that precision is generally fairly low for this model; for nearly all of the range of thresholds, the precision, or portion of positive classifications that are correct, is less than half. We can calculate the area under the precision-recall curve as a way to compare this classifier with other models or feature sets we may consider.

Scikit-learn offers functionality for calculating an AUC for any set of **x-y** data, using the trapezoid rule, which you may recall from calculus: **metrics.auc**. We used this functionality to get the area under the precision-recall curve.

9. Now recalculate the ROC AUC, except this time do it for the training data. How is this different, conceptually and quantitatively, from your earlier calculation?

   First, we need to calculate predicted probabilities using the training data, as opposed to the test data. Then we can calculate the ROC AUC using the training data labels. Here is the code:

```
y_train_2_pred_proba = example_lr.predict_proba(X_train_2)
metrics.roc_auc_score(y_train_2, y_train_2_pred_proba[:,1])
```

   You should obtain the following output:

```
0.6182918113358344
```

Quantitatively, we can see that this AUC is not all that different from the test data ROC AUC we calculated earlier. Both are about 0.62. Conceptually, what is the difference? When we calculate this metric on the training data, we are measuring the model's skill in predicting the same data that "taught" the model how to make predictions. We are seeing *how well the model fits the data*. On the other hand, test data metrics indicate performance on out-of-sample data the model hasn't "seen" before. If there was much of a difference in these scores, which usually would come in the form of a higher training score than the test score, it would indicate that while the model fits the data well, the trained model does not generalize well to new, unseen data.

In this case, the training and test scores are similar, meaning the model does about as well on out-of-sample data as it does on the same data used in model training. We will learn more about the insights we can gain by comparing training and test scores in *Chapter 4, The Bias-Variance Trade-Off*.

# CHAPTER 03: DETAILS OF LOGISTIC REGRESSION AND FEATURE EXPLORATION

## ACTIVITY 3.01: FITTING A LOGISTIC REGRESSION MODEL AND DIRECTLY USING THE COEFFICIENTS

**Solution:**

The first few steps are similar to things we've done in previous activities:

1. Create a train/test split (80/20) with **PAY_1** and **LIMIT_BAL** as features:

```
from sklearn.model_selection import train_test_split
X_train, X_test, y_train, y_test = train_test_split(
    df[['PAY_1', 'LIMIT_BAL']].values,
    df['default payment next month'].values,
    test_size=0.2, random_state=24)
```

2. Import **LogisticRegression**, with the default options, but set the solver to **'liblinear'**:

```
from sklearn.linear_model import LogisticRegression
lr_model = LogisticRegression(solver='liblinear')
```

3. Train on the training data and obtain predicted classes, as well as class probabilities, using the test data:

```
lr_model.fit(X_train, y_train)
y_pred = lr_model.predict(X_test)
y_pred_proba = lr_model.predict_proba(X_test)
```

4. Pull out the coefficients and intercept from the trained model and manually calculate predicted probabilities. You'll need to add a column of ones to your features, to multiply by the intercept.

   First, let's create the array of features, with a column of ones added, using horizontal stacking:

```
ones_and_features = np.hstack\
                    ([np.ones((X_test.shape[0],1)), X_test])
```

Now we need the intercept and coefficients, which we reshape and concatenate from scikit-learn output:

```
intercept_and_coefs = np.concatenate\
                ([lr_model.intercept_.reshape(1,1), \
                lr_model.coef_], axis=1)
```

To repeatedly multiply the intercept and coefficients by all the rows of **ones_and_features**, and take the sum of each row (that is, find the linear combination), you could write this all out using multiplication and addition. However, it's much faster to use the dot product:

```
X_lin_comb = np.dot(intercept_and_coefs,\
                np.transpose(ones_and_features))
```

Now **X_lin_comb** has the argument we need to pass to the sigmoid function we defined, in order to calculate predicted probabilities:

```
y_pred_proba_manual = sigmoid(X_lin_comb)
```

5. Using a threshold of **0.5**, manually calculate predicted classes. Compare this to the class predictions outputted by scikit-learn.

   The manually predicted probabilities, **y_pred_proba_manual**, should be the same as **y_pred_proba**; we'll check that momentarily. First, manually predict the classes with the threshold:

```
y_pred_manual = y_pred_proba_manual >= 0.5
```

   This array will have a different shape than **y_pred**, but it should contain the same values. We can check whether all the elements of two arrays are equal like this:

```
np.array_equal(y_pred.reshape(1,-1), y_pred_manual)
```

   This should return a logical **True** if the arrays are equal.

6. Calculate ROC AUC using both scikit-learn's predicted probabilities and your manually predicted probabilities, and compare them.

First, import the following:

```
from sklearn.metrics import roc_auc_score
```

Then, calculate this metric on both versions, taking care to access the correct column, or reshape as necessary:

```
roc_auc_score(y_test, y_pred_proba_manual.reshape(y_pred_proba_manual.shape[1],))
```

```
0.627207450280691
```

```
roc_auc_score(y_test, y_pred_proba[:,1])
```

```
0.627207450280691
```

**Figure 3.37: Calculating the ROC AUC from predicted probabilities**

The AUCs are, in fact, the same. What have we done here? We've confirmed that all we really need from this fitted scikit-learn model is three numbers: the intercept and the two coefficients. Once we have these, we could create model predictions using a few lines of code, with mathematical functions, that are equivalent to the predictions directly made from scikit-learn.

This is good to confirm your understanding, but otherwise, why would you ever want to do this? We'll talk about **model deployment** in the final chapter. However, depending on your circumstances, you may be in a situation where you don't have access to Python in the environment where new features will need to be input into the model for prediction. For example, you may need to make predictions entirely in SQL. While this is a limitation in general, with logistic regression you can use mathematical functions that are available in SQL to re-create the logistic regression prediction, only needing to copy and paste the intercept and coefficients somewhere in your SQL code. The dot product may not be available, but you can use multiplication and addition to accomplish the same purpose.

Now, what about the results themselves? What we've seen here is that we can slightly boost model performance above our previous efforts: using just **LIMIT_BAL** as a feature in the previous chapter's activity, the ROC AUC was a bit less at 0.62, instead of 0.63 here. In the next chapter, we'll learn advanced techniques with logistic regression that we can use to further improve performance.

# CHAPTER 04: THE BIAS-VARIANCE TRADE-OFF

## ACTIVITY 4.01: CROSS-VALIDATION AND FEATURE ENGINEERING WITH THE CASE STUDY DATA

**Solution:**

1. Select out the features from the DataFrame of the case study data.

   You can use the list of feature names that we've already created in this chapter, but be sure not to include the response variable, which would be a very good (but entirely inappropriate) feature:

   ```
   features = features_response[:-1]
   X = df[features].values
   ```

2. Make a training/test split using a random seed of 24:

   ```
   X_train, X_test, y_train, y_test = \
   train_test_split(X, df['default payment next month'].values,
                   test_size=0.2, random_state=24)
   ```

   We'll use this going forward and reserve this test data as the unseen test set. By specifying the random seed, we can easily create separate notebooks with other modeling approaches using the same training data.

3. Instantiate **MinMaxScaler** to scale the data, as shown in the following code:

   ```
   from sklearn.preprocessing import MinMaxScaler
   min_max_sc = MinMaxScaler()
   ```

4. Instantiate a logistic regression model with the **saga** solver, L1 penalty, and set **max_iter** to **1000**, as we'd like to allow the solver enough iterations to find a good solution:

   ```
   lr = LogisticRegression(solver='saga', penalty='l1',
                         max_iter=1000)
   ```

5. Import the **Pipeline** class and create a pipeline with the scaler and the logistic regression model, using the names **'scaler'** and **'model'** for the steps, respectively:

   ```
   from sklearn.pipeline import Pipeline
   scale_lr_pipeline = Pipeline(
       steps=[('scaler', min_max_sc), ('model', lr)])
   ```

6. Use the **get_params** and **set_params** methods to see how to view the parameters from each stage of the pipeline and change them (execute each of the following lines in a separate cell in your notebook and observe the output):

```
scale_lr_pipeline.get_params()
scale_lr_pipeline.get_params()['model__C']
scale_lr_pipeline.set_params(model__C = 2)
```

7. Create a smaller range of *C* values to test with cross-validation, as these models will take longer to train and test with more data than our previous exercise; we recommend $C = [10^2, 10, 1, 10^{-1}, 10^{-2}, 10^{-3}]$:

```
C_val_exponents = np.linspace(2,-3,6)
C_vals = np.float(10)**C_val_exponents
```

8. Make a new version of the **cross_val_C_search** function, called **cross_val_C_search_pipe**. Instead of the **model** argument, this function will take a **pipeline** argument. The changes inside the function will be to set the *C* value using **set_params(model__C = <value you want to test>)** on the pipeline, replacing the model with the pipeline for the **fit** and **predict_proba** methods, and accessing the *C* value using **pipeline.get_params()['model__C']** for the printed status update.

The changes are as follows:

```
def cross_val_C_search_pipe(k_folds, C_vals, pipeline, X, Y):
    ## [...]
    pipeline.set_params(model__C = C_vals[c_val_counter])
    ## [...]
    pipeline.fit(X_cv_train, y_cv_train)
    ## [...]
    y_cv_train_predict_proba = pipeline.predict_proba(X_cv_train)
    ## [...]
    y_cv_test_predict_proba = pipeline.predict_proba(X_cv_test)
    ## [...]
    print('Done with C = {}'.format(pipeline.get_params()\
                        ['model__C']))
```

> **NOTE**
>
> For the complete code, refer to https://packt.link/AsQmK.

9. Run this function as in the previous exercise, but using the new range of *C* values, the pipeline you created, and the features and response variable from the training split of the case study data. You may see warnings here, or in later steps, regarding the non-convergence of the solver; you could experiment with the **tol** or **max_iter** options to try and achieve convergence, although the results you obtain with **max_iter = 1000** are likely to be sufficient. Here is the code to do this:

```
cv_train_roc_auc, cv_test_roc_auc, cv_test_roc = \
cross_val_C_search_pipe(k_folds, C_vals, scale_lr_pipeline,
                        X_train, y_train)
```

You will obtain the following output:

```
Done with C = 100.0
Done with C = 10.0
Done with C = 1.0
Done with C = 0.1
Done with C = 0.01
Done with C = 0.001
```

10. Plot the average training and test ROC AUC across folds, for each *C* value, using the following code:

```
plt.plot(C_val_exponents, np.mean(cv_train_roc_auc, axis=0),
         '-o', label='Average training score')
plt.plot(C_val_exponents, np.mean(cv_test_roc_auc, axis=0),
         '-x', label='Average testing score')
plt.ylabel('ROC AUC')
plt.xlabel('log$_{10}$(C)')
plt.legend()
plt.title('Cross-validation on Case Study problem')
```

You will obtain the following output:

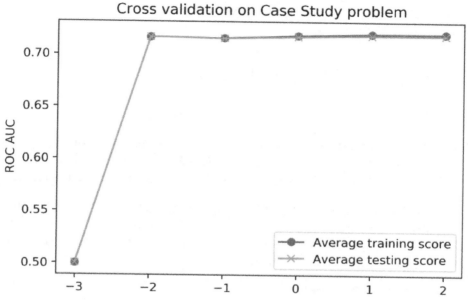

Figure 4.25: Cross-validation test performance

You should notice that regularization does not impart much benefit here, as may be expected: for lower *C* values, which correspond to stronger regularization, model testing (as well as training) performance decreases. While we are able to increase model performance over our previous efforts by using all the features available, it appears there is no overfitting going on. Instead, the training and test scores are about the same. Instead of overfitting, it's possible that we may be underfitting. Let's try engineering some interaction features to see if they can improve performance.

11. Create interaction features for the case study data and confirm that the number of new features makes sense using the following code:

```
from sklearn.preprocessing import PolynomialFeatures
make_interactions = PolynomialFeatures(degree=2,
                                       interaction_only=True,
                                       include_bias=False)
X_interact = make_interactions.fit_transform(X)
```

```
X_train, X_test, y_train, y_test = train_test_split(
    X_interact, df['default payment next month'].values,
    test_size=0.2, random_state=24)
print(X_train.shape)
print(X_test.shape)
```

You will obtain the following output:

```
(21331, 153)
(5333, 153)
```

From this you should see the new number of features is 153, which is *17 + "17 choose 2"* = 17 + 136 = 153. The *"17 choose 2"* part comes from choosing all possible combinations of 2 features to interact from the 17 original features.

12. Repeat the cross-validation procedure and observe the model performance when using interaction features; that is, repeat *steps 9* and *10*. Note that this will take substantially more time, due to the larger number of features, but it will probably take less than 10 minutes.

    You will obtain the following output:

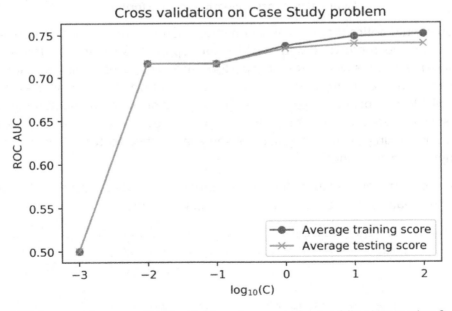

**Figure 4.26: Improved cross-validation test performance from adding interaction features**

So, does the average cross-validation test performance improve with the interaction features? Is regularization useful?

Engineering the interaction features increases the best model test score to about *ROC AUC = 0.74* on average across the folds, from about 0.72 without including interactions. These scores happen at *C = 100*, that is, with negligible regularization. On the plot of training versus test scores for the model with interactions, you can see that the training score is a bit higher than the test score, so it could be said that some amount of overfitting is going on. However, we cannot increase the test score through regularization here, so this may not be a problematic instance of overfitting. In most cases, whatever strategy yields the highest test score is the best strategy.

In summary, adding interaction features improved cross-validation performance, and regularization appears not to be useful for the case study at this point, using a logistic regression model. We will reserve the step of fitting on all the training data for later when we've tried other models in cross-validation to find the best model.

# CHAPTER 05: DECISION TREES AND RANDOM FORESTS

## ACTIVITY 5.01: CROSS-VALIDATION GRID SEARCH WITH RANDOM FOREST

**Solution:**

1. Create a dictionary representing the grid for the **max_depth** and **n_estimators** hyperparameters that will be searched. Include depths of 3, 6, 9, and 12, and 10, 50, 100, and 200 trees. Leave the other hyperparameters at their defaults. Create the dictionary using this code:

```
rf_params = {'max_depth':[3, 6, 9, 12],
             'n_estimators':[10, 50, 100, 200]}
```

> **NOTE**
>
> There are many other possible hyperparameters to search over. In particular, the scikit-learn documentation for random forest indicates that "The main parameters to adjust when using these methods are **n_estimators** and **max_features**" and that "Empirical good default values are … **max_features=sqrt(n_features)** for classification tasks."
>
> Source: https://scikit-learn.org/stable/modules/ensemble.html#parameters
>
> For the purposes of this book, we will use **max_features='auto'** (which is equal to **sqrt(n_features)**) and limit our exploration to **max_depth** and **n_estimators** for the sake of a shorter runtime. In a real-world situation, you should explore other hyperparameters according to how much computational time you can afford. Remember that in order to search in especially large parameter spaces, you can use **RandomizedSearchCV** to avoid exhaustively calculating metrics for every combination of hyperparameters in the grid.

2. Instantiate a **GridSearchCV** object using the same options that we have previously used in this chapter, but with the dictionary of hyperparameters created in step 1 here. Set **verbose=2** to see the output for each fit performed. You can reuse the same random forest model object, **rf**, that we have been using or create a new one. Create a new random forest object and instantiate the **GridSearchCV** class using this code:

```
rf = RandomForestClassifier(n_estimators=10,\
                            criterion='gini',\
                            max_depth=3,\
                            min_samples_split=2,\
                            min_samples_leaf=1,\
                            min_weight_fraction_leaf=0.0,\
                            max_features='auto',\
                            max_leaf_nodes=None,\
                            min_impurity_decrease=0.0,\
                            min_impurity_split=None,\
                            bootstrap=True,\
                            oob_score=False,\
                            n_jobs=None,
                            random_state=4,\
                            verbose=0,\
                            warm_start=False,\
                            class_weight=None)

cv_rf = GridSearchCV(rf, param_grid=rf_params,\
                     scoring='roc_auc',\
                     n_jobs=-1,\
                     refit=True,\
                     cv=4,\
                     verbose=2,\
                     error_score=np.nan,\
                     return_train_score=True)
```

3. Fit the **GridSearchCV** object on the training data. Perform the grid search using this code:

```
cv_rf.fit(X_train, y_train)
```

Because we chose the **verbose=2** option, you will see a relatively large amount of output in the notebook. There will be output for each combination of hyperparameters and, for each fold, as it is fitted and tested. Here are the first few lines of output:

```
Fitting 4 folds for each of 16 candidates, totalling 64 fits
[CV] max_depth=3, n_estimators=10 ....................................
[CV] .................... max_depth=3, n_estimators=10, total=   0.1s
[CV] max_depth=3, n_estimators=10 ....................................

[Parallel(n_jobs=1)]: Using backend SequentialBackend with 1 concurrent workers.
[Parallel(n_jobs=1)]: Done   1 out of   1 | elapsed:   0.1s remaining:   0.0s

[CV] .................... max_depth=3, n_estimators=10, total=   0.1s
[CV] max_depth=3, n_estimators=10 ....................................
[CV] .................... max_depth=3, n_estimators=10, total=   0.1s
[CV] max_depth=3, n_estimators=10 ....................................
[CV] .................... max_depth=3, n_estimators=10, total=   0.1s
[CV] max_depth=3, n_estimators=50 ....................................
[CV] .................... max_depth=3, n_estimators=50, total=   0.5s
```

Figure 5.22: The verbose output from cross-validation

While it's not necessary to see all this output for shorter cross-validation procedures, for longer ones, it can be reassuring to see that the cross-validation is working and to give you an idea of how long the fits are taking for various combinations of hyperparameters. If things are taking too long, you may want to interrupt the kernel by pushing the stop button (square) at the top of the notebook and choosing hyperparameters that will take less time to run, or use a more limited set of hyperparameters.

When this is all done, you should see the following output:

```
[Parallel(n_jobs=1)]: Done  64 out of  64 | elapsed:   2.3min finished

GridSearchCV(cv=4,
             estimator=RandomForestClassifier(max_depth=3, n_estimators=10,
                                               random_state=4),
             n_jobs=1,
             param_grid={'max_depth': [3, 6, 9, 12],
                         'n_estimators': [10, 50, 100, 200]},
             return_train_score=True, scoring='roc_auc', verbose=2)
```

Figure 5.23: The cross-validation output upon completion

This cross-validation job took about 2 minutes to run. As your jobs grow, you may wish to explore parallel processing with the **n_jobs** parameter to see whether it's possible to speed up the search. Using **n_jobs=-1** for parallel processing, you should be able to achieve shorter runtimes than with serial processing. However, with parallel processing, you won't be able to see the output of each individual model fitting operation, as shown in *Figure 5.23*.

4.  Put the results of the grid search in a pandas DataFrame. Use this code to put the results in a DataFrame:

```
cv_rf_results_df = pd.DataFrame(cv_rf.cv_results_)
```

5.  Create a **pcolormesh** visualization of the mean testing score for each combination of hyperparameters. Here is the code to create a mesh graph of cross-validation results. It's similar to the example graph that we created previously, but with annotation that is specific to the cross-validation we performed here:

```
ax_rf = plt.axes()
pcolor_graph = ax_rf.pcolormesh\
                (xx_rf, yy_rf,\
                 cv_rf_results_df['mean_test_score']\
                .values.reshape((4,4)), cmap=cm_rf)
plt.colorbar(pcolor_graph, label='Average testing ROC AUC')
ax_rf.set_aspect('equal')
ax_rf.set_xticks([0.5, 1.5, 2.5, 3.5])
ax_rf.set_yticks([0.5, 1.5, 2.5, 3.5])
ax_rf.set_xticklabels\
([str(tick_label) for tick_label in rf_params['n_estimators']])
ax_rf.set_yticklabels\
([str(tick_label) for tick_label in rf_params['max_depth']])
ax_rf.set_xlabel('Number of trees')
ax_rf.set_ylabel('Maximum depth')
```

The main change from our previous example is that instead of plotting the integers from 1 to 16, we're plotting the mean testing scores that we've retrieved and reshaped with `cv_rf_results_df['mean_test_score'].values.reshape((4,4))`. The other new things here are that we are using list comprehensions to create lists of strings for tick labels, based on the numerical values of hyperparameters in the grid. We access them from the dictionary that we defined, and then convert them individually to the `str` (string) data type within the list comprehension, for example, `ax_rf.set_xticklabels([str(tick_label) for tick_label in rf_params['n_estimators']])`. We have already set the tick locations to the places where we want the ticks using `set_xticks`. Also, we make a square-shaped graph using `ax_rf.set_aspect('equal')`. The graph should appear as follows:

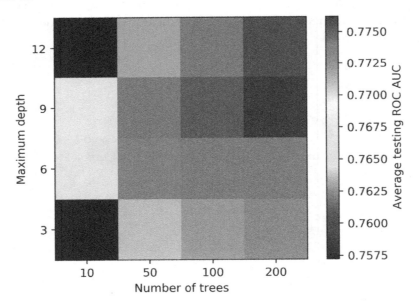

Figure 5.24: Results of cross-validation of a random forest over a grid with two hyperparameters

6.  Conclude which set of hyperparameters to use.

    What can we conclude from our grid search? There certainly seems to be an advantage to using trees with a depth of more than 3. Of the parameter combinations that we tried, **max_depth=9** with 200 trees yields the best average testing score, which you can look up in the DataFrame and confirm is ROC AUC = 0.776.

    This is the best model we've found from all of our efforts so far.

    In a real-world scenario, we'd likely do a more thorough search. Some good next steps would be to try a larger number of trees and not spend any more time with **n_estimators** < 200, since we know that we need at least 200 trees to get the best performance. You may search a more granular space of **max_depth** instead of jumping by 3s, as we've done here, and try a couple of other hyperparameters, such as **max_features**. For our purposes, however, we will assume that we've found the optimal hyperparameters here and move forward..

# CHAPTER 06: GRADIENT BOOSTING, XGBOOST, AND SHAP VALUES

## ACTIVITY 6.01: MODELING THE CASE STUDY DATA WITH XGBOOST AND EXPLAINING THE MODEL WITH SHAP

**Solution:**

In this activity, we'll take what we've learned in this chapter with a synthetic dataset and apply it to the case study data. We'll see how an XGBoost model performs on a validation set and explain the model predictions using SHAP values. We have prepared the dataset for this activity by replacing the samples that had missing values for the **PAY_1** feature, that we had previously ignored, while maintaining the same train/test split for the samples with no missing values. You can see how the data was prepared in the Appendix to the notebook for this activity.

1. Load the case study data that has been prepared for this exercise. The file path is **../../Data/Activity_6_01_data.pkl** and the variables are: **features_response**, **X_train_all**, **y_train_all**, **X_test_all**, **y_test_all**:

```
with open('../../Data/Activity_6_01_data.pkl', 'rb') as f:
    features_response, X_train_all, y_train_all, X_test_all,\
    y_test_all = pickle.load(f)
```

2. Define a validation set to train XGBoost with early stopping:

```
from sklearn.model_selection import train_test_split
X_train_2, X_val_2, y_train_2, y_val_2 = \
train_test_split(X_train_all, y_train_all,\
                 test_size=0.2, random_state=24)
```

3. Instantiate an XGBoost model. We'll use the **lossguide** grow policy and examine validation set performance for several values of **max_leaves**:

```
xgb_model_4 = xgb.XGBClassifier(
    n_estimators=1000,
    max_depth=0,
    learning_rate=0.1,
    verbosity=1,
```

```
objective='binary:logistic',
use_label_encoder=False,
n_jobs=-1,
tree_method='hist',
grow_policy='lossguide')
```

4. Search values of **max_leaves** from 5 to 200, counting by 5's:

```
max_leaves_values = list(range(5,205,5))
```

5. Create the evaluation set for early stopping:

```
eval_set_2 = [(X_train_2, y_train_2), (X_val_2, y_val_2)]
```

6. Loop through hyperparameter values and create a list of validation ROC AUCs, using the same technique as in *Exercise 6.01: Randomized Grid Search for Tuning XGBoost Hyperparameters*:

```
%%time
val_aucs = []
for max_leaves in max_leaves_values:
    #Set parameter and fit model
    xgb_model_4.set_params(**{'max_leaves':max_leaves})
    xgb_model_4.fit(X_train_2, y_train_2,\
                    eval_set=eval_set_2,\
                    eval_metric='auc',\
                    verbose=False,\
                    early_stopping_rounds=30)

    #Get validation score
    val_set_pred_proba = xgb_model_4.predict_proba(X_val_2)[:,1]
    val_aucs.append(roc_auc_score(y_val_2, val_set_pred_proba))
```

7. Create a data frame of the hyperparameter search results and plot the validation AUC against **max_leaves**:

```
max_leaves_df_2 = \
pd.DataFrame({'Max leaves':max_leaves_values,\
             'Validation AUC':val_aucs})
mpl.rcParams['figure.dpi'] = 400
max_leaves_df_2.set_index('Max leaves').plot()
```

The plot should look something like this:

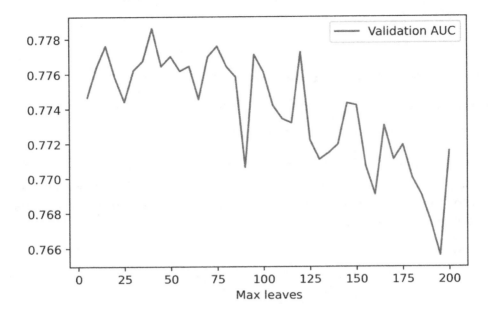

Figure 6.15: Validation AUC versus **max_leaves** for the case study data

Although the relationship is somewhat noisy, we see that in general, lower values of **max_leaves** result in a higher validation set ROC AUC. This is because limiting the complexity of trees by allowing fewer leaves results in less overfitting, and increases the validation set score.

8.  Observe the number of **max_leaves** corresponding to the highest ROC AUC on the validation set:

```
max_auc_2 = max_leaves_df_2['Validation AUC'].max()
max_auc_2
max_ix_2 = max_leaves_df_2['Validation AUC'] == max_auc_2
max_leaves_df_2[max_ix_2]
```

The result should be as follows:

|   | Max leaves | Validation AUC |
|---|---|---|
| **7** | 40 | 0.778592 |

Figure 6.16: Optimal **max_leaves** and validation set AUC for the case study data

We would like to interpret these results in light of our previous efforts in modeling the case study data. This is not a perfect comparison, because here we have missing values in the training and validation data, while previously we ignored them, and here we only have one validation set, as opposed to the k-folds cross-validation used earlier (although the interested reader could try using k-folds cross-validation for multiple training/validation splits in XGBoost with early stopping).

However, even given these limitations, the validation results here should provide a measure of out-of-sample performance similar to the k-folds cross-validation we performed earlier. We note that the validation ROC AUC here of 0.779 here is a bit higher than the 0.776 obtained previously with random forest in *Activity 5.01, Cross-Validation Grid Search with Random Forest*, from *Chapter 5, Decision Trees and Random Forests*. These validation scores are fairly similar and it would probably be fine to use either model in practice. We'll now move forward with the XGBoost model.

9. Refit the XGBoost model with the optimal hyperparameter:

```
xgb_model_4.set_params(**{'max_leaves':40})
xgb_model_4.fit(X_train_2, y_train_2, eval_set=eval_set_2,
                eval_metric='auc',
                verbose=False, early_stopping_rounds=30)
```

10. So that we can examine SHAP values for the validation set, make a data frame of this data:

```
X_val_2_df = pd.DataFrame(data=X_val_2,
                          columns=features_response[:-1])
```

11. Create an SHAP explainer for our new model using the validation data as the background dataset, obtain the SHAP values, and make a summary plot:

```
explainer_2 = shap.explainers.Tree(xgb_model_4, data=X_val_2_df)
shap_values_2 = explainer_2(X_val_2_df)
mpl.rcParams['figure.dpi'] = 75
shap.summary_plot(shap_values_2.values, X_val_2_df)
```

The plot should look like this:

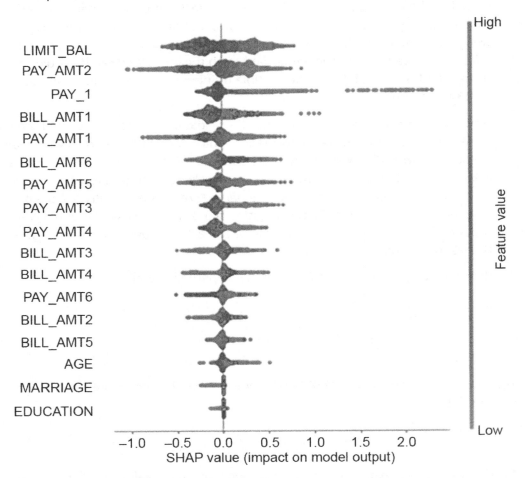

**Figure 6.17: SHAP values for the XGBoost model of the case study data on the validation set**

From *Figure 6.17*, we can see that the most important features in the XGBoost model are somewhat different from those in the random forest model we explored in *Chapter 5, Decision Trees and Random Forests* (*Figure 5.15*). No longer is **PAY_1** the most important feature, although it is still quite important at number 3. **LIMIT_BAL**, the borrower's credit limit, is now the most important feature. This makes sense as an important feature as the lender has likely based the credit limit on how risky a borrower is, so it should be a good predictor of the risk of default.

Let's explore whether **LIMIT_BAL** has any interesting SHAP interactions with other features. Instead of specifying which feature to color the scatter plot by, we can let the **shap** package pick the feature that has the most interaction by not indexing the explainer object for the color argument.

12. Make a scatter plot of **LIMIT_BAL** SHAP values, colored by the feature with the strongest interaction:

```
shap.plots.scatter(shap_values_2[:,'LIMIT_BAL'],
                   color=shap_values_2)
```

The plot should look like this:

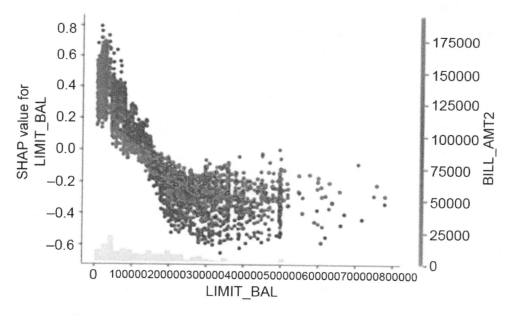

Figure 6.18: Scatter plot of SHAP values of **LIMIT_BAL** and the feature with the strongest interaction

**BILL_AMT2**, the amount of the bill from two months previous, has the strongest interaction with **LIMIT_BAL**. We can see that for most values of **LIMIT_BAL**, if the bill was particularly high, this leads to more positive SHAP values, meaning an increased risk of default. This can be observed by noting that most of the reddest colored dots appear along the top of the band of dots in *Figure 6.18*. This makes intuitive sense: even if a borrower was given a large credit limit, if their bill becomes very large, this may signal an increased risk of default.

Finally, we will save the model along with the training and test data for analysis and delivery to our business partner. We accomplish this using Python's **pickle** functionality.

13. Save the trained model along with the training and test data to a file:

```
with open('../Data/xgb_model_w_data.pkl', 'wb') as f:
    pickle.dump([X_train_all, y_train_all,\
                 X_test_all, y_test_all,\
                 xgb_model_4], f)
```

# CHAPTER 07: TEST SET ANALYSIS, FINANCIAL INSIGHTS, AND DELIVERY TO THE CLIENT

## ACTIVITY 7.01: DERIVING FINANCIAL INSIGHTS

**Solution:**

1. Using the testing set, calculate the cost of all defaults if there were no counseling program.

   Use this code for the calculation:

   ```
   cost_of_defaults = np.sum(y_test_all * X_test_all[:,5])
   cost_of_defaults
   ```

   The output should be this:

   ```
   60587763.0
   ```

2. Calculate by what percent the cost of defaults can be decreased by the counseling program.

   The potential decrease in the cost of default is the greatest possible net savings of the counseling program, divided by the cost of all defaults in the absence of a program:

   ```
   net_savings[max_savings_ix]/cost_of_defaults
   ```

   The output should be this:

   ```
   0.2214260658542551
   ```

   Results indicate that we can decrease the cost of defaults by 22% using a counseling program, guided by predictive modeling.

3. Calculate the net savings per account (considering all accounts it might be possible to counsel, in other words relative to the whole test set) at the optimal threshold.

   Use this code for the calculation:

   ```
   net_savings[max_savings_ix]/len(y_test_all)
   ```

The output should be as follows:

```
2259.2977433479286
```

Results like these help the client scale the potential amount of savings they could create with the counseling program, to as many accounts as they serve.

4. Plot the net savings per account against the cost of counseling per account for each threshold.

   Create the plot with this code:

```
plt.plot(total_cost/len(y_test_all),
         net_savings/len(y_test_all))
plt.xlabel\
('Upfront investment: cost of counselings per account (NT$)')
plt.ylabel('Net savings per account (NT$)')
```

The resulting plot should appear like this:

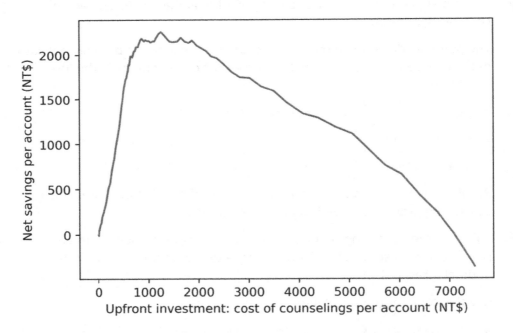

Figure 7.14: The initial cost of the counseling program needed
to achieve a given amount of savings

This indicates how much money the client needs to budget to the counseling program in a given month, to achieve a given amount of savings. It looks like the greatest benefit can be created by budgeting up to about NT$1300 per account (you could find the exact budgeted amount corresponding to maximum net savings using **np.argmax**). However, net savings are relatively flat for upfront investments between NT$1000 and 2000, being lower outside that range. The client may not actually be able to budget this much for the program. However, this graphic gives them evidence to argue for a larger budget if they need to.

This result corresponds to our graphic from the previous exercise. Although we've shown the optimal threshold is 0.36, it may be fine for the client to use a higher threshold up to about 0.5, thus making fewer positive predictions, offering counseling to fewer account holders, and having a smaller upfront program cost. *Figure 7.14* shows how this plays out in terms of cost and net savings per account.

5. Plot the fraction of accounts predicted as positive (this is called the "flag rate") at each threshold.

   Use this code to plot the flag rate against the threshold:

```
plt.plot(thresholds, n_pos_pred/len(y_test_all))
plt.ylabel('Flag rate')
plt.xlabel('Threshold')
```

The plot should appear as follows:

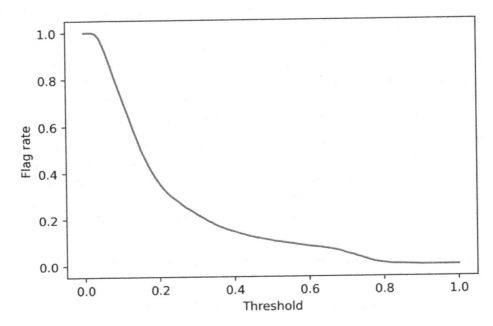

**Figure 7.15: Flag rate against threshold for the credit counseling program**

This plot shows the fraction of people who will be predicted to default and therefore will be recommended outreach at each threshold. It appears that at the optimal threshold of 0.36, only about 20% of accounts will be flagged for counseling. This shows how using a model to prioritize accounts for counseling can help focus on the right accounts and reduce wasted resources. Higher thresholds, which may result in nearly optimal savings up to a threshold of about 0.5 as shown in *Figure 7.12* (*Chapter 7, Test Set Analysis, Financial Insights, and Delivery to the Client*) result in lower flag rates.

6.  Plot a precision-recall curve for the testing data using the following code:

```
plt.plot(n_true_pos/sum(y_test_all),\
         np.divide(n_true_pos, n_pos_pred))
plt.xlabel('Recall')
plt.ylabel('Precision')
```

The plot should look like this:

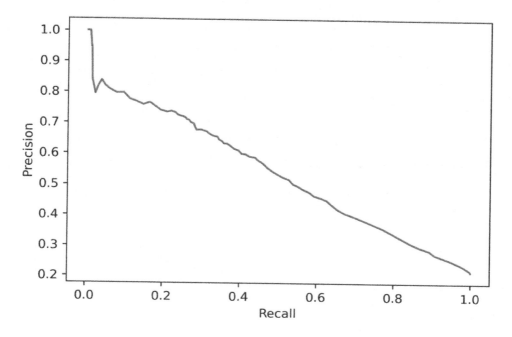

**Figure 7.16: Precision-recall curve**

*Figure 7.16* shows that in order to start getting a true positive rate (that is, recall) much above 0, we need to accept a precision of about 0.8 or lower.

Precision and recall have a direct link to the cost and savings of the program: the more precise our predictions are, the less money we are wasting on counseling due to incorrect model predictions. And, the higher the recall, the more savings we can create by successfully identifying accounts that would default. Compare the code in this step to the code used to calculate costs and savings in the previous exercise to see this.

To see the connection of precision and recall with the threshold used to define positive and negative predictions, it can be instructive to plot them separately.

7. Plot precision and recall separately on the *y*-axis against threshold on the *x*-axis.

   Use this code to produce the plot:

```
plt.plot(thresholds, np.divide(n_true_pos, n_pos_pred),
        label='Precision')
plt.plot(thresholds, n_true_pos/sum(y_test_all),
        label='Recall')
plt.xlabel('Threshold')
plt.legend()
```

   The plot should appear as follows:

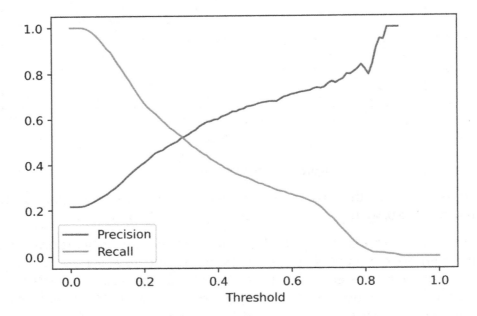

Figure 7.17: Precision and recall plotted separately against the threshold

This plot sheds some light on why the optimal threshold turned out to be 0.36. While the optimal threshold also depends on the financial analysis of costs and savings, we can see here that the steepest part of the initial increase in precision, which represents the correctness of positive predictions and is therefore a measure of how cost-effective the model-guided counseling can be, happens up to a threshold of about 0.36.

**Stephen Klosterman**

## HEY!

I am Stephen Klosterman, the author of this book. I really hope you enjoyed reading my book and found it useful.

It would really help me (and other potential readers!) if you could leave a review on Amazon sharing your thoughts on *Data Science Projects with Python, Second Edition*.

Go to the link https://packt.link/r/1800564481.

OR

Scan the QR code to leave your review.

Your review will help me to understand what's worked well in this book and what could be improved upon for future editions, so it really is appreciated.


Best wishes,

Stephen Klosterman

# INDEX

Made in the USA
Monee, IL
09 December 2023

48710774R00240